The CD ROM Handbook

The CD ROM Handbook

Chris Sherman

Intertext Publications
McGraw-Hill Book Company
New York, N.Y.

This book is dedicated to my goddaughter, Taylor Darlington Daynes.

Every effort has been made to assure accuracy in this book, and to protect the company names, products, services and intellectual property cited herein. Trademarks and service marks referred to in this book are the exclusive property of their respective owners. Listed trademarks were derived from various sources.

The publisher, editor, and contributors assume no responsibility for errors or omissions, and make no warranty of any kind, implied or expressed, and shall not be liable in any event for damages connected with or arising from the information published in this book.

Library of Congress Catalog Card Number 87-83103

10 9 8 7 6 5 4 3 2 1

ISBN 0-07-056578-3

Intertext Publications/Multiscience Press, Inc.
One Lincoln Plaza
New York, NY 10023

McGraw-Hill Book Company
1221 Avenue of the Americas
New York, NY 10020

Composed in Ventura Publisher by Context, Inc.

Contents

Acknowledgments

There is a true pioneer spirit among CD ROM developers, in the literal sense of exploration and discovery, but also in the profound cooperative attitude shared by most people involved in the industry. Many of these pioneers have contributed significant amounts of time and energy during the past two and a half years to help create this book.

Linda Helgerson is an exemplar of this pioneer spirit. Linda frequently and unselfishly shared her knowledge of industry resources, and directed me to a number of the *Handbook*'s contributors. She also wrote important sections of the book, and helped in uncountable other ways. Thank you, Linda.

Others who spent a significant amount of time helping various parts of this book come together include Matt Danielson, Howard Kaikow, Jean Kaplan, Ram Nomula, Larry Schwartz, and Bill Zoellick.

Special thanks to my "Interactive Mentor" Rod Daynes, and to my attorney, Wendy Daynes, for their unshakable faith in this book.

Other people in the CD ROM industry who contributed to this project include Terri Adkins, Edwin Brownrigg, Doug Carson, James DeVries, Kent Ekberg, Brian Eno, Rick Fisher, Robert Fisher, Joe Florio, Edward Fox, David Gimbel, Bill Harlow, John Hartigan, George Knapp, Maria Laskey, John Lowe, Bernie Luskin, Donna Lynn, Jerry McFaul, Fred Meyer, Andy Poggio, Franz Raetzer, Greg Reiker, Wink Saville, Ed Schmid, Dave Shen, Marcia Watson, and Chuck Weatherall.

On the home front, thanks to Randy Baker, Larry Barber, Stan Benedict, Henry Bertram, Beverly Butler, Lauralee Butler, Aireen Edilon, Harley Hahn, Julie Hymes, Jeneth McClure, Michael McClure, Mary Ann McClure, Jack Porter, Glenda Porter, and Crosby M. S. Porter.

Dr. Paul Hersey and Leadership Studies provided invaluable resources and support during the production of this book. Courseware, Inc., and IVID Communications also supported this project.

For vital production help thanks to Alan Rose of Intertext Publications, Ann Roberts of Context, Inc., and K. Blair Benson.

Finally, special thanks to the contributors themselves — though it's obvious, it needs to be stated: without them this book would not exist.

Trademarks

APPLE II® is a registered trademark and Macintosh™, Hyper-Card™, and Mac II™ are trademarks of Apple Computer Company.

UNIX is a trademark of AT&T Bell Laboratories.

DIALOG® is a registered trademark of DIALOG Information Service, Inc.

Unibus® is a registered trademark and QBUS™ and VAX™, VTX™, MicroVAX™ and VMS™ are trademarks of Digital Equipment Corporation.

GEM™ is a trademark of Digital Research Inc.

IBM® and IBM PC® are registered trademarks and IBM PC-AT™, IBM PC-XT™ and IBM PS/2™ are trademarks of International Business Machines Corporation.

LOTUS 1-2-3® is a registered trademark and Lotus Financial™ and One Source™ are trademarks of Lotus Development Corporation.

Sound Vision Authoring System™, VideoWorks II™, and Music-Works™ are trademarks of MacroMind.

LEXIS® is a registered trademark of Mead Data Control.

WORDSTAR® is a registered trademark of MicroPro International Corporation.

MS-WINDOWS®, MS-DOS®, and XENIX® are registered trademarks of Microsoft Corporation.

MC 68000® is a registered trademark of Motorola, Inc.

XEROX Star® is a registered trademark and SMALL TALK-80™ is a trademark of the Xerox Corporation.

The Electronic Encyclopedia™ is a trademark of Grolier Incorporated.

GEOVISION is a trademark of GEOVISION, Inc.

Datext™, Corporate Database™, and CD/Newsline™ are trademarks of Datext Inc.

Dow Jones News/Retrieval® is a registered trademark of Dow Jones and Company, Inc.

Clasix™ is a trademark of Reference Technology, Inc.

OCLC® is a registered trademark of Online Computer Library Center, Inc.

CVD™ is a trademark of SOCS Research, Inc.

Preface

CD ROM, or *Compact Disc Read-Only Memory*, is a significant new technology that enables millions of bytes of data to be stored on an ordinary compact disc. CD ROM provides numerous benefits compared with other forms of information storage and retrieval. Perhaps most significant is cost: Massive databases incorporating powerful search and retrieval software can be replicated and distributed for a fraction of the cost of other types of storage media. Even greater savings are gained by using the CD ROM database on personal workstations, diminishing the need for expensive access to large mainframe systems.

Another significant benefit is realized through CD ROM's multimedia capability. Conventional text or numeric data can coexist on a CD ROM disc with audio, computer graphics, and even video or digitized photographic images. Further, each type of data can be accessed *simultaneously*, allowing imaginative presentations of information not possible with other data storage media.

The CD ROM Handbook addresses the technical details of this exciting new technology. In these pages you will find out what Compact Disc Read-Only Memory is, how it works, and how to use it. The contributors are all acknowledged experts in their respective fields. More importantly, they are all deeply involved in the CD ROM industry. They have hands-on experience and expertise with the technology — in fact, many were influential in developing the current CD ROM format.

The CD ROM Handbook will help you understand the details of CD ROM technology so that you can use it effectively. The *Handbook* will help you makc informed decisions about hardware and software. Issues and techniques encountered in the different phases of CD ROM design and production are covered in great detail. You will gain a sense of the economic factors involved in creating, producing, and using CD ROM technology. And finally, the *Handbook* offers a look at the future, and how we can anticipate and prepare for tomorrow.

Interest in CD ROM is skyrocketing. More and more applications are being developed as hardware costs continue to drop and production techniques evolve. Pioneering CD ROM publishers are seeing increasing sales of their products and acceptance even in marketplaces that traditionally have avoided high-tech products. These "information products" were successful for two reasons: first, because the CD ROM publishers understood the technology and created useful, well-made products, and second, perhaps most importantly, because the CD ROM applications directly and specifically addressed a consumer *need*.

The CD ROM Handbook deals with the first half of the success equation, providing a detailed understanding of the technology. With a solid understanding of CD ROM's unique capabilities and its relative ease of use and portability, what people end up *doing* with CD ROM may drastically change our lives — perhaps even the way we think.

Chris Sherman

Introduction

Chris Sherman

What is CD ROM?

CD ROM is *compact disc read-only memory*. Compact discs were originally developed as a more durable, digital alternative to prerecorded phonograph records and cassette tapes used for audio playback. Read-only memory is a generic term for a permanent, unmodifiable computer data storage device.

CD ROM discs are circular, 120-mm diameter objects made from bulletproof polycarbonate, with a shiny underlayer that stores digital information. Only one side of the disc is used for data storage.

A CD ROM disc can store up to 660 Mbytes of information. This is about 260,000 pages of text, or 74 minutes of music or video.

Another way of looking at these mind-numbing statistics is to compare CD ROM to its ubiquitous relative, the floppy disk. Squeezing 660,000 Mbytes onto a single floppy disk using the 9 tracks per inch format of a standard MS DOS 360K diskette would require a diskette approximately 800 ft across[1]!

Building applications that harness the power of CD ROM technology, yet are easy to use, is a significant challenge for developers and publishers. To meet the challenge, developers must have a thorough, intimate understanding of CD ROM technology. *The CD ROM Handbook* provides that understanding.

---

1 Thanks to Steve Holder for this comparison.

About *The CD ROM Handbook*

The CD ROM Handbook focuses primarily on the technical aspects of CD ROM. In its chapters you will read about hardware and software, various CD ROM formats, and methods and techniques for manipulating data for different types of applications. You will read about the processes and issues involved in mastering and replicating CD ROM discs. Present-day applications and future directions are discussed, to provide you with the necessary tools and information to make your own decisions about CD ROM.

The *CD ROM Handbook* is organized into several major sections. Part A, *An Introduction to CD ROM*, provides an overview of the CD ROM industry.

Linda Helgerson begins with Chapter 1, *The CD ROM Industry: Past, Present, and Future*. Helgerson is the preeminent observer of the CD ROM industry, observing the course of events as editor of the prestigious *CD Data Report*, and helping shape the industry through her consulting firm Diversified Data Resources, Inc.

Still in its early phases, the CD ROM industry has been punctuated by annual leaps and bounds. The Microsoft CD ROM Conference held each year has been the traditional jumping-off point for a significant amount of CD ROM technology. In Chapter 2, David Traub offers a historical perspective of these seminal conferences and how they have helped define and nurture the CD ROM industry. Traub's chapter clearly highlights the dramatic, yet carefully controlled, leaps of technology that are characteristic of the CD ROM industry.

In Chapter 3, *The New Gutenbergs*, Steve Holder surveys current CD ROM applications, analyzing what types of information current applications are placing into the CD ROM format. Holder's survey also covers price, public availability, and other useful information.

Part B, *The CD ROM Format*, covers the technical specifications that define CD ROM delivery systems.

The fundamental component of any CD ROM system, of course, is the hardware. In Chapter 4, *CD ROM Hardware*, Jeffrey Nadler and Robert Weisenberg describe in detail how CD ROM drives are designed and how they work. Beyond simply describing the mechanical aspects of the devices, however, Nadler and Weisenberg discuss the critical aspects of error detection and correction built into CD ROM drives. The ability to cope with improperly retrieved data is intimately related to CD ROM's tremendous storage capacity.

CD ROM drives must be connected to some kind of computer system to be useful. Jack Spiegelberg discusses the challenges confronting developers in using CD ROM systems on microcomputers, which were not originally designed to handle massive amounts of data. In Chapter 5, *CD ROM Device Integration,* Spiegelberg talks about single systems, and the operating system extensions required to use a CD ROM drive. He also discusses the implications of using more than one CD ROM drive networked in a workstation environment.

Beyond the basic CD ROM format, several manufacturers have proposed multimedia standards that allow a CD ROM system to transcend an ordinary data retrieval device. Part C, *CD ROM Formats,* discusses these multimedia formats.

Compact Disc–Interactive, or CD-I, is described in Chapter 6 by Richard Bruno, one of the originators of the format. Philips and Sony hope to drive the CD-I format as a consumer product, using high-resolution graphics and sound capabilities combined with a powerful microprocessor to create a new type of home information appliance.

Another multimedia CD ROM format is Digital Video Interactive, or DVI. DVI differs from CD-I in that it is intended to be a computer peripheral, not a consumer product, and it emphasizes full motion video rather than high-resolution graphics. DVI is described in Chapter 7 by Arch Luther, a key member of the team at GE/RCA who developed the technology. Luther, who holds numerous patents on basic color television technology, describes the data compression techniques required to store the detailed information contained in a video image.

Completing Part C, we look at the future of optical media. David Davies, Director of 3M's Optical Recording Project, discusses the capabilities and potential of optical recording in Chapter 8, *Future Possibilities of CD ROM.*

Part D, *Information Storage and Retrieval,* deals with the software issues involved in CD ROM applications.

Because CD ROM is a data storage medium, *how* data is structured and stored on a disc directly affects the success of an application. In Chapter 9, *Designing a CD ROM Information Structure,* Bradley Watson, Terry Noreault, and Howard Turtle of OCLC discuss capabilities and restrictions of a read-only medium, and how to take maximum advantage of these characteristics when designing an application.

Most CD ROM applications use existing data. Often that data is not in electronic format, or if it is, it is not in an optimum format for use with CD ROM. John Bottoms and Linda Helgerson discuss this challenge in Chapter 10, *Data Conversion: The First Step toward Publishing on CD ROM*, offering techniques for dealing with all kinds of data.

Once data has been encoded on a disc, the user needs an easy, yet powerful means of access. John Bottoms describes the concepts surrounding retrieval systems in Chapter 11, *Full Text Indexed Retrieval Systems*.

CD ROM technology and artificial intelligence are natural partners, for two main reasons. First, a human trying to deal with the mass quantities of information available in a typical CD ROM application can often use help in narrowing a field of inquiry. Second, powerful artificial intelligence systems require large amounts of data, known as *knowledge bases*, to operate effectively. Michael Pincus, Kathy Pincus, and James Golden discuss current uses of artificial intelligence and CD ROM in Chapter 12.

Part E, *Creating a CD ROM: The Process*, covers the final steps in actually producing a CD ROM application.

The physical process of *Data Preparation and Premastering* (Chapter 13) is described by Allen Adkins. Different types of data have unique requirements in the preparation and premastering stage, and Adkins covers many of these different requirements.

Once data has been prepared and premastered, a master copy for replication must be created. Robert Harley provides a step-by-step look at *CD ROM Mastering* (Chapter 14), describing the special care that must be exercised at this point in the process to assure the highest quality master for duplication.

In *CD ROM Manufacturing* (Chapter 15), Robert Harley, Dwight Bancroft, Al Weeks, and Theodore Lindberg continue describing the production process involved in mass-producing discs. This chapter describes the steps and processes involved in creating finished copies of the master disc.

Part F, *Resources*, offers suggestions on where to go next for additional sources of information.

Beverly Butler and Bradley Watson complete the book (Chapter 17) with a selected bibliography of CD ROM information. This bibliography was created by searching several CD ROM databases. Butler and Watson comment on the process involved in using CD ROM for this kind of task.

CD ROM Is Here to Stay

CD ROM is a technology that is here to stay. The medium has attracted hundreds of top-caliber people from around the world who are defining, standardizing, and spearheading enthusiasm for its capabilities.

An Introduction to CD ROM

The CD ROM Industry: Past, Present and Future

Linda W. Helgerson

In November 1984, Denon, Hitachi, and Philips demonstrated prototype CD ROM drives with promises of production quantities to be delivered in the first quarter of 1985. Consumers then were buying up quantities of CD audio players at newly reduced prices for the holiday season. Philips/Sony licensees were awaiting a final version of *The Yellow Book* containing CD ROM physical specs; discussions concerning a standard interface between the CD ROM drive and microcomputers were just beginning; and the first commercial CD ROM disc was in final preparation by The Library Corporation. 1985 through 1987 were years of learning, testing, and reasonable growth for this newly introduced optical read-only storage media.

Now, more than 3 years later, the climate and industry surrounding CD ROM is changing. We no longer have to wait for things to happen (for example, the completion of a worldwide standard for the logical file format or the delivery of production units of the em-

This article appeared in the February, 1988 issue of CD Data Report and is reprinted here with permission of Langley Publications, Inc.

bedded, 5 1/4-inch half-height drives) — these expectations are now a reality. Also, the basic hurdles — a.k.a. learning curves — have been surpassed by users. Publishers, large and well-established firms, and smaller, heretofore unknown firms, have passed the initial CD ROM disc prototype stage and are well on their way to full production with detailed plans, market analyses, and sales projections. The situation has changed, and the "early years" of this read-only media is giving way to adoption of CD ROM by intermediaries and users with microcomputers and firms needing to disseminate large quantities of information internally or to customers.

A Review of 1984–1987 for the CD ROM Format

Standardization of File Format

With the initial hard work of the High Sierra team, and then the later deliberations of NISO, ANSI, ECMA, and ISO,[1] the standard for placing digital data on a CD ROM disc was adopted in October 1987.[2] This worldwide and industry wide cooperative effort allowed those firms waiting in the wings to commence with their CD ROM publishing and distributing plans.

Vertical Markets

Given the storage capacity and the economics of distributing data on CD ROM versus other media, most publishers have selected vertical markets as most promising for their CD ROM products during these years. The library, financial, legal, and medical markets have been the initial targets.

---

1 The High Sierra Group was an ad hoc assembly of industry representatives who developed the initial logical file format structure for CD ROM. NISO (National Information Standards Organization), ECMA (European Computer Manufacturers Association), ANSI (American National Standards Institute), ISO (International Standards Organization).

2 *Volume and File Structure of CD ROM for Information Interchange,* ISO Standard 9660.

Broadening Interest

Initially limited to those looking for a unique delivery mechanism or those firms not molded in a traditional industry, CD ROM publishing gained a wider audience than anticipated. The technology now appears to be well understood within the traditional publishing industry as well. Some major publishers, online database providers, and computer manufacturers have announced their intent to move products to CD ROM or to configure CD ROM as part of their product delivery system. McGraw-Hill, West Publishing, Dialog Information Services, Lotus Development Corporation, Apple Computer, Hewlett Packard, and Atari Corporation are examples. Others are in the process of developing their plans and products, and those still waiting in the wings are furiously assessing the risk of not using or providing CD ROM technology.

Hardware Availability

Hitachi, Laser Magnetic Storage (Philips), and Sony supply the production quantities of drives. Behind these three, there are other Japanese and U.S. firms ready to move into production or developing the necessary in-house production capabilities. Half-height drives, SCSI[3] interfaces as standard (but sometimes optional) items with drives, and audio output became available. Prices dropped, particularly with the half-height drives and with quantity orders. Originally priced around $1200, single units are now available for half this amount.

Developing Infrastructure

Large, as well as small, publishers now have a variety of options among service firms. Those companies that supply services to the CD ROM industry, such as data conversion, tagging and preparation, retrieval software and replicating houses, now face heightened competition. The growing sophistication of this infrastructure of service organizations is another indicator of positive movement of the CD

---

3 Small Computer Standard Interface.

ROM industry, and tools are already on the market that allow publishers to perform these operations themselves.

Industry Activity

One significant gauge of the health of any particular technology, such as CD ROM, is the almost disproportionate proliferation of conferences, seminars, market forecasts, articles in established periodicals, new publications, and industry experts all devoted to one topic — CD ROM. Not only has this indicated the interest of those special interest groups but it also points to heightened expectation of forthcoming profits for authors, analysts, conference organizers themselves, to say nothing of the industry.

International Activity

Spurred by internationally accepted physical and logical file format standards for CD ROM media, titles have been produced on several continents. More significantly, however, cross-marketing activities are already in place with notable organizations in joint-venture relationships with very big plans. Philips and Sony began the trend with the development of the Compact Disc Physical Standard, commonly known as The Red Book. Microsoft, Olivetti, and STET (the Italian telecommunications monopoly) formed a consortium in Italy, setting a trend for CD ROM publishing and disc distribution with accompanying computer and CD ROM drives in that country beyond that of any other European country. Disctronics, having launched its own manufacturing facility in Australia, soon acquired three additional facilities in two other continents. The ADONIS Project, a consortium of publishers of medical references and journals, now distributes reprints of articles to end users using CD ROM as the distribution device to document centers located worldwide. Firms of all sizes with varied products and services are merging efforts and capabilities.

Major Players

CD ROM has attracted large, multinational corporations. N. V. Philips, the Victor Company of Japan, Matsushita, Du Pont, 3M,

Mobay, and GE are among them. Other "big names" have publicly announced their CD ROM plans and products — Microsoft, Lotus, Apple, Hewlett Packard, Reed International, Elsevier Science Publishers, McGraw-Hill, John Wiley & Sons, Springer-Verlag, for example.

Titles Available

The most frequently asked question is, "What titles are available?" The answers vary, depending on whether the individual responding knows only of those titles described in trade journals or whether the respondent tracks all developments in each of the very well established and "hidden" vertical and niche markets. By mid 1988, more than 300 CD ROM titles were commercially available, compared with less than 100 the previous year. The next logical question is, "Why haven't I heard of them?" The answer: The data on the majority of these CD ROM discs are specific to a particular audience and would not necessarily be advertised or described in general-interest publications.

Some examples of industry-specific applications include the following:

- *Florists*: A CD ROM directory of FTD florists across the United States
- *Geophysicists*: The highly regarded Geophysical Data disc.
- *Geologists*: The Mass Spectral Data disc or the Powder Diffraction disc
- *Airline industry*: The series of discs containing both U.S. and international transportation statistics
- *Manufacturing or parts sales*: A proliferation of technical manuals or parts catalogs now available in increasing numbers on CD ROM systems
- *Astronomy:* The International Halley Watch will produce 20+ discs containing all data and images from the recent appearance of Halley's Comet in 1990.

Many discs initially were manufactured in quantities of 10 to 25 for internal evaluation or for use at beta test sites. By the end of 1987, publishers began to contract for larger runs. One division of McGraw-Hill intends an initial distribution of 34,000 titles with drives in 1989.[4] Major launches such as this will become more commonplace as publishers — such as the federal government — understand the economics of disc distribution.

Sales

Given an appropriate application and pricing structure, end users are willing to buy software with accompanying hardware. In the early days, a CD ROM drive was often acquired first and a disc, any disc, was purchased to try out the retrieval possibilities. Publishers learned from these early tests, and large databases became more "user friendly." By the end of 1987, products had not only the boolean operators associated with professional searching but also menu-driven techniques for the end user. Titles, introduced during 1985–1986 and updated in 1987, offered more capabilities, complimentary databases on the same disc, and integration capabilities with application software and writable storage devices. The mere quantity of these improved versions depicts the first 3 years of the CD ROM industry as years of learning, trial and enhancement, and steady growth.

Looking Beyond 1988

From this point forward, the theme of the CD ROM industry is still one of growth, but exponential growth, accompanied by a maturing infrastructure. Although CD ROM technology is now established, widespread numbers of applications in vertical markets are forthcoming.

Any Disc/Any Drive

With the physical and logical file format standards in place, only a few minor items need to be addressed before publishers and buyers can put aside any concern about using a disc produced at any

---

4 *Electronic Sweet's* — an index and retrieval program accompanying the CD ROM version of the *Sweet's Catalog* for the construction and building industries.

manufacturing facility on any drive produced by any vendor with any software on any computer.

The MS-DOS Extensions announced in the fall of 1986 by Microsoft are available under license to CD ROM drive manufacturers. This additional software eliminates the 32 megabyte file-size limitation and hardware dependency. The delivery of these MS-DOS Extensions by drive manufacturers will play a key role for buyers deciding among drives and drive features. In fact, it is expected that the Extensions will be used by vendors as leverage for acquiring quantity orders.

SCSI interfaces are now either standard or optional components with the half-height drives. Given the push for universality in CD ROM technology, firms that try to differentiate their products or services by producing a unique or possibly limiting interface design face embarrassment. In the long run, the buying public, rather than marketing muscle, will be the deciding factor for these kinds of issues.

Unfortunately, in the short term (hopefully), there are some integration issues still to be ironed out. For example, although SCSI is a standard, the SCSI interfaces supplied with CD ROM drives do not necessarily work with other SCSI peripherals, or vice versa (see Chapter 5). Early in 1988, a universal SCSI interface was introduced that would work with any CD ROM drive. This is a first step, but the larger and far more important step is a universal SCSI interface that will work with any CD ROM drive *and* other SCSI peripherals simultaneously.

Another step toward the any disc/any drive effort is the elimination of multiple and incompatible cartridges used with discs inserted into the half-height drive. One would have thought that drive manufacturers would have worked this all out prior to announcements. Since this is not the case, the market will decide, and undoubtedly it will decide in favor of the disc cartridge which is easiest to use, i.e., the one you can open without destroying the disc, the one which the majority of drive manufacturers have selected already — in short, the Sony cartridge. Lack of compatibility of disc cartridges should be viewed in the long term as a tactical error.

Maturity of Infrastructure

Much growth will occur in the service portion of the CD ROM industry in the next 2 years. Data conversion, preparation, database indexing, and premastering — like printing tasks — will be handled in house (with the purchase of component parts and software or of an integrated system) or by a dedicated service firm. The choice will depend on the amount, type, and frequency of disc publishing required, and the business interests of the publishing firm.

Retrieval software, off the shelf or application specific, will move beyond what existed during the first 3+ years. Already, the next wave of build and retrieval software capabilities is evident. Rather than being limited to search and retrieval software that can be modified to fit the requirements of the database and the end user, the software used to prepare the data (i.e., tagging for document structure, creation of lateral connections between databases, documents, or related subject areas) will *itself* become as if not the more important part of the equation.

Although concentration during the formative CD ROM years was primarily on the user interface and the retrieval side of the equation, the emphasis will change to the initial developmental side of the equation. Programs — just like application software — will become available to assist publishers of all sizes and interests to develop their own databases beyond what is now considered state of the art, i.e., management database systems (MDBS) and records management programs.

This need and soon-to-become requirement has occurred as a result of the inherent nature of CD ROM — a storage device for DIGITAL data. If publishers are to produce these digital (i.e., ASCII as well as raster[5]) discs and nonspecialist users are to use the data from these discs, then the *art* of producing must become a known act. The future of companies in the CD ROM business — software developers/suppliers and disc publishers — will survive or not as a result of attending to this very issue.

Replication of discs will be a certain area for technological improvements. New techniques, faster production, and higher yields will make discs a true commodity item — as affordable to the small publisher as to the large. There is already heavy competition among disc manufacturers in the form of pricing structures, services, and often-discussed quality of discs produced. This is not, however, the

---

5 ASCII: American Standard Code for Information Interchange, used to store text or other character data; raster refers to a graphic representation of data stored in a bit-mapped format.

area where competition will stay. It will move to other areas, such as replication of CD ROM discs using holography, which will yield a *standard* CD ROM disc with a greatly increased storage capacity.

New services based on a maturing infrastructure will prosper and grow. The most obvious one is in the area of authoring systems, software, and tools. A half dozen such integrated products have already been announced, and they are being purchased. But, like the next-generation build and retrieval programs, "you ain't seen nothin' yet."

The distribution and fulfillment segment of the industry is another area just beginning and ready to grow — *big*. Firms are already creating the mechanisms for answering questions such as "Where do I get a drive?" or "How do I buy a certain disc title?" What has already been determined is how different the process of distributing CD ROM products, hardware or software, is from any previous distribution activity. Book distributors find themselves in the business of selling hardware. Drive manufacturers, most all of whom are consumer electronics firms used to selling to the retail consumer market, are now faced with integrating their CD ROM drives with computers (with all the associated incompatibility issues), having to develop device drivers for each newly announced drive, having to license and supply MS-DOS Extensions and device drivers, having to figure out how to sell drives to customers rather than to retail wholesaler/distributors. Serial and magazine subscription houses have to learn about the world of computer peripherals and markets other than the known academic or corporate library markets. In short, known ways of accomplishing distribution and fulfillment activities and servicing and supplying traditional markets are dissolving into a maze of opportunities and headaches.

Finally, the multitude of conferences that deal with "what the CD ROM industry is all about" is already giving way to workshops training individuals and companies on how to produce their own CD ROM product lines. Meridian Data, Microsoft, and Philips–Du Pont Optical (PDO) began this type of activity with a series of workshops in 1987. Multiple expensive industrywide, generalizable conferences will be looked upon as useful only to those hauling in cash for registrations and exhibits. Instead, there will be one or two U.S. and/or international CD ROM conferences where the industry will announce new products and services, and preen in the face of competition.

Instead of the generalizable, all-things-to-all-people type gatherings, more pertinent discussions specific to the listening audience will occur at industry-specific conferences and meetings. Introductory-type seminars will change to training programs, and introductory "how to" training programs will then move to more technical "how to" programs as the CD ROM industry moves from learning how to store, produce, and distribute essentially textual data to producing standard CD ROM discs with text and graphics and audio and video still and motion images.

Possibly more than any other activity, the maturing of the infrastructure has been, and will be, the key indicator of the growth and maturity of the CD ROM industry over the next several years.

Mass Markets

Manufacturers of the lower-priced, mass-market computers will introduce systems with increased processing speeds, enhanced graphic capabilities, higher-resolution displays, and more embedded storage. CD ROM drives, either embedded or freestanding, with faster access times and lower prices will be available as standard or optional items to mass markets. They may even be bundled with the delivery of appropriate titles before 1989. Not limited to the business or professional community, CD ROM will rival other large-capacity information delivery vehicles because of its low-cost replication and sturdy nature. All this assumes that the costs of making discs, from beginning through mastering and replication, will become less expensive, and it will.

Copyright Resolution

Many publishers are already working on titles containing multiple sources, and for them the greatest barrier is confusion about the applicability of copyright laws, both nationally and internationally. By necessity, resolution will be sought, and in so doing, new avenues for publication of multiple-source CD ROM titles to vertical markets will open.

Decreased Prices

Increased demand for CD ROM hardware will reduce the variable costs of manufacturing and distribution, which will increase competition through pricing strategies. Given the price drops already experienced in single purchases of CD ROM, unit retail prices will be close to $300 in 2 years.

The Government as Publisher

With the standardization of CD ROM, governments have already started to publish and will soon seriously commit to publishing on disc throughout many agencies. CD ROM offers governments the opportunity for more efficient and timely distribution of their vast databases, both for use within the government and by the general public. For governments, CD ROM will be more than just an alternative or replacement for magnetic tape. It will be considered as the only means to cut the costs of data distribution. Increased paper costs, storage requirements, and postal rates will provide a strong incentive for this change.

Software on CD ROM

Software publishers have already begun distributing programs on CD ROM. The economics of distributing software programs on discs compared with magnetic tape, for example, are easily calculated. To assure legitimate use, however, issues such as access to application programs and security of the packages must be resolved. Much progress has already been achieved in the area of data encryption, although few firms are willing to venture forth into the limelight quite yet.

"The All-Purpose, Personal Publishing Machine"

In 1986, Fran Spigai dubbed the microcomputer as "the all-purpose personal information machine" in her speech on trends in electronic publishing.[6] She also reported, based on a survey of online database service executives, that CD ROM as a publishing medium was tops on the trends list.

Time passes and times change. Fran's personal information machine, or as some say, information delivery/retrieval system, is still in the process of "becoming" and the characteristics of this new

---

6   Online Conference, Chicago, November 1986.

all-purpose tool combines all earlier capabilities — those of a microcomputer per se and of an information retrieval system — but now adds a third function previously considered as separate. The third function is publishing and the corresponding result is knowledge.

To understand this progression, one must view the transition in two simultaneous paths. One path is the movement from data to information to knowledge — an amorphous sequence dealing with communications. The second path deals with a physical system, both hardware and software. The movement from PC to a retrieval-of-information system to a publishing system is tangible and therefore more easily understood.

As a result of having an all-purpose personal publishing system, individuals may acquire data, seek information, and gain knowledge. The hardware with appropriate software may be a combination of many known peripherals, but the intent will be total integration of functions and capabilities.

The personal publishing system does not yet exist. It will, but only after a period of time when publishers and distributors and system integrators and end users have had sufficient experience producing and using information retrieval systems begin to understand that — once again — the surface has only been scratched.

Multimedia CD ROMs

Just as the first year for CD ROM centered around getting used to having so much textual data on a 12-cm disc, the second year focused on retrieving and displaying the data. The third year firms attempted to combine text with images and audio. Future years for CD ROM will see a constant evolution of changes, based sometimes on the introduction and use of new products such as Digital Video Interactive (DVI), often on the ingenuity of those developing software, and increasingly because end users will constantly voice a desire for new features and capabilities having purchased and used earlier products. The movement will be steady, uphill, and unending.

The Standard User Interface

A standard user interface would probably make life easier for both publishers and users of CD ROMs, but it will not happen — really —

nor should it. Certainly, there will be more consistencies among user interfaces. Apple's HyperCard is an attempt at a standard, but early standard setting and adoption usually means later changes and enhancements.

Almost by definition, a user interface must be unique — for the database, for the user, for the application, and so on. What will become standard, maybe assumed is the better term, is the existence of certain capabilities, without which an interface and the corresponding retrieval capabilities would be considered less than sufficient.

Large Databases in Small Spaces

This overall trend has many themes — data compression, distributed information systems, from library shelves to desktops, from mainframes to micros, from file rooms to optical media, from cartonsfull delivered by freight to a sturdy envelopes delivered by courier, from volumes to a disc, from days to minutes, from unwieldy to utilitarian.

The book *Small Is Beautiful* by E. F. Schumacher contains many provocative and pertinent points relating to this issue. Schumacher writes, "What is it that we really require from the scientists and the technologists? I should answer: We need methods and equipment which are cheap enough so that they are accessible to virtually everyone; suitable for small-scale application; and compatible with man's need for creativity."[7]

The book was published in 1973. The thought remains viable. With CD ROM, the coast is clear.

About the Author

Linda W. Helgerson is president of Diversified Data Resources, Inc. (DDRI), a consulting firm in Northern Virginia that specializes in optical storage technologies and directly related fields, and editor and publisher of *CD Data Report*, the leading CD ROM industry newsletter since 1984.

---

7 E. F. Schumacher: *Small Is Beautiful*, Perennial Library, Harper & Row, New York, 1973, p. 34.

Helgerson consults with large and small organizations worldwide, including electronics manufacturers, optical disc mastering and replication firms, software development companies, industry associations, traditional and electronic publishers, online database service firms, federal agencies, the Department of Defense as well as DoD contractors. The types of consulting projects include analysis of user requirements, market trend analysis, hardware and software evaluation for integration within specific systems, technology evaluation, competitive product analyses, as well as overall industry watchdog. For many clients, Helgerson provides a continuous series of industry reports on areas of specific interest.

Helgerson is co-Editor of *The CD ROM Sourcebook* and co-author of *The Scanning Sourcebook* and *The Optical Disk Sourcebook*, all three published by DDRI. She is the author of two books published by the Association for Information and Image Management: *The Introduction to Scanning* and *The Introduction to Optical Technology*. She is the author of a three-part series of analytical articles appearing in *Library Hi Tech Journal* — "CD ROM Public Access Catalogs" — describing the features, the database creation and maintenance, and the user interface for each existing CD ROM PAC system. She is also the publisher and coeditor of a new series of popular books for users and producers of CD ROM products, published by Langley Publications, Inc.

In addition to being a prolific contributor to trade and professional journals, a regular speaker at industry conferences and forums, and a well-recognized name in the industry, Linda Helgerson has consulted extensively for the past 8 years with both users and suppliers in the planning, marketing, and production of optical storage and dissemination technologies.

DDRI
6609 Rosecroft Place
Falls Church, VA 22043
703-237-0682

2

An Historical Perspective
of CD ROM

David C. Traub

Beyond the Compact Disc Audio

By now, most of us have realized the phenomenal success of the Compact Disc. It was the fastest growing consumer electronic device in history. It sold over 4 million units in its first 4 years.

CD ROM is the next of a long series of planned optical configurations for data manipulation, storage, and delivery. As the second format of this series, the CD ROM will serve for years to come as the optimal means of storing and delivering massive text and multimedia applications.

This chapter provides an analysis of the genesis of CD ROM technology. Using reportage of the first two of the premier CD ROM conference series as context, we list and detail the evolving CD ROM industry by product, standards, and market. While partial to Microsoft's important contribution as conference sponsor, the chapter describes how the CD ROM evolved from the drawing boards of Dutch Philips in the early 1970s to the announcements of nearly every major micro-related vendor today.

17

The Legacy of Conference

Perhaps "giving conference" is the third oldest business known to man (magnetic memory being the second). Defined as "a formal meeting of minds," the notion of conference has evolved from solemn evaluation of public nuisance to more popular culture-type forum for new and evolving products and technology. Conference has become a week-long event for information exchange, product evaluation, professional leisure — and occasionally for breakthrough innovation.

As a phenomena of consensus, the first recognized conferences for any new technology become part code for that technology's existence. And though this is a truth which declines as markets mature and other conferences flourish, it remains that the evolution of the early conferences is a significant artifact to the primacy of a new and evolving product area.

Macro analysis of these early congregations can tell us as much — or more — about an evolving technology as micro analysis of the ancillary products themselves. We study this Microsoft conference series to achieve these insights into CD ROM, and to prepare for the more technically oriented articles to follow in the upcoming pages of *The CD ROM Handbook*.

Our story begins in 1985.

Bill Gates and CD ROM

In an 1985 interview, Microsoft founder Bill Gates stated his vision — and that of his company: *"To put a microcomputer on every desk in every home with Microsoft software making that a reality."*[1] Since Microsoft was founded in 1977, the company has, in most cases, maintained this focus evenly with the development of its highly successful applications, languages, and systems software. The exception has been Microsoft's efforts with the CD ROM, toward which Bill Gates has turned an inordinate amount of personal attention and energy.

---

1   *Micro Marketworld*, December 2, 1985, p. 36.

Why CD ROM?

With the advent in mid-1984 of integrated systems software such as Quarterdeck's DESQ and IBM's TopView, major PC vendors began to anticipate the immediate need for greater micro-based magnetic storage media. In particular, they realized that these memory-intensive windowing systems, providing tremendous utility to the user, required so much floppy and RAM memory as to limit the amount and type of applications and data they were designed to support.

Microsoft had become particularly aware of this storage-paradox because of its own early development work with Microsoft Windows. While Windows was ultimately the successful bid to the first IBM windows standard, its early versions were particularly memory-intensive and somewhat slow. It defied practical integration with existing magnetic media.

Moreover, as Microsoft envisioned a future enabled by these windowing systems, they foresaw that integrated systems software would ultimately encourage users to desire access to exponentially larger amounts of data *as commodities*. Given the right delivery media, PC users would have access to several new classes of micro-based software previously in the realm of hypothesis.

First, the PC user might now have closed-loop access to very large encyclopedic, research, or financial databases currently available only by access to a mini or mainframe computer. Second, the common user might now have ready access to the much more data-intensive multimedia-type applications that integrated data, graphics, video, and sound which Microsoft believed to be the future of computer-mediated popular media — the type of software they hoped might finally enable the PC to become a mass-market phenomena.

Yet as Microsoft and others had come to realize that neither the floppy nor the hard disk could provide the greater storage and delivery needs required by these larger requirements, they continued their search for a more efficient and affordable alternative media that could. They looked to Philip' new optically based data media as the answer.

Enter the CD ROM

The CDDA (Compact Disc Digital Audio) had established itself as the strongest consumer electronic introduction in product history. Yet not long after its launch, Philips had already begun to prepare to launch the next of a logical series of CD-based products designed to utilize the voluminous storage capability of the sturdy and inexpensive 120-mm CD disc.

This second CD product was designed specifically for data storage and delivery. Philips felt that, because of its nonvolatility and durability, this product would be seen as an ideal media for the distribution of systems software and large applications. It would enable delivery and access to larger, more massive text databases previously accessible to the PC only by networked access to larger computers.

CD ROM was physically identical in form to the CD Audio, and made available nearly 3 miles of recordable data track. Upon this track, a producer could store digitally as much as 650 Mbytes of data and correction code. CD ROM could also store diverse data types such as scanned and computer-generated images, animation, various video format, and monoaural, stereo, and compressed audio.[2]

Alas, despite this far greater storage capacity, storage on CD ROM was also far less expensive than its magnetic equivalent because of the manufacturing process. Each disc was injection-molded from a single master disc in an automated process that would quickly amortize the cost of manufacturing.

An Industry at Birth

In 1985, the new CD ROM industry was experiencing the same problems typical of the early stages of any new hardware-intensive industry. As usual, although growth of early CD ROM prototypes and culture was spirited, the hardware remained relatively unknown outside development and R & D labs. More importantly, early CD ROM advocates found themselves suffering from two major problems: (1) a lack of greater industry commitment, particularly of the software providers required to drive hardware sales, and (2) the classic lack of product standards.

The success of nearly every new delivery technology depends on eventual consensus and commitment. No one company can bear the intensive cost of development and ramp-up without knowledge that the software and marketing will follow. Although the CD ROM manufacturers had sufficient R & D cash flow derived from their

---

2   Indirect reference to John Gales' article entitled "Multi-Media Imaging and Audio Strategies," Microsoft 1987 CD ROM Conference Developer's Reference Guide, Workshop A3.

success with the CDDA, a majority of the publishers who owned the appropriate knowledge assets did not. Publishers were skeptical of a media so voluminous as to defy the requirements of most text-oriented products, a phenomenon implying multivendor titles — and problems with protecting intellectual property. They were not sufficiently convinced of this new format to commit R & D monies to convert their databases to drive the first CD products.

Also, the lack of early standards for any new technology is typically the most critical roadblock to any widespread usage and support. This is primarily because a lack of standards generally acts to undermine the user's ability to exchange between the various media and hardware of different vendors as they first reach the market. Unlike those that developed the VCR and Videodisc, the first CDDA pioneers had come together to create such a standard, and in so doing perhaps ensured that media's success. Nearly all these same early players chose to do the same for CD ROM, hoping to create a media standard that would ensure ready exchange among all CD ROM media and players.

An ad hoc standards committee, called the High Sierra Group, was formed to consolidate agreements of a logical file format to include consideration of the following: drive interface, physical recording, boot and program load, volume table of contents, information indexing, information input, and finally, the CD ROM standard file format.[3]

Microsoft's Commitment

Prior to these early deliberations Microsoft was already determining the thrust of its early positioning to this young industry. The company anticipated the growth of an entirely new industry infrastructure and could see a strong need for front-end support.

It was Microsoft's decision — Bill Gates' decision — not to focus initially on capturing a market, but rather to help catalyze or "create" a market by which all could prosper upon an mutually expanding hardware and software base. Microsoft's initial goal, therefore, would be to work with qualified players as potential partners, not as competitors.

---

3 Indirect reference to John Einberger's session during "Unifying a Software Format Standard," Thursday, March 6, 1986, 8:30 a.m. (Microsoft 1986 "Notes from the Conference," p. 77).

To help the industry become reality, Microsoft took three actions:

1. As the first CD ROM products were preparing their bid to market, Microsoft consummated its own bid to its first-ever corporate buyout. In January 1986, Microsoft purchased Cytation, a small American company developing CD ROM retrieval software. Its president, Tom Lopez, became vice president of CD ROM at Microsoft. His new job was to preside over a new division quickly set up out of the Hardware Development Group to exploit opportunities expected of the CD ROM.[4]

   The mission of this division was to consolidate upon the existing in-house development of several CD ROM related utilities, such as DOS Extensions. DOS Extensions was a program to be licensed to CD ROM manufacturers; it created a software bridge between the PC and CD ROM player. Specifically, this utility was designed to overcome the 32-Mbyte file-size limitation of MS DOS and enable all DOS-compatible computers seamless access to the entire 650-MB capacity of the CD ROM as if it were a hard disk.

2. Microsoft made known its commitment to the CD ROM standard by joining with Apple, DEC, Philips, and the others of the above-mentioned High Sierra Group to set about to define, agree upon, commit to, and advocate file format standards.

3. In February of 1986, Microsoft decided that the timing was right for public action to focus the scattered interest in this new technology. To do so, Microsoft chose to facilitate a conference to create the support culture required of a new industry, and to catalyze a forum for the development of software titles vital to buyers' interest in CD ROM hardware.

Thus in March, Microsoft '86 was launched as the first major event devoted to CD ROM during which first products could find a forum and first participants could find each other.

This first CD event became known as the "Woodstock of CD ROM."

---

4 Indirect reference to *Computer Currents* article, February 11–24, 1986, p. 21.

Microsoft '86: The Start of a Revolution

Gary Kildahl, president of Knowledge Set and Chairman of Digital Research, opened this first Microsoft conference echoing Bill Gates in 1985. He stated: "CD ROM represents an information revolution that will get PCs into the home fast."[5] The evangelical tone was thus set for the types of information, activities, and precedent that would take place at the Seattle conference as 900 or so industry participants excitedly adjourned from work in their labs and office buildings to help determine the future of CD ROM.

Accordingly, the conference thrived with many activities, including holding forum for a number of seminars, gatherings, and announcements, each a salient element to the genesis of this new evolving business. The following is a list of some of the more important and representative occurrences which set the stage for the next year in CD ROM — and for Microsoft '87.[6]

1. *Standards.* John Einberger, vice president of Reference Technology, and spokesperson for the High Sierra Group, came forward with the first public definition of the tentative logical file format standard for industrywide dissemination. A similar statement was made by the American Association of Publishers (AAP) regarding an agreement on the Standardized Publishing Markup Language (SPML) that ensured the uniformity of database input, and therefore, the uniformity — and diversity — of output to all media, including CD ROM. Required next of both would be industrywide acceptance.

2. *Market size.* Pioneer optical memory consultant Edward Rothchild reported his first tallies on actual machines sold to date — over 11,000 shipped globally, with more than 400 master discs pressed, more than one-half of which were early in-house demos.[7] Sony came out with their own estimates of the future global markets, predicting over 1 million CD ROM machines to be sold by 1990.

---

5 *Computer Currents*, February 11–24, 1986, p. 16.

6 Announcements 1 through 5 (a through g) taken from Microsoft 1986 "Notes from the Conference."

7 Ibid, p. 5.

3. *European market.* There was exceptionally strong interest devoted to CD ROM in terms of the continent, in particular the activities of France. During a session devoted to international markets, it was pointed out that CD ROM was particularly appropriate to the culture of France for several reasons. For example, the French population had an existing familiarity with database manipulation through its use of the successful Minitel videotext service. Also discussed were a number of French CD ROM applications, including discs on chemistry, ceramics, the French census, and a disc on Franco-American opportunities in trade.

4. *Global marketing.* The future of multinational marketing strategies was quickly established by the number of cooperative joint ventures announced to address anticipated opportunities. For example, SONY and KnowledgeSet announced a joint venture for CD ROM premastering. It became quickly apparent that any early sales of this product would be the result of multivendor bundling of hardware and software.

5. *New products.* There were many significant product announcements. Most were "early adopter" versions of existing library and financial databases migrated to this new technology. The following were among those introduced:

   a. Grolier showed its CD ROM *Electronic Encyclopedia*, the entire Academic American Encyclopedia presented on a single CD, arguably the first CD ROM product targeted to the general mass market.

   b. Dialog Information Service displayed the *OnDisc* CD ROM product, significant because its simultaneous ROM and online capability represented an ideal hybrid of the two diverse delivery technologies.

   c. Micromedix showed its collection of pharmacological databases for drug evaluation, critical care abstracts, tablet and capsule identification, and toxicology, each accessible off the CD.

d. Disclosure of Maryland introduced *COMPACT DIS-CLOSURE*, a file of business and financial information extracted from reports filed with the U.S. Securities and Exchange Commission by over 10,000 public companies.

e. Owl Systems's *GUIDE* was demonstrated as a Macintosh-like text and graphics word processor prototype that supported the creation of hypertext documents which could link any word, phrase, or graphic stored on CD ROM to elements of text in an associative manner.

f. Cox Enterprises of Woburn, Massachusetts, introduced *DATEXT*, a series of six separate database products, targeted to financial analysts, corporate planners, research directors, or senior management. These would enable users to profile single companies or industries, and to prepare in-depth analyses of those companies. All the *DATEXT* products are readily integrated into a number of leading software packages for further analysis and reporting.

g. Lotus introduced *ONE SOURCE*, a complement of nine financial databases designed for the professional money manager, providing weekly CD ROM updates of these databases via Federal Express.

As might be expected, the majority of these discs were pressed by several of the larger financial houses. There were several reasons for this. The financial houses were interested in proving earlier claims that CD ROM would become the cheapest way to distribute large amounts of machine-readable financial data. They had the products of sufficient volume to rationalize the disc space. They were curious about whether CD ROM might remove the expense and other limitations of accessing financial databases through a modem. Finally, it was they, the financial houses, who typically had the money to buy these products — and to develop them. Perhaps this last reason was most noteworthy.

These announcements were significant in that they represented an actual product and existing market culture, however immature. Although these first products were strictly of a vertical nature, they

89-03102

had, in less than a year, established CD ROM as a technology that could provide unique value-added to products existing in other media. CD ROM had proven itself as a legitimate solution to a specific set of problems.

Between the staccato of these early announcements there emerged a group of activities and statements that were setting the real stage for Microsoft '86; these had more to do with markets than with technology.

The Highlight of Microsoft '86: CD for the Home?

During the concluding session of the conference, Ashton-Tate Chief Scientist Robert Carr described three separate and distinct markets that the CD ROM would address over the next year: (1) vertical markets, with specific product designed for specific needs; (2) PC peripheral markets, wherein new CD ROM–based software would upgrade or enhance existing workstation applications; and finally, (3) consumer markets, a new opportunity that had previously seen little public consideration.[8]

Throughout the earlier sessions and announcements, all product introductions had been of the first two vertically oriented categories. There had been little or no product-oriented reference to the more horizontal, broad-based applications that might eventually attract a mainstream consumer audience. No product spoke directly to the multimedia future Microsoft held of its vision.

Yet a review of quotes of a number of principal speakers throughout the conference revealed that there was indeed interest in the idea of CD ROM beyond the business arena. Numerous references to "multimedia," "CD video," and "CD consumer applications" were heard throughout the conference.

Consider the source and frequency of these references made to a hypothetical CD ROM home market during early-week seminars:[9]

Microsoft's first manager for CD ROM, Carl Roarke:

---

8   Ibid, p. 163.

9   Ibid. for all the quotes taken from "Notes from the Conference."

Microsoft believes in the multi-media CD ROM as the key to a home market.

Michael Liebhold, manager, Apple Computer's Advanced Optical Media Technology:

Apple perceives CD ROM as a window for the integration of the PC into the home.

Phillipe Kahn, president of Borland Software:

There will soon arise a consumer market for the CD ROM that would soon become the realm of the Lorimars and Warner Brothers.

Manager for Microsoft Publishing, Min Yee:

Consumer applications were seen by Microsoft as the pathway to putting CD ROM into the home.

How did the above sources anticipate such a crossover penetration by CD ROM? Nearly all the statements seemed to refer to some set of CD ROM applications that could extend itself beyond the conventions presented by the earlier CD ROM products. These continuous references to consumer and entertainment markets implied CD usage beyond mere database delivery.

Whatever the entertainment application, it would compete with TV. More than a revolution in micro-based media, this was probably the "revolution" in the conference Marque, a revolution in home entertainment technology that would be enabled by CD ROM. Perhaps this was what Tom Lopez was referring to when he opened the announcements with:

This is the start of a revolution. I hope this conference will serve as a catalyst for this revolution.

Arguably it was, for during the latter part of the product announcement session which Lopez opened, many allusions made to a CD ROM product for the home were actualized by the conference's most controversial — and not surprising — announcement, the introduction by Philips and Sony of the concept for a stand-alone multimedia CD player known as the "CD-I," or Compact Disc–Interactive.

The Compact Disc–Interactive

From the first, Philips had operated under the premise of a carefully orchestrated, graduated introduction of the evolving CD formats. First was the CDDA, aimed carefully for the audiophile. Next was CD ROM, tailored for the business database and applications-delivery market. CD-I, by Philips' rationale, was the third of the CD line-up — and the first of the CD series designed specifically for the home market.

Similar to CD ROM, the CD-I standard was quite unique from its predecessor in several ways. For one, CD-I comes far closer than CD ROM to using its entire disc storage capacity because of its extensive graphics orientation. Second, CD-I goes beyond specifying its delivery media to define an entire hardware and software system. This need for further specification is required to enable the player its more demanding simultaneous integration of multiple media types, including various grades of sound, audio, animation, graphics, and limited video.[10]

Also, the interactive, multimedia potential of the proposed CD-I standard would theoretically give new schools of user-dependent product a wide range of innovative capabilities. For example, a typical CD-I title might mix still-frame digital images with text, cartoon, and limited third-by-third screen full-motion video, all at one of two separate levels of resolution. At the same time, it could mix these visuals between a variety of special effects such as wipes, pans, and fades, and simultaneously juxtapose these images against a continuous mix of various grades of audio, voice, and music, all under the user's real-time interactive control.

CD-I was designed as a stand-alone system to include a CD-I drive, a CD-I disc for information product and application software, a Motorola 68000 series processor with 1 Mbyte of RAM, CD-RTOS — a real-time, multitasking operating system, an input device or

---

[10] From John Gales' article "Future 12 cm (CD) Media Microsoft '87 Developer's Workshop Conference Notes," Sec. A2.

devices, video and audio decoders, and a font module with extended ASCII and KANJI character sets.

What was most remarkable about the CD-I player was its mode of delivery. Unlike CD ROM, CD-I was not designed as a peripheral to computer and monitor. Rather, the CD-I was designed as a stand-alone system to be plugged into a standard television screen and hi-fi system as an adjunct to the home entertainment system. Packaged to be perceived as other than a "computer," CD-I was designed to support media products which would be interchangeable among an installed base of players that could theoretically extend itself to all the TVs and stereos throughout the world.

CD-I was not a computer. It was a TV adjunct.

The Reaction: CD-I Versus CD ROM

Thus the major announcement of the conference had little to do with the business of CD databases — or even CD ROM. The major announcement was instead CD-I, a hybrid CD player packaged as a stand-alone system for the home market. The major surprise of the conference was that Philips, the primary sponsor of CD ROM, had introduced yet another format to consider, to finance, to support.

The Reality of CD-I

It was not long before the reality of potential product limitations struck. As announced, this first version would be restricted to a window of video of less than one third screen, and even this could only be projected at 17 frames per second at best. Someone at Houghton-Mifflin said that lack of video would be a vital deterrent to getting the home audience to bridge from TV to the CD-I.

Nor were there existing software applications to support the anticipated introduction of this product to the market. In fact, Michael Liebhold of Apple pointed out that the CD-I couldn't even conduct satisfactory file exchange with any of the existing installed base of software products and PCs.

But the biggest problem for this new media soon became apparent: in reality, it did not yet exist as hardware. That it existed at all as the highlight of this first Microsoft conference was a marketing gamble by which Philips hoped to inspire a critical mass that would quickly stimulate both industry support and a developmental momentum that would be key to ensuring the new product's success.

As the conference ended, advocacy for both formats had begun to establish itself over the differences between the two media. But while both sides disagreed about whether a multimedia CD-I might eventually succeed in its address to the potential of the home market, they both agreed that CD ROM was here now, a sturdy and utilitarian address to the problems of handling and delivering massive databases and applications.

To the supporters of CD ROM, the question of the media's success was no longer a question of "if." It had become a question of "when": when might the CD ROM realize its full market advantage given the introduction of CD-I?

Microsoft '86 Conclusions

Microsoft '86 would long be remembered for a number of reasons: the promise of an official worldwide standard; Philips' "conceptual" introduction of the CD-I, a multimedia CD player packaged specifically for the home; the apparent growing stature of CD ROM; the first official introduction of a number of CD ROM products; and most of all, the excitement of the very first CD ROM conference.

After the Conference

Many questions remained with the attendees as they departed Seattle. Their focus marred by the introduction of CD-I, this moderate minority would mount further resistance to corporate commitment to CD ROM. In particular, many of the more conservative publishers would now wait until a more significant CD ROM hardware base was established before justifying resources to press their databases.

Others would choose the opposite tack, devoting themselves strictly to the concept of CD-I, their hopes buoyed by the lure of the greater consumer markets such facile multimedia product might serve. For most, however, the conference served to provide a renewed, perhaps even vibrant sense of devotion to the promise of CD ROM.

The following year would harbor a continuous series of developments and innovations that would reveal the efforts of individual companies in CD ROM — and would support the momentum of the evolving industry as a whole.

A Dearth of Announcements

After the conference, despite a large number of important break-throughs, the number of important announcements throughout the year was somewhat limited. Corporate strategists planning the intro-duction of new CD ROM products chose to wait until the next big CD ROM conference before making announcements. Both new and seasoned vendors would wait to orchestrate their introductions to maximize impact upon the first significant wave of actual consumers who were optimistically expected to converge upon the next Microsoft conference.

Microsoft '87: Making It Happen

As in 1986, the opening speech for Microsoft '87 set the tone for the conference. In his opening speech, Microsoft's Tom Lopez spoke of "Making it Happen," an allusion to the real-time nature of the work and commitment required of all to continue to support the rather strained rise of CD ROM.

Since Microsoft '86, the actual sale of CD ROM had been less than expected, somewhat less than 30,000 total units shipped to OEM vendors.[11] What was more, the larger publishers had, for the most part, continued to hold back their interest in producing the more broad-based, consumer-oriented CD ROMs that might fuel the media's greater acceptance, in part because of the confusion CD-I had cast upon the future of electronic CD ROM publishing.

Yet as of Microsoft '87, there was still no CD-I prototype to see.

However, the above is not to say that the conference was of a lesser status. In fact, what the CD ROM community had experienced in the wake of the first conference was the pragmatic genesis to a real industry with a much stronger sense of identity, more innova-tion, and an unexpectedly strong show of titles.

---

11 "Industry Analyst's Forum," Microsoft '87.

With more than 100 titles available at the start of the conference, there continued a steady rise in the number of new applications being pressed weekly by or for mainstream vendors such as Lotus and KnowledgeSet, including the first CD ROM product for the Macintosh.[12] To support the pressing of these titles, more of the existing CDDA media production capability was dedicated to CD ROM.

Of the increasingly available CD ROM drives, more were showing a greater diversity of configurations. For example, a number of 1/2-inch-high drive configurations were announced as PC-compatible.

Perhaps equally important, but less touted, was the demonstration by Philips of its CD-PROM (for "Programmable Read-Only") player, a hybrid CD ROM-WORM drive that revealed the impending direction of the future of optical-based ROM.

As for the standards issues raised at Microsoft '86, the High Sierra Group went far to solve the problems by formally announcing a completed CD ROM file format standard that had now been accepted by a majority of vendors.

Indeed, with such a steady flow of activity due to the business of CD databases, all that lacked for the more grand-scale success of CD ROM were more varied, horizontal-market applications to drive greater player sales, and to cause the lower hardware prices that would enable CD ROM to become a mass-market phenomenon.

Therein was established the ambience of Microsoft '87. Perhaps a bit more humble, witness to a little less of the excitement and optimism that had been experienced the year before, but certainly far more experienced and insightful into the realities and dynamics of what it would take to power this new industry into the maturity of its markets — a community that was already "making it happen."

The Sessions

This first few days of the conference provided a forum for a number of bustling seminars, gatherings and announcements, each a salient element to an evolving industry speaking not only of the present, but also the future.

---

12 Roy Endres, vice president marketing, Multi-Add Services.

Consider a summary of several of the more representative sessions which lent themselves to an efficient matrix of the proceedings:

1. *Market size:* Edward Rothchild of Rothchild Associates came forth with his tallies on actual machines sold to *users* to date — over 13,000 purchased.[13] This was significantly fewer than that which had been predicted a year earlier by Rothchild and other consultants.

2. Rothchild also gave a session called the *Future of Optical Memory* which he used as a forum to introduce other optical-based products competing for CD ROM's markets. These other devices were:[14]

   a. *Analog ROM, or Videodisc:* The standard in training field, it can hold standard video and/or up to 54,000 images.

   b. *Analog Writable, OMDR, or Optical Memory Drive Recorder:* Typically a portable field recording devices for recording still images and video to disc (also video and up to 54,000 images).

   c. *WORM, or Write Once Read Many* (or Philips' *CD-PROM*): Existing player allows recording, but not write-over, of digital data. That or other existing data. 50+ players competing for this and Erasible market with both large capacity stand-alone jukebox and smaller micro-based products for Macintosh and IBM series now available (capacity between 125 Mbytes and 2+ Gbytes).

   d. *Optical ROM, or O-ROM:* Developed by SONY, announced by IBM, a high-performance optical ROM version of 3.5-in. and 5.25-inch recordable WORM discs (capacity between 125 Mbytes and 2+ Gbytes).

---

13 "Industry Analysts's Forum," Microsoft '87, hand-out on CD ROM market projections.

14 The following taken from Edward Rothchild speech. Reference to "EDOD," IBM announcement of O-ROM, and a 3.5-in. O-ROM taken form *CD-ROM Review* (December '87, p. 19), and the reference to optical tape taken from *MIS Week*, 8 (26), June 29, 1987, p. 8.

e. *Erasable, or EDOD* (Erasable Digital Optical Disc): Using magneto-optics or phase-change technology, these products, due Spring 1988, will allow users to read, write, erase, and write again over data. Erasable products are another area of fierce competition among storage vendors, primarily because Erasable media is expected to dominate the recordable market — *and will probably relegate the WORM to niche markets requiring audit trail* (125 Mbytes to 2+ Gbytes).

f. Laser card: Credit-card-sized cards for customer/patient information with optical capacity now of 2Mbytes; soon 200+ Mbytes.

g. Optical tape: Used primarily for research requiring super-mass-storage that needs only static access (up to 1000+Gbytes).

Rothchild was asked by the audience how CD ROM would fare against the above formats, and how all optical formats would fare against the increasingly voluminous storage capacity of evolving new magnetic hard-disk products. In terms of the first question, there were several responses: (1) CD ROM was here now; (2) there are a number of applications suited only to a read-only nature, particularly applications which require copyright protection, (3) Erasable might eventually outdo WORM because of its continued recordability; and (4) a hybrid Erasable-WORM-ROM format would evolve optimizing the best of each media, a concept similar to the CD-Programmable Read Only Memory format being shown at the conference by Philips.

Responding to the second issue of evolving magnetic hard-disk storage, Rothchild noted that hard disks could now store in excess of 750 Mbytes — more than the touted CD ROM. He also noted that the hard disk was faster, though this would eventually change. He went on to acknowledge several of the CD ROM's key assets over magnetic media: (1) Unlike magnetic media, CD ROM discs can be removed from their drives, enabling single drive multiple discs of information; (2) such removal also enables protection of discs holding sensitive information; (3) CD ROM discs are far more stable and durable than magnetic media, and thus, far less prone to crashes and loss of data; and (4) optical media are far less expensive.

It should be noted that a number of the major magnetic drive manufacturers such as Maxtor, Tallgrass, and Drexler are all now manufacturing writable optical media products in anticipation of that market's maturity.

3. *The CD family of products.*[15] John Gales of the Information Workstation Group detailed the evolving family of CD formats which had evolved from Philips first announcement of the concept of the Compact Disc in 1978:[16]

   a. *CD-DA, or Compact Disc–Digital Audio.* The first of the Com-pact Disc Series, introduced in 1978, the most successful consumer electronic introduction to date.

   b. *CD ROM, or Compact Disc–Read Only Memory.* The data version of the CD Audio with added error correction, announced October 1983, first shown November 1985.

   c. *CD-I, or Compact Disc-Interactive.* The multimedia, stand-alone system for the home, announced February 1986, expected for Christmas 1988 release.

   d. *CD-V, or Compact Disc-Video.* A hybrid digital-analog player that combines 20 minutes of digital music with 5 minutes of analog video. It was quickly announced February 1987 for availability the second half of 1987, possibly to compensate for the unexpected late start of CD-I.

   e. *CD-PROM, or Compact Disc Programmable-Read Only Memory.* A WORM/ROM hybrid that will allow a mix of

---

15 CD-G for "Graphics" and CD-WO for "WORM" are some of the latest to enter the expanding CD family of acronyms, the first a hybrid CD-DA player with limited graphics capability, the second a writable CD disc player that will also play CD ROM discs CD-"Common" is another supposed acronym for a CD format that will play on both MS-DOS and Apple players.

16 The following taken form John Gales' article, "Future 12 cm (CD) Media Microsoft '87 Developer's Workshop Conference Notes," Sec. A2.

read-only and writability on one disc, and might eventually play on a CD ROM player. First shown in public at Microsoft '87, it will be available sometime in 1988. *CD-PROM was one of the most significant announcements of the conference as it reflected the likely direction of future ROM products.*

f. *CD-IV, or Compact Disc-Interactive Video* A product proposed for 1989 that will combine a small videodisc with a full CD-I channel to add the full-motion video requirement lacking of the CD-I. The follow-up CD-IV product — likely to be the as yet unidentified "CD-X" product — will be upgraded to an all-digital 30 frames/minutes video version by 1993, more likely sooner if a competing technology or still-born CD-I market demands it because of full-motion video requirement.

4. There was a lot of expectation about *CD-I*. Primarily, there was the hope that there might be an actual demonstration of the product. However, although there were many announcements, sessions, and special interest groups dedicated to CD-I, this was not to be the case. Instead, the biggest CD-I-related announcement was that it would be at least another year before the product would be revealed. Philips found itself with a product concept that had gained and was slowly losing vital industry support before its product was even launched.

5. Perhaps more significant to the home market were sessions discussing *multimedia applications* for the more advanced CD ROM format known as mode 2. It was pointed out that the CD ROM player, as with the proposed CD-I, had the ability to combine images, sound, and text together into an interactive multimedia format, though perhaps initially with a bit less facility. One of these sessions was particularly exciting because it highlighted an actual prototype demonstration of a multimedia, multilingual visual database product for CD ROM developed by Editions Quebec/Amerique of Toronto and the Software Mart of Houston. This product was called *A VISUAL DICTIONARY* and consisted of 72 Mbytes of information, including 115 images and 1660 terms in French and English, any of which could be shown and heard on screen on demand.

6. Equally portentious to the future of CD ROM was a session which discussed *hypertext* and *hypermedia*, two terms recognizing the evolving linguistic of an unified, associative grammar of graphics and text. This was significant because mass storage of CD ROM would enable massive amounts of diverse media types that would require more efficient browsing, consideration, linkage, and implementation in a manner closer to the way the user actually thinks. Gary Kildahl said, "The advantage of CD ROM over print is that you don't have to treat knowledge as linear."[17] Hypermedia would be the grammar of this multiplanar access to CD ROM multimedia.

Announcements

Consider the following list of several of the more representative announcements of the 1987 conference:

1. John Einberger of Reference Technology again came public for the High Sierra Group Standards Committee, this time with the finalized definition of the logical file format standards for CD ROM. He urged expanding cooperation for all of those vendors who had not yet agreed to accept the standard.

2. Multi-Add Services made one of the more significant announcements of the conference with its introduction of the *first CD ROM application for the Macintosh*, a syndicated electronic art product called "Kwikee In-house Graphics Services." The product delivered an extremely large database of product, seasonal, atmosphere, and thematic art, together with the company's own DeskTop-Publishing page layout software, which allows users to produce their own ads and page layout inhouse. This product was particularly interesting because it also supported other existing Macintosh software.

---

17 Taken loosely from Kildahl opening speech, Microsoft '86 "Notes from the Conference," p. 10–13.

3. For its *CD-I,* Philips announced a series of joint ventures designed to facilitate software development, including the formation of AIM (American Interactive Media) and EIM (European Interactive Media). Both companies were created, and are actively seeding a number of CD-I titles, to ensure that sufficient software would be available upon product introduction to fuel early-adopter purchases.

   Philips also announced the finalization of the "Yellow Book" standards, the industrywide specification for CD-I ("Red Book" for CD-DA, "Green Book" for CD ROM, "Blue Book" for CD PROM). Finally, they also announced two other joint ventures to facilitate CD-I, including a venture with SUN Microsystems to produce CD-I authoring systems, and a venture with R. R. Donnelly Publishers to form Optimage, a liaison production house for publishers interested in writing to CD-I.

4. Other JV examples of strategic alliance were announced:

   a. The formation of Eikon Corporation, a joint venture of Microsoft, Oliveti, and SEAT based in Rome to provide CD ROM production services to Europe. Eikon was also formed to enhance Microsoft's distribution in Europe's expanding PC market. Tom Lopez would become chairman of that company.

   b. Sony and KnowledgeSet joined to announce the formation of Publishers Data Service (PDSC), a joint venture designed to provide "one-stop" CD ROM data preparation to convert raw data into ready-to-master computer tapes utilizing any industry file structure.

5. There were slow major auto projects, signifying a potential massive hardware base:

   a. Reynolds & Reynolds announced and displayed a CD ROM system for the control and inventory of parts distribution for Ford dealerships.

   b. Bell & Howell announced its IDB200 CD ROM disc containing an electronic parts catalog installed in General Motors dealerships, it allows mechanics to look up every part for every variety of car and light truck made over the last 10 years. Bell & Howell also announced it would try to market a similar system to Chrysler.[18]

(Note: the July 1988 *CD ROM Review* reported rumor of three additional major CD ROM orders: an order by ADP (Automatic Data Processing) of 5000 portable CD ROM systems for repair shops use, a Hewlett-Packard system designed to automate Ford dealership maintenance procedures, and a major CD ROM order of a system by Nissan of Japan.[19])

6. ADP also announced a *CD ROM-based portable computer system*, based on CD ROM technology to be used by insurance estimators when assessing claims.[20]

7. Dialog Information Service announced "OnDisc," a CD ROM product that shows the potential future of optical-storage melded with alternative communication resources, in this on-line access to Dialog's mainframe database. The user gets the best of both worlds: inexpensive, efficient access to the static CD ROM, and up-to-the-minute access to dynamic mainframe.

8. Owl Systems introduced *GUIDE*, a software product originally demonstrated in beta form by Brown University at Microsoft '86. GUIDE is primarily a concept-processor, with Macintosh-like interface, that is particularly adroit at the creation of hypertext and hypermedia documents which can link any graphic, word, phrase, or chunk of text imported or designed on the PC by means of interconnected buttons.[21] GUIDE 2.0 for the MAC and PC, a more multimedia-oriented processor, will soon follow. Hypermedia is fast becoming a term synonymous with the grammar and production of text, graphics, and sound-intensive CD ROM databases.

---

18 *CD-ROM Review*, October 1987, p. 36

19 Ibid. p. 36

20 Ibid. p. 36

21 Boston Computer Society, *Optical Insights*, Fall 1987, p. 20.

9. Lotus Development Corporation announced its *purchase of Computer Access Corp.*, developer and owner of the Bluefush retrieval software for the CD ROM. This purchase extended Lotus' positioning from a one-product CD ROM vendor (ONE SOURCE) to publisher of optical media in the finance field.

10. DEC's demonstration of a *CD ROM network* connecting dispersed workstations with up to 10 CD ROM drives showed that CD ROM could be accessible from both multiple DEC VAX-mate and IBM PC workstations.[22] This was a very significant announcement since it concerned the future the CD ROM player might have in relation to its place in already existing LAN environments.

11. One of the two most significant announcements of the conference was Microsoft's announcement of its *Microsoft Bookshelf* product, a word-processor utility that contained a library of 10 major reference works and writing aids on a single CD ROM disc — the first CD ROM product for the consumer market. Distribution deals with AMDEC and Sears Business Systems would enable *Bookshelf*, bundled with a Hitachi/AMDEC player, to be made available to the public at $1399 through 100 Sears outlets in the fall of 1987.[23]

The buying public would have its first exposure to CD ROM.

Product Reflections

As in 1986, the above announcements and sessions continued to add to the evolutionary stature of the CD ROM. The notion of voluminous optically based ROM was often the most appropriate solution to a number of specific problems. CD ROM provided the most cost-efficient means of delivering large databases to remote sites. CD ROM provided the most optimal means of housing the larger multimedia applications too large and unstable for storage on magnetic. More CD products were coming down the line, including several which would be recordable. Finally, software was being writ-

---

22 *CD-ROM Review*, July/August 1987, p. 20.

23 Ibid.

ten for swift and efficient navigation amongst these voluminous discs.

The question remained: Would the CD ROM succeed as a mainstream product? And indeed, would titles be written to encourage this acceptance, titles whose content, service, and facility might encourage an expanding hardware base to raise in volume, drop prices, and promote even further penetration? The conference had more to give.

The Conference Legacy

Microsoft '86 had set a precedent for surprise announcements. During the announcement session, within an ambience of excitement carefully sculptured by the conference producers, each vendor had introduced its product to the greatest dramatic effect possible. This was how the stage had been set for Philips' finale CD-I coup to their first-time audience of insiders.

Thus it was that Wednesday's full-house crowd sat expectantly through the first several announcements for the 1987 conference waiting to be shocked, surprised — and hopefully inspired, maybe even shown definitively how or why their media might soon thrive.

They would neither be disappointed this year nor suffer the "smoke and mirrors" Apple Evangelist Martha Steppen had declared of the CD-I introduction the year before.[24] They were about to see the ultimate insurance to the success of the CD ROM and its subsequent optical brethren, a bridge between the computer and the most popular delivery system on the planet — the television.

DVI: True Video on a CD ROM

At about 2 P.M. this day, General Electric/RCA actually demonstrated what Philips had earlier in the day said was not yet possible — full-screen, full-motion 30 frame/second video directly off a CD ROM disc. They called this "DVI" for Digital Video Interactive, a VLSI chip-set on a circuit board, rather than a standard like CD-I, that could enable an IBM PC-AT to display more than an hour of

---

24 *Computer Currents*, April 7–20, 1987, p. 24.

full-motion video, text, 3-D graphics, still images, special effects, and multitrack audio voice and music played from a highly compressed digital data stored on a single, standard CD ROM disc.

The essence of RCA's approach to solving the video-inhibiting problem of a limited data transfer rate was to compress the original visual information in non-real-time on a VAX 780 to produce a much smaller memory representation of the original images. Specifically, the RCA process updates only the difference, or delta change, between succeeding images off the CD ROM disc. The video display chips then decompress and play back the data as video in real time.

The problems with DVI were the following: (1) the initial poor resolution afforded it by the RCA compression process — a feature pointed out by Philips in defense of CD-I's carefully crafted and superior resolution; (2) DVI's lack of identification as an existing or autonomous system standard, (3) DVI's identification as a computer versus home entertainment technology — a burden to consumer acceptance, and (4) the anticipated exceptionally high cost of the early DVI circuit boards and production processes.[25]

As for the first, RCA claimed its available resolution would soon be shown to improve dramatically (RCA has more recently demonstrated a much improved resolution performance). As for the issue of standards, it was to DVI's advantage *not* to be a standard, but rather, to be a hardware-based innovation transparent to all existing software and hardware. The DVI technology should soon be easily migrated to any of the existing bases of the tens of millions of IBMs, Macintosh, and compatibles already on the market. As for its high cost and computer identity, the multimedia DVI would not initially be a consumer product, but rather a delivery system ideally suited to the industrial and corporate training and educational markets. And as for costs relative to mass markets, RCA felt that when consumer markets finally revealed themselves with high-volume CD-I sales, DVI could be cost modified to address that market as a stand-alone adjunct similar in programming concept to the CD-I.

Toward the end of his presentation, Art Kaiman, the RCA executive in charge of DVI, turned to a PC-AT on the podium, turned it on and installed an actual DVI CD ROM disc. As the live DVI

25 Boston Computer Society, p. 31.

demonstration unfolded before the baited audience, periodic cheers arose that eventually concluded as a standing ovation.

DVI Versus CD-I In Summary

DVI represents the advent of the first true multimedia CD ROM because of its facility with dexterous, full-motion digital video. Initially, it will compete in the institutional and corporate markets to create, automate, or enhance existing educational and marketing presentations currently relegated to text and graphics, videodisc, and videotape. In particular it will take full advantage of the color features of the new visually acuitous PS/2's and Macintosh II's that are now being introduced to professional markets.

Subsequently, as we enter the early 1990s, a less expensive stand-alone version of the DVI player will compete with CD-I in a market evolving under the acronym "ITV" (Interactive Television). However, they will not share this market alone. Both DVI and CD-I will face competition from other impending interactive multimedia products such as Mattel/SOCS Management's CVD (CD-IV) player, Warner New Media's CD+G, one of several multitrack "IVT" (interactive videotape) products, and whatever CD writeable/eraseables will follow. All these products are targeted to "bridge" a computer-phobic mass market that would currently prefer to purchase an "intelligent television toy" rather than a computer.

Of the differences between DVI and CD-I, Tom Lopez said:

> You have to understand each for what they are. CD-I is a computing device, an operating system with ROM and RAM that runs off of CD ROM storage media and looks like a TV set. DVI is a chip set which happens to run a MS-DOS based system which gives it an advantage since developers are used to it. As for the markets, CD-I will start at the consumers level and work its way out; DVI will start in business arenas and work out to other more general (mass) markets.[26]

---

26 *Computer Currents*, p. 25.

Ultimately, the multimedia capabilities of both DVI and CD-I — and their successive ITV technologies — will greatly enable the major computer vendors to put a computer in every home.

Of the masses, Nancy Woodhill, president of Gannet Company, said:

You can't change the way people live, you have to marry the medium with the way people live.

Inevitably this will mean the marriage of computer and television.

Microsoft '87 Conclusions: Bill Gates on the Future

In his closing speech, Bill Gates reviewed Microsoft's perception of the evolution of CD ROM through the succession of 1986 and 1987 conference highlights. He also predicted milestones for Microsoft '88.

Of the 1986 conference, he pointed out the three most important milestones were the introduction of the High Sierra Group standards, the connectivity of CD ROM to MS-DOS, and the surprising number of early applications already in use.

Of Microsoft '87, he again pointed to the activities of the High Sierra Group, this time ending with its final format definition; the introduction of the MS-DOS extension, providing seamless connectivity between PC and CD ROM; and the expanding number and diversity of applications for the CD ROM. He referred specifically to Microsoft Bookshelf as the first consumer-oriented CD ROM product, and to DVI's video capability as a doorway to the new types of multimedia applications that would entice the consumer's interest in the PC.

As for Microsoft '88, he predicted that we would see:

1. Definitive audio and video standards for DVI
2. Lower cost for all CD ROM drives, including half-height
3. Volume of sales to justify lower pricing overall
4. More agreements on codevelopment of CD hardware and software
5. Far richer graphics for hypertext and hypermedia browsing
6. Streamlined authoring tools for input and editing of various data
7. Other efficiency-oriented development tools

Finally, he concluded by again declaring the dire need for commitment to the creative development of broad-based applications that would appeal to the mass consumer; sales that would further decrease hardware costs, fuel the evolution of the media — and bring a return on investment for the early CD ROM investors.

Bill Gates always seems to know. It will be interesting to see which of his predictions come true by or before the next conference — and which of the new optical acronyms might be the CD-I or DVI of 1988.

Since Microsoft '87: The Once and Future of CD ROM

Today, less than 2 years since the first drives were sold commercially, CD ROM has evolved from a technology to market. Micromedix is shipping nearly 200 CD ROM systems per month to hospital emergency rooms. Grolier has sold its CD ROM to more than 2000 libraries. The most recent 1988 Microsoft Conference saw Apple Computer's full-court entrance into the CD ROM arena with its combination AppleCD SC CD ROM drive and user-friendly HyperCard — a hypertext-oriented thought processor capable of driving multimedia CD ROMs and videodiscs, bringing with it a dedicated million-fold user-base, an extremely mature marketing and development infrastructure, and a strong consumer and educational orientation.

More importantly, the High Sierra Standard has now been accepted by the vast majority of microcomputer vendors, nearly all of which now or will soon support CD ROM — including IBM which showed a CD ROM product at Microsoft '88 and enabled two of its PS/2 series support CD ROM, WORM, and 3.5-in. O-ROM drives.

CD ROM's Future Becomes Questionable

Yet even as the fourth Microsoft Conference approaches, there remain strong doubts from several quarters about the ultimate ascension of CD ROM as the commodity-oriented storage mainstay it was predicted to become, particularly in lieu of continued disappointing sales that remain well below the early optimistic predictions that 100,000 units would be sold by 1989. A recent analysis published by the Boston Computer Society suggests several of the reasons why the immediate growth of CD ROM remains sluggish:[27]

1. The cost of drives remains prohibitive for casual dissemination, though these will fall as more broad-based, consumer-oriented products appear.

2. CD ROM drives have not yet been embraced by the major PC LAN suppliers as single-drive network servers.

3. There are insufficient broad-based titles to inspire consumer sales.

4. There are insufficient non-graphics-oriented titles to allow publishers to rationalize employing the massive storage of CD ROM, a capacity that portends the complexity and conflict of multititle and multivendor products.

5. General public reluctance remains against accepting a read-only medium, particularly given today's obsession with recordability, and given the impending advent of WORM and Erasible discs as the key to the popular notion of a "paperless office."

That optical media in general will succeed and thrive is certainly no longer a question. However, whether one or the other of the optical media will dominate is another question. *Indeed there are growing arguments that both WORM and CD ROM will eventually bow to the Erasable as the ultimate optical media.* This advocacy will continue to rise in crescendo as the Erasible products arrive and gain market share beginning early next 1989.

The basis for these arguments will soon be proven — with exceptions. These exceptions represent the specific advantage over Erasable each of the other optical media provides to specific niche re-

---

27 Numbers 1 through 3 and 5 taken from Boston Computer Society, *Optical Insights*, Fall 1987, p. 1.

quirements. For example, WORM will reign as the ideal format for customers who have large amounts of paper documents, technical drawings, and high density images to continually update, track, and audit.[28]

As for CD ROM, the advantage of non-erasable nonvolatile read-only data will ensure the success of the optical ROM format for decades to come. This is for several reasons, all due to the fact that certain types of product require that their deliverables remain intact. For example, most financial, library, and pedagogical databases can only remain effective if the integrity of their content is maintained. The nonvolatility of certain types of products is to both the legal and financial advantage of its publisher because the proprietary nature of certain intellectual property precludes user compromise, and because nonvolatility will allow for effective usage accounting.

The Real Issue

Most important, what must be considered is that CD ROM is only the first of the CD data formats to be introduced to the market. Its read-only nature is only the first of many optical advantages to be developed and offered — and it won't be the last. Its impending success as a pervasive machine base will be a symbiotic function of increasing sales volumes, more favorable pricing, and variety of applications — a synergistic circumstance that has yet to arrive.

In terms of CD ROM's long-term success, it is important to remember is that it is far more than a product. It is a media standard that will ultimately thrive of its own efficacy as the most appropriate solution to a wide variety of storage and delivery requirements.

Conclusion

CD ROM is only the beginning. As it maintains its service, we will continue to see more and more optical formats available, each of the newer somehow accessible to those they upgrade. We will see

---

28 General concept of CD ROM versus WORM comparison inspired by same article in Boston Computer Society, *Optical Insights*, Fall 1987, pp. 1, 4, 5.

erasable CDs that re-record twice as much video as a VCR, 3.5-in. CD ROMs, and WORM discs that are carried as employee artifacts. Particularly, we will see hybrid formats with specific capabilities pressed as needs require — such as Writable *and* ROM *and* Erasable media.

Together, these collective optical formats shall serve the evolving storage and delivery needs of an ever expanding, information dependent and feature convergent Mac, PC, and PS user base the world over.

About the Author

David C. Traub is currently a contributing editor and associate publisher of *HyperMedia Guide*, a print, videodisc, and CD ROM–based interactive magazine produced in San Francisco. He is also Senior Partner of Sourcelynx, a San Francisco firm that has provided management and computer consulting to Pacific Bell, Drexler Burnham Lambert, and six start-up firms, including three involved in the fields of CD ROM and interactive CD.

His media experience spans video production, feature films, sound engineering and journalism. He has degrees and has done thesis work in the fields of film, rhetoric, and educational cinema. He has spoken internationally on such topics as CD ROM, online retrieval, desktop video, the Microsoft Conference Series, and Hypermedia.

SourceLynx
2560 Bancroft Way, Suite 1
Berkeley, CA 94704
415–540–0480

References

Books

Buddine, Laura and Elizabeth Young *The Brady Guide To CD ROM*, New York: Prentice Hall, 1987.

Susan Ropiequet, *ROM Optical Publishing*, Redmond, WA: Microsoft Press, 1987.

Periodicals

CD Data Report, Suite 1115-324, 1350 Beverly Rd, McLean, VA 22101

CD-I News, Link Resources, 79 Fifth Avenue, New York, NY 10003.

CD ROM Review, P.O. Box 921, Farmingdale, NY 11737–9621.

Optical Information Systems, Meckler Publishing, 520 Riverside Ave., Westport, CN 06880.

Optical Insights, Boston Computer Society, 1 Center Plaza, Boston, MA 02108.

Optical Memory News, Rothchild Consultants, P.O. Box 14817, San Francisco, CA 94114.

Memoires Optiques, Francis Pelletier, Vanne, France.

Video Computing, P.O. Box 3415, Indialantic, FL 32903.

The Videodisc Monitor, P.O. Box 26, Falls Church, VA 22046.

3

The New Gutenbergs

Steve Holder

In the first 3 years since CD ROM applications began to appear, well over 300 titles have been published. What are these CD ROMs being used for? Who is using them and why? Who publishes CD ROMs and what kind of information do they put on them? The answers to questions such as these are valuable to our study of CD ROM technology because it is the practical application of a technology that drives its future development.

To understand the implications of compact disc data storage, we'll examine the major application areas, the publishing community, the different forms of data being recorded, the predominant audiences, and other characteristics of the first wave of CD ROM releases. With this background, we will be better able to understand the current user environment and the possible future directions of CD ROM technology.

The Major Application Areas

Technology promoters tout a broad list of hypothetical applications, but the actual uses of CD ROM have already given the industry its own distinct character. Not surprisingly, information distribution characterizes the most frequent CD ROM applications, and traditional information suppliers are the largest class of CD ROM publishers.

But even though information distribution is the predominant use, optical data discs are also significant in special-purpose computer systems, and to a lesser extent, they are showing up in academic research and internal corporate information systems.

Information Distribution

The sale of information is a business transaction with CD ROM becoming an economical and convenient medium for delivery. Typifying the information available on compact disc are abstract databases, bibliographies, directories, and periodical indexes; financial, demographic, cartographic, scientific, and engineering databases; the full text of federal and state regulations, and other legal references; and to a limited extent, encyclopedias, dictionaries, books, and other literary collections.

Generally, these products are sold as individual discs, or on an annual subscription basis providing updated discs at regular intervals. Software is provided (most often for PC-class computers but occasionally for MacIntosh) enabling easy access to the data contained on the disc. The software usually supports most of the major manufacturers' CD ROM drives connected to personal computers.

Special-Purpose Systems

While the transmittal of information is the most common commercial use of CD data discs, another significant commercial application is in special-purpose computer systems. In special-purpose systems, the optical disc is usually not available as a standalone product. Instead, it is viewed as an integral data storage component of a proprietary computer system enabling it to be used for specialized applications.

Typical applications of this type (frequently built around personal computers) are library cataloging and patron access systems, air and sea navigation systems, parts catalog systems, and cartographic systems.

Academic Research Systems

A small but potentially growing application area for CD ROM is in academic research. Similar to special-purpose systems, but unique in their noncommercial nature, these applications feature a work station enabling students and other researchers to access and perform studies on large databases.

The few existing and planned applications in this category are oriented toward studies of classical literature, but the potential extends into other areas of research as well.

Internal Applications

Another significant application area for optical data storage is noncommercial and archival uses.

While the possibility of reducing warehouses full of paper documents to a stack of optical discs is very real, our survey turned up no applications of this type for CD ROM. Because of the continuous nature of archival projects, they seem better suited to WORM technologies, where data can be easily recorded on optical media using document scanners.

A few large companies, however, are using CD ROM for internal information systems. Though intracompany distribution may be a factor, internal applications are more often driven by the need for compact storage and rapid access to information.

The CD ROM Publishing Community

The more than 100 organizations that have ventured into CD ROM publishing are an extremely diverse group, ranging from the Fortune 100 to one-person operations, from mail-order distributors to the federal government, and from Japan to Europe. These pioneering industry leaders consist primarily of the traditional publishers and electronic data services, the new optical publishers, the CD ROM service industry, special-purpose computer system vendors, and public agencies.

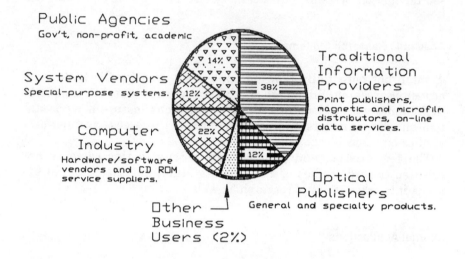

Public Agencies
Gov't, non-profit, academic

System Vendors
Special-purpose systems.

Computer
Industry
Hardware/software
vendors and CD ROM
service suppliers.

Traditional
Information
Providers
Print publishers,
magnetic and microfilm
distributors, on-line
data services.

Optical
Publishers
General and specialty products.

Other
Business
Users (2%)

Figure 3-1   The CD ROM publishing community.

Traditional Information Providers

With the ability to compress hundreds of books or mainframes full of data into the size of a greeting card at the cost of a few dollars per copy, print publishers, data service companies, and on-line data base services are flocking to the new medium.

These traditional information suppliers, numbering some 40 companies, have converted varying portions of their information offerings to the optical disc format, accounting for nearly 45 percent of the currently available CD ROMs. While their initial motivations might be considered a defensive reaction to protect their established markets, the optical medium is nonetheless becoming an obvious extension of their primary product line.

Recognizable names in this category are Dialog, Disclosure, Grolier, Ingram Books, McGraw-Hill, Prentice-Hall, Standard & Poor's, and John Wiley. The list includes many other significant information providers whose names are becoming more widely known in CD ROM circles, such as R. R. Bowker, Cambridge Scientific Abstracts, Datext, Diversified Data Resources, Donnelly Marketing, Harris Information, the Globe and Mail newspaper, International

Computaprint, Micromedex, Dun's Marketing Services, Slater Hall, University Microfilms, Utlas International, and H. W. Wilson. (A complete list is available in the Appendixes.)

Holding the record for most CD ROMs is H. W Wilson with 12 titles representing much of its line of bibliographies and periodical indexes. Of the remaining information distributors, many have produced 2 to 4 CD ROMs, but the vast majority have shown their tentativeness by producing only one disc. As a group, the traditional information providers have produced an average of nearly two CD ROM discs each.

The trend indicates that many more traditional publishers will be offering at least token CD ROM products, and the majority of those who have machine readable data will eventually convert much of their wares to optical disc format. Even though their average output may remain low, traditional information suppliers will account for more CD ROM products than any other publishing segment because of the great number of participants.

Optical Publishers

The optical data disc has also spawned many new companies who are dedicated to optical publishing. These companies' product lines range from the general to the more specific markets.

The general optical publisher often buys the CD publishing rights outright or joint ventures with information suppliers to produce and distribute CD data discs of all types. SilverPlatter Information, Inc. is the archetypal example with nine titles at the time of our survey, spanning a wide range of subject areas. Knowledge Access, Quantum Access, and Tri-Star Publishing are similar companies in the general CD ROM publishing arena.

These general optical publishers are similar to the CD ROM service bureaus except that they assume some degree of ownership and marketing rights, whereas the service bureaus prepare CD ROMs solely for fees.

Other optical publishers, focused on narrower markets, produce CD ROM products only for particular subject areas. Geovision provides cartographic databases; Newsreel Access Systems produces a database of newsreel footage; VLS, Inc. offers complete federal regulations on disc; and Ad Art distributes a disc containing graphic images of commercial clip art.

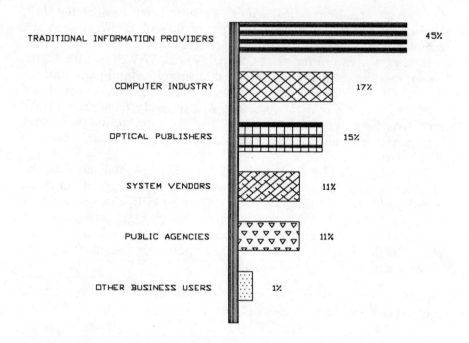

Figure 3-2   Percent of total CD ROM output.

Many other publishers are also specialized in their products, such as Micromedex' line of CD ROM medical diagnostic databases, but they are considered more traditional information suppliers because they also offer their products in other forms such as computer tapes.

The general and specialty optical publishers comprise about 12 percent of the publishing publishing community, and have produced 15 percent of existing CD ROM titles. Currently, the general publishers are averaging nearly 2.5 titles per publisher, while the specialty publishers average almost 1.5 titles each.

The total volume of CD ROM titles produced by the optical publishing segment may never reach the volume produced by the traditional publishers, but their average output can be expected to be higher. Over time, the difference between an optical publisher and a traditional publisher will become less distinct as both groups begin to distribute information in both optical and nonoptical forms.

CD ROM Service Industry

The CD ROM service bureaus, hardware vendors, and developers of CD ROM–related software have each developed at least one disc to demonstrate their products or capabilities. Many of these demonstration discs are available at very nominal prices.

Some companies have parleyed their computer expertise into full-fledged CD ROM products, such as Lotus Development's One Source, the only CD ROM subscription with weekly updates, conveniently interfacing numerous financial databases with Lotus' "1-2-3" spreadsheet product.

Microsoft also has a unique product, the Microsoft Bookshelf. This ultimate horizontal CD ROM application features dictionary, thesaurus, quotations, style manual, almanac, spelling checker, form letters, zip code directory and several other eminantly useful publications for the general computer user.

As the CD ROM service industry develops a greater output of applications for real clients, we can expect these demonstration products to become a less significant part of the overall CD ROM offerings.

Special-Purpose Computer System Vendors

Many existing and newly organized companies are offering special-purpose computer systems that feature CD ROM for data storage. Library Corporation, Brodart Automation, and General Research specialize in library cataloging and patron access systems that use CD ROM.

In the transportation industry, Disc Navigation, a European company, sells a maritime navigation system with 2500 sea charts recorded on a set of CD ROMs accessed through a proprietary computer system that can be tied into various standard maritime navigational systems.

LaserPlot and LaserTrak also offer sea and air navigation systems, respectively. More portable in nature, these systems include navigational charts and trip planning software.

DeLorme Mapping Systems provides a specialized cartographic system that includes a world atlas at 15 miles to the inch which is used as a supplement to more detailed mapping projects.

Optical Media International produces a CD ROM disc, the Universe of Sounds, used as a digital audio data source for its proprietary music synthesizer system.

Public Agencies

Another segment of the publishing community is composed of government, academic, and nonprofit agencies. Academic, research, and scientific institutions are an important, but small component of this category, most often developing CD ROMs for internal use, but also making them available for outside consumption.

Thesauraus Linquae Graecae, led by Theodore Brunner of the University of California at Irvine, has been converting Greek language texts to machine readable form since 1972. Previously stored on tape and used in mainframe environments, TLG has since published two CD ROMs, the first with 212 Mbytes of Greek text, the second adding an additional 173 Mbytes of indices.

Each of the TLG discs has been the centerpiece of experimental scholastic research stations. Ibycus Systems used TLG CD ROM #A in its Ibycus Scholarly Computer system. CD ROM #B was used in the Isocrates Project, a collaborative effort for the development of a research and document preparation system led by Paul Kahn of the Institute for Research in Information and Scholarship (IRIS).

Other scholarly projects underway include Perseus (Harvard) which will add a variety of maps and other related images to a database of ancient literature; Computer Assisted Tools for Septuagint Studies (University of Pennsylvania) which will combine classical, religious, and medieval texts in a CD ROM–based retrieval system; and the Black Fiction Project (Cornell University) cataloging black literature of this century.

In the government sector, data previously supplied on magnetic tapes is now being offered on compact disc. The U.S. Geological Survey, the National Geophysical Data Center, and the Census Bureau typify traditional public information sources now publishing data on CD ROM. The Jet Propulsion Laboratory has also joined in with its publication of Voyager Images of Uranus on CD ROM.

The National Technical Information Service, an organization of the U.S. Department of Commerce, is also licensing its on-line database of scientific, technical, and engineering abstracts for distribution on CD ROM.

The diversity of public and nonprofit publishers is further illustrated by the likes of the American Psychology Association, the British Library, the Commonwealth Agricultural Bureau (U.K.), the Canadian Center for Occupational Health and Safety, the Minnesota Department of Education, the Royal Society of Chemistry (U.K.), and the Western Library Network (Olympia, Washington).

Indications are that government agencies of all types will become prominent members of the CD ROM publishing community, and that CD ROMs will even find military applications in combat systems.

Content Format of the Typical CD ROM

The content of CD ROMs can be viewed in many different ways. One method distinguishes information format, such as data, text, images, audio, and software. Another compares the CD ROM to its original print or computer analog form, such as a directory, anthology, bibliography, catalog, index, manual, encyclopedia, or database.

Both these views lead to the same inescapable conclusion — that CD ROMs are much more likely to contain computer databases than text, images, or audio; and that bibliographies, indexes, and abstracts, as a group, are the most common type of database.

Abstracts

Images, audio, and software are fairly distinct information forms. Many applications, however, tend to blur the difference between pure data and pure text. In a pure sense, data is considered the highly structured record/field organization of typical databases, while text is the full unstructured text of articles and books.

Because of the large number of CD ROMs that contain mostly field- oriented data, but include large fields of text within the same database structure, it was necessary to designate a distinct format classification we called the abstract.

In nearly every case, the abstract form applies to bibliographies, periodical indexes, and financial databases, as well as actual databases of abstracts in a wide variety of subject areas. More than 50 percent of the current CD ROM offerings are of this form, with only about 5 percent being financial applications.

While it is impractical to list them all here (a complete listing is in the Appendixes), a representative sample includes:

Applied Sciences and Technology Index
Art Index
A-V Online
Biography Index
Books in Print
Business Periodicals Index
Commonwealth Agricultural Bureaux Abstracts
Cumulative Book Index
Current Biotechnology Abstracts
Dialog On-Disc ERIC
Education Index
Embase
General Science Index
Humanities Index
Index to Legal Periodicals
Library Literature
Life Sciences Collection
Pollution/Ecology/Toxicology
Psyclit
Social Sciences Index
Sociofile
Ulrich's International Periodicals Directory

We conclude from this finding that a majority of CD ROM applications do not actually contain end-user data, but rather they contain pointers to information in existing print forms. This shouldn't be construed as a characteristic of the optical medium itself, however. Rather, it seems that this type of data, being readily available in electronic form, has lent itself to expedient conversion to CD ROM formats for the first wave of applications.

Databases

Approximately one-third of the CD ROMs surveyed are simple databases, primarily demographic, but also including product catalogs, business/consumer directories, and medical and scientific databases.

Typical data access is via selection of fields and keywords that reduce the database to a selected subset meeting specified criteria. Several of these databases are discussed in more detail in the following section on Popular Audiences.

In most cases, these databases are straight conversions from their mainframe forms, with the addition of special indexes, and access software to compensate for the inherent slowness of seeking on CD ROM. User interfaces are also typically customized for PC environments.

One of the most unique CD ROM databases, created by the Minnesota Department of Education, is dubbed the First National Itembank & Test Development System. It contains over 100,000 test questions for developing test instruments in five basic skill areas.

Full Text

Less than 15 percent of the CD ROM applications are devoted to full text replication of print media. Significantly, most of these are legal applications, typically containing the complete text of federal and state regulations. The remainder are demonstration products and various types of encyclopedic information taking advantage of large quantities of existing text in electronic form. Many such full text applications are described in the following sections on Legal and General Reference applications.

Full text applications are typically supported by inverted indexes that pinpoint every occurrence of every significant word in the text. This preprocessing allows rapid location of any specified keyword in the texts, simply by looking it up in the index.

In many cases, the user interface mimics popular mainframe search and retrieval software, so that users who have previously used on-line services feel comfortable with the CD ROM implementations.

Images

The CD ROMs containing images (about 10 percent of those surveyed) are mostly demonstration products, cartographic applications, and navigational systems. However, a few applications are significant in their uniqueness.

Ad Art publishes its catalog of product clip art on CD ROM, providing high-resolution images of common name-brand consumer products for retail advertising applications. Indexed by company, brand name, product category, or Universal Product Code, the disc is provided to newspapers, retail stores, and ad agencies at virtually no cost, with manufacturers paying for inclusion on the disc.

Combining images and text, the Merriam Webster Dictionary, from Highlighted Data, includes the illustrations from the original print version as part of its database of definitions.

Similarly, the Visual Dictionary depicts 3000 line drawings along with the definitions of terms related to objects in each picture. Based on the book of the same title, it is produced by a consortium of companies under direction of Software Mart.

MasterSearch TM, a trademark information database from Tri Star Publishing, includes images of trademarks as well as data from trademark registrations and applications. These images can be printed to support research and litigation efforts.

Using a combination image base and database, Geovision produces three classes of cartographic disc. The Metro Series offers maps at 1:24,000 scale for major metropolitan areas, in conjunction with other source data. The State Series includes a complete state map at 1:100,000 scale plus utilities, roads, railroads, hydrography, place names, hypsography, and county boundaries. The U.S. Series provides similar data with a complete U.S. map at 1:2,000,000 scale.

In a related application area, navigational systems such as those designed by Disc Navigation, LaserPlot, and LaserTrak offer images of air and sea navigation charts on CD ROM as an integral part of flight planning and maritime navigational computer systems.

Perhaps the most unique image-based application is produced by Image Storage/Retrieval Systems for the insurance claims adjustment industry. Using a lap-top computer with 640 X 400 pixel plasma touch screen, claims adjusters can input automobile make and model to access parts diagrams for cars involved in accidents. By touching the damaged parts in the diagrams, they can obtain repair estimates and settle claims on the scene within 20 minutes.

Audio

Because of CD ROM's audio parentage, it would seem that aural information would be a natural supplement to CD data. Yet fewer than 4 percent of the initial CD ROMs include audio data formats.

Perhaps because compact disc audio consumes nearly 10 Mbytes of data space for each minute of audio, economics dictate that CD audio is less valuable than CD data for computer applications. But digital audio boards that provide up to 40 minutes of lower fidelity audio per 10 Mbytes of data present a very real possibility that audio will become a more common characteristic of future CD ROM applications.

Of the existing applications offering audio, several are demonstration products. However, two dictionaries, the Visual Dictionary from Facts-On-File, and the Merriam Webster Dictionary from Highlighted Data, include audio pronunciations of defined words, which may portend the audio applications of future CD ROM products.

The Visual Dictionary (a joint product of U.S. and Canadian companies) includes pronunciations in both French and English, but is planned to include Spanish, Chinese, German, Japanese, and Italian versions in the future.

In a different application, Optical Media International has produced the Universe of Sounds, a disc containing the digital data for use in its proprietary music synthesizer system.

Hitachi, whose CD ROM players include standard compact disc audio capabilities, includes 30 minutes of classical music in CD audio form on its CD ROM Test Disc #3. As far as we have been able to determine, this is the only application that mixes standard CD audio (greenbook standard) and computer data on a single disc.

Software

As Rockley Miller pointed out in a CD ROM editorial in *The Videodisc Monitor*, the immense capacity of CD ROM creates a vast disparity between perceived and actual value. While CD ROM can store the equivalent of hundreds of thousands of dollars of software, who would be willing to pay that price for a 4 3/4-inch disc? Perhaps that is why very little software is being supplied on CD ROM.

Except for demonstration products, and the occasional inclusion of software necessary for the particular CD ROM application, only one disc offers software as its primary product — the PC-SIG CD ROM Disc. This library of public domain and shareware programs is a unique instance of software being supplied on CD ROM because of the low cost of the source material.

Yet the possibilities for future distribution of programs using optical discs are attractive in many cases. Computer manufacturers sup-

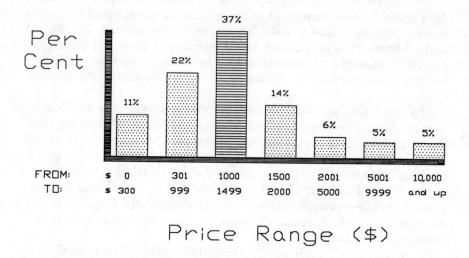

Figure 3-3   CD ROM prices.

plying operating systems and utility software on reels of magnetic
tape could easily and economically convert to the CD medium for future distribution.

Popular Audiences

As with books, CD ROMs often contain information appealing to
many different types of users, complicating efforts to neatly classify
them according to audience. Nonetheless, the first wave of CD ROMs
includes a large selection of titles clearly targeted to specifically
identifiable audiences: marketing, finance, legal, medical, scien-
tific/engineering, and library professions.

On the other hand, a growing number of CD ROM applications
have such broad appeal that they cannot be relegated to clearly
defined user categories. Classified as general reference, these typically include catalogs, directories, encyclopedias, dictionaries, and other
general reference works.

Marketing

Market Statistics and Knowledge Access have teamed to produce Your Marketing Consultant, a two-disc set containing data on consumers and businesses. The Consumer disc offers demographic profiles, economic factors and retail store figures, while the Business-to-Business disc contains data by type of business, employee count, and occupational factors. Data for the United State is selectable by metropolitan area, county, or other geographic regions.

The Infomark Laser PC System from National Decision Systems provides geodemographic population statistics, facts on 7 million businesses, customer targeting and lifestyle segmentation data, shopping center reports, customer expenditure figures, color mapping, and site location tools. The system uses NDS' specially configured AT computer, also offering data on a 12-inch laser disc in addition to CD ROM.

Harris Information Services' Selectory of American Electronics Manufacturers is a more targeted marketing application, permitting generation of mailing labels, sales lead cards, and company profiles on electronics firms meeting user-specified criteria.

CD/Corporate and CD/Corptech, offered by Datext, Inc., consists of five CD ROMs, providing complete financial, analytical and statistical data on technology, service, consumer, industrial and high-tech companies.

Conquest, a consumer information system from Donnelly Marketing Information Services, contains economic, demographic, and other data variables for the entire U.S. It allows analysis of spending patterns, consumer profiles by geographic area, and preparation of maps showing geographic distribution of target markets.

Other databases marketers may find appealing are the County and Metro Compendium, and Population Disc provided by Slater Hall Information Products. These discs detail data on health, education, retail, banking, personal income, poverty, labor, population, housing, age, race, sex, and other topics for all counties and metropolitan areas.

Companies with Canadian markets would be interested in Homebase and Business Plan, two discs produced by Tetragon of Canada. The first lists names, addresses, and phone numbers for all residences in Canada; the second lists over 1/2 million Canadian businesses.

Business Statistics, from Slater Hall Information Products, contains three databases originally published by the Department of Commerce Bureau of Economic Analysis. These are the National Income and Product Accounts (GNP) 1929–1986; Business Statistics (the Blue Pages from the Survey of Current Business), annual from 1961 to 1985 and monthly beginning in 1981; and Income and Employment by state, annual from 1969 to 1985.

Financial

Because databases of consumer and business information often combine both marketing and financial data, many of the products described above as marketing oriented are also of interest to financial analysts. For instance, the previously described CD/Corporate also contains 7 years of financial statements, 11 years of stock prices and trading data, and Form 10-Ks for each company in its database.

But in addition to the marketing/financial applications above, several other CD ROM products are focused more specifically on providing financial information. CD/Banking, another Datext product, details deposits, loans, profits, liquidity, and other information for more than 15,000 U.S. commercial banks.

Disclosure's database of financial data and SEC filings for more than 10,000 public companies is also available on optical disc. Called Compact Disclosure, the database can be searched using more than 200 different financial and business variables.

Standard & Poor's provides its Compustat financial databases on CD as Compustat PC Plus. The historical fundamentals are used for portfolio management, securities and credit analyses, and merger and acquisitions.

The most ambitious financial database product has to be One Source from Lotus Development Corporation. With eight industry standard historical financial databases (including Compustat and Disclosure), updated discs are delivered weekly via Federal Express. During the week, data can be updated daily in about 10 minutes by modem. Accompanying software allows access to CD ROM data while using Lotus' 1-2-3 spreadsheet, or through a separate research and analysis package.

SilverPlatter Information distributes the CD ROM version of JA Micropublishing's Corporate and Industry Research Reports (CIRR). This database indexes more than 70,000 abstracts on corporate and industry reports written by securities and investment banking firms.

A different segment of the financial community would be interested in the CD ROMs containing tax information. These include Phinet Tax Resource, from Prentice-Hall Information Network, Tax Library, from Tax Analysts, and Tax Forms on Demand, from On-Line Computer Systems.

Legal

For the legal community, the first wave of CD ROMs offers complete federal and state regulations and other legal reference works in a desktop electronic form.

VLS, Inc. publishes Optext, a three-disc set containing the Code of Federal Regulations (Titles 1–50) and the Federal Register. With federal regulations in electronic form, legal researchers can easily locate all references to any given keyword, such as "product liability," and instantly call up each reference. This tiny set of CD ROMs replaces 22 feet of printed volumes.

In addition to its own issue of the Federal Regulations, ERM Computer Services also publishes state regulations for Pennsylvania, New Jersey, and other major industrial states for use in its Enflex Info computer system.

Demonstrating more specialized legal applications, Quantum Access produces The Texas Attorney General Documents, a compilation of the official opinions issued by the Texas Attorney General, and State Education Encyclopedia containing all regulations, statutes, and appeals related to running a school district in Texas. And in another niche area, Tri-Star Publishing is producing a database of patent information.

For the dedicated legal researcher, H. W. Wilson offers its Index to Legal Periodicals on CD ROM, cataloging articles from 476 leading legal periodicals in English, French, and Spanish. Searches can be performed by cases or statutes, as well as by topic.

In a very different legal application, Tri-Star Publishing produces MasterSearch TM, a database of trademark information from the U.S. Patent and Trademark Office. This database includes the text of active trademark registrations and applications, as well as actual trademark images. Useful in marketing research or litigation support, the database can be searched for any keyword appearing in any field of the trademark filing.

Medical and Health

The medical and health professions are also benefitting from CD ROM technology. Leading the field in medical applications is Micromedex, Inc., with its four-disc Computerized Clinical Information System (CCIS).

Micromedex' first disc, Poisindex, is a database of over 410,000 toxic substances, including identification, ingredient, and treatment information accessible by brand/trade name, manufacturer, generic or chemical name, street slang terminology, botanical, or common name.

Drugdex contains drug evaluations and consults on over 4000 investigational and foreign, FDA approved and over-the-counter preparations, indexed by U.S. and foreign brand/trade names; disease states; and drug information terms.

For acute care, Emergindex provides access to information dealing with medical/surgical disease and traumatic injury. Using a 40,000 word dictionary of medical terms, information can be rapidly retrieved from a database of clinical reviews, clinical abstracts, differential reviews, and EKG demonstration strips.

The fourth disc in the CCIS set, Identidex, is a tablet and capsule identification system using manufacturer imprint codes as the primary identification resource. With more than 33,000 entries, the data base covers U.S. and foreign ethical/prescription drugs, over-the-counter preparations, generic drugs, and look-alike or rip-off drugs, including color and physical descriptions, and slang/street terminology.

For the health professional, the oustanding bargain of the year is the CCINFOdisc from the Canadian Centre for Occupational Health and Safety. At $100 per year for a two-disc set, including four quarterly updates, this CD ROM currently provides 17 databases, 6 videotex information packages, and 18 full text publications addressing hazardous chemicals and other occupational health and safety information.

Among the many CD ROMs available from SilverPlatter Information Services is OSH-ROM, a collection of three occupational health and safety databases. Together, they contain 240,000 abstracts of articles from 500 journals and 100,000 monographs/reports, spanning nearly 30 years and more than 50 countries. The subject areas include toxicology, epidemiology, occupational medicine, pathology, physiology, metabolism, and many more.

The International Association for Scientific Computing is releasing CD/Biotech, a journal containing the NIH-sponsored Genetic Sequences Databank (Genbank), the National Biomedical Research Foundation's Protein Identification Resource, the European Molecular Biology Laboratory's Data Library, articles of interest to the biotech community, and operational software of scientific interest.

In a more general vein, John Wiley & Sons publishes the International Dictionary of Medicine and Biology, containing definitions of more than 160,000 terms.

Many databases of medical abstracts are also available. Digital Diagnostics offers Bibliomed, a thesaurus-oriented retrieval system for the National Library of Medicine's Medline database of medical abstracts, and SilverPlatter distributes Elsevier Scientific Publishers' Embase, a database of abstracts in clinical medicine and biomedical research.

Cambridge Scientific Abstracts produces Compact Cambridge Medline, indexing articles from more than 3000 publications covering all areas of biomedicine, and the Royal Society of Chemistry (U.K.) published its Current Biotechnology Abstracts database on CD ROM.

Scientific/Engineering

John Wiley & Sons has three CD ROM products in the scientific field. The Kirk-Othmer Encyclopedia of Chemical Technology is a CD ROM version of Wiley's 24-volume reference set on chemistry and related industries.

The CD ROM version of Wiley's 19-volume Mark Encyclopedia of Polymer Science and Engineering covers polymer and plastics technology, while Wiley's Registry of Mass-Spectral Data is a valuable collection of data in the field of mass spectrometry.

Hydrodata, a set of CD ROM discs produced by US WEST Knowledge Engineering, provides access to 100 years of daily flows on U.S. rivers for flood-plain planning, water supply analysis, environmental decision making, water law, reservoir operation, and utility siting. The data can be exported to popular spreadsheets or analyzed using the accompanying utilities.

The National Technical Information Service (an agency of the U.S. Department of Commerce), collects the scientific, engineering, and technical reports produced by federal agencies and government con-

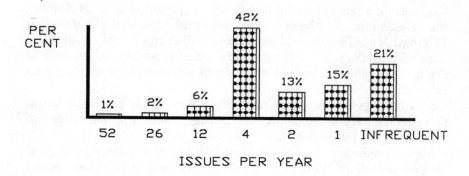

Figure 3-4   Frequency of updates.

tractors. The abstracts of these reports have been available on-line, and will soon be available on CD ROM.

Other databases of scientific abstracts and periodical indexes include the Applied Science and Technology Index, from H.W. Wilson; the Compact Cambridge Pollution/Ecology/Toxicology abstract database from Cambridge Scientific Abstracts; and the General Science Index, also from H. W. Wilson.

Library

Library applications divide into two primary areas: cataloging and patron access systems. For cataloging, librarians use CD ROMs as an administrative tool, retrieving electronic file cards from a database of catalog records, then editing and printing them to generate the cards for the library's central catalog.

Library Corporation's Bibliofile Catalog Production System features two CD ROM databases for catalog production, and book identification and ordering. The LC MARC English Language Discs contain Library of Congress English-Language cataloging data, including monographs, serials, Government Printing Office publications, maps, film, and music. Also available is the LC MARC Foreign Language Discs containing Library of Congress foreign language cataloging data.

Other catalog production systems include LaserQuest from General Research Corporation, and DisCon from Utlas International. The GRC Resource Database contains over 4 million catalog records on four CD ROM discs, and is available for a one-time fee plus annual maintenance costs. Discon contains 6 million catalog records, and is provided on a monthly rental basis plus a small fee based on the number of records retrieved.

The Western Library Network, a 250-member library association spanning the Western U.S. and Canada, has produced LaserCat. These three CD ROM discs contain 1.9 million records of its membership's holdings plus 2 years of records from the Library of Congress. The database, covering books, serials, films, music, maps, and other formats, is used in preparing cards, labels, and bibliographies.

For book identification and ordering, the Any-Book CD ROM from Library Corporation provides 1,500,000 titles available from 22,000 publishers. In addition to providing complete data on both books and publishers, accompanying software will generate orders and accounting records, and monitor the status of all orders and accounts.

In patron access systems, the physical card catalog is replaced by one or more personal computers with the library's entire card catalog contained on CD ROM. Catalog updates can be stored on hard disk until it becomes necessary to master a new CD ROM. Using a very simplified design for user input, library patrons can search the CD ROM card catalog for specific titles, authors, or subjects.

For patron access, Brodart Automation supplies Le Pac, a customized personal computer with a protective faceplate installed over the disk drives, and an optional, specially designed 10-key pad instead of a keyboard. For each library, Brodart prepares a custom CD ROM containing the library's unique card catalog.

General Research Corporation's patron access system, LaserGuide, includes library floor plans giving users a map to any book's location. A unique browsing mode also allows users to scan books that are physically near others previously found in searching. With this facility, patrons can actually browse "closed" stacks, and shelves located in branch libraries.

Library Corporation also offers a complete patron access work station including the stand. Called the Intelligent Catalog, it applies inference techniques to search titles, subjects, and authors without being directed, and makes recommendations of additional subject material or titles it "thinks" the user would enjoy.

Other CD ROM products aimed at library audiences, though in a very different way, are databases of abstracts in library science. Library Literature, from H. W. Wilson, indexes 189 foreign and domestic publications in English and a dozen foreign languages, covering all aspects of library and information science. LISA, compiled by Library Association Publishing, Ltd., and published on CD ROM by SilverPlatter, contains abstracts of the world's literature in librarianship, information science, and related disciplines.

Though not a library application, per se, we include here the bibliographic databases currently being used in retail bookstores. The Del Mar Group has created the Bookseller's Assistant for bookstore customer's to look up books, and LaserSearch, an in- store book identification and ordering system available exclusively from Ingram Book Company.

General Reference

Because of the volume and breadth of data they contain, many CD ROM applications are useful to a wide variety of audiences in businesses, schools, and government agencies. And even though a consumer market does not yet exist, many could be considered consumer-oriented products.

For shipping and mailing applications, any U.S. address can be quickly retrieved using the Address Verification System from Information Design. This CD ROM contains the entire 47-volume National Directory of the U.S. Postal Service.

Product catalogs include Parts-Master, NSA's database of over 12 million parts and products procured by the U.S. government, and McGraw-Hill's Sweet's Catalog Files, an indexed listing of manufacturers' product catalogs including Sweet's Byline Service, Sweet's Update Service, and Sweet's Specification System.

Where necessary, users can scan Newsbank's file of 700,000 news clippings, or Newsreel Access Systems' News Scan database of over 200,000 pieces of news film. In addition, the Canadian Globe and Mail newspaper has archived all of its 1985 newspapers on a single CD ROM for external distribution.

General reference encyclopedias include Grolier's Electronic Encyclopedia on CD ROM, the McGraw-Hill Science and Technical Reference Set, and the Gran Enciclopedia del Mundo from ComCal of

Spain. Each of these are full text CD ROM versions of the original printed references.

CD ROM dictionaries are also available. The Visual Dictionary, available from Facts-On-File, contains 3000 line drawings with audio pronunciations and definitions for all of the parts in the illustrations. Currently in French and English, other languages are to be added soon.

The Merriam Webster Dictionary, from Highlighted Data, contains the illustrations of the original print version, as well as audio pronunciations for each word. In addition, it contains a geographic database of the United States, allowing the user to focus in on areas of interest. Similarly, Tri-Star Publishing and the Oxford University Press are copublishing the Oxford English Dictionary.

For the everyday PC user, the Microsoft Bookshelf contains 10 reference works: the *American Heritage Dictionary, Bartlett's Quotations, Chicago Manual of Style, World Almanac, Roget's Thesaurus, Houghton-Mifflin Spelling Verifier and Corrector, Forms and Letters, Houghton-Mifflin Usage Alert, Business Information Sources,* and *US Postal Service ZIP Code Directory.*

Though no marketable products have yet been released, a variety of companies are experimenting with CD ROM telephone directories. NYNEX has been testing a prototype CD ROM directory through selected companies, while Pacific Bell Directory is investigating coupling yellow page directories with auto-dial software. Compact Discoveries, a Florida optical publisher, has produced a demonstration disc called the Illustrated Yellow Pages.

Demonstration and Prototype Discs

It would be unfair to conclude any examination of ground-breaking CD ROM applications without noting the significant number of prototype and demonstration discs that have been produced, especially since many of these can be obtained for very, very nominal prices.

In the category of books-on-disc, Reteaco has distributed Communications Excellence and The Brady Guide to CD ROM on compact disc to promote its FindIT retrieval software. Similarly, Computer Access Corporation produced CD ROM: The New Papyrus, a fully indexed version of the original printed book, illustrating its

Bluefish access software. (Computer Access has since been acquired by Lotus Development Corporation.)

Diversified Data Resources has published the CD ROM Sourcedisc, containing all the data in its printed CD ROM Sourcebook, plus industry-related market studies, periodicals, reference sources, services, and samples of CD ROM related software.

To demonstrate their capabilities and services in CD ROM data preparation, Amtec Information Services created the OPTI/Search Sampler Disc, Reference Technology produced Samplers I, II, and III, Earth View released Interactive Audiomation, and Information Dimensions pressed the Compact Video Demonstration Disc.

As a demonstration of rapid publishing capability, Disc in a Day was produced during the Second Annual CD ROM Conference by Lo-Down, Optical Media International, and LaserVideo. At the same time, Meridian Data, Computer Access, Info Express, iBase Systems, and Philips DuPont Optical joined forces to publish The Conference Disc, containing articles on CD ROM with sample databases and retrieval software.

For testing its CD ROM drives, Hitachi has CD ROM Test Disc #3, which includes 30 minutes of classical music in CD Audio format, as well as many megabytes of graphic images, text, and software.

During development of the Visual Dictionary, Software Mart produced a prototype disc containing 117 drawings, with definitions and audio pronunciations in English and French for 1660 terms. Compact Discoveries also produced a prototype disc for its Illustrated Yellow Pages containing images, maps, and directory information for the South Florida area.

Several government agencies have also produced prototype discs. The National Geophysical Data Center created the NOAA/NESDIS Demonstration Disc containing a collection of data from the National Oceanic and Atmospheric Administration. The USGS Prototype Demonstration Disc from the U.S. Geological Survey contains several USGS databases and samples of six different retrieval packages.

The U.S. Census Bureau produced two CD ROM test discs. Census Test Disc #1 contains demographic data for zip codes, location of manufacturing plants, county level agricultural data, 1983 County Business Patterns, and 1984 Population Estimates for Government Units. Census Test Disc #2 contains latitude and longitude for the centroids of census statistical areas, demographic and housing data for all places over 10,000 population, and a longitudinal, county-level data file.

Dawning of the Optical Information Age

Mankind's progressing intellect has been characterized by labels such as the Stone Age, the Iron Age, the Machine Age, the Electronic Age, the Space Age, and the Information Age. Each period lasting geometrically less time before the next arrives. Though we are yet on the forefront of the Information Age, perhaps we are already seeing the beginning of the next major milestone in human progress.

By expanding our vision to take in the entire optical landscape, we see fiber optic communications and optical computers combining with optical data storage to create a completely new information environment, one in which all information is created, processed, transmitted, and stored optically.

And when we look back upon the late twentieth century as the dawn of the Optical Information Age, it'll not be the new medium we salute, but the pioneering efforts of those who put the new medium to work. It's not the new papyrus we'll remember, but the New Gutenbergs.

About the Author

Steve Holder is Vice President and co-founder of IVID Communications, an applications development and systems integration firm. IVID specializes in interactive videodisc and CD ROM application design and software development.

IVID Communications
4340 Viewridge Ave., Suite B
San Diego, CA 92123
619–576–0611

References

Crane, Gregory, V. Judson Harward, Frederick Hemans, Albert Henrichs, Thomas Martin, Gregory Nagy, D. Neel Smith (1986). "Perseus: An Interactive Curriculum on Ancient Greek Civilization, A Proposal to the Annenberg/CPB Project," Harvard University, September.

Helgerson, Linda (1986). "CD-ROM: The Basis for Scholarly Research in Higher Education," *The CD Data Report*, Langley Publications, McLean, Va., December.

Kahn, Paul (1986). "A Description of Isocrates: All of Greek Literature on a CD ROM," Brown University, July.

Kraft, Robert A. (1986). "Gearing Up for CD ROM," Religious Studies News, September.

Martin, Brian (1987). "The First CD ROM Publication." In: *CD ROM*, vol. 2, Suzanne Ropiequet (ed.) Redmond, Wash.: Microsoft Press.

B

The CD ROM Format

4

CD ROM Hardware

Jeffrey N. Nadler and Robert J. Wiesenberg

The design of the CD ROM hardware device is perhaps more astonishing than the technologies used to employ 550 Mbytes of data on the 120-mm CD ROM disc. The ability to precisely access and reconstruct encoded data make the CD ROM drive a powerful tool for the personal computer environment. The development of the CD ROM drive hardware has given users the freedom to reign over tremendous volumes of information. No other hardware device provides such a cost effective means for accessing vast volumes of information via a personal computer.

The intention of this chapter is to explain how CD ROM hardware reconstructs the data encoded on the CD ROM disc. The description will cover the origin of the technology, an overview of the CD ROM drive and workstation, optical components, servo control systems, EFM demodulation, error correction, descrambling, interface, and system control.

Overview

Origin of CD ROM Drive Technology

The development of CD ROM technology is greatly attributed to the emergence of CD Audio. Not only the disc manufacturing aspects but the mass production of the optical and other components of CD Audio players has helped to bring CD ROM hardware to a cost-effective level.

It has been a natural progression to adapt the CD Audio player for the computer environment. The basic modifications include the design of superior error correction techniques and the adaptation to provide an interface to allow connection to the personal computer.

CD ROM drives require sophisticated error correction capabilities because of the extreme importance of accuracy when handling electronic data. A computer user cannot afford the error rates that are acceptable in the CD Audio environment. For this reason, additional error correction schemes have been incorporated into the CD ROM hardware and software systems.

The addition of interface circuitry provides the necessary linkage that CD ROM drives require to enter into the world of computer peripherals. Various interface designs provide compatibility with a number of different computers.

Other changes have been made to the CD Audio player to ready it for the computer peripheral market. Due to different demands made by the computer market versus the consumer electronics market, component selection and design integrity may differ between CD ROM drives and CD Audio players.

The CD ROM drive eliminates the manual buttons used on CD Audio players for searching the disc and puts the power to precisely randomly access the disc's 550 Mbytes of information in the hands of the personal computer user.

Relationship with the Personal Computer

One of the great attractions of CD ROM hardware is that it can be used with existing personal computer systems. The basic CD ROM system includes a personal computer containing a minimum of 256K memory, monitor, CD ROM drive, interface cable, and controller card. The simple installation of a single slot controller card into the motherboard joins the user with this powerful device. After installation, the PC recognizes the CD ROM drive the same way floppy disk drives or other magnetic drives are recognized. More complex workstations have been designed to link multiple drives to one or more PCs.

Different Types of Drives

The design parameters for CD ROM drives are outlined by the Yellow Book standard developed by N. V. Philips and the Sony Corporation in 1983. The purpose of the Yellow Book standard is to outline the manufacturing requirements for CD ROM discs. This standard is to ensure that all discs are manufactured in the same way. The CD ROM drive specifications are an outgrowth of the disc standard. They are the minimum requirements necessary to read a standard disc.

Today, there are several manufacturers of drives on the market, each differs slightly in performance and features. However, each conforms with the requirements outlined by the Yellow Book standard. All drives must be able to read 550 Mbytes of data encoded on the 120 mm disc in a constant linear velocity (CLV) mode, blocks of data consisting of a total of 2352 bytes (288 bytes of error correction and error detection coding and 2048 bytes of user data.) The standard also requires that the drive be able to transfer sequential blocks of data from the disc at a rate of 150 kbytes/second.

The first drives to reach the market were the stand-alone and full-height built-in models. These vary in design from manufacturer to manufacturer. Some are designed to be placed next to the personal computer while others can be stacked on top of the computer under the monitor. Stand alone drives contain 110- or 220-volt power supplies and plug into an AC outlet. Most of the external drives have multiple connectors for daisy chaining several drives to one controller card. Depending on the drive and the controller card it is possible to daisy chain as many as eight drives to one controller card and personal computer.

For users who prefer the CD ROM to be mounted internally in their personal computer, manufacturers offer built-in models that conform to the form factor for a full-height floppy disk drive or hard disk drive. In this case the drive does not need an independent power supply; it is connected internally to four pin DC connectors used for floppy or hard disk drives. The second generation CD ROM drives are designed to fit into a half-height disk drive space in the personal computer.

Features

A variety of features has given each of the drive manufacturers distinction. One issue that has received considerable attention is the different disk loading mechanisms. Several drives use an electronic front-loading door modeled after the CD Audio player. Others use a mechanical front-loading door or a manual front-loading protective cartridge. Philips has been the only manufacturer to use a top loading mechanism.

Additional capabilities such as vertical mounting and durability for extreme environmental conditions are obtainable from some of the vendors. All manufacturers also offer models with audio capabilities. In the case of some stand alone models there is a front miniheadphone jack and a volume control or two RCA jacks on the rear panel of the drive. Other manufacturers have implemented the audio capabilities on the controller card. It should be noted that the audio reproduction in the CD ROM drive is not the same high-quality audio produced by the CD Audio drives. Drives also take on distinct characteristics depending on the method of interface used to communicate with the host computer. These are addressed later in the chapter.

Optical Pickup

The function of the optical pickup in the CD ROM drive is to translate the optically stored information on the CD ROM disc into electrical signals. The information is read by shining a laser beam onto the disc and detecting the strength of the reflection. The intensity of the reflected beam is dependent upon the presence of pits and lands on the disc. The depth of the pit was chosen to be one-quarter the wavelength of the laser beam in the transparent substrate (refractive index $n = 1.5$) of the disc. The reflected light from such a pit ends up 180° out of phase with the light reflected from the adjacent reflective surface causing destructive interference between the two reflections.

Since the diameter of the laser spot on the disc is considerably larger than the diameter of the pit, the light reflected from a pit is actually partially from the pit and partially from the nearby reflective surface. The end result is that the reflected light from a pit is much less intense than the reflected light from a nearby land (see Figure 4-1). The reflected light beams from the pits and lands are read by photodiodes that can detect the intensity differences and convert them into electrical signals.

Laser

A low-power semiconductor laser is used in the CD ROM drive to produce the light beams needed to read the data from the disc. A semiconductor laser is very similar to a light emitting diode (LED) except that the light emitted from a laser is one wavelength only and is coherent in phase while the LED output is many wavelengths and is incoherent with regard to phase.

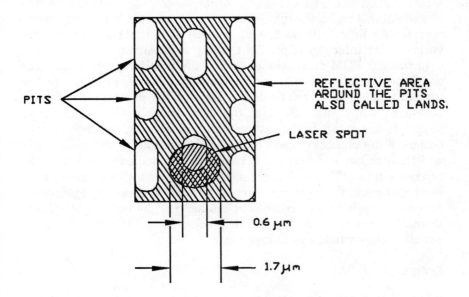

Figure 4-1 Laser spot touching a pit and adjacent land. The reflections from the pit and the land will interfere with each other.

Light is emitted from a semiconductor *pn* junction when a large enough forward bias placed across the junction causes minority carriers in the junction to spontaneously recombine with majority carriers. The light emission is a result of the carriers falling to a lower energy state when they recombine. For the semiconductor laser *pn* junction used in the CD ROM drive, a combination of AlGaAs is used in a heterojunction format that emits coherent light with a wavelength of 790 nanometers at a very low power of approximately 5 milliwatts. It is worth noting that the laser used in the CD ROM drive and most semiconductor lasers are low power lasers and are not very dangerous. If someone were to shine the laser directly into one's eye, however, the eye would indeed be damaged. There are safety locks built into the drive such that when the drawer is open for disc loading, the laser is turned off even though it would still be nearly impossible to look directly at the laser.

The output from a semiconductor laser can vary with changes in temperature or simply with age. To prevent problems reading the data, a photodiode is placed near the laser to monitor the intensity of the light (this is not the photodiode used to read the data). The monitor photodiode, as well as the other photodiodes that will be discussed later, can be thought of as a semiconductor laser working in reverse: As light falls on the photodiode it outputs a current that varies as the intensity of the light falling on it varies.

In the CD ROM drive, the output of the monitor photodiode feeds one input to a semiconductor comparator. The other input to the comparator is a fixed reference voltage that the photodiode output is compared with. The output of the comparator controls the power supply to the laser. If the intensity of the laser light decreases, the output of the photodiode will decrease. The output of the comparator will then reflect a difference between the photodiode input and the reference input. This difference signal will increase the power to the laser and cause the light intensity to increase to its normal intensity. A similar result would occur if the intensity of the laser light were to increase above the reference level. A schematic of the monitor diode circuit is shown below in Figure 4-2.

Optics

Inside the optical pickup there is considerably more than just a semiconductor laser (see Figure 4-3). An intricate optical system alters various characteristics of the laser light to properly read the data

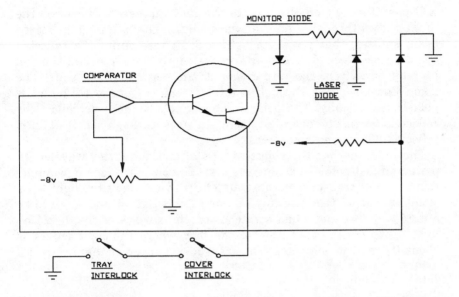

Figure 4-2 Schematic of circuit monitoring and controlling amount of light emitted by laser diode.

and to keep the laser spot vertically in focus and radially on track. Without vertical focusing and radial tracking systems, the optical pickup would never be able to read the tiny pits and lands on the disc.

After leaving the laser, the beam first goes through a diffraction grating plate where two small side beams are formed on either side of the main beam. This produces the popular "three beam" style, also used in the CD Audio systems. It will be shown later how these side beams are used for radial tracking. Another style designed by Philips N.V. uses only one beam for reading and tracking. After being diffracted, the light goes through a collimator lens that makes the light beams parallel so they can be properly focused onto the disc by the objective lens. After the collimator lens the light encounters a polarized beam splitter. The job of the polarized beam splitter is to allow the incident beams to pass through to the disc but to redirect the reflected beam 90° to the photodiodes where the reflections can be interpreted. The polarized beam splitter is designed to allow horizontally polarized light to pass directly through unchanged. The light beam from the laser is at this point polarized horizontally so it will pass through on the way to the disc unaltered. However, the beam passes through a quarter wavelength plate, after the polarized beam splitter, that gives the light a 90° phase shift. The reflected beam passes through the quarter wavelength plate a second time on its way back from the disc giving it another 90° phase shift. The beam has now gone through a total of 180° in phase shift and is polarized vertically. The polarized beam splitter does not allow the reflected vertically polarized beam to pass through. Instead it is reflected 90° to the photodiodes.

The light reaches the objective lens after the quarter wavelength plate and just before reaching the disc. The objective lens in conjunction with the transparent substrate of the disc focuses the light to be small enough to read the tiny pits and lands but not too small to be affected by dirt and small scratches on the surface of the disc. The light spot on the outer edge of the disc where the light enters is about 0.8 mm in diameter. The transparent layer of the disc is 1.2

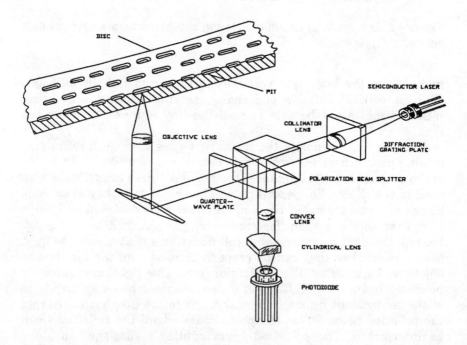

Figure 4-3 The internal parts of the optical pickup unit.

mm thick with a refractive index of $n = 1.5$. This means that the 0.8-mm-diameter light spot on the surface of the disc is reduced to a spot 1.7 μm in diameter on the reflective layer of the disc (see Figure 4-4). Any dirt or marks on the surface of the disc that are in the path of the light beam are reduced by six orders of magnitude in size at the reflective layer of the disc. Thus, any dirt smaller than 0.5 mm will have no effect on the laser spot at the pits and lands.

The reflection of the finely focused light beam will travel back through the objective lens and quarter wavelength plate but will be deflected by the polarized beam splitter onto the photodiodes through a convex lens and a cylindrical lens. These two lenses, together with the objective lens, are used to maintain the proper focus of the spot on the disc. The range of focus of the optical pickup is only 4 μm. Thus, a greater variation in the flatness of the disc would result in errors. It turns out that disc warp can cause height variations as large as 500 to 1000 μm. Therefore, an automatic focus correction servo system must be employed in the player.

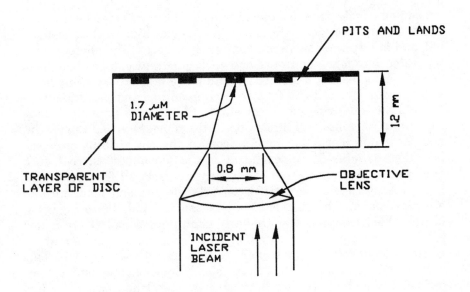

Figure 4-4 Diagram of laser light on disc surface.

Focusing Servo

The focusing servo uses the reflection from the main laser beam to detect and correct focusing errors and maintain the laser spot on the disc within its 4 μm range of focus. As the light beam passes through the convex lens, the vertical component of the beam is focused at the focal point of the lens while the horizontal component is unaffected. At the cylindrical lens, the horizontal component is focused and the vertical component is unaffected. As a result of separately focusing the horizontal and vertical components, two different focal points are produced — one for the horizontal and one for the vertical. A photodiode placed halfway between these two focal points will have a circular spot on it. The system is designed to produce a near-perfect round spot on the photodiode when the laser beam spot on the disc is perfectly in focus. When a height variation on the disc, due to an imperfectly flat disc, is encountered, the reflected beams are no longer perfectly aligned and an elliptical spot forms on the photodiode. When the disc is closer to the objective lens, the spot is elongated vertically, and vice versa when the disc is further from the objective lens (see Figures 4-5A–C).

The photodiode performs two functions on the reflected light beam: It translates the optical information on the disc into an electrical signal, and it keeps the lens system properly in focus. The photodiode is separated into four quadrants and each quadrant can be thought of as one photodiode. If a perfectly round circle falls on the photodiode, an equal amount of light falls on each quadrant and each quadrant outputs an equal current. If an ellipse falls on the four quadrants, the output currents will differ due to the unequal amounts of light, and these differences are used to correct the out of focus situation (see Figures 4-5A–C). Independent of the amount of current each quadrant produces, the sum of the currents from all four quadrants is used as the main signal that converts the pits and lands into an electrical signal. The signals from quadrants A and C (see Figure 4-6) are added together, and similarly quadrants B and D are added together. These combined signals feed a differential amplifier which generates the focus error signal [FER = (A + C) − (B + D)]. This focus error signal controls an electronically movable magnetic coil attached to the objective lens that can move the lens closer to or further away from the disc. It will be seen later that the objective lens can also be moved side to side for proper tracking control. The focus error signal will be zero when the beam is in focus and will be a

5A: Four quadrant
    diode with laser
    spot when disc
    and detective
    lens are too
    close.

5B: Four quadrant
    diode with laser
    spot when disc
    is in focus.

5C: Four quadrant
    diode with laser
    spot when disc
    and objective
    lens are too far
    apart.

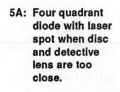
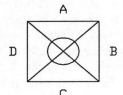
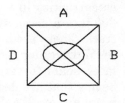

Figure 4-5A–C

varying positive or negative signal depending upon how close to or
how far away from the disc the objective lens is. The focus error signal will continuously move the coil that moves the objective lens
until the focus error signal is zero, i.e., until the system is in focus.
When the objective lens is too close to the disc, quadrants A and C
will receive more light than quadrants B and D. Thus FER = $(A + C)$
$- (B + D)$ will be positive and will move the lens away from the disc
until FER = 0. When the reverse occurs, $(A + C) - (B + D)$ will be
negative and will move the lens in the opposite direction. It should
be noted that this method used to focus the beam is not standard
among all drives although the different approaches are similar.

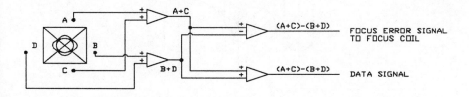

Figure 4-6 Four quadrant diode, focus error signal, and data signal.

Tracking Servo

Another problem the optical pickup needs to address is radial mistracking. The pits and lands on the disc are organized in radial tracks. The width of each pit is 0.6 μm and the radial distance between tracks is 1.6 μm. Considering these very small distances and eccentricities in the disc which can cause radial swings as large as 300 μm, a servo system is required to keep the laser on the proper track. There are basically two different designs currently used in CD ROM drives for radial tracking correction. One system uses the main laser beam to stay on track, and another uses two additional side beams that are dedicated to maintaining proper tracking. The three-beam approach will be examined here (see Figure 4-7).

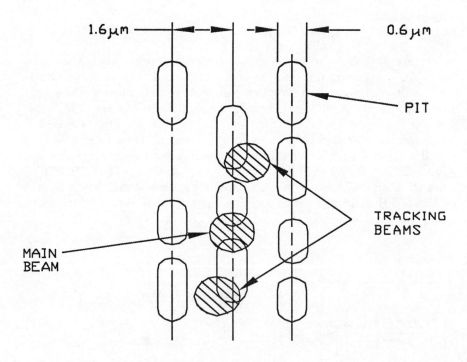

Figure 4-7 Main beams with radial tracking beams as they appear on the disc.

It has already been shown how the main laser beam is split into three beams by the diffraction grating plate. The two side beams follow the main beam through the entire optical pickup and end up falling on either side of the four quadrant photodiode onto two additional photodiodes (see Figure 4-8). The radial tracking correction system is similar to the focusing correction system; the intensity of the two reflected side beams is used to maintain proper tracking. One side beam is positioned to touch some of the pit track and some of the reflective surface in between the pit tracks on the left side of the main beam. The other side beam is positioned similarly on the right side of the main beam. If the main beam is correctly on track, the intensity of the reflection from the two side beams will be equal and their difference will be zero. If the main beam is not centered on the

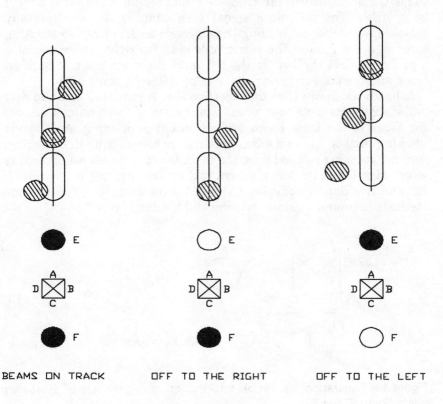

BEAMS ON TRACK   OFF TO THE RIGHT   OFF TO THE LEFT

Figure 4-8 Two radial tracking photo diodes.

pit track, one side beam will touch more of the pit track and the other side beam will touch more of the reflective area in between pit tracks. Since the reflection from the pit is weaker than the reflection from the reflective land area, the outputs of the two radial tracking photodiodes will be unequal. Each of the side beams reflect onto a photodiode. Similar to the focusing servo, the outputs of these photodiodes go to a differential amplifier that produces the tracking error signal. Since the two beams do not cross the same radial position at the same time, the bottom beam is delayed 30 ms from the differential amplifier.

The tracking judgment made by the differential amplifier then represents the radial tracking accuracy at exactly the same spot. When the main beam is properly on track, the difference signal $(F - E)$ equals zero and no adjustment is necessary. When the beam is off to the left, more light will fall on diode F and the difference $(F - E)$ will be positive. The difference signal then controls the electronically movable magnetic coil holding the objective lens. A positive tracking error signal will move the objective lens to the right, and a negative signal will move the lens to the left until the main beam is back on track and the tracking error signal is zero (see Figure 4-9).

It has been shown that the objective lens is mounted in a two-axis adjustable system so that small movements of the lens can control the focus of the laser beam and its radial positioning. A different tracking method uses an adjustable mirror to fine-tune the tracking. Another focusing method uses the main beam to decide whether it is in or out of focus. Despite different methods of ensuring proper focusing and tracking, all existing CD ROM drive manufacturers provide methods to protect against focusing and tracking errors.

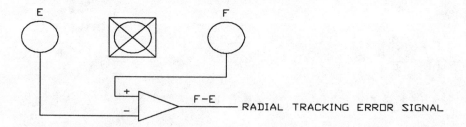

Figure 4-9 Generation of radial tracking error signal using sidebeam photodiodes E and F.

In addition to fixing radial tracking errors, all CD ROM drives need to move the entire optical pickup unit radially across the disc. Different kinds of searches may require the optical pickup to go to any one of up to 20,000 different radial tracks. One system has the optical pickup mounted on an electrically movable sled that moves linearly across the disc. Another system uses an optical pickup mounted to a rotating arm that sweeps across the disc. In the rotating arm design, the radial tracking servos adjust the radial tracking errors by moving the entire arm in very small increments. The different systems are analogous to the linear and radial pickup arms in different record turntable designs (see Figure 4-10). While searching for a particular track on the disc, the radial tracking servo system is disabled by the microprocessor, and the microprocessor moves the optical pickup until it is on the desired track. The servo system is then reengaged to fine-tune the position.

CLV Servo

Unlike typical magnetic disc storage mediums that rotate with constant angular velocity (CAV), the CD ROM disc is rotated at a constant linear velocity (CLV). This means that the speed of the disc

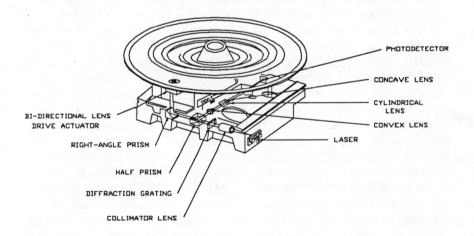

Figure 4-10a Slide pickup design.

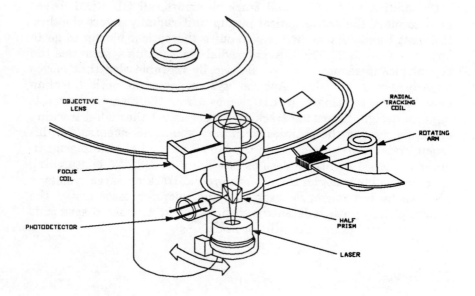

OBJECTIVE
LENS

RADIAL
TRACKING
COIL

ROTATING
ARM

FOCUS
COIL

PHOTODETECTOR

HALF
PRISM

LASER

Figure 4-10b Rotating arm pickup design.

motor varies depending upon the position of the optical pickup unit.
The disc motor speed is varied to maintain a constant speed between
the disc and the optical pickup unit regardless of whether the optical
pickup is at the center of the disc or on the outer edge. In a CAV system the speed of the disc motor remains constant. However, in CAV
the relative speed between the disc and the optical pickup is constantly changing depending upon the radial distance away from the
center of the disc. The relationship can be expressed in a simple
equation: $v = wr$, where v is the linear speed or the speed of the disc
underneath the optical pickup, w is the angular speed or the speed of
the disc motor, and r is the distance from the center of the disc. It
can easily be seen that in a CAV system, w is held constant; so the
linear speed v must change as r changes. In a CLV system, v is held
constant so as r changes, the disc motor speed w must change. It can
also easily be seen that in CLV as the radius r increases (the optical
pickup moves from the center toward the outer edge), w the disc
motor speed w must decrease to maintain a constant linear velocity v
between the disc and the optical pickup.

The advantage of CLV over CAV is the amount of information that can be stored using CLV. In a CAV system the data on the disc is more dense at the center of the disc than at the outer edge. Thus space at the outer edge is wasted. In a CLV system the density of the data on the disc is the same at every point on the disc. The disadvantage of the CLV system is that in order to read the data stored, the disc motor speed must constantly be changed. Searches and jumps to different locations on the disc can be done much quicker in a CAV system compared with a CLV system because there is no waiting for the disc motor speed to adjust.

In the CD ROM standard, the constant linear velocity v is 1.3 meters/second. To accomplish the constant linear velocity, the rotational speed of the disc w changes from 500 rpm at the center of the disc to 200 rpm at the outer edge. More important than the actual rpm of the disc is the rate at which data is read from the disc. There is an electronic servo system that controls the speed of the disc. It works by allowing the data read from the disc to enter a memory buffer at whatever rate the optical pickup is reading it. The data is then clocked out of the memory buffer at a precisely controlled rate of 4.32 Mbytes/second by a quartz crystal oscillator. The data path in, data path out, and memory buffer were designed to maintain the buffer 50 percent full. If it is less than 50 percent full, a signal is sent to the spindle motor to increase its velocity until the buffer is 50 percent full again. This procedure works in reverse when the buffer is more than 50 percent full. The quartz controlled oscillator ensures that the data is handled at a very precisely controlled rate, and the CLV servo system maintains the constant linear velocity of 1.3 m/s. Figure 4-11 shows a block diagram of the different servo systems.

Eight to Fourteen Demodulation

The sum of the outputs from the four-quadrant diode constitutes the data signal in modulated form. The output from the photodiodes is not a perfect square wave although it is a digital signal. Because the laser spot on the disc is slightly larger than the pit width and since the pit edges cannot be made perfectly vertical, the output wave from the photodiodes looks more like a sine wave than a square wave. However, it is easy to recover the digital signal from the photodiode output commonly called the HF signal, the RF signal, or the EFM signal.

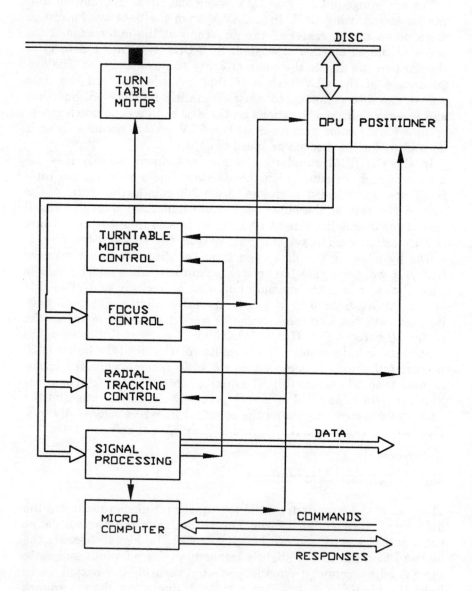

Figure 4-11 Servo systems and signal processing. Compliments of Laser Magnetic Storage.

The EFM signal is amplified and passed through a low frequency filter that helps maintain the digital quality of the signal. Dirt or fingermarks on the disc will reduce the amplitude of the reflected signal. This can cause the reflected signals from both pits and lands to both look like pits. The low-frequency filter removes low-frequency components and maintains the signal about the threshold between pit or land (see Figure 4-12). The EFM signal is reshaped to its original digital form using a comparator and data strobe. The system clock is regenerated from the signal using a phase-locked loop tuned to the channel bit frequency 4.3218 MHz. Once the clock has been regenerated, various other timing signals are generated that separate the information into data and control information.

The digital signal will go through EFM demodulation which returns the signal back into its original format. As discussed previously, the information is placed into a buffer that is used to control the rotational speed of the disc (see the preceding section). The information in CD ROM is organized into blocks (see Figure 4-16), and each block is the equivalent of 98 frames of CD Audio data (see Figure 4-13). As part of the modulation process, additional bits, called merging bits, are added to the data that prevent consecutive ones from occurring and also reduce the low-frequency content of the data. The different servo systems in the CD ROM player operate using low frequency signals. Any low frequency noise generated by the data itself will interfere with the servo systems and can cause improper focusing, tracking, or CLV control (more on this later in the section on Descrambling).

In the data processing circuits the control and display information, data, and error correction code must be demodulated from 14 bits

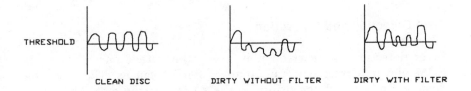

THRESHOLD

CLEAN DISC   DIRTY WITHOUT FILTER   DIRTY WITH FILTER

Figure 4-12 The affect of low frequency filter on the data signal. Compliments of Laser Magnetic Storage

24	14	168	56	168	56	102
SYNC	CONTROL AND DISPLAY	DATA	PARITY	DATA	PARITY	MERGING
BITS	BITS	BITS	BITS	BITS	BITS	BITS

Figure 4-13 One frame comprised of 588 channel bits.

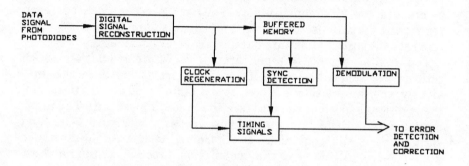

Figure 4-14 Block diagam of demodulation.

per byte to 8 bits per byte. The demodulation will return the information back to its original form and is precisely EFM encoding in reverse. The demodulation can be done with a lookup table in ROM or by using a logic array. Upon completion of demodulation the data is now ready for error detection and correction processing. Figures 4-14 and 4-15 are block diagrams of the signal processing in the CD ROM drive.

Error Detection and Correction

Error detection and correction is a very important part of the CD ROM player. Errors can have many different causes. There can be dust, scratches, or fingerprints on the surface of the disc. There can also be bubbles or contaminants in the substrate of the disc. Errors might also occur when there are tracking or focusing problems. Regardless of the cause, errors must be detected and corrected. The accepted error rate in the computer industry is 1 error in 10 to the

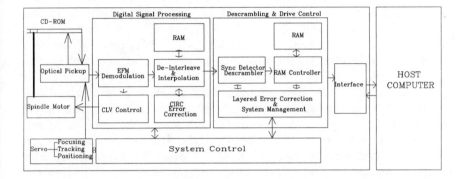

Figure 4-15 Signal processing in the CD ROM player. (Courtesy of Sony.)

12 bytes of information. Using the same error detection and correction scheme used in CD Audio, CD ROM would only achieve an error rate of 10^{-9}. But an additional layer of error correction is used that brings the error rate to 10^{-12}. In CD Audio, errors that cannot be corrected can just be muted unknowingly to the listener. However, in CD ROM, a portion of the information cannot simply be ignored.

Errors can be classified into three different categories: (1) random single-bit errors, (2) burst bit errors, or (3) word or block errors. A random single-bit error needs no explanation. Burst bit errors are multiple random single-bit errors, and word or block errors are when random or burst errors occur on entire words or blocks. Various methods exist for detecting and correcting errors. One of the most basic ways of detecting errors is to have redundant data and compare the original data with the redundant data. However, the overhead is expensive when providing for two sets of the same information, and when an error is detected it cannot be determined whether the error is in the original data or the redundant data. The data can be repeated three times and then the majority of the three would be the "true" data, but the expense is even greater.

Another basic form of error detection in computer devices is the use of a parity bit. An extra bit is generated for each word that tells whether the number of 1s present in the word is even (or odd as long as consistency is maintained). The parity bit can be used to make each word have an even number of 1s. If the number of 1s in the word is even, the parity bit will be a 0, and if the number of 1s in the word is odd the parity bit will be a 1. Unfortunately, the use of 1 parity bit is limited to the detection of errors and does nothing to correct them.

Multiple parity bits are commonly used for error detection and correction. A simple example of this is shown below with three 3-bit words of data organized in a matrix. A fourth row and a fourth column are added to make a 4 by 4 matrix. The fourth place in each row or column represents the sum of the previous three places. Any single error can be easily detected and corrected using the redundant data. In the matrix below, if the number 6 were transmitted as a 5, then the sum at the end of row 2 would be 14, and the sum at the end of column 3 would be 17. These two numbers would contradict the transmitted parity sums of 15 and 18. The error would be easily identified and corrected. This form of error detection and correction is called block code, where several words are grouped together in blocks before the parity words are generated. The drawback of this example is when multiple errors occur.

```
1 | 2 | 3 | 6
4 | 5 | 6 | 15
7 | 8 | 9 | 24
-----------------
12| 15 | 18 | 45
```

In CD Audio and CD ROM, a common source of error is dust or scratches on the disc, and the type of error produced is usually a burst error (several consecutive word errors). To help prevent burst errors in compact disc technologies, the data goes through a process called interleaving before being placed onto the disc. Interleaving rearranges the data so that consecutive pieces of information are not placed in consecutive locations on the disc. Consequently, any dust or scratches on the disc will not affect many consecutive pieces of information. When many consecutive pieces of information are damaged, the probability is increased that the data and its corresponding parity words both get damaged. Interleaving will disperse burst errors among the data, reducing the chances of a word and its corresponding correction word being damaged.

Interleaving is the last part of the error detection and correction that the data receives before being written to the disc. Interleaving is part of a standardized process called cross-interleaved Reed-Solomon (CIRC) coding used in both the CD- ROM and CD Audio. Since interleaving is the last stage in the encoding process, it is the first process performed in the decoding process. The data is written into RAM and read out in the reverse of the interleaving algorithm performed during encoding. Deinterleaving returns the consecutive pieces of information back into their original sequence along with the corresponding redundant data generated for error detection and correction.

In the CD ROM, cross-interleave Reed-Solomon code is the first part of the two stages of error detection and correction used. The second part is the additional error correction code developed to lower the error rate to 10^{-12}. The Reed-Solomon codes (named for the inventors of this type of error correction codes) used in the CIRC method belong to a class of coding known as block code. In block code, groups of words are joined together in a block before parity words are added to the block itself.

The CD ROM data is organized into blocks. One block of data consists of 12 bytes of synchronization information that identify the block, 4 bytes for the block address, 2048 bytes of data, and 288 bytes for the error detection and correction. Of these 288 bytes, 4 are used for error detection, 276 for error correction, and the remaining 8 bytes are currently unused (see Figure 4-16). Within each block, the data is organized into a matrix and parity words are generated for each row and column that are used to detect and correct any errors that have occurred.

The first stage of error detection and correction can correct 1 error in 10 to the ninth bytes of information. In CD Audio, if there is still

12	4	2048	288 LAYERED ECC BYTES		
SYNC BYTES	BLOCK ADDRESS BYTES	DATA BYTES	4 DETECTION BYTES	276 CORRECTION BYTES	8 UNUSED BYTES

Figure 4-16 One block = 2352 bytes = 98 frames.

unreliable data, interpolation and muting circuits will either fake the data using the previous words or simply mute the sound. However, in the CD ROM system the layered ECC goes to work. The extra error detection and correction information in the 288 bytes is applied to each block. As previously mentioned, of the 288 bytes used for error detection and correction, 4 bytes are for detection, 8 bytes are unused, and 276 bytes are used for error correction. Many CD ROM drives let the host computer apply the extra layer of error correction and some drives perform the extra correction inside the drive. At this time, however, the point where the layered error correction is applied has not been standardized in the industry.

Sync Detection and Descrambling

The CD ROM drive must be able to access any one of the approximately 270,000 different blocks of information. Therefore, each block has its own address. Following the CD Audio format, each block address is identified by a number that represents minutes (0 to 60), seconds (0 to 59), and a block number (0 to 74). The block address is contained in 4 bytes of each block. Each block is separated by 12 bytes of synchronization code. After the address and synchronization information, 2336 bytes of user information, 288 of which are error detection and correction codes, remain in each block. In total, there are nearly 550 Mbytes of user information available on the CD ROM disc.

The 2336 bytes of data in each block are scrambled to reduce low-frequency noise. As discussed in the interleaving section, low-frequency noise can be produced by the data that interferes with the different servo systems in the CD ROM drive. If the lengths of the pits and lands were equal, no low-frequency signals would exist. Unfortunately, the data cannot be represented in this way. One of the functions of the merging bits is to equalize the lengths of the pits and lands. In addition, the 2336 bytes of user data are scrambled to decrease the DC content of the data. It should be noted that scrambling is completely independent of interleaving.

The sync pattern must be detected before the data can be descrambled in the CD ROM drive. The 12 bytes of sync pattern are all 1s except for the first and last bytes which are 0s. Descrambling is performed using a RAM prior to the interface that connects the drive to the host computer.

Interface

The interface bus of the CD ROM drive serves as the communication line to carry signals to and from the drive and the host system. Without the interface the drive cannot be controlled nor can the host communicate with the drive to take advantage of the CD ROM application.

Each of the drive manufacturers has designed their interface bus differently; however, many of the signals that are used are consistent among the different drives. The interface bus is responsible for transferring three types of signals: command signals, status signals, and data signals. Command signals are used to instruct the drive to perform various functions such as jumps and searches. Status signals inform the host of the drive that commands have been received, or that particular functions have been initiated or terminated. Most importantly, data signals transfer requested data from the drive to the host system.

Three types of bus lines are used to transfer different signals. Bidirectional lines carry signals originating from either the host system or the CD ROM drive. One-way lines are devoted to transferring signals in one direction only, either originating from the host or the drive.

User data is transferred via the bidirectional bus lines. One-way lines are designated to handle specific commands or status signals, but no user data.

About the Authors

Jeffrey N. Nadler and Robert J. Wiesenberg are the cofounders of Rommates Inc., a company dedicated to CD ROM services and technology. Rommates Inc. provides complete CD ROM publishing services and full text and image retrieval solutions for both CD ROM and magnetic media.

Jeffrey N. Nadler holds a B.S. degree in Electrical Engineering from Union College in Schenectady, New York and is a member of the Tau Beta Pi and Eta Kappa Nu engineering societies. He worked in VLSI semiconductor development with the IBM Corporation prior to cofounding Rommates Inc.

Robert J. Wiesenberg received a B.A. in Political Science from Union College. Before cofounding Rommates, he worked in Tokyo,

Japan as a production-marketing liaison between the Japanese and American divisions of Kaga Electronics Co. Ltd., a computer peripheral manufacturer.

Rommates Inc.
P.O. Box 447
Cross River, New York 10518
(914)763–8277

Bibliography

Carasso, M.G., J. B. H. Peck, J. P. Sinjou: "The Compact Digital Audio System," *Philips Technical Review*, vol. 40, no. 6, 1982.

Chen, Peter Pin-Shan, "The Compact Disk ROM: How It Works," *IEEE Spectrum*, April 1986.

Heemskerk, J.P.J., K.A. Immick, and Schouhamer: "Compact Disc: System Aspects and Modulation," *Philips Technical Review*, vol. 40, no. 6, 1982.

Hoeve, H., J. Timmermans, and L. B. Vriess: "Error Correction and Concealment in the Compact Disc System," *Philips Technical Review*, vol. 40, no. 6, 1982.

Lambert, Steve and Suzanne Ropiequet (eds.):CD ROM: The New Papyrus. Redmond, Wash.: Microsoft Press, 1986.

Lenk, John D.: "Repairing Compact Disc Players," reprint from *Radio-Electronics*, Gernsbeack Publications, Inc., 1986.

Miyaoka, Senri: "Digital Audio is Compact and Rugged," *IEEE Spectrum*, March 1984.

Nippon Columbia Co., Ltd.: "Denon Controller for DRD-550 CD ROM Drive" (technical manual), 1985.

——————————————— "Denon DRD-550 CD ROM Drive Series" (specifications), 1986.

——————————————— "Denon Full-Height CD ROM Interface Manual," Revision 0, 1987.

Panasonic Industrial Company: *CD ROM Drive System Technical Operations Manual.*

Peek, J.B.H.: "Communications Aspects of the Compact Disc Digital Audio System," *IEEE Communications Magazine*, vol. 23, no. 2, February 1985.

Philips Export B.V.: "Philips Compact Disc ROM: The Economic and Flexible Medium for Distributing Information," 1984.

Pohlmann, Ken C.: *Principles of Digital Audio.* Indianapolis, Ind.: Howard W. Sams and Company, 1985.

Sako, Yoichiro, and Tadao Suzuki: "Data Structure of the Compact Disk-Read Only Memory System," *Applied Optics*, vol. 25, no. 22, November 1986.

Sony CRB85-131: "Note of CD ROM System (version 1.4.1)," Sony Corporation, 1985.

Sony Corp. Engineers, "Digital Disk Recording and Reproduction" in The McGraw-Hill Audio Engineering Handbook, K. Blair Benson, ed. New York: McGraw-Hill, in press.

Streetman, Ben G.: *Solid State Electronic Devices.* Englewood Cliffs, N.J.: Prentice-Hall, 1980.

Tsurushima, Katsuaki: "Sony Compact Disc Digital Audio: All About the Compact Disc System" (Sony Corporation document).

Watkinson, J.R.: "Channel Code and Disc Format-1," *Electronics and Wireless World*, May 1985.

——————————————— "Compact Disc Players," *Electronics and Wireless World*, August 1985.

——————————————— "The Compact Disc System," *Electronics and Wireless World*, January 1985.

——————————————— "Principles   of   Optical   Storage,"
Electronics and Wireless World, March 1985.

Zoellick, B.: "CD ROM Software Development," *Byte*, May 1986.

5

CD ROM Device Integration: From Chaos to Standards

Jack Spiegelberg

In the early days of CD ROM, device integration problems made most CD ROM applications incompatible with most CD ROM systems. Applications were made to run on very specific system configurations, and there was little commonality between CD ROM interface methods and software support.

The result was chaos: developers struggled to host their applications on multiple different drive types and interface cards while many potential buyers became confused and rightfully postponed purchase decisions until the smoke cleared. In effect, the poor state of CD ROM device integration was severely restricting industry growth.

Many of the problems have now been solved, and their solutions have become widely accepted and used throughout the industry. Available technical solutions to other problems are yet to gain broad user acceptance, and still other difficulties remain unresolved.

This chapter examines the evolution of CD ROM device integration It also addresses the dramatic impact that CD ROM device integration has on the health and growth potential of the CD ROM industry.

CD ROM Users Ask:

"Can I use my CD ROM drive with my new IBM PS/2?"

"Why don't our Dialog and Datext CD ROM programs work on our XT class machines? They work fine on our AT class machines."

"None of these CD ROMs work on my PC clone. Why?"

"Can I attach several PCs to a single CD ROM drive?"

"Why won't the CD ROM drive work with PCs that are on our network? They work with PCs that aren't attached to the network."

CD ROM Application Developers Complain:

"This product must be marketable on as many differing PC configurations as possible, including networked systems as well as stand-alone PCs. How much development effort will be required?"

"A major reason why our product cost is so high and our development time so long is because we have to support several incompatible CD ROM drives, interface cards, and software device drivers. Is there some way to avoid this, even if only to a limited degree?"

"We don't want to be, nor can we afford to be, in the position of having to integrate our software with a multitude of low-level CD ROM device drivers. But is there any real alternative?"

Answers to these and other similar questions were not what users, developers, or the CD ROM industry in general would have liked. It was indicative of the immature state of CD ROM device integration at that time.

As we will uncover in this chapter, however, technical solutions to many of these problems are now available. Widespread awareness, acceptance, and use of these solutions is occurring and will facilitate the continued rapid growth of CD ROM.

Understanding Device Integration

Device integration involves the *linking together of parts* that enable application programs to control and access information from a particular type of device, such as CD ROM.

In the case of CD ROM, the linking components are depicted in Figure 5-1. But there is much more to device integration than merely connecting the parts and making a few specific hardware/software configurations work.

A well-integrated device is characterized by hardware and software components and standards that shield application developers from differences in the various makes and models of the device. End users benefit through an abundance of high-quality application programs. In particular, well-integrated devices *do not* ensnarl application developers or end users in a mass of hardware and software incompatibility issues.

Hard disk drives for IBM-compatible PCs are one example of a well-integrated device. It is generally the case that any commonly available hard disk drive can be readily attached to any IBM-compatible PC with the justified expectation that it will work with any MS-DOS application program. There is no concern that certain programs operate only with certain types of drives or that a par-

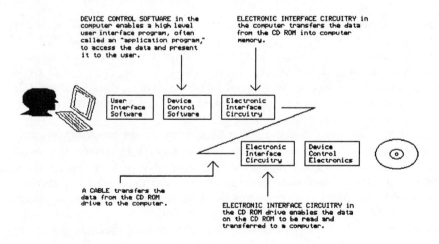

Figure 5-1 CD ROM device integration.

ticular interface card is required in order to access some particular data file. In effect, the only significant differentiating factors between hard disk drives are capacity, access speed, reputation of the vendor and manufacturer and of course, cost.

By virtue of these factors, hard disk technology is fully exploitable without any artificial restrictions. It is a very-well integrated device for PCs because users and developers alike are free to focus their attention and spend their resources where they should — on application programs that satisfy needs.

CD ROM Drives Becoming Better Integrated

In contrast to the mature state of hard disk integration on PCs, CD ROM is still in the process of becoming a well-integrated device.

Figure 5-2 compares the system configurations of an application which in one case uses a hard disk, and in the other case uses a CD ROM. Although not representative of all CD ROM programs, the figure accurately depicts the recent immature state of CD ROM device integration

Lack of a Common Operating System Interface

As illustrated, a major characteristic of the level of CD ROM device integration was that most CD ROM programs accessed the CD ROM drive directly, bypassing the more standard method of making calls through an operating system to the device. In most cases, CD ROM application developers wrote software which interfaced directly to device driver software modules provided by the hardware manufacturers.

Since there were many different hardware interface adapters and software driver modules, application developers inherited the enormous task of providing unique support for each of their products on many different hardware configurations. Additionally, as interface problems occurred and were resolved, developers incurred substantial program update and redistribution tasks.

As application developers will attest, providing direct support for several different types of device interfaces is outside of their primary area of expertise, and it severely impacts their development of effective application programs.

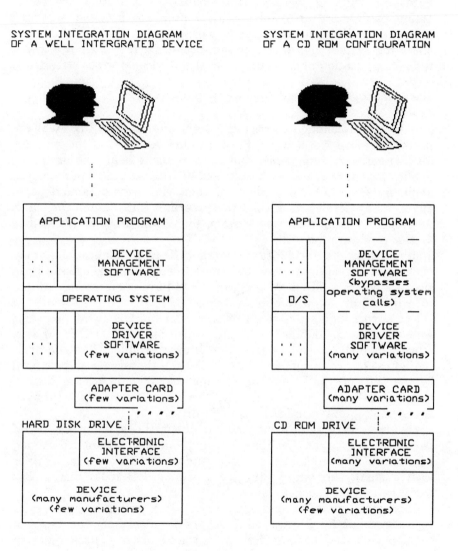

Figure 5-2 Comparison of a well-integrated device with CD ROM.

In the case of well-integrated devices, the various software and hardware "building blocks" which make up a system are better defined and there are well specified interfaces between adjoining components. Efficiencies are achieved because a limited number of operating system and device driver specialists, rather than a multitude of application programmers, develop device interface software.

The Effects of Nonstandard Software Integration

The lack of a common operating system interface for CD ROM impacts users in several ways. First, the inefficiencies of the multiple diverse software integration and support tasks being performed by application developers were reflected in higher costs and delayed availability of CD ROM products. Second, end users became dependent on many developers of CD ROM programs, rather than the single developer of their operating system, to resolve problems related to system configuration.

In addition, the possibility of adopting CD ROM applications to unusual system configurations became severely limited, especially in systems where a CD ROM program could have operated in addition to or in conjunction with other software.

Not surprisingly, almost all of the available CD ROM programs were provided in "bundled" packages which included a CD ROM disc, a program diskette and a description of exactly which CD ROM drive configurations were supported. The CD ROM data could only be used by the software package that accompanied it, only with a limited range of CD ROM units, and only with a specific interface card between the computer and the CD ROM drive.

This was very telling information about the state of CD ROM device integration at that time. No single interface standard existed which would have enabled product vendors to support a majority or even a small subgroup of the most popular CD ROM drives that were then on the market.

In contrast, products developed for use with well-integrated device types, such as hard disks on PCs, are isolated from the types of development and support issues indicated above. These types of products interface through an operating system to control any manufacturer's device which adheres to a well defined set of interface standards for that device type.

Hardware Incompatibilities

As Table 5-1 indicates, there were a myriad of differing and incompatible ways in which CD ROM drives were connected to PCs, with even more hardware interface alternatives available than there were CD ROM drive manufacturers. Even SCSI (small computer system interface) interfaces were not fully compatible between the various manufacturers.

In some instances there as many as three incompatible interface cards available for a single model CD ROM drive depending on whether the drive was to be configured as a stand alone unit, or as part of a multidrive CD ROM subsystem. Perhaps the only interface standard that existed for CD ROM was that all manufacturers provide at least some method with which the drive could be attached to either IBM-compatible personal computers or to the SCSI port of Apple Macintoshs and Apple II GSs.

Effects of Hardware Incompatibilities on End Users

From an end user's point of view, CD ROM hardware incompatibilities do not seem too problematic at first since a reasonable selection of the major manufacturers' drives are supported by most

Table 5-1   CD ROM Drive Interfaces for PCs

| | Type of CD ROM Interface | | |
Manufacturer	SCSI(*)	Custom Parallel	Other
Denon	✓	✓	
Digital Equipment Corp.		✓	
Hitachi	✓	✓	
Knowledgeset Corp.		✓	
Laser Magnetic Storage Int.	✓		✓ (RS–422)
OnLine		✓	
Panasonic	✓		
Philips	✓		✓ (Serial)
Reference Technology, Inc.		✓	
Sanyo		✓	
Sony	✓	✓	
Toshiba	✓		

(*) SCSI interfaces by differing manufacturers are not compatible in all cases.

CD ROM products. Furthermore, most products seem to lend themselves well to stand-alone use.

Consider, for example, CD ROM–based reference catalogs intended for use in libraries. The information basically includes book titles, author names, book classifications, and brief abstracts of each book. They are used to identify references that are available in a user's specific area of interest.

There seems little need for this type of product to be used in conjunction with some other type of PC application such as a word processor or electronic spreadsheet, or that it be supported on every available CD ROM drive. The product serves a very specific function on an adequate hardware base, and it meets a specific and well defined need. Its lack of extensibility does not seem to be very limiting.

But what about instances where:

- A particular user's hardware configuration won't support the CD ROM program that he or she would like to use?
- A CD ROM hardware adapter cannot coexist with some other adapter in a user's PC due to conflicts with Interrupt address or DMA channel assignments?
- A CD ROM product does lend itself to use with other software packages, but can only be run in a stand-alone mode?
- A particular CD ROM product can only be run in stand alone mode yet the system it is attached to is on a network with many potential users.

These types of situations occur frequently and until recently there were few easy solutions.

Case Study

By examining a specific CD ROM problem and its resolution, some of the effects of the poor CD ROM device integration become painfully apparent.

The example involves the original Grolier Electronic Encyclopedia, in which was released one of the first CD ROM products aimed at a broad user market. As such, it naturally encountered some of the thorniest CD ROM device integration issues.

A user experienced difficulties during a keyword search with the product operating on an IBM PC XT-286 with a Hitachi 1503S CD ROM drive. The CD ROM occasionally appeared to operate unusually fast and the system would subsequently either halt or output scrambled text to the screen.

Since two other CD ROM products operated successfully on the same system, it seemed unlikely that system hardware was at fault. But neither did the software or CD ROM seem to be the cause since the same CD ROM disc and program diskette operated properly on another PC.

After many phone calls to the system hardware vendor, to Grolier's, to the software firm that assisted Grolier in developing the search software, and to Hitachi, the problem was identified as a CD ROM software device driver incompatibility with certain PCs that utilized 80286 (PC-AT type) processors.

More specifically, the problem involved the software technique used to transfer data from the CD ROM to the memory of the computer. The data transfer rate on that particular model of PC did not fall within the limits programmed into the software device driver for that CD ROM drive. A simple software modification corrected the problem. Even after the software solution was available, however, it was no simple task to upgrade the user's system with the modified software.

The Grolier Electronic Encyclopedia product included separate software device driver modules for each CD ROM unit which it supported. Each module contained software developed in part by CD ROM hardware manufacturers with the remainder being developed by the Grolier software development team. Consequently, participation by both software development organizations was required to generate an upgraded, replacement software driver.

Due to the manner in which the Hitachi device driver software was linked into other device control software, a simple software module replacement by Hitachi was not possible. Instead, the upgraded Hitachi software had to be incorporated into other device control software, and a new device driver module generated.

Ultimately, the upgraded software was included in a revised version of the program diskette which accompanied the Grolier CD ROM, and the user's problem was resolved. However, the solution required the involvement of every organization that participated in the software development and hardware support of the original product!

And this addressed only a single instance of a system configuration problem with a single CD ROM product!

Unfortunately this scenario was not unique and it exemplified the poor state of CD ROM device integration at that time. Given the many variations in device drivers and system configurations that were then in use, this type of problem was common and industry growth suffered as a result.

In Perspective

Before looking at some of the solutions to the problems of CD ROM device integration, it is useful to quickly review the two major factors which facilitated the incredibly rapid growth and acceptance of CD ROM as an industry standard for read-only mass storage.

1. *CD Audio created the opportunity.* The phenomenal success of Compact Disc Audio as a consumer product provided the opportunity to attach massive 550-Mbyte storage units to personal computers at low cost. It also established many of the hardware and media standards that provided the platform for stable growth.

2. *Data format standards facilitated rapid growth.* The Yellow Book media format standard and the High Sierra file format standard were developed by early pioneers of the CD ROM industry who accurately perceived both the potential of the technology and the need for standards to facilitate growth.

The Yellow Book established physical format standards for CD ROM discs so they could be physically readable on CD ROM drives made by different manufacturers. Building on this, the High Sierra Group (HSG) file format standard for CD ROM discs enabled data placed on discs by different developers and manufacturers to be readable on different computers using different operating systems and configured with different CD ROM drives.

Together, these standards have proven invaluable in that were both timely and technically well conceived. They provided the necessary direction for rapid and stable growth that would otherwise have become chaotically fragmented.

From this background, CD ROM quickly became widely accepted and put to effective use. The issues of improved CD ROM connectability and device integration loomed as the next major barriers to realizing the full potential of the technology.

Emerging Solutions

Given the very rapid growth of CD ROM, it is not surprising that the demand for improved device connectability and better device integration surpassed the availability of suitable solutions. There existed a clear need, but no clear solutions.

SCSI Controllers for CD ROM

The Small Computer System Interface or SCSI (pronounced "Scuzzy") is emerging as a much needed solution to some of the problems of connecting CD ROM drives to personal computers. It has already achieved a broad enough acceptance within the CD ROM industry to become the de-facto standard for interfacing CD ROM drives to Apple personal computers and, to a lesser but still significant degree, with IBM-compatible PCs.

SCSI is the specification of a small computer input/output bus interface that is commonly used to connect other types of storage devices to small computers — devices such as hard disks, floppy disks, magnetic tape drives and printers.

A Brief History of SCSI

SCSI had its origins in the very early days of personal computing. It was formally named in 1982 as a formalization and extension of a popular, commercial small system parallel bus named "SASI," the Shugart Associates System Interface, which generally met small system requirements for a device-independent peripheral or system bus. SASI enjoyed significant market success as a *de facto* standard for interfacing peripheral devices, such as floppy disk drives, to small computers.

Since that time, an ANSI (American National Standards Institute) technical committee, the X3T9.2 Task Group, has extended and refined the SCSI specification to the point that, in 1986, a SCSI standard (American National Standard X3.131-1986) was released.

At present, a draft document defining an enhanced version of the SCSI Interface, entitled SCSI-2, is currently being reviewed prior to its anticipated acceptance as an upgrade and extension to the original SCSI standard. SCSI-2 includes support for optical memory devices such as CD ROM.

SCSI: An "Intelligent" Device Interface

The SCSI interface standard is a set of mechanical, electrical, and functional specifications that define a shared means of communication between small computers and intelligent peripheral devices, particularly mass storage devices. The major goal of SCSI is to facilitate the integration of these types of system components into any small computer system.

SCSI supports communications between computers and peripherals using a technique that is independent of both the specific devices being accessed as well as the specific type of computer or computers configured into a system. To accomplish this, SCSI defines an "intelligent," system-level interface which provides host computers with device-independent control of entire classes of devices.

SCSI command sets for peripheral device types are "device-independent"; that is, they largely hide the internal structure of the device (e.g., cylinders, heads, and sectors) from the interface. This facilitates the development of "generic" device driver software that can control all devices of a particular type. Hence, with SCSI, a single software driver and hardware interface can be used to support a single type of device, such as CD ROM drives, hard disk drives, or printers, regardless of the manufacturer, model, speed, or other unique characteristics of the specific device being used.

SCSI devices are classified as either Initiators or Targets. Initiators originate operations between devices on the SCSI bus, while Targets perform operations in response to commands received from the bus.

Up to eight SCSI devices can be supported on a single SCSI bus, and any combination of Initiators and Targets may be configured on the same bus. A SCSI option provides for the attachment of multiple devices to each Target device. Hence, the sample SCSI configurations shown in Figure 5-3 are possible.

SCSI is an extremely versatile device interface that addresses several of the problems with CD ROM device integration. Not only can many devices of a single type be attached to the bus, multiple different device types may share a single SCSI bus. Rather than dedicating a single slot for each device, an entire subsystem of mixed device types may be chained together. And, since SCSI is a very fast interface, it can support high-speed devices such as hard disks with no degradation in performance.

SCSI also provides virtually unlimited expandability to systems which have reached their capacity of plug-in adapter cards. This is particularly important in systems such as the IBM PS/2 Model 30 which has only three expansion slots. In addition, SCSI expandability is achieved without the risk of introducing device address conflicts between the new device and previously existing devices.

Most importantly, SCSI provides a standard for connecting devices such as CD ROM drives to computers. It explicitly defines every ele-

SINGLE INITIATOR / SINGLE TARGET

```
                                   ┌─ DEVICE WITH CONTROLLER ─┐
 ┌──────────┬──────────┐           │ ┌───────────┐            │
 │          │   SCSI   │ ⟨SCSI BUS⟩│ │   SCSI    │            │   ┌────────┐
 │ COMPUTER │ ADAPTER  │           │ │ CONTROLLER│            │   │ DEVICE │
 │          │          │           │ │           │ ┌────────┐ │   └────────┘
 └──────────┴──────────┘           │ └───────────┘ │ DEVICE │ │
                                   │               └────────┘ │
                                   └───────────────────────────┘
```

SINGLE INITIATOR / MULTIPLE TARGETS

```
                                   ┌─ DEVICE WITH CONTROLLER ─┐
 ┌──────────┬──────────┐           │ ┌───────────┐            │
 │          │   SCSI   │ ⟨SCSI BUS⟩│ │   SCSI    │            │   ┌────────┐
 │ COMPUTER │ ADAPTER  │           │ │ CONTROLLER│            │   │ DEVICE │
 │          │          │           │ │    #1     │ ┌────────┐ │   └────────┘
 └──────────┴──────────┘           │ └───────────┘ │ DEVICE │ │
                                   │               └────────┘ │
                                   └───────────────────────────┘

                                   ┌─ DEVICE WITH CONTROLLER ─┐
                                   │ ┌───────────┐            │
                                   │ │   SCSI    │            │   ┌────────┐
                                   │ │ CONTROLLER│            │   │ DEVICE │
                                   │ │    #2     │ ┌────────┐ │   └────────┘
                                   │ └───────────┘ │ DEVICE │ │
                                   │               └────────┘ │
                                   └───────────────────────────┘
```

Figure 5-3   Sample SCSI configurations.

MULTIPLE INITIATORS / MULTIPLE TARGETS

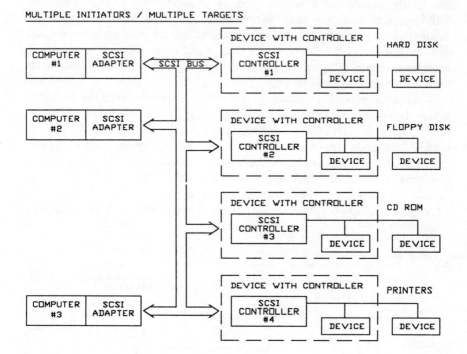

Figure 5-3   Sample SCSI configurations (continued).

ment of the interface from connector pin assignments to the specific functional requirements of "generic" device driver software. Without SCSI, the number of specific controllers needed to make most CD ROM drives operate with most small computers is virtually unbounded, as are the associated hardware and software development and support costs.

Unfortunately, SCSI is not the ideal solution in all cases. On IBM compatible PCs, SCSI devices are more costly than their custom interface counterparts. This is partially due to the fact that they are housed in external units and require their own chassis and power supplies, and also because they utilize a greater number of more complex integrated circuits than non-SCSI devices. Also, since SCSI devices are external units, they result in less streamlined configurations than comparable devices which can be mounted inside a computer chassis.

Standardization between manufacturers is also an issue with SCSI devices. The SCSI-2 specification still lacks minute details in certain areas regarding support of optical storage devices and it is not yet a formally approved ANSI specification. Consequently, there are slight incompatibilities between one manufacturer's implementation of SCSI and anothers.

Nonetheless, the many virtues of SCSI make it an ideal solution to many of the problems of CD ROM device integration.

Summarizing, SCSI provides the following:

- A versatile standard for physically connecting CD ROMs and other devices to a broad range of computers including PCs, Apples, Amigas, and many others
- A standard for the software control of CD ROM drives made by different manufacturers
- Easy and virtually unlimited ability to add new devices to computers which have limited expansion capabilities

The Microsoft CD ROM Extensions

Just as SCSI is emerging as a solution to many of the CD ROM hardware integrations issues, the Microsoft CD ROM Extension software is bringing much needed order to the software integration issues of CD ROM.

The Microsoft CD ROM Extensions enable IBM-compatible personal computers using the MS-DOS operating system to access CD ROM in a very simple and familiar manner, treating it as a large, read-only hard disk drive. As with hard disks, MS-DOS commands such as "DIR," "COPY," and "TYPE" can be used to access files on CD ROM. Differences exist, of course, in the ways in which each device can be used, but the basic data access and retrieval functions common to both CD ROM and hard disks are supported through widely used MS-DOS commands and standard MS-DOS software.

Configuring Systems with the Extensions

As illustrated in Figure 5-4, the CD ROM Extensions consist of two software components. Microsoft provides a device-independent CD ROM control program — "MSCDEX" — and CD ROM manufacturers provide device-specific software drivers. MSCDEX interfaces at the high-order end with CD ROM application software, and at the low-order end with device driver software modules. The device driver modules, in turn, interface with CD ROM hardware adapter cards to control the CD ROM drives.

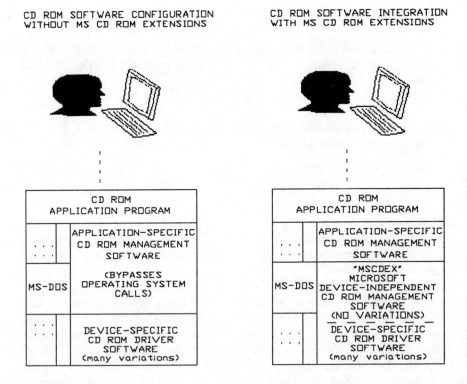

Figure 5-4 Configuration comparison — Microsoft CD ROM extensions.

Technical Characteristics of the Extensions

The CD ROM Extensions support several unique characteristics of CD ROM, including audio on/off control and techniques which accommodate the relatively slow seek time of CD ROM drives.

An example of a performance-enhancing feature of the Extensions is a command entitled "READ LONG PREFETCH." This command instructs the device driver to seek to a particular area on the CD ROM disc and read in data but, unlike most commands, it is only an advisory command. The device driver is not obligated to perform the function but can instead consider the command a "hint" that the designated data is likely to be read. The requests are low priority and are preemptible by other requests for service. If a "demand" service request is issued, the advisory command is aborted and the new function is performed immediately. Conversely, if the advisory function is successfully completed before another service request is issued, the requested data is made immediately available to the application program. With this technique, average seek time is reduced and performance is improved.

The technical restrictions mandated by the use of the CD ROM Extensions are minimal: The CD ROM discs must be in ISO 9660 or High Sierra (HSG) format, and the MS-DOS 3.1 or higher operating system must be used.

Benefits of the CD ROM Extensions

The major benefit of the CD ROM Extension software is to provide a standard software interface between CD ROM application software and the multitude of incompatible software and hardware components on which the applications run. CD ROM applications can be developed to run on a wide base of CD ROM system configurations without the need for developers to directly interface with, and support a myriad of differing and incompatible hardware and software components. In effect, the Extensions insulate developers from the many complexities of broad-based device support.

Additionally, since CD ROM units are accessible much like hard disks, sophisticated software originally developed for use with hard disk systems can be readily adapted for use with CD ROM. Systems which use Local Area Networks, or LANs, exemplify this.

A large and rapidly growing segment of the PC industry is linking PCs together using LAN networks in order to share common databases and other system resources such as printers. As illustrated in Figure 5-5, a typical LAN configuration includes a master station operating as a "file server" to other stations on the network. Remote workstations access data files contained on mass storage devices attached to the master station.

Since the Extensions provide hard-disk-like support of CD ROMs, network software developed for LAN systems with hard disks can be easily adapted for use with CD ROM based LAN systems provided, of course, that they can adapt to a read-only mass storage environment.

A Simple "Before and After" Case for the CD ROM Extensions

A California company, Education Systems Corporation, has implemented networked CD ROM based systems both with the CD ROM Extension software and without it. With over 1800 computerized lessons in their 300 Mbyte curriculum, ESC has found small network configurations, with a single CD ROM drive attached to a master station, to be the most effective way to host their product.

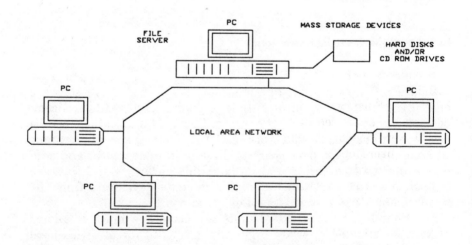

Figure 5-5 Networked PC/CD ROM system configuration.

The ESC system makes very simple use of the CD ROM. Using the LAN network, lessons are transferred in their entirety from the CD ROM to requesting workstations where they are run. Once loaded in the workstation, no further access to the CD ROM is required in order to operate the lesson.

Using the MS-DOS Extensions and a networking operating system, a simple file copy operation is all that is required to load a course from the CD ROM to one of the workstations. However, prior to the availability of the CD ROM Extensions, sophisticated custom software in both the master network workstation and the remote workstations was required in order to access courses from the CD ROM.

More Advanced CD ROM Configurations

As solutions to the fundamental issues of CD ROM device integration emerge and gain market acceptance, they become the building blocks for more complex system configurations.

Potential users of networked CD ROM applications expect to be able to concurrently share CD ROM databases, and expect only minimal performance degradation as other users become active on the network. Due to slow CD ROM seek times, realistic planning must go into the design and use of CD ROM network applications. Nonetheless, with good planning, CD ROM networks can be put to very effective use. And, due to the existence and broad acceptance of the CD ROM Extensions and network standards, well integrated CD ROM based LAN systems became readily achievable.

Specialized CD ROM networking products are already becoming available. Such products build on pre-existing standards in order to provide the enhanced functionality.

CD Net, developed by Meridian Data Inc. of Capitola, California, enables users on a network to access up to four CD ROM drives using standard MS-DOS drive designation letters. CD ROM Extension software is one of the fundamental building blocks of this system, providing a key component of the interface between the CD ROM drive's and the user stations on the network. Building on this approach, CD Net supports a variety of network configurations including Ethernet, ARCnet and Token-Ring network hardware operating under both Novell and MS Net network software environments.

Opti-Net, developed by Online Products Corporation of German-town, Maryland, provides a similar capability using a different approach. With Optinet software and an Online CD ROM interface card on the network server, up to eight CD ROM drives can be supported on the network. CD ROM's are accessible as though they are hard disk drives. This is achieved through compatibility with Netbios — a widely used operating system interface standard for local area networks. In this case, Netbios compatibility provides the standardized interface between the network and the CD ROM subsystem.

In both instances, stable and well-accepted standards provided the essential foundation on which widely useable CD ROM network configurations could be implemented.

Conclusion

The incredibly rapid evolution of CD ROM was made possible by the timely adaptation of standards which allowed for stable growth rather than fragmented and chaotic expansion.

Looking back, the phenomenal commercial success of CD Audio created the opportunity for CD ROM. The Yellow Book established fundamental physical formatting standards for CD ROM so that manufacturers could build compatible CD ROM drives. And the High Sierra Group provided file format standards so that different computers and different operating systems could interchange CD ROMs created by CD ROM developers.

The industry was then at the threshold of a major barrier to the achievement of the full potential of the technology. It had to resolve a multitude of troublesome issues concerning CD ROM device integration — issues which had encumbered product development, caused confusion and slowed growth.

Strong solutions are at hand in the form of SCSI interfaces for CD ROM drives and the Microsoft CD ROM Extensions. The CD ROM industry and users are now moving steadily forward with the implementation of solutions that will enable the channeled and unencumbered growth of CD ROM.

About the Author

Jack Spiegelberg is president of IVID Communications, a San Diego–based firm specializing in the design and development of highly customized CD ROM products and interactive videodisc programs.

Acknowledgments

I wish to thank the following people for the information provided: Monti Basar, Online Products Corp., for network configuration information; Henry Burgess, Microsoft Corp., for information on the Microsoft CD ROM Extensions; Wink Saville, Meridian Data, for information on Interface Characteristics of CD ROM systems.

References

American National Standard for Information Systems — Small Computer System Interface (SCSI), New York, American National Standards Instutite, Inc., 1986.

Buddine, Laura, and Elizabeth Young. *The Brady Guide to CD ROM*. New York: Brady Books, 1987.

Denon Controller for Denon CD ROM Drive (SCSI/SASI Protocol) Technical Manual. Tokyo, Japan: Nippon Columbia Incorporated, 1987.

Microsoft MS DOS CD ROM Extensions Function Requests. Redmond, Wash.: Microsoft Inc., January 15, 1988.

Microsoft MS DOS CD ROM Extensions Hardware Dependent Device Driver Specifications. Redmond, Wash.: Microsoft Inc.,January 27, 1987.

Warren, Carl, "SCSI Bus Eases Device Integration," in *CD ROM: The New Papyrus*, Steve Lambert and Suzanne Ropiequet, eds., Redmond, Wash.: Microsoft Press, 1986.

Advanced CD ROM Formats

6

Compact Disc–Interactive

Richard Bruno

Introduction

For disc-based optical media there are no direct means of "viewing" the information stored on the disc's surface. By magnifying the sequence of pits and lands on the disc's surface, one cannot see a picture, "hear" any sound, or visualize a string of alphanumeric data! The end user's information has not only been placed on the disc's surface in a microscopic form but it has also been coded in a fashion that is particular to the medium itself and the data types it holds. As such, the end user can locate and "view" information stored on the disc's surface if — and only if — equipment is provided that can exercise six basic functions.

At the end user or dialogue level one requires a means of command or man-machine stimulus (e.g., keys) on input and one obtains a man-machine response (e.g., display) on output. At the machine or equipment level commands need be encoded or machine interpretable (e.g., hard wired or software), and on output decoded or man-interpretable. Finally, at the physical level one must access the right start location on the disc and read the signals contained thereon.

Level	Function	
	Input	Output
End User/Dialogue	Command	Response
Machine	Interpret	Decode
Physical	Access	Read

Figure 6-1   Usability functions for optical systems.

This chapter will not cover the physical level in any significant fashion since this is part of the Compact Disc–Digital Audio (CD-DA) Standard Specification, the so-called "Red Book." Nor will this chapter focus on the CD ROM Standard Specification since the byte level format is already a part of the Compact Disc–Interactive (CD-I) Standard Specification, the so-called "Green Book." As such, this chapter will focus on CD-I and cover byte level formats, the machine level as well as the base-case functionality for the end user level.

Compact Disc–Digital Audio (CD-DA)

CD-DA was introduced to the world market in 1982. By the end of 1987 there were about 30 million players and 450 million discs in use around the world.[1] CD-DA was accepted by the consumer electronics marketplace more readily than any other product ever produced.

The basic reason for this acceptance was that CD-DA offered very high quality sound reproduction at an attractive price via an easy to use system that fit existing conditions in a large base of homes. Moreover, CD-DA ensured end user worldwide compatibility between discs and systems. The latter is a consequence of industry adoption of one standard specification for CD-DA.

---

1   Estimates N.V. Philips.

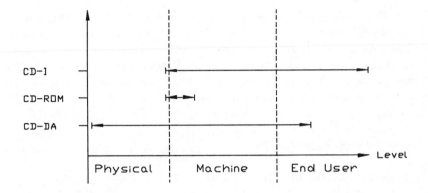

Figure 6-2 Target of standard specifications for optical systems.

A CD-DA disc measures 12 centimeters or 4.75 inches in diameter and can carry, for all practical purposes, up to 72 minutes of high quality audio per side. It should be noted that typically only one side is used on CD-DA discs as the printed disc label is on the nonactive side. The standard specification for CD-DA is, in fact, the source specification for CD ROM and CD-I. It contains all the physical level specifications for the media and the system as well as the machine level and end user level specification related to decoding Pulse Coded Modulation (PCM) audio.

Compact Disc Read Only Memory (CD ROM)

Unlike CD-DA, CD ROM is not a system that is usable at all three levels. A CD ROM unit is a peripheral device. It operates, beyond the CD-DA interface, at both the physical and low-level machine levels in order to access and read data as well as ensure the integrity of data. Coupling the end user to the CD ROM disc's content requires the interfacing of a computer to a CD ROM peripheral. This situation is analogous to a floppy disk drive. Most computers on the market are in one form or another, e.g., file and data format, incompatible. This is evidenced by the case of software distribution via floppy discs. As such CD ROM disc to CD ROM based systems compatibility cannot be compared to that of CD-DA.

CD ROM was introduced on the market in 1985. By the end of 1987 there were some 40,000 CD ROM peripherals and about 150,000 discs in use worldwide.[2]

A CD ROM disc is the same size as a CD-DA disc and also has the same physical characteristics. Such discs can be replicated in the same plants and can use the same equipment used for CD-DA discs.

Multimedia on a Compact Disc

The term *multimedia* originated from the audiovisual industry to denote a multiple slide projector show coupled to a sound track under processor control. Another interpretation of multimedia is the blending together or two or more data types, such as text, audio, visual, and binary (e.g., computer instructions) data on one common storage medium.

Multimedia on a compact disc implies that several dissimilar data types could be simultaneously stored on and sensibly retrieved from a CD. Moreover, the equipment that is necessary to provide the six basic functions (Figure 6-1) will need to decode some of those data types in real-time and present tightly coupled data, or multiple types, to the end user via well established interfaces (e.g., HiFi system, TV) in real-time.

What are these various data types and what factors influence them? To begin with it is useful to consider the factors. Some data types such as audio and video or pictures (still or moving) can be interpolated to remove or disguise hard or soft errors that emanate from the disc. However, for alphanumeric, graphic, or binary data such concealment cannot be used due to the non-continuous temporal or spatial nature of these data types.

For some data types the inherent limitations of the CD (in terms of data rate and space) may be a constraint to developing a full or broad range of CD based multimedia applications. For pictures this is always the case be it for stills or motion, whereas for audio only space limits potential applications. Constraints related to these factors imply data compression need be used.

Not all data have the same inherent or application dependent temporal requirements. Clearly audio is a real-time data type, whereas

---

2 Estimates N.V. Philips.

Factors	Data Type				
	α-Numeric	Audio	Visual Graphics	Pictures	Binary
Data Integrity -Concealment		●		●	
-ECC required	●		●		●
CD Data Rate Limitation				●	
CD Space Limitation		●		●	
Real Time Data		●		●	
Real Time Tight Coupling		●		●	●
Language Dependent	●	●			
File/Record Standards Exist	●		●		●
Dependent on Existing Interface Standards	●	●	●	●	

Figure 6-3   Factors influencing multimedia data types.

motion pictures, a subset of the picture category, is also real-time in nature. This, plus the fact that certain multimedia data types may be constrained to tight coupling in real-time (e.g., audiovisual synchronization) imposes real-time event handling on any multimedia CD-based system. Beyond real-time event handling, multilanguage use of CD systems in general, and for real-time data, in particular, implies that a real-time interleaving and deinterleaving mechanism must be available.

The existence of viable national standards or worldwide industry standards for the CD medium's application to multimedia data requires due consideration. This is particularly true if a piggyback strategy to existing standards and equipment is adopted. Here standards from the computer industry will impact alphanumeric, graphic, and binary data types, while national or international standards in the audio/video world will impose requirements mainly for analog video output.

It's under these conditions and constraints that the specification of multimedia Compact Discs needs to be defined and, indeed, Compact Disc–Interactive (CD-I) took its form.

CD-I Standard Specification

A standard specification is by the very nature of this term a snapshot in time. Indeed, once it is frozen, the world of technology has already moved a step further. Yet, once a standard specification has been adopted and is in place, it takes decades to replace it. This is witnessed in many industries such as broadcast TV (e.g., PAL versus EMAC) and even in the audio industry (e.g., the phonograph versus CD-DA). It is said that a new standard will only depose an established one if two of three key factors, i.e., cost, performance, or functionality, have been appropriately changed by about an order of magnitude or more. This concept of "substantial leverage" of a new specification over the old one is what causes vested interest to adopt the standard.

A multi-industry standard specification is a self-consistent set of agreements on the technical specification of a product. It is, in a sense, the best compromise specification for a product that will satisfy the required functions and performance characteristics in a compatible and cost effective fashion for a global market. Of essence in bringing about the adoption of such a standard is its timely specification and introduction. Compact Disc–Interactive which is based on the CD-DA specification is such a standard specification.

This specification was initially conceived and prototyped by Philips in 1983–1984 and then proposed to the CD licensees in 1986 by Philips and Sony. After a suggestion period where over 2000 questions and comments from licensees were taken in account, the final specification was released to Philips' and Sony's 150 licensees in 1987.

CD-I Functions and Features

From 1983 to 1987 scientists and engineers at Philips and Sony were working on a CD-based multimedia standard specification. Feasibility projects for a consumer and semiprofessional/institutional multimedia system started, independently, during the course of 1983 at Philips, Sony, and Matsushita Electric Industrial. By 1985 Philips and Sony began to cooperate on an applications based consumer oriented CD multimedia system and standard specification. This standard specification is known today as Compact Disc–Interactive, or CD-I. The full functional specification for CD-I was released to the Philips-Sony licensees in March 1987.

This chapter describes the various parts of the CD-I specification in terms of the functions available as well as the features of the CD-I base case system. These capabilities are a consequence of a basic set of requirements:

Multimedia applications target
— Consumer
  • Real-time audiovisual capabilities
— Semiprofessional/institutional
  • Expandability

Disc producability
— Ease of authoring
— Same mastering and replications process as CD-DA

Piggyback on existing consumer electronics products
— Television systems
— HiFi system

Compatibility
— CD-DA discs and systems
— Upward and downward
— International (NTSC/PAL/SECAM independence)

Consumer cost target
— All these considerations were used to establish principles and ground rules to guide the specification process.

Disc Structure

CD-I discs are compatible with CD-DA discs and players in terms of the Eight to Fourteen Modulation (EFM) and Cross-Interleaved Reed-Solomon Code (CIRC) use, and their ability to hold CD-DA tracks and PCM coding. This will become more evident in this section on disc structure.

All compact disc formats (e.g., CD-DA, CD ROM, and CD-I contain a lead-in area, a program area, and a lead-out area (Figure 6-4). The lead-in area (Figure 6-5) of a CD-I disc is composed of empty sectors which allows for easy identification of the program area start. The program area of a CD-I disc (Figure 6-5) can hold, as does a CD-DA disc, up to 99 tracks numbered 1 to 99. Although a CD-I disc can contain CD-DA tracks, the first track of a CD-I disc's program area must be a CD-I track. Any CD-DA track on a CD-I disc must be positioned after the final CD-I track on the disc. Typically a CD-I disc need only contain one CD-I track because the data and programs on a CD-I disc can be segmented into files and records. As such, there can be one or more (i.e., ≤ 98) CD-DA tracks on a CD-I disc. A track can be any length between 4 seconds (300 sectors) and the total available space for the program area (maximum approximately 72 minutes or 325,000 sectors).

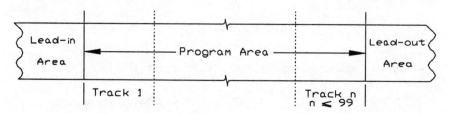

Figure 6-4   CD disc structure.

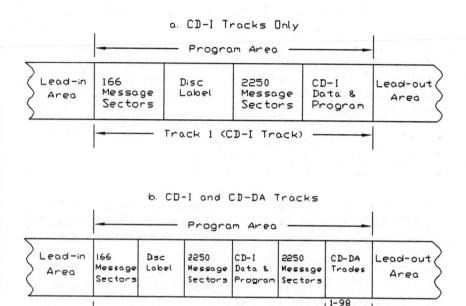

Figure 6-5 CD-I disc structure.

The lead-out area of a CD-I disc contains CD-I empty sectors if the last track is a CD-I track and CD-DA silent frames if the last track is a CD-DA track.

All sectors in a CD-I track are mode 2 sectors (see the next section). Some of these sectors are used for warning messages that can only be heard on older model CD-DA players and are skipped by a CD-I system. These sectors are called message sectors. Message sectors contain a spoken message warning the user at play start that he has unintentionally loaded a CD-I disc on an old model CD-DA player.

When a CD-I disc is put in a CD-I system and played, the first sectors that are read are the Disc Label sectors. The disc label contains a description of all the files on a CD-I disc, its contents, size, creator, etc., as well as the location of any software modules which must be loaded into the system, the boot file if necessary and the path table which allows access to those files. The disc label is comprised of three records: the File Structure Volume Descriptor, the Boot Record, and the Terminator Record.

A path table (Figures 6-6 and 6-7), which gives a list of all directories, must be put on each CD-I disc. This table gives an index of the directory structure on the disc which typically follows the disc label. The location of this table on the disc is given in the disc label. Each entry has the following fields:

* Location of the directory file
* Parent directory name
* Directory name

Each directory is a file containing file descriptor records.

All data and programs on a CD-I disc are divided into files. Any file may be accessed through the path table on the disc. Each file has a file descriptor record which is located in the appropriate directory file. This file contains the file name, number, size, address, owner, attributes, software interleave factor, and the access permissions for read. There are three types of files:

* Directory files
* Real-time files
* "Ordinary" files

Sector Format

CD-I data are divided into "atomic" units called sectors. Globally the sector structure of CD-I sectors is similar to that for CD ROM mode 2. One CD-I sector is, on disc, the same size as one CD-DA frame. CD-I sectors are read at a rate of 75 sectors per second.

The size of a CD-I sector (Figure 6-8) is 2352 bytes and is broken up into three basic parts: the header, the subheader, and the data area. The header of a CD-I sector is the same as a mode 2 header for a CD ROM sector. It contains a 12-byte synchronization pattern, a 3-byte sector address in minutes, seconds, and sector number, and a 1-byte mode descriptor. The latter is always set to 2 for CD-I. The eight byte subheader contains all the data necessary for real-time switching and transfer of CD-I data on a sector by sector basis. It contains information such as the file interleave data (i.e., as required

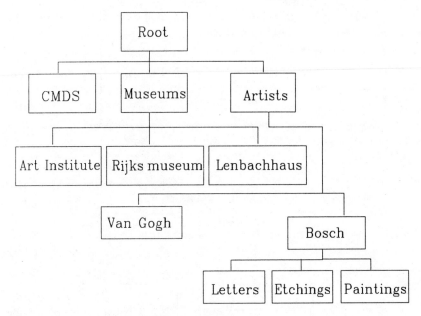

Figure 6-6 Example directory structure.

Relative Position	Parent Directory Number	Directory File Name
1	1	Root
2	1	CMSD
3	1	Museums
4	1	Artists
5	3	Art Institute
6	3	Rÿks museum
7	3	Lenbachhaus
8	4	Van Gogh
9	4	Bosch
10	9	Letters
11	9	Etchings
12	9	Paintings

Figure 6-7 Example path table.

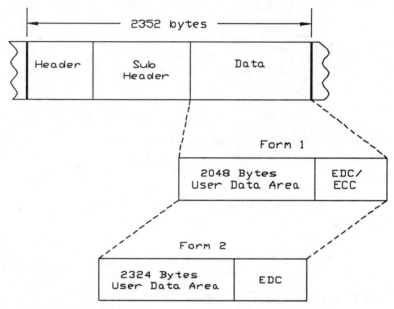

Figure 6-8   Sector format.

for a hardware deinterleaving), sector channel data, data type bits (i.e., real-time, non-real-time, audio, video, or program related data), the form bit (i.e., form 1 or form 2), trigger bit, end of record (EOR) and end of file (EOF) bits, and coding information data (i.e., the detailed data type and format in which the data in the data area is in).

The structure of the data area depends on the sector forms (Figure 6-8). Form 1 sectors contain 2048 bytes of user data as well as 280 bytes of error detection and correction code. Form 1 sectors are used for data whose integrity is essential, such as text, application programs, and control data. In these cases there is no built-in prediction capability or redundancy to allow a means of recovery from errors. Form 2 sectors contain 2324 bytes of user data and no additional layer of error correction beyond the CIRC. The use of form 2 sectors is more suited for data where concealment can be invoked, e.g., audio and video data. Since form 2 sectors allow for error detection, concealment strategies can be used effectively here. Moreover, form 2 allows for 15 percent more data bandwidth than do form 1 sectors. For audio this is equivalent to having audio limited to a 14.4-kHz bandwidth (form 1) or 17 kHz (form 2).

Level	Quality	Maximum Duration of Play
Real-Time CD-DA (Stereo only)	Super HiFi	1.2 hours
Level A -Stereo -mono	HiFi	2.4 hours 4.8 hours
Level B -Stereo -mono	FM	4.8 hours 9.6 hours
Level C -Stereo -mono	AM	9.6 hours 19.2 hours
Non-Real-Time Phonetic	Telephone	~10,000 hours

Figure 6-9   CD-I Audio levels.

CD-I Audio

CD-I offers four standard real-time audio quality levels and one non-real-time level (Figure 6-9). The first of these levels is the CD-DA level. This level is the standard CD-DA 44.1-kHz sampling rate 16 bit PCM coded audio (Figure 6-10). This level allows for one super Hi-Fi stereo channel with a maximum playing time of about 72 minutes. The bandwidth of this level is 20 kHz and the signal-to-noise (S/N) and dynamic range are 96 decibels.

The subsequent three real-time levels are Adaptive Delta Pulse Code Modulation (ADPCM) coded audio, wither stereo or mono, that is put in CD-I form 2 sectors. These three levels are called levels A, B, and C. Level A has a quality better than the Deutsches Industrie Norm (DIN) HiFi norms. Its maximum playing time per channel is 72 minutes; however, with two stereo and four mono channels its effective net maximum playing time is 2.4 and 4.8 hours, respectively. It should be noted that the concept of a "channel" in CD-I can be used in two ways. The first is for extended playing time (Figure 6-

Level	Sampling Rate (KHz)	Coding	Bits per Sample	Bandwidth (KHz)	Number of Channels	Percent of Data Rate
CD-DA	44.1	PCM	16	20	1 stereo	100
A	37.8	ADPCM	8	17	2 stereo 4 mono	50 25
B	37.8	ADPCM	4	17	4 stereo 8 mono	25 12.5
C	18.9	ADPCM	4	8.5	8 stereo 16 mono	12.5 6.25

Figure 6-10 Characteristics of real-time CD-I Audio levels.

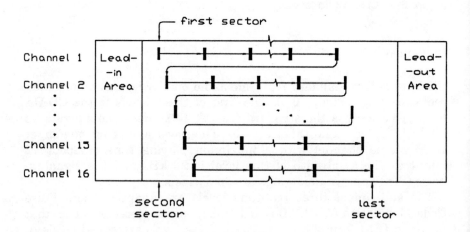

Figure 6-11   Channel extended playing time.

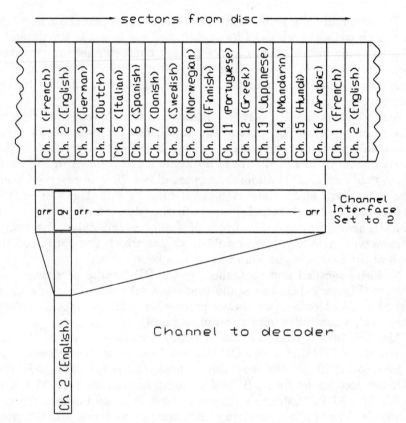

Figure 6-12 Multi-channel real-time access.

11), and the second is for real-time access to parallel audio data streams (Figure 6-12).

The two other ADPCM levels are levels B and C. Both use 4-bit significance for their range value and data differences. Level B has a quality superior to direct broadcast FM sound and level C's quality is comparable to or better than direct broadcast AM sound. Using one or another of these levels on a CD-I disc depends on the:

• Application's requirements in terms of sound quality
• Bandwidth left over in the data stream for a particular audio channel.

The non-real-time level is the phonetic coding level. This is a text to speech coding level. CD-I has two interfaces to assist the decoding of such audio information, i.e., the default character set (upper interface) and 8 bit PCM decoding in real-time (lower interface). The translation from the upper to the lower interface is handled by the microprocessor.

Audio data on a CD-I disc is contained in form 2 real-time sectors. The coding information part of the subheader for audio sectors contians information on emphasis setting, quality level and mode (i.e. mono or stero). The structure of an audio sector, shown in Figure 6-13, is made up of 2304 audio data bytes plus a 20 byte reserved area. The 2304 byte audio data is divided into 18 sound groups of 128 bytes, each and each sound group is further divided into 16 bytes for sound parameters and 112 bytes of actual sound data. The sound parameters include range and filter values which are optimized for each of the four or eight sound units in a sound group.

Audio is decoded and controlled by the CD-I audio processor subsystem (Figure 6-14). The audio processor subsystem is made up of an ADPCM decoder, an audio processing unit, a special effects processor, a controller, and a soundmap unit.

ADPCM data is passed to the ADPCM decoder either directly (see 1 in Figure 6-14) from the CD-Control Unit or indirectly (see 2 in Figure 6-14) from the soundmap unit (memory). The ADPCM decoder decodes levels A, B, and C audio as well as 8-bit 37.8 kHz PCM. The ADPCM decoder outputs 16-bit PCM audio data for two channels. The audio processing unit accepts as input CD-DA data directly after the CIRC or PCM data from the ADPCM decoder. The audio processing unit is essentially a Digital to Analog Converter (DAC), but when combined with the special effects processor functions, like a two-channel audio mixer with loudness control under central processor unit (CPU) control. It should be noted that the combination of CPU and soundmap use is allowable in a CD-I application to decode data to any of these standard audio modes.

CD-I Video

As for audio, video data are contained in form 2 real-time sectors. The coding information for video sectors is made up of the resolution of the video data, the coding method used, and an even/odd line flag for error concealment.

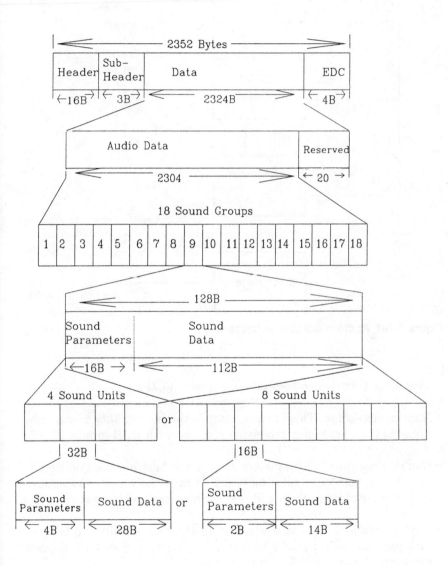

Figure 6-13   Audio sector structure.

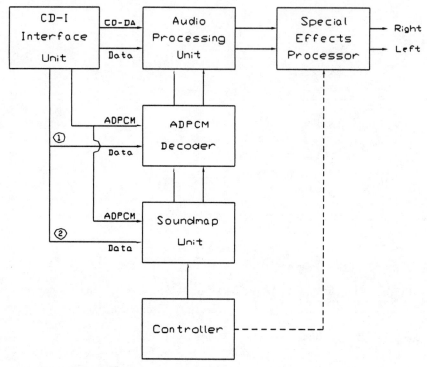

Figure 6-14   Audio processor subsystem.

There are three video resolutions offered in CD-I:

* *Normal resolution.* This is equivalent to the best quality picture obtainable from broadcast television receiver with RGB inputs.

* *Double resolution.* This is equivalent to the best picture quality obtainable on computer color monitors. It provides a better reproduction of computer graphics and text than normal resolution.

* *High resolution.* This is equivalent to the best quality digital picture generated in a studio to Audio Engineering Society/European Broadcast Union (AES/EBU) standards.

The lower CD-I interface can decode four types of coding schemes in real-time. The first is Delta Y (luminance or brightness), UV

Resolution	Display System			
	525 Line		625 Line	
	Horizontal	Vertical	Horizontal	Vertical
Normal	360	240	384	280
Double	720	240	768	280
High	720	480	768	560

Figure 6-15   Screen resolution in pixels.

(chroma), or DYUV, which is best suited for photographic images. The second is Color Look-Up Table (CLUT) coding which is best suited for quality text and graphics. The third is run length coding which can be used to compress CLUT coded images further. This is of particular relevance for cartoon like images used in motion animation. The final coding scheme is RGB555, which is best suited for images or complex graphics that the user will manipulate.

The combination of DYUV and run-length coding allows for one additional coding method known as Quantized High Resolution Y (QHY). This method results in excellent high resolution DYUV pictures with only a 30 percent, as opposed to 300 percent, increase in image storage size beyond normal resolution. The allowable combinations of coding schemes and picture resolutions are shown in Figure 6-16. This shows that all basic coding schemes are available in base case CD-I systems. It should be noted that, as in audio, applications specific video decoding via the CPU and memory is allowed in a CD-I application as long as the decoded data can then be transferred for the next level of decoding and display to one of the standard video modes.

The coding on disc for DYUV images is shown in Figure 6-17. Here each pixel pair is represented by 2 bytes. The difference values for luminance and the two chroma values are given by DY, DU, and DV respectively. Each 4 bit value is converted to an 8 bit value to adding the present pixel's difference to the previous pixel's predicted value (along the same video scan line) in the decoder.

There are several different CLUT modes. Figure 6-18 shows the coding on disc for CLUT8, CLUT7, and CLUT4. CLUT8 uses 8 bits

Coding Scheme	Resolution		
	Normal	Double	High
DYUV	B	——	E
QHY	——	B	E
CLUT 8 bit	B	——	E
CLUT 7 bit	B	——	E
CLUT 4 bit	——	B	——
RL 7 bit	B	——	E
RL 3 bit	——	B	——
RGB 555	B	——	——

B= Base case system
E= Extended system

Figure 6-16 Combination of coding schemes and resolution.

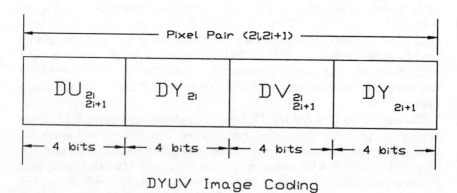

DYUV Image Coding

Figure 6-17   DYUV image coding.

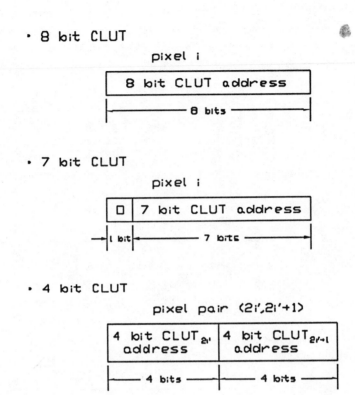

Figure 6-18   CLUT Image coding.

to define the accessible palette of 256 colors, while CLUT7 uses 7 bits for 128 colors and CLUT4 uses 4 bits for defining 16 colors.

For run-length images Figure 6-19 shows the representation of the image coding format. In the case of normal and high resolution, 2 bytes of data are used to define the pixel color (from a predefined CLUT) and then the number of pixels (the run) of this same color. In double resolution pixel pairs are taken together.

The on disc coding for RGB555 images is shown in Figure 6-20. The structure of the RGB values are given as a transparency bit and 5 bits for each of R, G, and B in 2 bytes of data.

CD-I Images as viewed by the end user are, like CD-I's digital audio, composed of multiple planes. In the case of audio, two input planes L_{in} (left) and R_{in} (right) are available and can, under CPU

• 7 bit Run-length

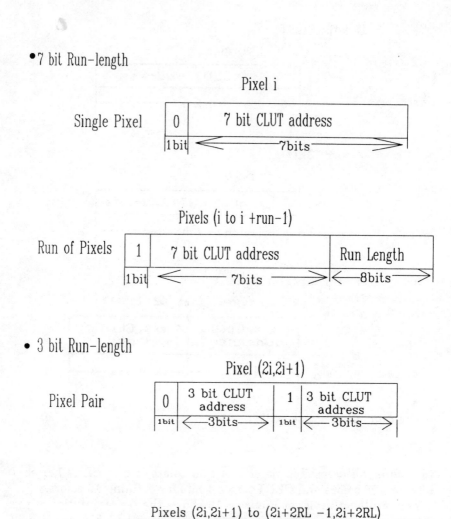

Figure 6-19   Run-length Image coding.

Pixel i

T	Red	Green (High bits)	Green (Low bits)	Blue
1b	⟵ 5 bits ⟶	⟵ 2 bits ⟶	⟵ 3 bits ⟶	⟵ 5 bits ⟶

Figure 6-20   RGB 555 image coding.

control, be mixed in any fashion into two output planes L_{out} (left) and R_{out} (right). At a conceptual level there is a symmetry between digital audio planes and digital video planes. CD-I allows for two digital video planes, that is, a "foreground plane" (plane A) and a "background plane" (plane B) (Figure 6-21). However, unlike audio these planes can be combined pixel by pixel in any fashion into one output plane, i.e., the display's visual plane.

Apart from the two digital video planes CD-I video has, like CD-I audio[3] an external optional analog input plane, and unlike audio, a hardware cursor plane. The analog plane, if active, can be combined

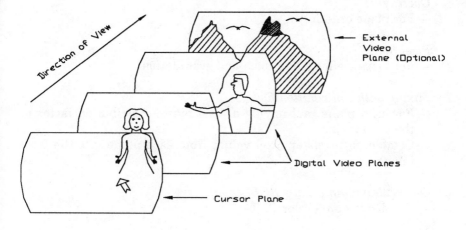

Figure 6-21   CD-I visual planes.

---

3 In the case of CD-I audio the external optional analog input plane is composed of two distinct planes $L_{ext\ in}$ (left) and $R_{ext\ in}$ (right).

with the digital planes and the cursor plane in any fashion into one output displayed image. The cursor plane contains a 16 × 16 pixel cursor which is hardware controlled in accordance to user/superuser cursor positioning pattern and color.

Video that is encoded and placed on a CD-I disc is decoded by a CD-I video processor subsystem as shown in Figure 6-22. The video processor subsystem has two banks of RAM, bank 0 and bank 1, coupled to it. Bank 0 contains visual information for plane A, and bank 1 contains visual information for plane B.

The video processor subsystem is capable of several basic functions:

Decoding
DYUV ---> YUV ---> RGB 888 (min DAC 666)
CLUT ---> RGB 888 (min DAC 666)
RL ---> CLUT ---> RGB 888 (min DAC 666)
RGB 555 ---> RGB 888 (min DAC 666)

Color keying per pixel
— For creating transparent areas in any plane

Overlay
— For plane ordering

Pixel hold
— For mosaic effects like zoom and granulation

Mixing with contribution factors
— For each plane multiplying a pixel by its contribution factor to the total image
— Combining pixels or pixel values from each plane into the total image

Outputting to an analog RGB signal
— For display on a color CRT

These functions in the video processor subsystem, under disc, user, or superuser control, give a CD-I system the ability not only to display quality digital video images and full motion sequences but also to carry out an array of special effects without consuming precious data bandwidth.

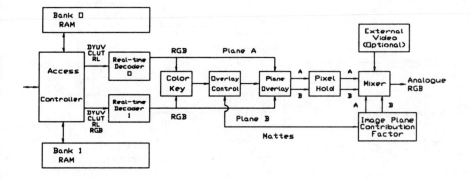

Figure 6-22   Video processor subsystem.

As shown in Figure 6-22, the video processor subsystem has two real-time decoders. Each of these decoders (e.g., DYUV part of a real-time decoder, shown in Figure 6-23) is capable of decoding CD-I visual images. In particular, real-time decoder 0 decodes DYUV, CLUT and run-length coded images, while real-time decoder 1 decodes DYUV, CLUT, run-length and RGB images. Also, since a CD-I system has two planes but only one 8-bit CLUT arranged in four banks, the allowable coding combinations of plane A overlaid with plane B is given in Figure 6-24.

The hardware cursor plane is 16 pixels square. Each pixel of this cursor plane can be set to be either transparent or to a cursor color. There are 16 colors to choose from. The cursor may appear as a solid program defined shape on the display or may be caused to blink. The cursor is available at all CD-I resolutions and may be positioned at any point on the CD-I full-screen area under disc, user, and/or super-user control.

Loading and displaying pixel data is only one aspect of the video display program. The control of visual content includes the loading of CLUT RGB values, defining matte areas, image contribution factors, etc. This is all done in CD-I via a display control program (DCP). Such programs, which can be distributed over or localized on one area of the CD-I disc, consist of a set of display control instructions which are carried out on every video line or field scan. As such, these instructions are placed in two tables which are called the field con-

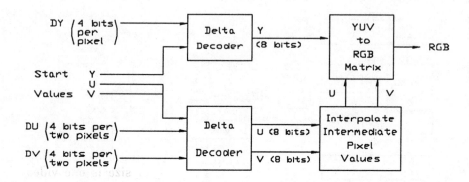

Figure 6-23 DYUV part of the real-time decoder.

trol table (FCT), which is executed once every field and can be renewed if desired once every field, and the line control table (LCT), which is executed on a per line basis and may be different for each line of each field. Each visual plane has an FCT and an LCT associated with it for each scan. These may remain static or may be modified over time, e.g., for each field. The field control table can

		Plane A						
		Off	DYUV	CLUT			Run length	
				4	7	8	3	7
Plane B	Off							
	DYUV							
	CLUT 4					▨		
	7					▨		
	8					▨		
	Run length 3					▨		
	7					▨		
	RGB 555		▨	▨	▨	▨	▨	▨

☐ = Available

▨ = Not available

Figure 6-24   Allowable coding combinations.

hold up to 1024 instructions and is used for setting up the display parameters at the start of each field. The line control table can hold up to 8 instructions per line. These allow one to change the display parameters from one line to another as the scan progresses. As a result of this basic structure of a DCP and the fact that CD-I is a line-oriented system from memory and for control, and a pixel-oriented system for decoding overlay and special effects, it is possible to allocate separate screens to each line of each visual plane. These separate hardware supported screens are called subscreens. Subscreens can be treated as distinct and separate visual entities in terms of their content, coding scheme, and manipulation (e.g., scrolling and special effects). The minimum subscreen size is one video line in each visual plane and the maximum size depends only on memory size (i.e., it can be greater than a full screen).

One example of a DCP is shown in Figure 6-25. This is an example of matte creation. There are three overlapping mattes in this example and an area of image contribution factor (ICF) change. Considering just one display line in Figure 6-25, it is clear that it requires the maximum of 8 LCT instructions to carry out this effect.

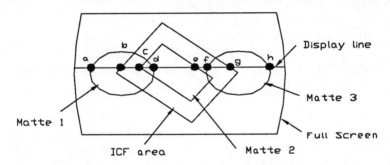

a: Start Matte 1
b: change ICF
c: Start Matte 2
d: End Matte 1
e: End Matte 2
f: Start Matte 3
g: Change ICF
h: End Matte 3

Figure 6-25   DSP example.

Other examples of DCP instruction
— Subscreen object movement synchronized to display scanning
— Image coding per subscreen
— Reloading CLUT colors per scan line: this would increase the maximum possible number of colors on a display from:
  • CLUT 8 (Normal Resolution) 256 to 2488
  • CLUT 7 (Normal Resolution) 128 to 2360
  • CLUT 4 (Double Resolution)16 to 2248 out of 16.8 million colors.
— Loading a new backdrop color in the place of external video

In closing the CD-I video section it should be noted that the philosophy behind CD-I is to offer a real-time interface with a breadth of capabilities. The application can always be used to produce higher level interfaces as long as the latter at some point transfers data to the former.

CD-I Program Related Data Representations

Program-related CD-I data can be:

• Binary data (e.g., the application program in executable object code)
• Text
• Phonetic coding

The CD-I operating system does not restrict the format or the content of the data to be processed by the application. All CD-I program related data are stored in form 1 sectors.
· All CD-I programs are stored in executable object code to ensure real-time performance. Each loadable program is put in a file which may contain one or more software modules. These files are usually placed in a directory named "CMDS" and may be located anywhere within the CD-I file system. The instruction set for CD-I programs is defined in the M68000 Programmers Reference Manual. The data related to a CD-I program is stored in form 1 sectors. Such data may be included in real-time records at the beginning of a record. If the data is non-real-time, it would be positioned at any point in a non-real-time record or in front of a real-time record.

CD-I players must at least support the CD-I default character set[4]. The font module of a CD-I player contains at least four fonts in the CD-I's system ROM, one of which can be a local font set. For character sets other than the default character set, the font module for that character set must first reside in memory before any characters can be displayed. Any font module other than the one supporting ISO/DIS 8859/1 must reside on the CD-I disc.

The last program-related data representation is phonetic coding. The text representing phonetic code may be placed on a CD-I disc as CD-I default characters. This text is read by the application which converts it to 8 bit PCM that can be decoded by the audio processing subsystem.

CD-Real-time Operating System (CD-RTOS)

CD-RTOS is another CD-I component. It is the real-time operating system that hides the details of the hardware from the application and so provides the disc-borne application with a uniform interface for all CD-I systems. CD-RTOS is an operating system that was evolved from an existing operating system called OS9. The latter has found wide use in process control, remote entry terminals, and personal computers.

The CD-I system playing a CD-I application must support multiple data types and streams (i.e., audio, video, text, control, and application program) as well as several I/O devices (e.g., keyboard, pixel pointing device, display) in real-time.[5] These data streams may demand the invocation of several separate and distinct processes. These processes may be "synchronous" or "asynchronous" and need be carried out within certain real-time constraints. CD-RTOS provides this basic multitasking event-driven support to the application. The architecture of CD-RTOS is modular. As additional functionality is required, calls are made to one or another module in the base case CD-RTOS. If a new function beyond the base case CD-

---

4   ISO/DIS Standard Document 8859/1.

5   "Real-time" refers to three times:
    Video: less than or equal to a field update (1/60 second)
    Audio: less than or equal to a sector update (1/75 second)
    Event: less than or equal to an interrupt (1/100 second)

RTOS is required by the application, the new CD-RTOS module is loaded from disc onto the CD-I system.

The organization of CD-RTOS is shown in Figure 6-26. The application program with its associated data and libraries are located on disc. They are loaded by CD-RTOS, as needed by the application, into the CD-I system and executed by CD-RTOS in accordance to the applications scheduling. At the top of CD-RTOS are some basic libraries (e.g., math, user interface). Below these is the CD-RTOS kernel which handles the multitasking, task control, interprocess communication, memory management, interrupt handling, the system's service requests, I/O calls, and task synchronization. Alongside the kernel are connected various housekeeping and initialization modules, as well as the Configuration Status Descriptor (CSD) module. This module can be queried by the application to determine the CD-I system's configuration. Below the kernel are the key file manager modules, i.e.:

• Compact Disc File Manager (CD-FM)
• Nonvolatile RAM File Manager (NRF)

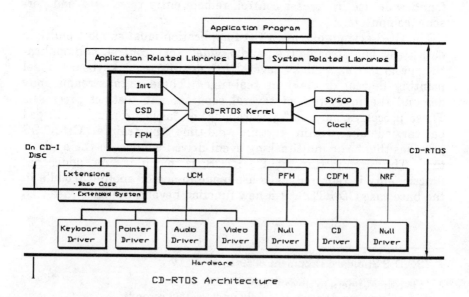

Figure 6-26   CD-RTOS architecture.

- Pipe File Manager (PFM)
- User Communications Manager (UCM)

The upper interface of these file managers are hardware independent while the lower interface is coupled to various device drivers for:

- Keyboard
- Pointing device
- Compact Disc player
- Audio subsystem
- Video subsystem
- CPU subsystem
- Non-volatile RAM (NVRAM)

The device drivers take account of any differences in devices from different manufacturers. These drivers handle all low level functions. Extensions to CD-I system base case level functionality are handled by either placing the extension manager on a disc since it is relevant to the base case systems or in the system for extended systems.

When a CD-I system is turned on and a disc is inserted, CD-RTOS initiates a startup procedure (see Figure 6-27). This procedure initializes the hardware, starts up the CD-RTOS kernel, displays the system copyright message, and if necessary, loads a boot file from disc and compiles the Configuration Status Descriptor (CSD). After this, the file system is initialized after the disc label is read, the manufacturer's logo and copyright message is displayed, and the initial disc based application is executed. If the end user removes the disc and inserts another disc, this procedure is started from the Load Boot File point again.

The CSD allows an application to find out what devices are available and what their status is as resources for the application that is resident on a particular CD-I system. Each device on the system has an entry in the CSD. This is stored in either RAM or ROM with user settings stored in NVRAM. Each CSD entry is known as a device status descriptor (DSD), and consists of four parts:

- Device type
- Device name
- Active status
- Device parameter set

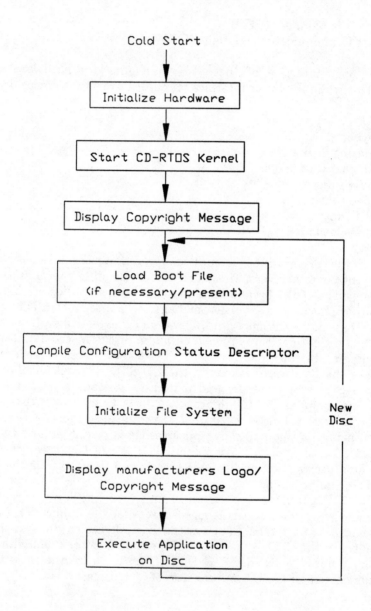

Figure 6-27   Startup procedure.

The devices considered in the CSD include CD-I base case resources such as the video decoder, display type, audio decoder, x-y device, as well as extensions such as floppy disc drives, printers, modems.

A basic mechanism that is available in all CD-I systems is the File Protection Mechanism (FPM). This mechanism allows the content owner or publisher of a CD-I disc to protect up to 32 different file sets on a CD-I disc through access codes. As such, a disc can be produced to contain several applications to which access can be individually controlled through separate, per customer and application, access codes. Thus, the customer may buy the disc and pay for as many applications upon initial purchase as he or she desires, with the option of accessing others, for a fee, at a later date. This kind of protection is enabled by having each CD-I player and protected disc application contain unique codes. The encryption method handled by the kernel match the player/disc decrypted codes with the access codes in order to control access to the application.

As already mentioned, file managers are modules that assure hardware independence for the application. The Compact Disc File Manager (CDFM) converts high-level commands from the application to the CD player device driver commands. This file manager provides access to the disc based file system and schedules and executes any disc access.

The service requests processed by CDFM are:

- Open path to specified file.
- Change user's default directories.
- Change current file/record position pointer.
- Read data from file.
- Get specified status information.
- Set status information.
- Perform special function.
- Close file.

A special CDFM command is used to play CD-DA files. This command routes CD-DA data directly from the CD to the audio processing unit. All other files are CD-I files. These have a directory hierarchy and can be opened and read by CDFM in any order. Files/records containing ADPCM audio data that is to be directly decoded by the ADPCM decoder are passed by CD FM to the audio processor subsystem directly.

The second file manager, the NVRAM file manager (NRF), manages the access to files for the application in the CD-I system's NVRAM. This file manager provides a basic directory structure with only one NVRAM directory and no subdirectories. File names may be defined by the application and no duplication is allowed.

The last CD-I file manager is the User Communications Manager (UCM). This manager is responsible for the four main devices that are used to dialogue with the user, i.e., keyboard, x-y or pointing device, audio, and video. For the keyboard, when a read request is obtained, UCM will return the characters typed at the keyboard. A program can either issue a read and wait for input or ask UCM to send it a signal when the input from the keyboard arrives. A list of some of the keyboard functions available via UCM are:

- read line
- read
- signal on data ready
- release device
- check for data ready.

If an application must follow the position of the pointing device, it must poll UCM for the current pointer position frequently enough to respond smoothly to pointer position changes. UCM does this efficiently in that it allows the application to ask it to send a signal every time the pointer location changes. In this way the program checks the pointer position often enough to track it accurately without wasting unnecessary time in polling.

Some of the pointer device functions that are available via UCM are:

- get pointer coordinates
- signal on pointer change
- release device

The audio module of UCM controls the flow of ADPCM sound data into and out of memory, as well as control signals from the CPU to the audio processor subsystem. This module supports non-real-time audio output and application-created sounds, and assists in the manipulation of sound data in memory as well as via hardware in the audio processing subsystem. Hardware real-time manipulation is restricted to two channel mixing, panning, and four channel attenuation. The audio data structure stored in memory is called a soundmap. UCM operates on soundmaps. The basic operations that UCM can perform on soundmaps are:

- merge two soundmaps
- loop soundmaps
- generate PCM soundmap[6]

When soundmaps are directed at the audio processor subsystem, UCM can control soundmap output attenuation via the aforementioned hardware control mechanism. Some of the commands available via UCM for the audio module are:

- create soundmap
- output soundmap
- stop audio processor
- conceal soundmap error
- close soundmap
- mix mono to stereo
- mix stereo to stereo
- set soundmap looping
- set attenuation

The video data structure in memory is called a drawmap. UCM's video module operates on and controls the output of drawmaps. UCM operations can combine and control drawmaps, handle characters or graphics, and display drawmaps for multiple planes under UCM control.

The video module of UCM supports multiple text fonts. These can be treated as character based fonts or as a bit mapped object. The former uses UCM's terminal emulation mode which supports both line editing and the use of character attributes. In this case the display is controlled by writing text and control codes using the I$Write command. In the latter case text is drawn from the drawmap as a text string of bit mapped fonts. Since control codes are not used here the application must control the location of text. CD-I fonts are data modules that must be in memory when the use of the font set is ac-

---

6   Level A ADPCM with filter coefficients set to zero is 8-bit PCM data.

tive. A CD-I system can have up to four fonts active in ROM at any time.

UCM has three modes of interpreting character codes. Eight-bit codes, like the CD-I default character set range from 0 to 255, which is sufficient for most character based languages. Seven/fifteen-bit codes represent 128 characters in 8 bits with the high bit reserved as a mode switch. If it is on, 15 bits are used for the character code. This latter case gives enough characters for oriental videogram-based languages and multiple font types. UCM requires that each font/character pair have its own unique number.

Some of the font drawing and terminal emulation functions available via UCM are:

- draw text
- character code mapping
- get font
- activate font
- deactivate font
- release font
- draw justified text
- set interlace mode
- calculate text length
- relative character positions
- return font data
- return glyph data
- justified character positions
- pointer in region
- get region location
- write
- write line
- set output drawmap
- set mapping mode
- activate font
- deactivate font

CD-I hardware supports a 16 by 16 bit hardware cursor. This hardware cursor plane is the first of four CD-I video planes. UCM offers a high level interface to the cursor hardware. This includes functions to control the cursor status, location, shape, color, and blink rate. A partial list of the cursor functions that are available is:

- position cursor
- show cursor
- hide cursor
- set cursor pattern
- set cursor color
- set cursor blink

Beyond the hardware cursor, CD-I can support any number of software graphics cursors.

An area of a drawmap can be named. Such an area is called a region. Two or more regions can be combined with various operations such as region intersection, union, difference, or exclusive OR. Moreover, regions can be repositioned in a drawmap. As such, regions can be used as clipping regions or they can be drawn on the drawmap. When one sets a clipping region in a drawmap, no drawing operation is allowed to change the drawmap outside of the clipping region. This capability is useful for supporting windows and a variety of graphics operations. Some of the clipping region functions supported by UCM are:

- create region
- region intersection
- region union
- region difference
- region exclusive-OR
- move region
- delete region

UCM supports a basic set of graphics functions. A partial list of the drawing commands are:

- set drawing pattern
- set pattern alignment
- set color register
- set clipping region
- set pen size
- set pen style
- draw a dot
- draw a line
- draw a polyline
- draw a circular arc

- draw an elliptical arc
- draw a rectangle
- draw a rounded rectangle
- draw a polygon
- draw a circle
- draw a circular wedge
- draw an ellipse
- draw an elliptical wedge
- draw a region
- bounded fill
- flood fill
- copy drawmap to drawmap

A variety of operations on drawmaps are also supported by UCM. There are special exchange and copy operations that accept a transparent color setting. These operations will not copy pixels that represent the transparent color. The latter remain unchanged. For such operations rectangular areas (a line is a special case of a rectangle) or individual pixels can be copied into or out of a drawmap. UCM transforms image data into a standard array, e.g., hardware interpretable, or pixel information when it reads from a drawmap and transforms image data from its pixel form to the drawmap's internal representation when it writes data into the drawmap. A write operation for an irregular area changes selected parts of a drawmap. This operation updates each line in a given range with the location and extent of the update specified on a line-by-line basis. Lines that are not updated have a zero-length update. Some of the drawmap operations that are available via the UCM are:

- create drawmap
- set drawing origin
- copy drawmap to drawmap
- exchange data between drawmaps
- copy with transparency
- exchange data with transparency
- irregular write to drawmap
- read drawmap
- write pixel
- read pixel
- conceal drawmap error
- close drawmap

To display a drawmap, UCM invokes a display control program (DCP) which is executed by the video processor subsystem. One part of the DCP is executed every video field, i.e., 50 or 60 times per second. This program is called the field control table (FCT). A second part of the DCP is executed for each scan line. This is called the line control table (LCT). The same program codes are used for both the FCT and LCT. FCT instructions are executed each time the display is refreshed. The FCT must include an instruction that points the video processor subsystem to the LCT of the first line to be displayed.

For each of the two digital image planes there must be a DCP. Each of these DCPs controls the parameters that effect the output of the visual information to the display from the drawmap for that visual plane. UCM has a series of commands that manage the two parts of a DCP. These commands provide a uniform interface; however, the application program is responsible for the setup and modification of the DCPs.

The DCP instructions that link the LCT to the FCT and the LCTs to LCTs are instructions that are supported by UCM. These instructions are useful for functions such as scrolling and subscreens. Most special effects are, in fact, performed by manipulating the DCP. The display parameters controlled by the DCP are:

* image coding method
* transparency control
* plane order
* external video plane color
* transparent color per plane
* mask color per plane
* image contribution factors per plane
* mosaic control (mosaic effects) per plane
* color look up table values per plane
* mattes per plane.

DCP instructions control video parameters for each plane on a line by line basis in real-time. The basic set of DCP functions are:

* create FCT
* read FCT
* write FCT
* read FCT instruction

- write FCT instruction
- delete FCT instruction
- create LCT
- read LCT
- write LCT
- read LCT column
- write LCT column
- read LCT instruction
- write LCT instruction
- delete LCT
- link LCT to FCT
- link LCT to LCT
- execute DCP

Most of the CD-I special effects are performed by the DCP. A cut from one image to another can be done by changing plane order in the FCT. A wipe is performed by changing from the top plane's visual data to the bottom plane's visual data one line at a time or by using a matte function. A dissolve is performed by increasing the contribution factors of one plane while decreasing the contribution factors of the other plane.

Audio played from a CD-I disc is always real-time. Moreover, audio accompanied by video or video that has precise and sequenced time constraints is also real-time. The smallest noninterruptable (except abort) "atomic" unit of real-time data is called a real-time record. Real-time files are made up of real-time records. Non-real-time data or control data relevant to real-time records typically precede the real-time record or are a part of a real-time record but are placed at the head of the record. The control of the flow of data through a CD-I system is handled by the play control structure, and the synchronization (e.g., of audio and video) is achieved by using the trigger settings in sectors and the use of timers. The play system call of the play control structure, is used to play real-time records and files by selecting sectors by file number, channel number, and data type. The play system call also controls the destination of data via the Play Control Blocks (PCB) and Play Control Lists (PCL), and signals the application whenever a specific event occurs. The PCB deinterleaves data and also provides the channel mask for channel selection. The PCL points to the appropriate parts of memory where the data is to be directed such as a soundmap or a drawmap.

The PCL buffer includes text and control data. Control data is usually in the form of a real-time control area (RTCA) which is located at the head of a real-time record (see Figure 6-28) and is loaded into the system prior to the real-time data. The RTCA is interpreted by a real-time record interpreter (RTRI) which is used to control the real-time playback and synchronization of data from a real-time record. The RTCA contains commands used to control the playing of real-time records, the loading of record data, the manipulation and display of visual data, the manipulation and output of audio data, and the synchronization of various real-time data types. The RTRI, which is contained in an ordinary file on the CD-I disc, is a multitasking interpreter that is written to decode the function codes contained in the RTCAs.

Synchronization which typically is used between audio and video data can be achieved in several ways, i.e., via:

- A software timer which can be instructed to generate a signal after a given time
- A user input which can generate a signal
- A signal from the application or a "concurrent" application

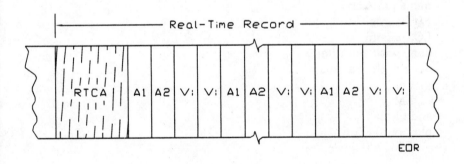

A1 = Audio sector data audio channel 1
A2 = Audio sector data video channel 2
Vi = Video sector data video channel 1
     V1 can be seen with A1 or A2 syncronized

Figure 6-28   Example real-time record.

- A trigger list, end of record bit, or end of file bit in the sector sub-header
- A full buffer signal from a PCL buffer
- An end of transfer of requested data

Every CD-RTOS file manager makes use of signals to communicate with the application. When a signal is sent to a process, the normal execution of the process is interrupted and control is transferred to the process's signal handler. A process can give the operating system the address of a function which the operating system will call each time a signal is directed at the process. If a process does not want to receive a signal, it can mask it. This is done automatically. Signals that are not received are queued for later attention. If a process does not handle a signal or mask it or catch and ignore it, then any nonzero signal will kill the process. For CD-RTOS interprocess signals function in the same way as signals from file managers. Signals can come from:

- UCM
  keyboard interrupt
  keyboard kill
  keyboard data ready
  mouse motion
  FCT signal
  LCT signal
  done with soundmap
  done with drawmap

- CDFM
  end of play
  play buffer full
  play hit a trigger

- Kernel
  alarm signals

- Other programs
  application specific

Another synchronization method support by CD-RTOS is via events and event handling. Events have names and values and are accessible to any process that calls their name. A process can wait for an event to attain a given value or value within a given range. Commands can be used to set or increment the value of an event.

CD-I Base Case

The CD-I base case defines the greatest common denominator among all CD-I systems and CD-DA players. A system can be called a CD-I system if, at the very least, it behaves like a CD-I base case system. A CD-I application running on a CD-I system must, at least, behave as if it was running on a "stand-alone" base case system. This approach allows all CD-DA and CD-I discs to play on all CD-I systems.

The CD-I base case system is made up of a well defined set of components (see Figure 6-29). These components are:

- A compact disc player
- A CD-DA controller/interface unit
- A CD-I interface
- A system bus
- A CD-I audio processing subsystem
- A CD-I video processing subsystem
- A microprocessing unit (MPU)
- A Direct Memory Addressing (DMA) Controller
- RAM
- An Access Controller
- NVRAM
- CD-RTOS, CSD and Font Module ROM
- A pointing device
- A keyboard (optional)
- A clock/calendar

The compact disc player can access data or CD-DA music on any part of a CD-DA and CD-I disc within a maximum of 3 seconds. The player can be controlled by functions such as:

- jump to address
- pause
- continue
- stop
- eject

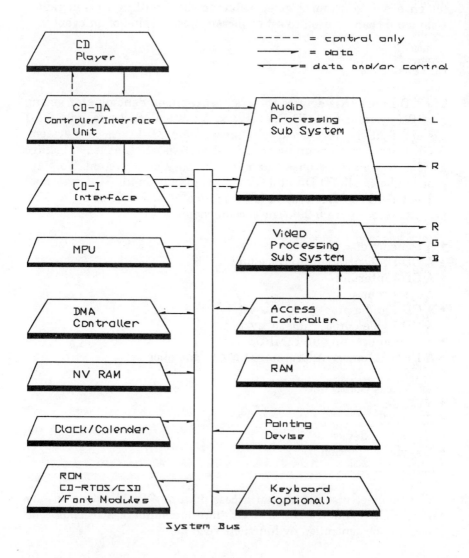

Figure 6-29   The CD-I base case system.

The CD-DA controller/interface unit delivers data, after the CIRC (Cross Interleaved Reed-Solomon Code) error correction, to:

• The audio processing subsystem if it is 16 bit PCM CD-DA audio data
• The CD-I interface if it is CD ROM or CD-I data
• The CD-DA controller/interface unit also controls the compact disc player.

The CD-I interface passes control information from the MPU via the bus to the CD-DA controller/interface unit as well as passing 'filtered' sectorized data to the system bus. The CD-I interface filters the data it passes to the bus by:

• Selecting the data belonging to the requested file
• Selecting the data belonging to the requested channel
• Selecting the data to be passed to one or another coprocessor by checking its data type
• Checking the data's status

As such the CD-I interface deinterleaves the data streams, generates selective interrupts and passes the resultant data to the appropriate processor/coprocessor. All this is done by interpreting the subheader information in real-time.

The system bus must be at least 16 bits wide and is used to couple all the aforementioned components, apart from the CD-DA controller/interface unit, together. Furthermore, the bus may be used as an interface to extend the CD-I system.

The CD-I audio processing subsystem, video processing subsystem and access controller have been previously discussed in this chapter, with one exception. The exception for the video processing subsystem is that it can decode all resolutions except non-interlaced high resolution images.

For both audio and video the input and processing of external signals in addition to CD borne signals is optional. However, for video an external video plane is available in the base case and can always be used as a backdrop color for the other video planes. A variety of backdrop colors are available for the external video plane.

The CD-I base case system is capable of reading and decoding CD-DA PCM data from either CD-DA tracks on a CD-I or CD ROM disc or CD-DA tracks on a CD-DA disc. Furthermore, a base case system is able to read CD ROM mode 1 discs, but, in general, cannot decode them. As such both the CD-I and the ISO 9660 file structure are supported by the base case system data transfer.

All CD-I systems must have two mechanisms available such that:

- Data can be transferred from the CD-I interface unit to RAM independently of the MPU
- Contiguous areas of memory can be copied independent of the MPU.

One example of this is a peripheral-to-memory DMA as well as a memory-to-memory DMA.

The code on CD-I discs must always be in M68000 executable object code format. The MPU must be at least a 16 bit data bus version of a 68000 family member. The total RAM (audio, video, and system) must be a minimum of 1 Mbytes and organized into at least two banks of 512 kbytes each. Beyond volatile RAM a minimum amount of CD-I NVRAM must be available. The CD-I base case system must have at least 8 kbytes of nonvolatile memory.

A CD-I base case must have at least one x-y pointing device. This pointing device must be capable of accessing each pixel of a normal resolution display. Furthermore, the pointing device must have at least two trigger buttons.

A battery backup clock/calendar is also available on each CD-I base case system. This clock/calendar must have a resolution of at least 1 second and must be capable of counting from seconds up to and including years and accommodate leap years.

All CD-I base case systems must have the CD-I default character set and at least four font modules in ROM. Beyond this the ROM must also contain the base case CD-RTOS and libraries, and CD-FM must also support the ISO 9660 file structure for CD ROM mode 1 discs. All internalized base case devices must be defined by entries in the ROM-based CSD.

All CD-I base case devices are interrupt-driven.

Extensions and Examples

CD-I Peripherals and Extensions

An extended CD-I system is a CD-I system which conforms to the CD-I base case, and has any number of additional CD-I extensions (e.g., memory and peripherals such as a floppy disk drive) added to its capabilities (see Figure 6-30). Since the CD-I base case system was specified to ensure CD-I disc/system compatibility, it's capabilities must, at the very least, be at the core of each CD-I system extended or not. However, not all user needs can be satisfied by a base case system (see Figure 6-31). This is what CD-I peripherals and extensions intend to accomplish. Within the CD-I concept peripherals and extensions are specified in such a way that their addition to the base case system is self-consistent, and encompass cost effective extensions and peripherals that are available today and will be available in the future.

The Peripheral Status Descriptor (PSD) is central to developers wanting to use CD-I peripherals and extensions. The PSD is compiled into the CSD for each extension and peripheral. It is used by the application to recognize the CD-I system's configuration and accommodate for various possibilities such that the application (i.e., from the CD-I disc) will usefully play on the various CD-I systems.

The basic approach to peripherals in the CD-I concept is that any given CD-I peripheral is independent of any other CD-I peripheral. As such, all CD-I peripherals may be considered as self-contained I/O devices. A partial list of the devices supported as CD-I peripherals and extensions are:

- RAM
- NVRAM
- Graphics coprocessor
- Arithmetic coprocessor
- High resolution video processing subsystem
- Genlocked external video mixed to CD-I video
- External audio mixed to CD-I/CD-DA audio
- Higher than normal resolution displays
- 3.5-inch floppy disk drive
- Image printer
- Bidirectional modem

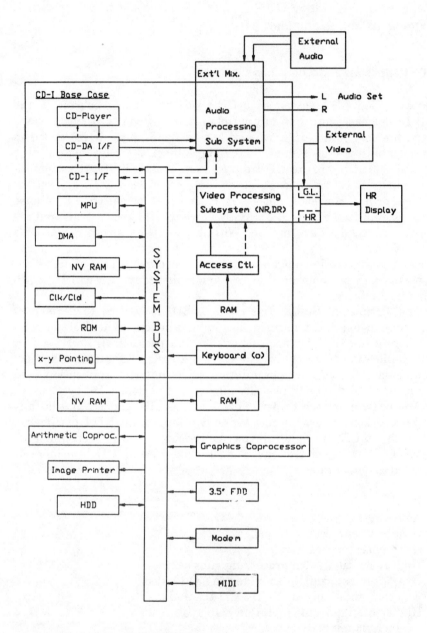

Figure 6-30   An example CD-I extended system.

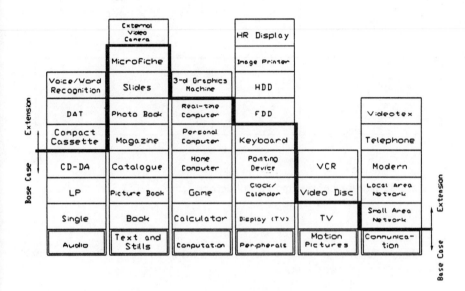

Figure 6-31 Product areas and CD-I capabilities.

- Hard disk drive
- Musical Instrument Digital Interface (MIDI)
- Local Area Network (LAN)

All CD-I extensions or peripherals must make available to the CD-I system their PSD device drivers and file manager. The PSD will be compiled by the CD-I system at startup into the CSD and a CD-I file manager can be used by the application as a hardware independent interface to the particular I/O device requested. The CD-I specification (the so-called Green Book) defines the file manager interface for all CD-I extensions or peripherals.

Specifications and Capabilities

Below is a list of the basic specifications and capabilities associated with the CD-I base case system:

System	Resolution (X 86400)		
	NR	DR	HR
525 line	1	2	4
625 line	1.24_4	2.48_8	4.97_7

Figure 6-32 Number of pixels in a full screen.[8]

Playing time
— Theoretical maximum = 74 minutes 33 seconds
— Practical playing time:
  • 66 minutes (CD ROM and CD-I form 1)
  • 72 minutes (CD-DA and CD-I form 2)

Disc data rate
— 75 sectors/second
— 150 kbyte/second (CD ROM and CD-I form 1 user data)
— 170.5 kbyte/second (CD-I form 2 user data)

Disc capacity
— Theoretical maximum = 335,475 sectors
  • 655 Mbytes (CD ROM and CD-I form 1 user data)
  • 745 Mbytes (CD-I form 2 user data)
— Practical capacity = 324,000 sectors
  • 580 Mbytes (CD ROM and CD-I form 1 user data)
  • 719 Mbytes (CD-I form 2 user data)

Maximum audio playing time (practical)
— CD-DA = 1.2 hours
— ADPCM levels
  • LEVEL A (HiFi; equivalent to a new, high-quality LP recording)
    — Stereo = 2.4 hours
    — Mono = 4.8 hours

- Level B (MidFi; equivalent to an FM radio broadcast)
  — Stereo = 4.8 hours
  — Mono = 9.6 hours
- Level C (voice[7], equivalent to an AM radio broadcast)
  — Stereo = 9.6 hours
  — Mono = 19.2 hours

Video
— Motion video picture size (525 line systems, NR, 15 frames/second input, 30 frames/second output, maximum playing time 72 minutes)
  - DYUV = 13.5 percent of full screen (i.e., 132 X 88 pixels)
  - Using application specific coding flag, e.g.:
    — DY (i.e., black and white movie) = 27 percent of full screen (i.e., 186 × 124 pixels)[8]
    — DY (interpolation and line repeat) = 100 percent of full screen (i.e., 360 × 240 pixels)
  - CLUT8 = 13.5 percent of full screen
  - CLUT8&7 animation = 100% of full screen
  - RL7 = 100% of full screen
  - RL3 = 100% of full screen
— Full-screen loading time: Approximately 0.495 seconds to load and display an 84.4 kbyte full screen image.
— (Refer to Figures 6-32 through 6-35.)

Audio and Video
— For motion video typically Level B mono to Level C stereo is sufficient. As such without audio preloading, the numbers above for full motion have to be decreased by 7/8, e.g: DYUV motion becomes 11.8 percent or 124 × 83 pixels.
— For still video the loading times are decreased by:

$$F = 1 - \sum_{i=1}^{N} L_i$$

---

7 Level C, although called the voice level, can be used for both voice and music.

8 A full screen extends beyond the visible area of a display. Typically the visible area is between 48 and 50 microseconds line sweep, while the full screen is about 52.4 microseconds.

Coding Scheme	Resolution (KB)		
	NR	DR	HR
DYUV	84.4	——	337.5
QHY (typical)	——	101KB	109KB
CLUT 8	84.4	——	337.5
CLUT 7	84.4	——	337.5
CLUT 4	——	84.4	——
RL 7 (typical)	10.5	——	28
RL 3 (typical)	——	8.5	——
RGB 555	168.8	——	——

Figure 6-33 Full screen picture size (525 line systems).

where N = number of audio channels used
L_i = bandwidth removal fraction for channel i.
   = 1/2 A stereo
   = 1/4 A mono/B stereo
   = 1/8 B mono/C stereo
   = 1/16 C mono

Special Effects

In the worst case CD-I special effects (525 line systems) using the full FCT, LCT, and resetting of registers for all CD-I planes require no more than 3.8 kbytes. Here the special effect would cover the full CD-I screen and would be made up of the maximum change of settings for each CD-I visual plane at any moment in time (i.e., frame time). As such, if these settings change at this maximum value from frame to frame, in the worst case CD-I disc-driven special effects would take up no more than three quarters of the disc data rate. Typically, special effects can either be pres-tored in RAM as an effects module, or if disc driven, they would rarely require more than 1 kbyte per frame or no more than 10 percent of the CD-I (form 1) data rate.

Text

The amount of text that can be placed on a CD-I disc is given in Figure 6-36.

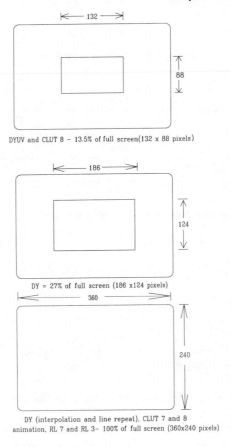

DYUV and CLUT 8 – 13.5% of full screen(132 x 88 pixels)

DY = 27% of full screen (186 x124 pixels)

DY (interpolation and line repeat), CLUT 7 and 8
animation, RL 7 and RL 3– 100% of full screen (360x240 pixels)

Figure 6-34 Motion video picture size.

Conclusion

There are many possible paths that a digital interactive multimedia
standard specification can follow. The choice of one or another path
depends less on the state of technology today and research wish-lists
for the future than on the requirements imposed by:

• Today's installed base of consumer electronics equipment (this is
the multimedia link to the end user!),
• The practical evolution of this installed base over the next decade,
• Cost considerations at market entry and during market growth,
• The intuition of those involved in the specification process.

Coding Scheme	Picture size (of full screen NR)		
	1	$\frac{1}{2} \times \frac{1}{2}$	$\frac{1}{3} \times \frac{1}{3}$
DYUV	8725	34900	78525
CLUT 8/7	8725	34900	78525
RL 7	70120	280480	631080
RGB 555	4362	17450	39262

Figure 6-35 Maximum number of pictures on a CD-I disc (525 line systems).

During the years that the process of defining the Green Book standard took place a large group of talented and multidisciplinary individuals from Matsushita, Microware, Philips and Sony worked at putting together this open and extendable standard specification. Without this mix of disciplines, cultures, corporate viewpoints, product commitment and product solutions, a viable robust specification could never have been fashioned. It is the work and dedication of all of these people that is embodied in this chapter on CD-I.

The contents of this chapter and, indeed, the contents of this book are about the beginning of a new industry. It is a long path from where we all are now to the market adoption of a new medium of expression that will form a viable industry. If a new and emergent in-

Character Type	Number of Characters	Page Equivalent Size
CD-I default 8 bit	$608 \cdot 10^6$	$297 \cdot 10^3$
Extended Sets 16 bit (multifont/ideograms)	$304 \cdot 10^6$	$148 \cdot 10^3$

Figure 6-36 Maximum amount of text on a CD-I disc.

dustry can be likened to a mountain than the successful climb can only be done step-by-step. Few of us doubt that optical media will be the pervasive and ubiquitous medium for both passive and interactive multimedia applications in the '90s and into the year 2000. So, we are all climbing up the same mountain together.

About the Author

At NV Philips, Richard Bruno was in charge of R & D for Home Interactive Systems where interactive optical media was one of the key R & D areas. Apart from CD ROM the author was responsible for and was the chief architect of CD-I, the development of which was jointly undertaken by Philips and Sony. In 1987 Dr. Bruno became Vice President Technical at OptImage Interactive Services Company, an interactive multimedia services and tools joint venture formed in Chicago by R. R. Donnelley & Sons and N.V. Philips. The author received his HBSc in mathematics and physics from McGill University in 1967 and his Ph.D. from McMaster University in Hamilton, Ontario in 1970.

Dr. Richard Bruno
V.P. Technical
OptImage
300W Adams St. Suite 601
Chicago, IL 60606
312–853–2626

References

Bruno, Richard. "Making Compact Discs Interactive," IEEE Spectrum, November 1987, pp 40-45.

Nishiguchi, Masayuki; Akagiri, Kenzo; Suzuki, Tadao. "The New Audio Bit Rate Reduction System for the CD-I Format," AES Journal, November 1986, 2375, pp. 1–10.

Philips International (1987). *Compact Disc–Interactive: A Designer's Overview*. Deventer, The Netherlands: Kluwer Technische Boeken B.V.

7

Digital Video Interactive

Arch Luther

Digital Video Interactive (DVI) is a new all-digital technology which is used with a computer to create a single system capable of interactive full-motion video, stereo audio, and powerful computer graphics. This technology offers the kind of interactivity that we associate with computers while presenting the kind of realistic audio and video that we get from television. DVI is basically a low-cost technology which will allow it to be used in high-volume consumer products. A system with DVI has the unique capability to reproduce full-screen motion video and audio from a standard digital CD ROM disc — up to 72 minutes playing time. In addition, it retains all the usual computer capabilities to control, store, and display all types of information from any digital source, including CD ROM. This chapter will describe the objectives of DVI technology, its concepts, its hardware, and its software.

Objectives for DVI

Systems already exist to combine a computer with audio and video — for example, a laser video disc which plays analog video and audio can be interfaced to a computer. Why do we need another new system to do that? Although video disc-plus-computer systems have generated a lot of interest in industrial, educational, training, and military fields, they have not reached mass appeal because of their cost, complexity, performance limitations, and large size. In spite of that, the application of these systems clearly demonstrates the existence of markets ready for a product with the right performance at the right price.

To achieve the right product, the major objectives of DVI technology for a combined audio-video-computer system are:

• *Flexibility* for widest application
• Potential for *low-cost* (consumer-priced) versions
• Possibility of *small-size* packaging
• *Realistic* video and audio from CD ROM and other media
• Computer *graphics* and synthetic video

The objective of *flexibility* is most important — it means that the system hardware design should limit the range of use as little as possible. In DVI technology, this is accomplished by making everything *digital*, and *programmable*. By doing everything digitally — not just the computer, but audio and video, too — there is only one hardware technology required, and the hardware design can utilize custom digital VLSI integrated circuits which will be the key to reaching the ultimate high-volume low cost. By being fully programmable, the system characteristics are controlled in software and the exact configuration of capabilities needed for any application can be established by the application itself when it starts, with the same hardware all the time. A software approach is essentially open-ended in that as new techniques or algorithms are developed, they can be programmed to run on existing hardware. In this respect, the DVI hardware is just like any other computer hardware.

DVI's objectives are better understood by examining some applications. For example, one application that has already been developed with DVI (a joint project with VideoDisc Publishing, Inc. in New York City) allows an interior decorator to create a room floor plan and select furniture, fabrics, wall coverings, carpets, etc. Then, using the "synthetic video" capability of DVI, a perspective rendering (Figure 7-1) of that room from any point of view may be quickly generated on the screen, showing all the furniture pieces, fabrics, and colors selected by the designer. The large data capacity of a CD

ROM is used in this application to store a catalog of furniture designs, fabrics for covering the furniture, paints, wall coverings, accessories, and carpets. The realistic rendering of room designs and fast interactivity for modifying the design allow the interior designer to more effectively communicate his or her design to the client.

The synthetic video capability is also applicable in other fields where realistic viewing of computer-based designs is required, such as CAD, architectural design, and landscape design. In the latter case, the computer can also be used to "grow" landscape plantings and then render the result to show what a particular plan will look like a number of years in the future.

The capability of DVI to store frames of real video on the CD ROM and retrieve them quickly is used to create a "surrogate travel" mode, where the user may move around a site in real time and visually and aurally explore the area. This capability has been demonstrated in the "Palenque" application (a joint project with the Bank Street College of Education in New York City) which takes the

Figure 7-1   Room design rendered by the Design and Decorate DVI application.

user to a Maya ruin site in Mexico. The user may walk many paths through the site and into the surrounding jungle while seeing the sights and hearing sounds captured from the actual site. A further feature of Palenque lets the user enter a panorama mode at selected spots during the travel. In this mode the user can — with joystick control — look up and down or look around through a full 360°. A single CD ROM disc has enough storage capacity for Palenque to also include an in-depth "museum" of audio and video information about the site in addition to several miles worth of surrogate travel.

Another class of applications is based on the small size of a CD ROM disc drive which will allow compact DVI systems to be built for use in vehicular on-board information systems containing video, audio, and computer data. This is of great interest to the military for solving their problem of keeping up-to-date maintenance and training information with a vehicle when it is deployed anywhere in the world. The prodigious data capacity of the CD ROM and DVI's ability to have video and audio, along with the data on the CD ROM are important in building effective field maintenance and training information systems. The low replication cost of the CD disc means that field updates are accomplished simply by periodically replacing all CD discs in the field. These same aspects make DVI of interest to the commercial aircraft and automotive industries.

DVI Hardware Concepts

DVI was developed at the David Sarnoff Research Center (formerly RCA Laboratories, now a subsidiary of SRI International) in Princeton, New Jersey, under contract from General Electric to meet the objective of a low-cost single system with flexible audio/video/computer capabilities.

DVI can be interfaced to any kind of computer system with appropriate power and storage characteristics. In the first implementation of the technology, DVI is packaged as three boards (Figure 7-2) which plug into an IBM PC/AT or compatible computer. The PC/AT platform was chosen because it has appropriate performance and it is widely available. The DVI boards for PC/AT are being marketed by the GE DVI Technology Venture. However, this board set is designed for professional markets, and it does not represent DVI's ultimate cost potential. The components of DVI will allow a complete

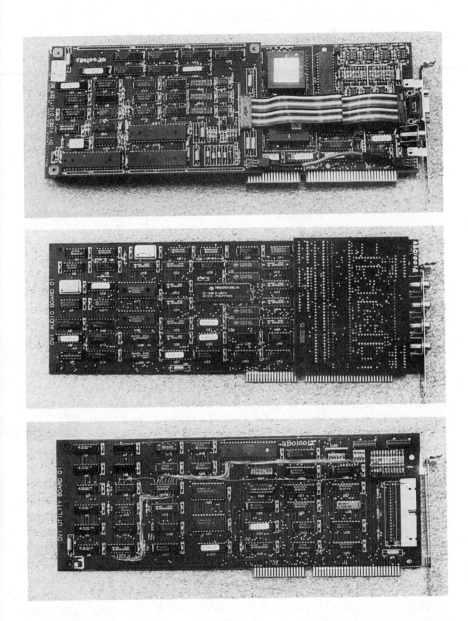

Figure 7-2   The three boards which implement DVI technology in an IBM PC/AT or compatible computer. From top to bottom: video, audio, and utility boards.

system to be mass-produced as a consumer product when the market is ready to support million-quantity volume of production.

The heart of DVI technology is a custom VLS1 processor which handles the video functions of the system. This is a two-chip set called the Video Display Processor (VDP), which includes a "pixel processor" (VDP1), and an "output display processor" (VDP2). The job of the pixel processor VDP1 is to operate on images stored in memory. VDP1 is a full microprocessor with its own unique instruction set and it runs at 12.5 million instructions per second (MIPS). That is roughly 10 times faster than a VAX minicomputer. The output display processor VDP2 is responsible for sending an image in memory to an RGB monitor. The DVI Video Board contains the VDP chip set, memory, and interfaces for the host computer and an analog RGB multisync monitor.

The memory used with the VDP is a special form of dynamic RAM called Video RAM (VRAM). VRAM chips are "dual-ported"; that is, in addition to the usual random- access parallel port that all RAM chips have, they have an independent serial output which can deliver sequential data from memory at high rates. The serial port is used by VDP2 to output data for the display monitor. VDP1 independently uses the parallel port for its processing of the data. In most systems, VRAM memory is made separate from the RAM used by the system CPU so that VDP1 and VRAM form a coprocessor system which operates in parallel with the system CPU. This arrangement gives the maximum possible speed for both VDP1 and the system CPU.

The second board of the DVI board set is for audio. The audio board uses a Texas Instruments TMS320C10 Digital Signal Processor chip as its CPU, and it is set up with its own memory and interface so that it gives an audio capability with programmability which is completely comparable to the programmability of the video board. The audio CPU with its dedicated memory operates as an independent coprocessor for audio functions. Two audio output channels are provided with 14-bit resolution D/A conversion and programmable filters.

For use in development, (or in applications which require audio or video input), there are plug-in digitizer options for both the audio and video boards. The video digitizer takes an NTSC video input and digitizes at 768 x 480 resolution. The audio digitizer has two channels for stereo and can digitize over a range of programmable sample rates. In both cases, software will handle processing of the digitized result to whatever format is necessary for storage.

The third board of the board set is called the Utility Board, and it contains a special buffered interface for the CD ROM drive, memory which can be optionally used to expand a PC/AT that has only 512 kbytes of RAM on the motherboard up to 640 kbytes, and interfaces for two analog joysticks. This board must be used when CD ROM is required in a DVI system. The other features of the board are there primarily to avoid having to use an additional board slot for these features in some systems.

DVI Software Concepts

DVI technology has extreme flexibility because the hardware is designed so that almost all the system features are defined by the software. This places a burden on the software design that it also should be designed for maximum flexibility. However, if every developer designed all his or her own software from the hardware level on up, there would be no compatibility between applications or systems. Therefore, the designers of DVI technology have written a system software package which brings the DVI capabilities up to a C language interface while still retaining most of the flexibility. This interface is intended to be part of the DVI industry standards which are being developed. The first implementation of the software, like the hardware, is for the PC/AT or compatible computers.

With the PC/AT embodiment of DVI the system software package of libraries makes all the capabilities available to DVI application programmers through subroutine calls in the C language. There are terminate-and-stay-resident drivers for the hardware, and the rest of the DVI system software is linked into the application code. With this arrangement, DVI applications will run in a standard DOS environment on the PC/AT or compatibles.

The DVI software uses standard DOS binary files for all audio and video data. Therefore, such data can be stored on any medium which looks like a disk drive to DOS. Hard disk, floppy disk, or RAM disks are all usable. Note that actual playing of motion video will work only with media which have a high enough data transfer rate. For example, floppy disks are too slow to play motion video directly — it would be necessary to copy to hard disk or to memory before playing in real time. In addition, CD ROM using the High Sierra format (which formats the CD ROM to also look like a DOS disk device) can be used to store DVI data. The Microsoft CD ROM Extension package is used for software interface of the CD ROM.

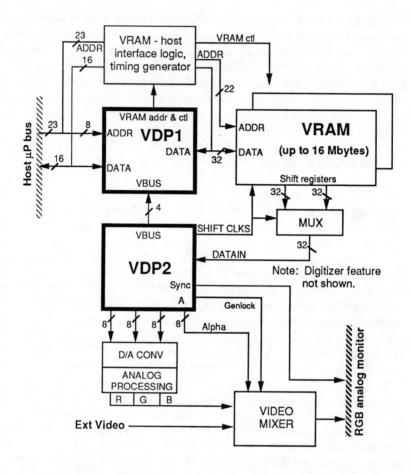

Figure 7-3 Hardware block diagram of interfacing of VDP1 and VDP2 in a PC/AT or compatible computer.

The DVI Video Chip Set (VDP)

Figure 7-3 is a hardware block diagram of how the two chips, VRAM, the video output, and the system CPU connect together. It is specific to the PC/AT embodiment. As already explained, VDP1 is a processor for images stored in VRAM and VDP2 is the output display processor which converts an image from VRAM into a signal suitable for driving a display monitor.

VRAM is shown at the top right in Figure 7-3 (using the currently available 256-kbit VRAM chips, it comes in 1- Mbyte modules); up to 4 VRAM modules can be piggybacked on the Video Board. (In the future 1-megabit VRAM chips will become available; then a VRAM module can be 4 Mbytes, and with four piggybacks the full 16- Mbyte address capability of VDP1 could be reached.) VDP1 connects to the VRAM *parallel* port with a 32-bit data bus. There is a separate interface between the host computer bus and VRAM which bypasses VDP1 (but is still arbitrated by VDP1). This path around VDP1 from the host bus is for data to load from the host into VRAM. The control interface to VDP1 is directly from the host bus through 256 16-bit registers. VDP1 is a microprocessor with its own instruction set and needs a program for running those instructions. Programs for VDP1 are in *microcode* — executed from an on-chip RAM in VDP1. Microcode gets to VDP1 by first being loaded by the host system into VRAM and VDP1 moves it into its own RAM from there.

VDP1 contains a general microprocessor bus interface which can be used with most kinds of computer bus structures. In the case of the PC/AT implementation, hardware on the video board (which has the VDP chip set) makes VDP1 (and the VRAM parallel port) appear in a window of the system's main memory. The video board also has an interrupt interface to the system bus. VDP2 does not access the system bus, but rather it connects to VDP1 and the VRAM serial port. Additional hardware on the video board handles the D/A conversion and processing for the analog RGB outputs which go to the display monitor.

VDP2 also interfaces to the *serial* port of VRAM with a 32-bit data connection. VDP2 processes the data internally in accordance with pixel format information which has been loaded into its registers. It delivers a 32-bit parallel output which is D/A converted off-chip to yield R, G, and B 8-bit signals and an 8-bit alpha-channel value which can be used off-chip for various purposes, for example, controlling a video mixer as shown in Figure 7-3.

VDP1 and VDP2 are connected together by the 4-bit VBUS. This is used only for control; as already explained, all data transfer between the chips is via VRAM.

Programmability: Video

Key to the flexibility of DVI is its *programmability*. Not only are the algorithms for video and audio programmable, but the system configuration is programmable. A good example of the latter is the way in which VRAM can be organized by software for a variety of video capabilities. As far as the hardware is concerned, VRAM is simply one large contiguous block of memory — up to 16 Mbytes. However, to the software VRAM can be any number of separate regions for image storage; these regions are called bitmaps.

Each bitmap is defined in software to represent a rectangular image of a size specified by x and y counts for number of pixels. The pixel format is defined in software to have a particular number of bits per pixel (8, 16, or 32), and to use one of several ways by which the pixel bits are converted to color values by VDP2. All the DVI system software functions recognize bitmaps and will act on them as separate entities even though they are actually all in the same contiguous memory.

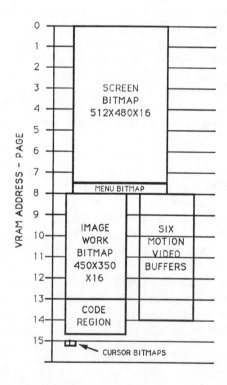

Figure 7-4 Diagram of VRAM layout for the example application, showing alternate usage between pages 8 and 15.

As an example of the use of multiple bitmaps, consider an application which has an on-screen menu and windows for presenting motion video or still images that the user selects from the menu. In this rather simple application, there could be need for five or six different bitmaps at the same time, and more at different times. Figure 7-4 shows the arrangement of VRAM which would be used by this application. Memory address 0 in VRAM is at the top of the figure, and address increases as you go down the figure. VRAM address is shown by *page*, where each page is 64 kbytes; so the diagram shows 1 Mbyte in total.

The first bitmap is reserved for the screen which is displayed by VDP2. This screen bitmap is 512 x 480 in resolution at 16 bits per pixel (bpp), and is at address page 0, as shown by Figure 7-4. That would use 480 kbytes of VRAM, going from address page 0 to address page 7.5. Note that the figure shows the bitmap as a rectangle so that its name can be written on it, although it is really just a one-dimensional range of memory address.

The menu bar is stored in another bitmap at a different address (page 7.5) in VRAM. For a bar across the top of the screen the menu might be 512 x 32 pixels and at 16 bpp this uses another 32k of VRAM. The menu is given its own separate bitmap so that it can be updated as necessary off-screen, and then copied to the screen area of VRAM by VDP1 when the update is to be shown. Such a copy takes place in a fraction of a frame time, so it appears instantaneous to the user.

The application also requires a cursor that moves with mouse or joystick. Handling of the cursor will need two small bitmaps: one to hold the cursor image and another to save the part of the screen which is behind the cursor. Every time the cursor is moved, VDP1 will restore the previous image from behind the cursor, save the image from the screen bitmap at the new cursor location, and then transparently copy the cursor image to the screen bitmap at the new location. These small bitmaps which are at address page 15, are 20 x 20 pixels at 16 bpp, which uses only 1.6 kbytes. (Bitmaps can be any size, even 1 pixel.)

Two more bitmaps are needed for the application to display compressed still images. In this case, one bitmap is needed to store the uncompressed image as it is being constructed by VDP1 running the decompression microcode, and a second region of VRAM (the compressed code buffer) is needed to hold the compressed image code that had been loaded from mass storage. (Remember that VDP1 works on images in VRAM only — the compressed code must be moved into VRAM before VDP1 can decompress it.) If the still image is displayed in a 450 x 350 window, the first bitmap would take 315 kbytes and is located at address page 8. When an image has been completely decompressed, it is then copied to the screen display bitmap — this allows smooth transitions between images. Depending on the degree of compression being used, the compressed code buffer might be another 100 kbytes, and is at page 13. As you can see, we have used up almost all of 1 Mbyte because all the bitmaps or regions explained so far need to exist simultaneously. (It is also necessary to allocate some amount of VRAM to system use; in this example, that would have to be in page 15.)

A further part of this application is to play motion video at 256 x 240 resolution and display that full-screen. This will require something like six buffers at the 256 x 240 resolution, but since the still image buffer and its code buffer will not be used at the same time, the system can reconfigure dynamically to use the same space in VRAM for either stills or motion, therefore the motion buffers will also begin at page 8.

The point of this example is that by having the VRAM layout configured in software, there is a lot of flexibility to create complex configurations to suit many kinds of applications, and to even change configuration on the fly during an application. The DVI system software libraries contain functions which facilitate doing that so the application programmer can accomplish anything within the limits of the VRAM size and the processing speed of VDP1.

Programmability: Audio

The DVI audio system has similar features of programmability. In the case of audio, the programmer is concerned with "channels" of audio. A number of audio channels may be specified and set up to mix to the two physical outputs from the audio board. One, two, or more channels may be used depending on the specific application requirements. Each channel is separately controllable by software for choice of selection, playing or stopping, audio level, and mix to the physical outputs. Channels can also be "looped" to repeat the same selection over and over. Audio can be played from any form of mass storage, or from system RAM, or EMS RAM. It can be played with video, or without video. The audio parameters and the system setup can be changed dynamically when needed. All of this is accomplished by the application programmer using the DVI system software library calls. The audio processor has its own internal program or "microcode," but here also the DVI system software makes that invisible to the programmer.

DVI audio uses compression to save storage space for audio. The algorithm used by the DVI system libraries is a form of Adaptive Differential Pulse Code Modulation (ADPCM), which delivers between 2:1 and 4:1 compression. The software provides four choices of data rate, from 32 to 256 kbits/second. The output bandwidth changes from approximately 50 to 4000 Hz to 50 to 15,000 Hz between these data rates. This gives quality ranging from roughly equivalent to AM radio to LP record quality. Because the audio algorithm is in software, the door is open for different algorithms to be used here.

Video Compression: Still Images

The VDP chip set handles compression and decompression of still images so quickly and effectively that this feature can always be used. There are two types of compression for stills available in the current microcode library (the qualifier "current" is used because further compression versions are sure to be developed). One is referred to as "lossless" compression and it works on 16-bpp images, compressing anywhere from 1.5:1 to about 7:1 depending on the complexity of the image. With lossless compression, the decompressed image is *exactly* the same as the original, bit for bit. Images that began as photographs will on the average compress about 2:1, whereas graphics images will typically compress much more. Lossless compression takes approximately 1 second to compress a 512 x 480 image. Even allowing for the decompression time, which is a fraction of a second, lossless compression serves to speed up access and to save storage space. The system software allows lossless compression to be built in to any application which requires saving of 16-bpp images.

The second form of still compression available in the current microcode does not give exact reproduction. There are errors in the reproduced image, but they are in places which may be difficult to see. This is called "lossy" compression because some information is lost. Lossy compression may be tuned with two parameters to give a compromise result that will be acceptable for many applications. A tool program is available for running lossy compression and adjusting the two parameters while interactively viewing the results. Once a choice has been made, the compressed file is stored by the tool. In the application, decompression occurs automatically, regardless of the tuning parameters. Lossy compression of stills gives compression ratios of 7:1 to 25:1.

Video Compression: Motion Video

Compression for motion video is quite a different problem from still compression because of the impact of *time* on the process. While it does not matter how long still compression or decompression takes (as long as it is fast enough that the user does not become impatient), motion processing has to be accomplished at the *frame rate* of the motion video — usually 30 frames per second. Therefore, in motion compression and decompression we are always concerned with speed.

The second major consideration for motion video compression is the matter of *data rate*. This is the reason that we need motion compression in the first place — raw digitizing of motion video creates very high data rates. For example, if we digitize a frame at 512 x 480 and 16 bpp, we obtain 480 kbytes of data. If this is repeated at 30 frames per second, we get a data rate of 30 * 480, or 14.4 Mbytes/second. There is no way that we can store data at that rate in a small computer. Therefore, we must compress, and we must do it before we store the data.

The DVI motion video compression approaches are tailored to working with the data rate of the standard CD ROM, which is 1.2 Mbits per second or 5 kbytes per frame at 30 frames per second. DVI compressed motion video files can be used with any medium that can handle this rate continuously; if a higher rate medium is used, it is possible to produce better results. However, the CD ROM rate is considered to be the point of entry, and the current algorithms are designed to produce good results at that rate.

The above numbers call for compression factors of the order of 100:1. This kind of compression cannot be made transparent (or "lossless"), but fortunately there is a lot of redundancy in motion video which can be exploited to reach large compression factors and still have usable pictures. There is redundancy in a single image *spatially* — this is used for still image compression; however spatial compression is not enough to reach anywhere near 100:1. We must also exploit the *temporal* redundancy, that is, the similarity that exists from one frame to the next. By using both of these approaches, the DVI motion video compression is successful with a reproduced resolution of 256 x 240 pixels, full-screen.

DVI motion video compression currently comes in two flavors: real-time *Edit-Level* compression which can be done on any DVI development system, and *Presentation-Level* compression which requires that the developer send his video material to a central site for compression. Presentation-Level compression takes many millions of computer cycles being devoted to each frame to figure out the optimum way to compress that frame. For example, a VAX super-mini-computer needs upward of 30 seconds per frame to do DVI compression. To perform compression at a more reasonable speed (a few seconds per frame), a special system using a Meiko parallel processor has been assembled and programmed for this task. Such a computing facility is too expensive for every DVI developer to have one, therefore this capability will be centralized at a number of locations around the world. However, it also would be too expensive and would take too long if all your video had to go through a central facility before you could see it in your application, even for testing or for selection of material.

Edit-Level compression solves the testing and preview problem by using the power of VDP1 to do the best it can at compressing in real time, right on the DVI system. The video digitizer option on the video board is used to capture from any NTSC video feed (camera, VCR, etc.), while VDP1 compresses simultaneously and stores the result on hard disk. The result is motion video at lower resolution and at lower frame rate than Presentation-Level, and with more artifacts; but the quality is good enough to test your application and choose the exact clips of video which will go out for Presentation-Level compression. There are some applications where Edit-Level compression will fill the bill without using Presentation-Level at all.

Both forms of compression create a standard DVI video file, which is playable by the same system software. Thus, the developer's application code can be completed and tested with Edit-Level video files. After deciding on the video segments to use, they are sent out for Presentation- Level compression. When the Presentation-Level files come back from the central facility, they are simply substituted in the application and everything will run just like it did in testing except that the video quality has become much better.

Because VDP1 is a programmable microprocessor with a full instruction set, VDP1 can be programmed to decompress any algorithm, even ones which may be invented in the future. In order to exploit this flexibility, the DVI system does not require any standardizing of compression algorithms which would limit the opportunity to make better algorithms in the future. This is accomplished by having the microcode necessary for decompressing a particular file of compressed video data go along with the file. As implemented in the DVI system software, the microcode itself is in a separate file and the compressed video data file identifies to the system the microcode file which must be used. This is more flexible than actually putting both of them into the same file, because the door is kept open to develop new microcode that might decompress the same data in a better way. It also allows the possibility to have future enhanced versions of VDP1 which could still play old code files, but may require different microcode to do that.

DVI System Software: PC/AT Version

The features of a DVI system are determined by the software that is used. For the PC/AT or compatible embodiment of DVI technology, a full set of system software has been developed and is being marketed to developers who want to create DVI applications for the PC/AT platform. This software — which will be described below — is only one of the many ways in which DVI system software might be written, however it is the first one and it is being marketed to developers for their use in creating applications and it will be the starting point for development of DVI standards. Other people working with different computer platforms or with different host computer software could choose to write their own system, in that case, they would have to be concerned with their hardware interfaces directly. The DVI system software that will be described here has a C language interface which is generalized and is expected to be easily ported to other platforms as they are developed. This interface will become the basis for the DVI standard which allows DVI applications from many developers to run on the hardware of multiple manufacturers. The technology will be best served if others writing systems do not depart from this generalized interface.

On the PC/AT the DVI system runs under the MSDOS operating system. When CD ROM is used, DVI requires the Microsoft CD ROM

Extension package for MSDOS. This package expects that the CD ROM disc is formatted according to the High Sierra format standard, in which case the CD drive looks like any other disc device to the system. All the files used by DVI are standard DOS files, and they are accessed through DOS regardless of what kind of storage device is actually used. Software access to the DVI hardware on the DVI boardset is through a set of drivers which are installed when the system boots up.

Since all the mass storage devices in a PC/AT are on the system bus, and these devices are used for storage of audio and video, it is clear that the audio and video data must move through the system bus on its way to VRAM or audio RAM. The system CPU is responsible for managing that data transfer as well as any other non audio/video computing required by the application. Therefore, the system requires a form of real-time multitasking because the audio and video boards must never run out of data while playing, regardless of the other demands placed on the system CPU. In the DVI system, these tasks are accomplished with the Real-Time Executive (RTX) software. RTX is part of the DVI system software libraries and includes a set of C functions which allow a DVI application to set up and run a number of real-time tasks. RTX runs within a DVI application only: It provides multitasking of the activities required inside a DVI application.

Playing of compressed audio and video is a complex task; it calls for management of large amounts of compressed data, delivery of microcode to the audio and video processors, and real-time control of the decompression operation. Another major part of the DVI system software library is responsible for these tasks — the Audio Video Support System (AVSS). AVSS calls RTX to set up the tasks it needs to handle the data transfer and other operations for playing of audio and video. The application programmer is only concerned with calling AVSS, and is not concerned with the internal mechanics of AVSS. AVSS also includes "hooks" which allow custom functions to be run in synchronism with AVSS; for example, a hook routine would be used to write subtitles on top of a moving video scene being played by AVSS. The hook capability provides the flexibility to combine any of the other capabilities of DVI with the playing of audio or video, limited only by the computing speed of the processors involved.

Another major part of the DVI system software library contains the graphics functions. DVI graphics includes functions for the usual items such as drawing lines, circles, rectangles, etc. either in line form or filled with colors, or with various logical operations performed between a source and destination bitmap, or with a drawing color. In addition to these functions, graphics also has a group of functions for loading and saving images, and for writing text on the DVI screen in a variety of fonts and sizes.

Many of the DVI system software library functions require loading of microcode to VDP1 or the audio processor. Routines for doing that are built in to the system software so that a programmer does not have to worry about microcode management at all. However, for some applications there will be a need to create custom microcode that the standard DVI system will not know about. Tools for microcode development are available, and custom microcode can be integrated into an application using a set of calls from the system library which are intended for that purpose. These same calls can be used to access some microcode functions which are available with the system software but have not been integrated into the graphics or other standard package. Some of these special microcode routines are for performing a variety of image processing tasks on rectangular regions of a bitmap, such as controlling hue, contrast, or brightness of an image, filtering the image, detecting edges. These routines operate very rapidly and often can be used directly on the screen image in real time.

Some of the most interesting DVI functions are the scale and warp routines which are part of the graphics library. With scale, a rectangular image can be changed in size by any amount in 1-pixel steps, with different scale factors for x and y. The scale function offers choice of filtering or not, and is used to adjust sizes of images with very little degradation.

The warp function is used for synthetic video applications, such as the Design and Decorate (D&D) application described earlier. In synthetic video, a scene is constructed as a computer model, defined by points in three-dimensional space. These points describe polygons which represent the surfaces of the objects in the computer model. The surfaces are flat, so a model for a curved object requires a lot of surfaces for a realistic rendering. The synthetic video scene is further defined by specifying a "texture" for each surface which will be used to cover the surface whenever it is displayed (see Figure 7-5). The textures are video images normally stored in rectangular shape; for example, in D&D the fabric textures for covering the furniture

Figure 7-5 An example of video texturing.

pieces are digitized photographs of real fabrics. The technique is called *video texturing*.

In order to display the scene from a particular point of view, the system CPU first does a 3-D transformation on the points of the computer model to calculate where on the screen to place each surface. Surfaces which are hidden or partially covered in the 3-D rendering are properly accounted for. Then the coordinates of each surface to display and its texture information are passed to the warp function, which tells VDP1 to draw each surface on the screen using the warp microcode. This fills each polygon with its texture adjusted to fit the shape of the polygon as it is seen on the screen. These operations happen rapidly, so that complex screens involving hundreds of polygons are drawn in a few seconds.

The use of video texturing often allows a relatively simple model to be rendered quite realistically, with much of the detail being contained in the textures. For example, the house rendering shown in Figure 7-5 involves only six polygons using only four textures. The video texturing technique leads to many applications such as a flight simulator where the computer models the terrain that is being flown above; mapping (where the map detail is a texture); surrogate travel through a computer model, which might be the inside of a building, or a submarine; exploded views, for equipment disassembly and repair; or animated scenes for modeling of laboratory experiments.

DVI's software-based flexibility extends to its use of the CD ROM storage capacity also. For example, if the entire CD ROM is devoted to full-screen motion video and accompanying audio, 72 minutes of video-with-audio can be stored. However, if the video is to be displayed in a window of one quarter screen, that takes one quarter as much data, which can still be packed on the CD ROM. In this case, we could have 288 minutes of video on a single CD ROM — nearly 5 hr! But all of the CD ROM does not have to be in the same format — in another example, we could store 5000 512 x 480 compressed still images, which would use about half of the CD ROM capacity. The rest of the CD ROM space might be clips of audio to be used with the still images — at the lowest audio rate (32 kbits/second) we would have room for a total of 20 hours of audio. Any other combination of the above numbers is possible.

Conclusion

The DVI system software as it now exists is a generalized, basic package that can be used for the design of many applications. However, like the DVI hardware itself, it is expected to be further developed and grow as the industry learns how to utilize all the power and flexibility that is contained in the basic concepts of DVI. The system design of DVI provides for the expected improvements of both hardware and software to be smoothly integrated in current and future systems. This open-endedness is the most important reason for DVI to be the standard for video and audio for personal computers.

About the Author

Arch C. Luther is a consultant, writer, and software designer. He worked on DVI technology as a senior staff scientist at the David Sarnoff Research Center in Princeton, NJ, and spent many years as an engineer and manager in the Broadcast Systems department of RCA Corp. He has a BSEE from Massachusetts Institute of Technology.

8

Future Possibilities of CD ROM

David H. Davies

The success of the compact disc format owes much to stand-ardization. Without a clear standard, there would be no industry today. The downside of a standard, however, is that it can impede progress. This trade-off is clearly evident in CD ROM when compared with present and future alternatives. This chapter focuses on drive and media issues and examines some basic limitations in today's format. Alternatives are discussed and reviewed. Particular emphasis is placed on the emerging user recordable forms of optical storage and on the CD and non-CD versions of these technologies. Within the recordable format, both write-once and erasable are considered, and appropriate applications for the CD versions of these technologies are identified.

Finally, the possibility of a multifunctional or universal drive is outlined; the problems and opportunities for this as yet unavailable device are significant.

Limitations In Current CD ROM Technology

Today's CD ROM drive is clearly limited as a CPU peripheral. These limitations were well understood by the inventors but arise from the limitations placed upon the system by the need for maximizing compatibility with CD Audio and by cost limitations. The major limitations are as follows:

1. *Limited access time (typically 0.5 to 1.0 second).* Access time is influenced by the limited rotation rate that affects the latency period; by the carriage jump mechanics and the acceleration properties of the positioning servos. In particular, the CLV (constant linear velocity) nature of the drive significantly slows the mechanism of the head-carriage jump. Image decompression, with error correction, can significantly degrade data retrieval time also. A good review of this aspect is given in Ref. 1. The open-loop nature of the coarse jump also detracts from access time since the head must make several fine seeks to finally locate itself.

2. *Data transfer rate limitations* [150 kbytes/second (continuous)]. This is set once again by the rotation rate and, in addition, by the error correction encoding and decoding time. Rotation rates vary from 200 to 500 rpm and are set to give a CLV of about 1.2–1.4 m/s.

3. *Format and encoding limitations.* The selected modulation coding scheme for CD ROM, Eight-to-Fourteen modulation code (EFM), is designed to allow for significant tolerance buildup in minimum "feature" separation. This stacking up of tolerances potentially results from spatial errors induced from the original master disc to a final worst case user disc in a user drive. It also derives from the optical numerical aperture (0.45) spot resolution limits in today's products.

   Alternative encoding schemes such as 2, 7 place greater constraints upon spatial tolerances but have definite advantages in that EFM code shows the worst signal roll off tendency when bits are crowded together. This results in a sacrifice of capacity potential. Reference 2 compares various coding options for optical storage.

4. *Error correction.* The CD ROM standard calls for a "two-layer" error correction scheme; the Cross-Interleaved Reed Solomon code (CIRC) system defined into all CD Audio players allows error correction from a raw 10^{-3}–10^{-4} region to a user level of 10^{-9}–10^{-10}. An error rate of 10^{-9} would result in occasional hard errors. Typically, in audio these are "muted" out as a final step. Basics of error correction are covered in Ref. 3, specifics of the CD Audio system are given in Ref. 4. The methodology adopted in CD ROM standards is to apply an extra step called the layered ECC. The layered system is an additional error correction over the audio CIRC system; it is a two-dimensional version of Reed Solomon and it allows a user practical error rate of 10^{-12} to be achieved. The trade-off is in data rate, if significant levels of errors occur that are not caught by the first CIRC level; then the system can be slowed by the need for correction. The alternative, adopted by part of the recordable disc industry, for example, is to require initial media error specification levels such that the second layer is not required. Table 8-1 illustrates the effect of two level ECC on CD ROM media under different stress conditions; the extra level, although rarely needed, is a worthwhile addition. The result has been a reliable, error-free system.

5. *Tracking systems.* Specific disc radial tracking schemes are not standardized. Even in CD ROM technology several schemes exist, but if you compare the typical CD ROM tracking methods with those employed in more advanced optical drives, then some trade-offs are apparent. Consider the open-loop nature of the track finding, for example: A typical CD ROM drive

Table 8-1 Typical Stress Test Results: CD ROM Media

	Bit error rate (BER)	Max. burst length (frames)
As produced	6.9×10^{-5}	4
1 year (office)	1.6×10^{-4}	4
Heavily scratched	1.0×10^{-3}	11
800 h, 60°C., 95% RH	5.0×10^{-4}	6

Result: Two-level ECC, designed to allow for 1×10^{-3} errors with maximum burst

does not count tracks during the rapid seek mode. This arises out of frequency band contention problems with the data signals. The subsequent hunting, or fine jumps can absorb significant time especially as the slow rotational latency compounds the problem. A further trade-off is the use of three spot tracking versus far field. In the former, the information itself provides a tracking medium which is located by multiple beams obtained from the single laser. However, the need to split the beams reduces the energy density in the read:write beam. In read-only devices, this is a negligible problem, but in recordable versions of optical storage this presents a limitation unless higher power lasers are available. On the other hand, far field tracking does result in higher risk of variability, disc to disc, since the replication of the continuous grooves is difficult. Further, the far field method does have the increased risk of data cross talk in the tracking channel. Generally, however, the far field can achieve higher track to track pitch densities. The major problem with the CD ROM system is the lack of flexibility in adaption to recordable media. This is explained below.

Table 8-2 summarizes the design trade-offs explained above. The comparisons have been made against a subset of alternatives generally used in the recordable 130mm drive industry. It should be remembered that these drives are generally an order of magnitude more expensive.

Future Possibilities: Prerecorded Optical Data Products

Given the trade-offs described above, it is obvious that a higher performance read only optical product is relatively straightforward to achieve. Using typical commercial 130-mm write-once drive specifications, it is simple to derive a pro forma specification for such a device. Table 8-3 lists expected performance parameters; the price for such a device would be higher than for CD ROM drives.

Technology Issues

Disc media for such advanced read only devices have already been discussed: generically, "O-ROM" (Ref. 5) (Optical Read-Only Memory), or more specifically, "Data ROM" (Ref. 6). The major

Table 8-2   Design Trade-offs in CD ROM[a]

Performance Variable	EFM Encoding	CLV Rotation Mode	CIRC ECC (2 level)	"Open loop" Track Finding	3 spot Tracking
Access time	0	–	0	–	0
Data rate[b]	–	–	–	0	0
Capacity	–	+	–	0	–
Error rates	+	0	+	0	0
Reliability	+	0	+	–	+
Multifunctionality	–	0	0	–	–
	vs 2.7	vs CAV	vs 1 level	vs track counting	vs far field

[a]In almost all cases shown in Table 8-2 cost trade-offs generally favor the design features selected for today's CD ROM drive. The exception is the use of the added layer of error correction.
[b]Disc to drive transfer rate.

0 = neutral
+ = advantage of the selected design variable
- = disadvantage of the selected design variable

Table 8-3   Predicted Read-Only Optical Disc Performances Compared with Today's CD ROM

	CD ROM	O ROM-I	O ROM-II
Disc diameter (mm)	130	130	90
Rotation format	CLV	CAV	MCAV (zoned)
Capacity per side (Mbytes) (user)	550	200	400
Data transfer rate (kbytes/s) (user data)	153	2000	5000 (avg.) (variable)
Average access time (ms)	500–1000	400	<<50
Track-to-track access	2	2	1
Date of first commercial shipment	1985	1989	1991–1992
Rotational rate (rpm)	200–500	900	3600

design differences in these media compared with CD ROM are as follows:

1. *Concentrically organized data rather than spiral.* This is to conform to normal magnetic standards and recognizes the fact that many applications involve repeated random access rather than continuous streaming data.

2. *130 mm versus 120 mm (or possibly 90 mm).* To obtain maximum capacity within the physical form factor provided in the PC package environment. This today this is determined by the small format magnetic drives and hence is 130 or 90 mm. The strong emergence of 90-mm (3.5-inch) form factor in recent years and the convenience of such a size makes it very likely to succeed provided sufficient capacity is available; see below.

3. *Hard sectored.* Preformatted with individual track numbers and sector numbers. To allow easy track counting while in rapid seek mode and to provide rapid random access.

4. *Tighter encoding.* Encoded with a stringent code such as 2, 7 or NRZ to maximize performance (see Ref. 2).

5. *CAV rotation mode.* To facilitate rapid random access. However, CAV mode reduces effective capacity by approximately 50 percent over CLV for equivalent formats. A more likely option for a next generation "ROM" product would be modified or zoned CAV. In this method the disc always rotates at constant radial rate but the data rate is varied in zones from i.d. to o.d. This preserves a constant disc feature size and density hence maximizing capacity. Reference 7 discusses modified CAV approaches. This is an excellent approach for high capacity 90-mm media.

6. *Construction and media materials.* The present media construction is well known, the next generation of media is possibly be double-sided with internal surfaces laminated; outer surfaces will be made of plastic with 1.2-mm optical path thickness. Several controversial aspects dominate the selection of

disc material. Many advocates for glass promote its life and physical stability while plastic proponents laud the fact that hundreds of millions of such discs have been successfully sold. Table 8-4 lists the relative merits of various possible plastic media materials. No major threat to polycarbonate is yet on the horizon nor are its deficiencies sufficient to warrant the kind of investment needed to develop such a material.

Data Compression and Read-Only Optical Data Disc Developments

Techniques to compress information have been extensively developed recently. The availability of gigabyte level storage paradoxically has increased the interest in compressed information since it has opened up the realistic possibility of extensive use of imaged data. Capacity needs are severely impacted by image storage; an A4 page at 400 dots per inch needs 2 Mbytes of storage capacity. The need for compression, however, must be traded off against error levels and access

Table 8-4 Candidate Materials for Future ROM Media

Property	Unit	PC	PMMA	Epoxy[a]	PO[b]	PC/PS[c]
Transmission (780–830 nm)	%	90	92	92	93	93
Refractive index	—	1.55–1.59	1.49–1.52	1.51–1.54	1.55	—
Birefringence	nm	<20	<10	<5	<20	<5
Glass transition temperature	°C	143–145	89–100	115–125	155	130
Deformation temperature	°C	125–136	80–88	125–135	129–136	—
Rockwell hardness	M-scale	5	82	85–90	75	—
Water absorption	%	0.2	0.3	0.25–0.3	0.01	0.15
Water vapor transmission	g/m^2 per 24 h	3.6	2.8	1.30–2.5	—	—

[a] Published data by Sumitomo Bakelite.
[b] Amorphous polyolefine, published data by Mitsui Petrochemical.
[c] PC/modif. PST 60/40, published data by Sumitomo Chemical.

Source: From Ref. 8.

times. The need to ensure data integrity has forced developments in error correction, and this then has reinforced the development in the entire storage field.

Compression is clearly a part of the CD ROM/O ROM future and must be examined. In essence, information is compressed by the recognition of patterns and repetition and by the use of predefined codes to exploit these. Also, it works through the elimination of redundancy and on trading off small but finite error possibilities against other variables. The pattern recognition capability of the human mind can allow for significant error in image input and still achieve errorless recognition. Compression must, however, take into account the needed error levels of the finally retrieved data, the kind of data transmission systems used, and for proper utility in a CD ROM environment, the time taken to compress and decompress. A good review of this topic is given in Ref. 9. A scheme favored in the optical area today is called M^2R, or modified (modified) READ. The READ method (Relative Element Address Designate) is based on comparative line-to-line analysis that basically encodes only changes. The international facsimile standard setting body (CCITT)(10) has defined standards and Group 4 of the fax standard fits well into optical data storage environments. It also allows for mixed images and is efficient; it does, however, assume high originating data integrity. Figure 8-1 shows the time to encode a standard page (CCITT text documents) using M^2R. It can be seen that depending on the content it can take well over a second. This restricts the utility but in a CD ROM user application it is not too disparate from other time requirements.

The compression possible in typical office documents can be up to 1 in 20, say, for a 400-dpi imaged textual document, or down to 1:5 for a 400-dpi complex drawing. The compression of video images (stationary or moving) is a related but separate field not considered here. Recent efforts such as DVI (RCA/GE) offer hope that this could hasten the broadening of the technology and the merger of data and video formats.

With more advanced computational methods and better LSI, coupled to image design that maximizes compression potential, it is certain that the ability to rapidly compress and decompress data with high integrity will be an important ingredient in the future of read-only optical disc storage.

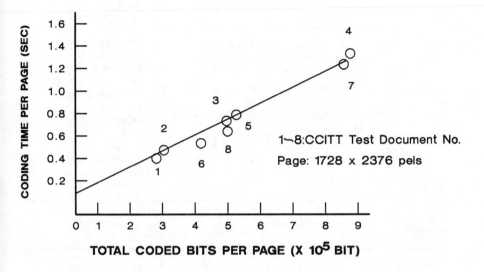

Figure 8-1   Data compression in M²R format (Ref. 11). Data from Hitachi HD 63085 LSI (G4 FAX Std).

Applications for Next Generation Read-Only Media

This chapter focuses on optical data products and hence does not discuss the variety of video and nondata formats such as CD-V, CD-I, and DVI.

Nevertheless, in the next generation, read only formats will take advantage of the flexibility of the medium and the emergence of digital video and the differences between data and video will blend. This factor will influence the emergence of specific applications that utilize both video and data on the same disc where appropriate.

In general, the evolution of the technology toward the versions of generically named "O ROM's" will broaden the application base for today's CD ROM. It is not anticipated that they will replace CD ROM at all. The added cost of both media and drive make it critical

Application Matrix

	Frequent Rapid Random Access	Semi-conscious Data Streams
Typical Applications	• Computer application software • Computer internal operational software • Relational data bases • Heavily cross indexed data • Interactive tutorial training • Highly interactive games & simulation • Machine accessed data banks • Data bases including embedded application software	• Encyclopedic data • Catalog data • Audio entertainment • Video entertainment • Archival storage (distributed) • Simple contiguous data bases • Tutorial training — limited interactive • Human accessed data bank
Avg. Number Access / Hr.	>> 60 / hr.	<< 60 / hr.
Technology	O-ROM <<----------------------------------->> CD-ROM	

Figure 8-2   **Read only applications compared to average access rates and appropriate technology.**

that only those applications requiring rapid and frequent random access will cost justify the newer technology. Figure 8-2 illustrates this principle and lists typical conceptual applications anticipated.

Figure 8-3 shows a generic applications chart for optical storage that breaks down the prerecorded *and* recordable technologies into a matrix of access frequency versus capacity required. This shows clearly that the recordable forms of the technology will have a clear place even in the restricted "CD" world. This chart is discussed in more detail below.

Future Possibilities for Write-Once "CD ROM" (CD WORM)

From now on we will depart from the strict adherence to the "CD" standard nomenclature and discuss future varieties of "CD" optical disc that are user recordable. At this time, the strict definition of Compact Disc as defined by the standard books would disallow this

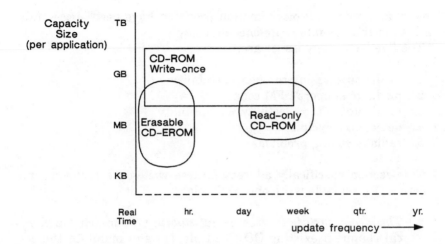

Figure 8-3   CD applications: Capacity vs. update needs as a function of technology.

usage. We believe these standards will be expanded, but for now we will define our terms as follows.

CD WORM. A write-once disc that is *readable* on a standard CD ROM drive. It will therefore have to obey all the rules of CD ROM in terms of ECC, encoding, physical standards, detection, etc.

Note that such a disc is writable once and then not rewritable; it can of course be altered but in a generally destructive mode only. It is not assumed that such a disc is *writable* on a *standard* CD ROM drive, only *readable*. However, the writing drive would be similar in many aspects except laser power, laser power stability, and recording pit precision.

Technology Issues

It is not our intent to review write-once technologies in depth. The reader is referred to Ref. 12 for that. This section outlines the problems and possibilities for CD WORM per se.

The technology issues involved in CD WORM are fivefold and are primarily media related. The hardware for writing such a disc in a user environment is relatively straightforward providing the additional cost is recognized. The problem of providing enhanced laser power, and obtaining pit formation precision have been successfully tackled in the 130-mm write-once industry.

The five technology issues are:

1. media surface environmental stability
2. media to support EFM code
3. media absolute reflectivity compatibility
4. detection principle
5. radial tracking problems

This section specifically addresses these write-once problems unique to a CD-readable write once technology.

1. *The media surface environmental stability.* To match the physical clamp on existing CD ROM players and maintain the correct information plane location requires that any CD disc match the CD Audio construction almost exactly. This requires that the reflector of the CD Audio disc be functionally replaced by the write-once active absorber. This is a problem in that it requires a write-once active layer that is stable for long periods (in excess of 10 years) protected only by a lacquer coating as in the CD disc. This requirement rules out almost all tellurium- and dye-based write-once coatings. Although recently the Tandy Corp., with ODI in Beaverton, Oregon, proposed a dye-based CD Audio system that would have limited cyclic rewrite potential, it is as yet uncertain as to whether this can be commercially realized. The media family developed by 3M being oxidation resistive and nontoxic is a possibility but it has problems with the detector and reflectivity issues. See Ref. 13 for more information on that particular media. Reference 14 discusses other CD WORM media possibilities including gallium antimonide, a possible candidate. This problem is the most difficult to solve with today's technology of all the issues detailed in this section. An alternative to a media materials solution is a very thin laminated glass cover sheet; this, however, raises serious potential issues of thermal expansion mismatch.

2. *Media to support EFM code.* The EFM code adopted for CD formats must be utilized in a CD WORM if it is to be compatible. The problem of code compatibility lies in the ability of the

media to sustain (i.e., reproduce) the smallest possible "feature" of the code. A particular problem with many optical medias is the tendency to be insensitive to short narrow laser pulses. There are two ways to avoid this problem: Develop a media with rapid response and high sensitivity and with small feature reproducibility, or alternatively modify the EFM code in a compatible way so that it does not use such short pulses. This is discussed for GaSb media by Philips in Ref. 14. Figure 8-4 shows block error rates (BLER) in a CD compatible EFM format for the GaSb media under different film thickness values. CNRs of >55 db for 720 kHz written signals at practical laser power densities were also obtained in EFM code for this media as shown in Figure 8-5.

3. *Media absolute reflectivity compatibility.* The CD ROM optical head is designed to track and focus off a surface that reflects >85 percent of the 820-nm infrared laser light. A recordable media, however, needs to efficiently absorb this same laser power. The incompatibility is severe for absorbing media based on layer interference structures operating at the media interference minimum. In practice, medias having approximately 60 percent reflectance work well with most detectors and CD-focusing optics. This is a compromise but one that should work. It does place another constraint on the media developer, however.

4. *Detection of pits.* The CD Audio/ROM system is based on the detection of physical (relief) pits on the surface through the resulting changes in the reflected light. A user recordable system requires the use of minimal laser power which preclude the formation of deep physical relief structures. A compatible media could be fabricated, however, through the use of a trilayer system where the absorbing layer is such that it melts to reveal the base reflector that is the correct interference depth to create the required phase change. This is shown in Figure 8-6.

5. *The radial tracking problem.* Last, but not least, is the need to track the information surface. The preembossed CD ROM media uses the data stream on the surface itself to track. An unrecorded media suitable for user playback and for recording

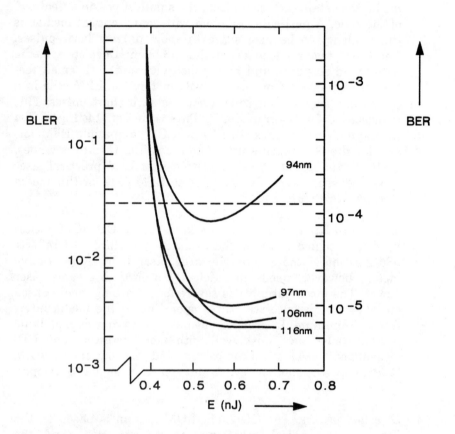

Figure 8-4   GaSb Media — CD WORM Media Candidate — 1986 Philips.
Block error rate (BLER) and bit error rate (BER) of written EFM signals as
a function of the unit pulse energy, E, for various values of the film
thickness.

on a low cost unit would have to find a way to provide some
tracking feature. Of course, if the user recorder is suitably expensive and can be made with servo writing capability using
precision feedback optics and accurate mechanics, then this is
no problem as the positioning accuracy is then recorded in at
the recorder level. This is not practical for a low cost recorder,
however.

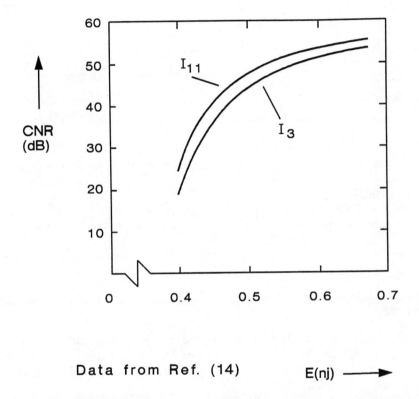

Data from Ref. (14)   E(nj) ⟶

Figure 8-5   CNR performance of CD WORM media. I_3 marks at 720 KHz. I_{11} marks at 196 KHz. CLV velocity at 1.25 m/sec.

A first-level solution is to preformat the media with the 18 bytes of "header" (sync and i.d.) per CD ROM block. A portion of the 288 bytes provided for the layered ECC could also be used to provide a reference location for the otherwise open loop data field. In addition, it should be possible to master record and preformat location marks along the "blank" data portion of the track edges and utilizing the 3-spot tracking signal, use the "flags" as signals in much the same way that sampled servo systems use today.

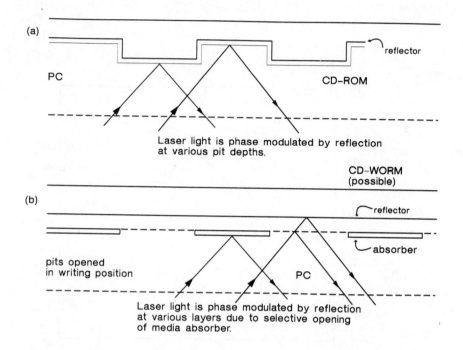

Figure 8-6 Comparison of detection principle CD ROM (a) vs. proposed CD WORM (b).

Obviously, much will be needed to verify any concept along these lines but the tracking problem does represent a stumbling block if true universal playability is to be achieved on a recordable CD ROM.

CD WORM Applications

Five facets of the application arena are relevant to CD WORM compared with CD ROM. (This is illustrated in Figure 8-7.) These are the five issues that could tilt the potential user in the CD WORM direction, compared to CD ROM:

1. Confidentiality
2. Cost-effective replica quantity requirements
3. Turnaround time (tape input to disc output)
4. Traceability of the record
5. Updatability of the information

THE CD-WORM APPLICATION ARENA

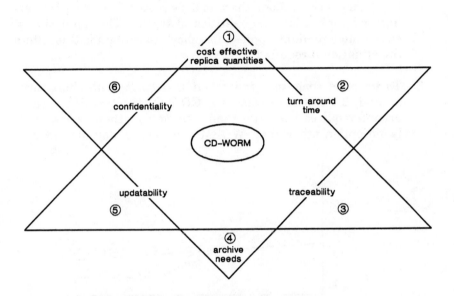

Figure 8-7   The CD WORM features versus CD ROM. Overlap of any two parts makes for a good potential CD WORM application . . . providing condition #1 is met.

1. *Confidentiality.* Until mastering and replication can be done cost effectively at remote small scale sites, the user faces the uncertainty of letting confidential information out of direct control. This, of course, applies especially to national security critical data. Although the record of the replication houses is excellent, this is always a cause for concern.

    In-house recording in a read only format of small quantities of media (see item 2 below) is very expensive and there is no doubt that confidentiality control is a good market rationale for CD WORM.

2. *Cost-effective replica quantity requirements.* Figure 8-8 shows
the trade-off of media cost between master/replication production of CD ROM and CD WORM. These calculations are heavily dependent on the specific cost assumptions shown, since
these costs are currently changing rapidly. Overall, however,
from a media cost alone there is a clear cutoff favoring mastering and replication in quantities above 50. This analysis assumes no premium applied for short turnaround; this alters
the situation if required.

3. *Turnaround time (tape input to disc output).* With short turnaround, the cost effectiveness of CD WORM alters. If the turnaround required is shorter than a single day, there is essentially no option other than WORM. Between 1 day and regular

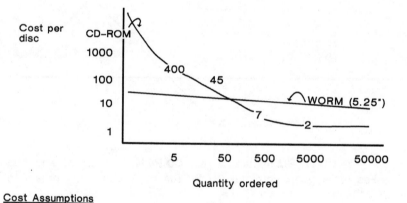

Cost Assumptions

Quantities	Mastering	Copies
<50	$2000	$5 ea.
>50 – <1000	$2000	$3 ea.
> 1000 – <5000	free	$3 ea.
>5000	free	$2 ea.

* 130mm WORM used as example.

*Cost analysis assumes a fully burdened operator for WORM duplication but that the
WORM recorder is fully amortized or trivial on a per disc basis.

Figure 8-8   Cost analysis (approx.); CD WORM versus CD ROM (normal
turn around).

turn (10 days generally), premiums are applied and the cost trade off issue moves up to approximately 100 copies depending on the specific turnaround. To be fully accurate, this analysis should look at the relative cost of the in-house WORM facility and allocate a premium for reserved capacity held open for short turns. The overall picture is not altered, however, and the approximate cutoff still applies.

4. *Nonalterability, traceability, and updatability.* This application issue distinguishes CD WORM from CD EROM [rewritable (see below)] as well as between CD WORM and CD ROM. If traceability and updatability of the record are required, then CD WORM is ideal; if total nonalterability is needed, then CD ROM is ideal. If rapid and frequent update is needed, then CD EROM is best. Figure 8-9 illustrates this matrix.

Issues of copyright notwithstanding, it is technologically straightforward to make a CD WORM drive; the media is more difficult but achievable. There are clear applications requiring the turnaround, traceability advantages, and updatability of CD WORM. There is no doubt that such a product will be available soon.

Feature Matrix for Recordable Products

	CD-WORM	CD-EROM	CD-ROM
Traceable	/////		
Updatable	/////	/////	
Non-alterable			/////

Figure 8-9   Applications for CD ROM versus CD WORM versus CD EROM.

Future Possibilities for Rewritable CD ROM (CD EROM)

The quest for a rewritable, so-called erasable, optical technology has been well documented; see Ref. 15, for example. Here we will examine briefly the prospect for "erasable CD ROM," or CD EROM, as we could call it (CD Erasable Read Only Memory).

Three technologies are currently being investigated for this function, (1) magneto-optic, (2) phase change, and (3) reversible dye polymer. Phase change and dye polymer techniques are today still research orientated and have major difficulty in meeting the industry expectation of 10^6 erase cycles without degradation. This section will focus on magneto-optics (M-O). The possible success of the Tandy/ODI dye approval to CD Audio could alter the technology dynamics significantly, the limited rewrite (10^3 cycles) is probably more than realistically sufficient but may not be enough to alter market perception in the data market.

The Technology

Figure 8-10 shows the fundamentals of the Magneto-Optic mechanism. The laser is used as a microheating element and alters the magnetic properties of a film of rare earth metals. Only where the films are heated does the magnetic coercivity alter, and hence the information "bit" is physically defined by the laser spot size. Hence, the usual approximate 1µm pit cell dimension present in most optical storage is maintained. Read-out of the information utilizes the Kerr-Faraday effect which is the fractional rotation of the axis of polarization of light by the internal and surface magnetic field of a material. The origins of this technology are quite old but in recent years extensive work has proven that a usable media can be developed from the principle (Ref. 16). The effort, however, to date has been directed at computer peripheral applications rather than at CD formats.

There are significant difficulties in making a CD EROM using magneto-optic technology:

1. Ensuring that the media has adequate performance and stability over many years in uncontrolled environments

2. Obtaining sufficient density and precision of recording to use EFM code

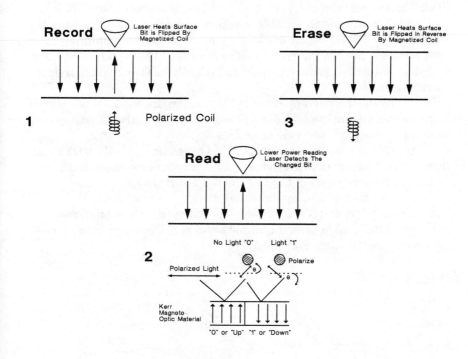

Figure 8-10   How Magneto-Optics works.

3. Obtaining sufficient carrier-to-noise ratio in an EFM mode

4. Creating and maintaining over life sufficiently low levels of errors that the CIRC-ECC and the 2-layer ECC is sufficient to correct-out to the 10^{12} level required for the data industry

5. Providing adequate protection for the M-O layers in a single plastic package compatible with today's CD ROM players

6. Allowing for single-bit rewrite (bit overwrite)

These problems can be overcome and indeed a prototype M-O system was demonstrated in 1984 (Ref. 17). However, no commercial device exists yet and the principal problem is item 5 above. It is unlikely that a sufficiently stable media will be developed so that the answer may lie in better packaging or in a revised clamp system that allows a double thickness media package. This would, of course, rule out interchangeability with today's CD ROM drives, a large compromise.

To illustrate the current state of the art, Figure 8-11 shows carrier to noise data from typical 3M M-O media; today the CNR is more than adequate from several companies.

Further, it is also true for certain M-O medias (Ref. 18) that a sufficient CNR value is achieved at write frequencies more than adequate to meet the need of the CD ROM specifications.

Regarding media life, as indicated above, it is not clear that with the existing "package" this can be achieved. In a conventional polycarbonate double sealed laminate the results shown in Figure 8-12 were obtained (data from Ref. 18).

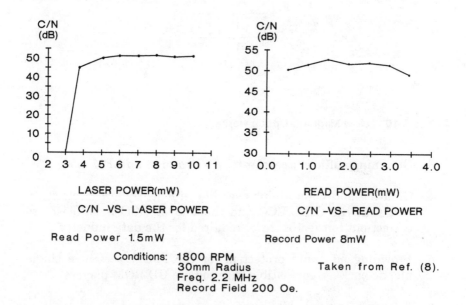

Figure 8-11   Magneto-Optic media — CNR data.

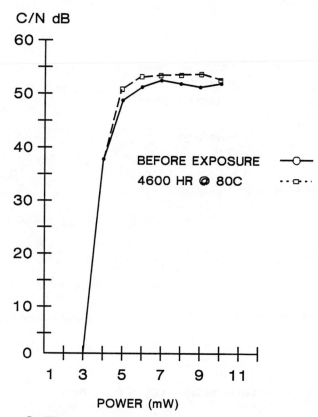

CNR vs. write power after 80°C.
Exposure for 4600 hrs. (Ref. 18).

Figure 8-12   M-O media life.

To meet the CD package needs, the media construction would have
to follow the construction principles shown in Figure 8-13, which is
taken from Ref. 19 which discusses aspects of erasable CD Audio
technology (E-DAD). The effectiveness of the air surface dielectric
would have to be exceptional, but with a glass disc with microglass
cover this could be achieved.

Regarding the ability to sustain an EFM code, in contrast to CD
WORM, no major problems are found. For example, Figure 8-14
shows bit jitter data taken with an EFM code above the CD required
linear velocity of 1.2 m/second. The media is within the 20 ns spec.

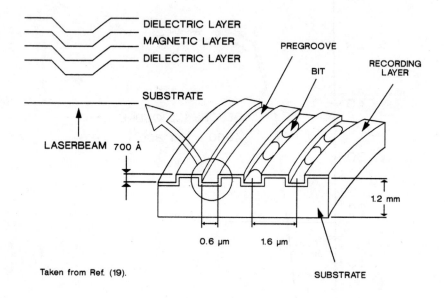

DIELECTRIC LAYER
MAGNETIC LAYER
DIELECTRIC LAYER
PREGROOVE
BIT
RECORDING LAYER
SUBSTRATE
LASERBEAM 700 Å
1.2 mm
0.6 μm   1.6 μm
Taken from Ref. (19).
SUBSTRATE

Figure 8-13   Proposed recordable (CD) media (Sanyo).

Also, actual block error rates (BLER) have been obtained for M-O media using EFM codes and at the required linear velocity; see Figure 8-15 taken from Ref. 19.

Applications for CD EROM

The write-once discussion in the section on CD WORM is very much relevant to CD EROM applications. The differences lie in the relative degree of importance of the following variables.

1. Cost of media compared with reusability inconvenience and erasure time. A relative high media cost favors rewritable media.

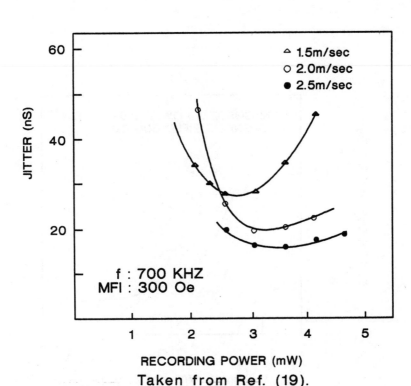

RECORDING POWER (mW)

Taken from Ref. (19).

Figure 8-14   Experimental bit jitter data taken with CD ROM compatible code (EFM) — erasable (M-O) media.

2. Need for traceability of the record and, possibly, legal admissibility in the future. This favors CD WORM/CD ROM over the rewritable option.

3. *Updatability requirements*. Very frequent update where the update obsoletes the prior information. This certainly makes CD EROM more cost effective than CD WORM and a better performance option than CD ROM.

4. *Data rate*. The physics of magneto-optic rewritability allows up to 24 Mbits/second. Of course, this is only usable with a modified CD specification; however, it is possible that recordable media players will be developed that have optional high data rate features when needed.

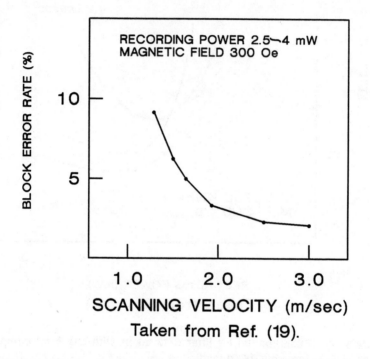

BLOCK ERROR RATE (%)

RECORDING POWER 2.5~4 mW
MAGNETIC FIELD 300 Oe

SCANNING VELOCITY (m/sec)

Taken from Ref. (19).

Figure 8-15   Block error rates taken with CD ROM compatible code (EFM) — erasable (M-O) media.

CD EROM as an option in a multifunctional system or as an adjunct to a CD ROM drive is obviously attractive. Once again, the issue is cost.

In Conclusion

There is no doubt that M-O technology can meet the performance needs of a rewritable CD technology. The media life and stability in the existing CD disc package are unproven as yet but within a 5-year time frame there is no doubt that this can be achieved.

Multifunctional CD Drives

The similarity in operation between read-only, write-once, and erasable optical media options has always intrigued the technical community and several proposals (see Ref. 5) have been made to create a "multifunctionality" option in the technology. Such devices are indeed in development in the computer optical drive community where cost constraints are less troublesome. Multifunctionality usually means the ability to achieve a drive capable of read only (distributed info), write once (archive, traceable record), and erasable (multiple write) in the same device — media interchange, and perhaps some form of simple mode selection, being the only requirement.

Technology

Even given that the individual CD WORM and CD EROM drive/media technologies are developed, combining them into a device that achieves both and has a read only function is not a trivial task.

The problems, even allowing for the assumption that the individual technologies are in place, are:

1. *Varying detection principles.* M-O erasable, for example, uses polarization phase change while the other techniques use amplitude detection. This is not as serious as it sounds since fundamentally all the detectors rely on intensity. Splitting the detector by phase and recombining for amplitude can be achieved.

2. *Varying signal level into the detector.* The detectors and options will need to handle medias that vary from highly IR reflective (85 percent) to low reflectivity (10 percent) and yet maintain focus and tracking servo operation.

3. *Variable bit window properties.* The device will need to operate over a worst case range of bit jitter and timing window.

4. *Tracking complications.* Depending on the method combining "phaseless" (i.e., physically flat) media such as M-O with relief structures as in prerecorded makes for complexity in tracking.

By far the best would be a sampled servo approach that separates the tracking function from the data function. This, however, is precluded by today's specification.

5. *Laser power levels.* Different laser power levels for read and the various writing options are inevitable. The laser diodes would need to operate with stability over a wide range.

Despite these issues, there is little doubt that this product will surface.

Applications

The application for this universal CD data drive depends upon the relative price. The disparate needs of the user community make it difficult to predict. In its simplest form, it is easy to envisage the ROM function providing the data base that is extracted, the EROM being the routine updated interactive local memory and the WORM function providing a backup function. More difficult to envisage is the degree of use contention for each function. Fundamentally, if the universal device were virtually identical in price, then it would dominate. For every few percentage points of premium in price, its attractiveness decreases.

Figure 8-16 is a representation of a comparative break out of technology and application; the shorter turnarounds favor the recordable technologies, the larger quantities the read only versions.

Conclusions

The avenues of possibility open to optical storage are very great. These include the merging of video, data, and audio, and interchanging between distributed publishing, archival storage and rewritable optical storage; the wealth of flexibility offered by lower and lower cost per bit of storage and greater and greater capacities available with rapid access is of major significance to the system designer.

Even newer techniques are on the horizon. These include holographic storage, which opens up a new degree of freedom based on the beam angle, or photochemical hole burning, which multiplexes the laser frequency.

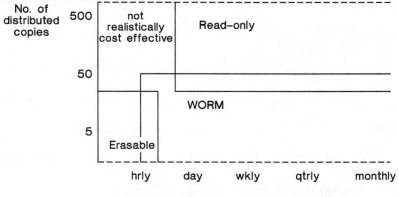

Update frequency also impacts this matrix.

Figure 8-16   Cost effectiveness of CD ROM and future recordable CD formats.

These methods offer the clear likelihood of several orders of magnitude of increased storage density in the years to come.

About the Author

David H. Davies is General Manager of the Optical Recording Project for 3M. He has responsibility for commercialization of all forms of laser-based prerecorded and recordable media. Dr. Davies obtained his Ph.D. in 1967 in Physical Chemistry (University College, London) and an M.B.A. in 1974 from the University of Pittsburgh. He is the author of over 50 technical publications and has eight issued U.S. patents. Prior to his 3M position, he was cofounder and vice president of Kylex Inc. which was acquired by 3M in 1981.

Dr. Davies is a member of the Optical Society of America, Materials Research Society, Society of Information Display, and the Institute of Electrical & Electronics Engineers.

3M Company
420 North Bernardo
Mountain View, CA 94043
415–969–5200

References

1.   T. Takeuchi, T. Murakami (Hitachi), et al. (1986), *JITE Japan*, *40*(6).
2.   J. Isailovic (1985). *Proc. SPIE*, *529*:161.
3.   E. R. Berlekamp (1968). *Algebraic Coding Theory*. New York: McGraw-Hill.
4.   Proceedings of the AES Premier Conference (Audio Eng. Society) (1980, 1982), Ryetown, New York.
5.   D. H. Davies (1983). Proceedings Technology Opportunity Conference, San Francisco: Rothchild Consultants Inc.
6.   S. Miyaoka (1985). Personal Communication (Sony Corp.).
7.   A. Ishihara, T. Yoshimaru, A. Chickamori (Toshiba) (1987). OSA Topical Meeting on Optical Data Storage, vol. 10, paper no. FB2.
8.   T. Takahashi, et al. (29 August 1986). "Performance of Magneto-Optic Media on Plastic Substrates," Personal Communication.
9.   T. J. Lynch (1985) *Data Compression*. Belmont, Calif.: Lifetree Publications.
10. Terminal Equipment and Protocol for Telematic Services (1984), CCITT Red Book, vol. VII.3, Geneva, CCITT.
11. Data from Hitachi HD 63085 LSI (G4 FAX Std).
12a. SPIE Proceedings "Optical Storage Media" (1983) Vol. 420.
12b. Proceedings OSA Topical Meeting on Optical Storage (1983), Optical Society of America, Incline Village.
13. S. Lu, et al. (1983), Vol. 420, paper no. 39 in Ref. 12a.
14. H. V. Tongeren and M. Sens (1983), Paper WC3-1 in Ref. 12b.
15. SPIE Proceedings (1985) Vol. 529.

16. For example, R. N. Gardner, T. A. Rinehart, L. H. Johnson, R. P. Freese, R. A. Lund (1983). *Proc. SPIE*, vol. 420.

17. K. Torazawa, S. Murata, S. Minechika (1985). *Sanyo Tech. Rev.* 17 (2).

18. R. P. Freese and T. Takahashi (1985). "High performance magneto-optic recording media," *JIEEE (Japan)*, Mag-85-88.

19. T. Murakami, K. Taira, M. Mori (1986). *Applied Optics*, 25: 3986

D

Information Storage and Retrieval

9

Designing a CD ROM
Information Structure

Bradley Watson, Terry Noreault, and Howard Turtle

Introduction

In designing an information storage structure for CD ROM, designers must change their built-in prejudices. For 30+ years designers
have optimized file structures for *erasable* media. With CD ROM,
erasability is gone and file structures do not need to be optimized for
insert, change, or delete operations. The only meaningful operation
for CD ROM data structures is the look-up operation.

A second critical aspect of CD ROM drives for an application designer is that CD ROM drive access times are slow, when compared
with Winchester-style disk drives.

Now, given that only the look-up is pertinent and that it is an inherently slow operation, a third aspect of CD ROM, one that is often
the primary reason for choosing CD ROM for an application, becomes important: CD ROM discs hold a large amount of data, at
least 55 times as much as a 10-Mbtye Winchester.

All of this means that the primary design consideration for files and file-layouts for CD ROM is to *optimize fetch times*. With this primary consideration in mind, this chapter will address the following:

Physical characteristics of CD ROM
　Disc capacity
　Physical block size
　Drive access speed
　Drive transfer speed
　Interleaving of blocks

Data access requirements
　CD ROM data types
　Data encoding characteristics
　Access methods

File attributes
　File placement on disc
　File structures
　　Sequential files
　　Indexed sequential access method files
　　B-Tree files
　　Hashed files

Alternatives to total in-house CD ROM application building

CD ROM example applications

Summary: Getting started from scratch

Physical Characteristics of CD ROM

The major physical characteristics of CD ROM are related to the fact that CD ROM drives use Constant Linear Velocity (CLV) encoding as opposed to Constant Angular Velocity (CAV) encoding, which is used with magnetic drives. On CLV units, bits are packed at the same density all over the disc, meaning that the motor that spins the disc on a CD ROM drive must change the angular velocity as the head moves over the disc. CD ROM discs spin from 200 to 530 rpm. Compared with magnetic media, this changing velocity causes seek times and latency times to be relatively high.

On the other hand, CAV units used on magnetic media pack bits closer together on the inner tracks of a disc than on the outer tracks. This allows the disc motor to rotate at a constant angular velocity as the head moves over the disc, reducing seek and latency times.

The most noticeable characteristic of CLV encoding (besides slower access times) is that the higher bit density on outer tracks results in greater byte capacities for equivalent disc sizes relative to CAV units.

The use of CLV technology in CD ROM introduces other oddities besides the denser data capacities and slower access times. First, CD ROM discs don't actually have "tracks" in the sense that magnetic disks have tracks, nor do they have "sectors."

CD ROM discs have only one spiral track, much like vinyl audio records. Moving from the inside to the outside of the disc reading data sequentially entails following that spiral. Data is recorded along the track in fixed length blocks, with block addresses beginning at the inner portion of the spiral, increasing toward the outer end of the spiral.

Random seeks on CD ROM are also somewhat different from on magnetic drives. Essentially, the head is moved "near" the correct area in one movement, then is more finely positioned by "peeking" at the blocks passing beneath the head. On magnetic drives the head is moved directly to the correct track. Latency time is then added, waiting for the correct data to come into position as the disc rotates.

CD ROM has inherited some nomenclature from CD Audio technology. Actual physical addresses are spoken of in terms of "minutes," "seconds," and "blocks." There are 74 minutes on one CD ROM disc, 60 seconds/minute, and 75 blocks per second. Because the CD format was designed to store audio, 1 minute of storage on a CD equals 1 minute of playing time which in turn equals 4500 blocks of digital data.

However, when an application provides an address to a CD ROM controller, it generally gives either the *logical record number* of the record within a given file, or the *byte offset* of the record from the beginning of the file. The driver software converts this *logical address* to minutes, seconds, and blocks, and then positions the head accordingly.

Disc Capacity

CD ROM discs have an extremely large raw capacity. However, over-head associated with block formatting, error detection, and error correction requirements cause that capacity to shrink slightly. Many current mastering processes allow only 60 minutes of data on a disc instead of the 74 minutes defined by the format.

To further complicate the capacity issue, there are two recording modes for CD ROM. Mode 1 is for general data; mode 2 is compatible with the audio data storage format of Compact Discs. Using mode 1 allows 2048 bytes of user data; mode 2 allows 2336 bytes. The difference is 288 bytes of error detection and correction information. Some forms of data, such as audio, do not need the same level of error protection that other types of data need, and can benefit from the extra storage gained by eliminating protection.

Both modes can be used on the same CD ROM disc. To support applications that require multiple data types (a music education program, for example) audio data (mode 2) can be combined with with executable code and textual data (mode 1).

Many conventional CD ROM mastering processes limit an application to 60 minutes or roughly 553 Mbytes in mode 1. However, some mastering processes allow more than 60 minutes; the artificial barrier having been broken by some mastering processes. Disc capacities will almost certainly increase in the future.

Physical Block Size

User data, in mode 1, is stored on a CD ROM in 2048-byte blocks. In addition to those bytes, each physical block has bytes allocated to identify the block and for error handling. At the beginning of each block, 12 bytes are set aside for drive synchronization and 4 bytes for the absolute address of the block. After the 2048 bytes of user data, there are 288 bytes of error correction coding (ECC) data. The ECC segment consists of 4 bytes for error detection, 8 bytes of 0's, and 276 bytes of error correction data. All together this makes for a physical block of 2352 bytes on a CD ROM disc.

The 2352 bytes per block for CD ROM is exactly the same as for CDs used in music reproduction, which use a format that is virtually identical to mode 2. The difference in the two formats is the error

Table 9-1   Disc Capacities for the Two Modes

	Usable Blocks	Usable Bytes
Mode 1		
60 minutes	270,000	552,960,000
74 minutes	333,000	681,984,000
Mode 2		
60 minutes	270,000	630,720,000
74 minutes	333,000	777,888,000

correction bytes. Digital music reproduction does not require as much error handling ability as data storage.

For many applications, the 2048 bytes of user data per physical block in mode 1 is the important number. The remaining 304 bytes of overhead added by the premastering and mastering process is a given that has to be accepted. Obviously, those bytes do effect access times, since the error data has to be analyzed each time a block is accessed, but this effect is constant and is often a hardware function.

A designer may also use mode 2 for audio, video, facsimile, or other data that can tolerate the increased error rate.

Drive Access Speed

CD ROM access time is slow. Drive manufacturers quote 500 to 700 milliseconds as an average access time, though recently announced drives are pushing the bottom end to 250 milliseconds. Maximum access times are 1000 to 1100 milliseconds. Average latency is quoted at 66 to 70 milliseconds for the inner tracks, with 150 milliseconds for the outer tracks. Compared with Winchester magnetic technology, with total access times routinely in the 13 to 75-millisecond range, latency times alone for CD ROM make it a much slower media, without even considering seek times.

Figure 9-1 compares access times for several devices. It is clear that CD ROM is much slower than conventional drives or write-once optical drives (WORM). Current microcomputer magnetic drives are slower than their mainframe counterparts (typically 35 to 40 mil-

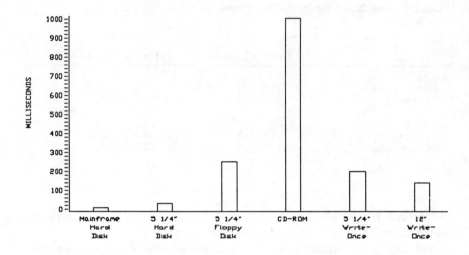

Figure 9-1   Drive access speeds.

liseconds compared with 13 to 15 milliseconds), but even at that, they far outperform most CD ROM drives.

Tests suggest that actual performance is somewhat slower than the manufacturers' quoted specifications. For a typical drive, moving from the inner to the outer tracks (or spanning 60 minutes of data, in CD ROM terminology) requires 1300 milliseconds. Moving the same 60 minutes in reverse required 1400 milliseconds. This suggests that to optimize access times you must minimize head movement (see Figure 9-2). One technique would be to place frequently used data on the inner tracks. This will reduce latency, with some expense in head movement. When planning the layout of files on the disc, the designer should take these factors into account.

Drive Transfer Speed

In most CD ROM drives, data is transferred at 176 kbytes/second for the entire physical block of 2352 bytes. However, user data is only 2048 bytes of that total, so the effective transfer rate is more like 150 kbytes/second during a continuous read. This compares with mainframe drives that are on the order of 3000 kbytes/second and personal computer drives that range from 400 to 1200 kbytes/second.

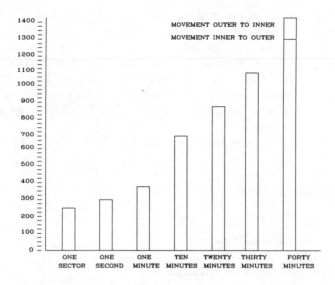

Figure 9-2   Drive transfer speeds.

Interleaving of Blocks

Normally, physical blocks are arranged on CD ROM tracks in a sequential manner. The first block is followed on the track by the second block, and so forth. This differs substantially from magnetic media. Transparent to user, magnetic disk controllers often format their media so that physical sectors are *interleaved*.

Interleaving is done when the time between sectors on magnetic disks is too short to allow a controller to clear its buffer. By skipping a couple of sectors between sequentially addressed sectors, the additional time allows the controller to empty its buffer and ready itself for the next sector. If interleaving was not used, then a full disc revolution would be required between sector reads.

Table 9-2   Drive Transfer Speed (Mode 1)

	Full Block	User Data
CD ROM	176 kbytes/sec	150 kbytes/sec
Mainframe drives	3000 kbytes/sec	—
PC drives	400–1200 kbytes/sec	—

CD ROM transfer speed and the assembly of data from its physical encoding is so slow that automatic interleaving by the controller is not needed. But there is an option during the premastering phase that allows blocks of files to be interleaved on tracks. One might choose to do this if the sequence of block accessing is known ahead of time and head movement is to be optimized. The provision of interleaving is part of the *logical* file structure for CD ROM, not part of the physical structure.

For example, if data is to be read in from three files in the following manner:

```
while data-needed

    get 2 blocks from file 1
    get 1 block from file 2
    get 3 blocks from file 3
    use data from files 1,2,3

end while
```

the file designer could specify an interleaving option assuring that after the two required blocks are read from file 1, the head will be in position to get the required block from file 2, which would then leave the head in position to get the required blocks from file 3. A well-designed pattern of interleaving could result in significant reductions in access time. A significant caveat is required here; this reduction in access tion depends entirely on predictable file usage patterns.

Data Access Requirements

Three basic classes of applications currently utilize CD ROM. The simplest class consists of a large database placed on CD ROM, such as New York Stock Exchange statistics for a given period of time. This data is then retrieved and selectively moved to magnetic media for access by a financial analysis program.

The second class is information retrieval, using search-and-retrieval software that directly accesses the data on the CD ROM. This category includes applications such as encyclopedias or other reference materials on a CD ROM disc for full-text searching.

The third class of application may use the full capabilities of CD ROM for storing different data types, such as audio, text, computer graphics, or compressed photographic or video images. Training or entertainment packages are an excellent example of this style of application.

CD ROM Data Types

CD ROM lends itself to these primary data types:

1. Audio
2. Video
3. Text
4. Binary

One can intermix these data types on one disc, achieving a multimedia effect. Compact Discs (CD) were originally developed and marketed for their audio capabilities. CD ROM's additional capabilities of handling video, text, and binary data give an application designer a broad palette for creating virtually any desired effect.

Data Encoding Characteristics

Data can be encoded on a CD ROM disc in several ways. For example, most microcomputer environments support ASCII data for text, while many mainframes are EBCDIC based. It is possible that a CD ROM designer might need to use both types of data encoding on the same disc in order to achieve efficient compatibility across machine types.

If the application is to be internationally distributed, then other character encodings become important. ASCII is not just one character set, but instead is a continuum of character sets, using redefinition of the 128 7-bit combinations used in ASCII. Reference documents ISO 646 and ISO 2022, international standards issued by the International Organization for Standardization (ISO), address these issues.

If the application is to be used in the Far East, then encodings of the Katakana and Kanji character sets must be used. Using Katakana and Kanji characters can have an impact on storage space, since typically more than one octet (8-bit byte) is needed to encode a character. Escape sequences are used, which can increase the space needed to store data. With ASCII, escape sequences are defined in the ISO standards for handling certain kinds of special characters and for switching character sets.

A second encoding consideration has to do with byte-ordering for binary integers. Many computers store integers with the least-significant byte first, and most-significant byte last. Other computers reverse this. If a compact disc is to be accessed on both types of computer, integers must be recorded twice (once with each method), or the software in the computer reading the data must know what order was used in the mastering of the disc, and interpret the number accordingly.

A final example of encoding considerations lies with the compression of images, both motion and nonmotion. International standards recommendation T.4 by Study Group XIV of the Consultative Committee on International Telephone and Telegraph (CCITT) exist for encoding black and white facsimile images, though not for color images. The encoding of motion images, i.e., video of any kind, black-white or color, has been done in a variety of ways. At this point, however, these methods are usually proprietary and no single standard exists.

Storage space is at a premium when capturing images for storage on CD ROM. Images must carry information regarding halftones and/or color, as well as motion or nonmotion. Encoding schemes for color images can take up to 15 bits per pixel, allowing 32,768 colors. Using 4 bits per pixel will give 16 colors. An image of an 8.5 by 11 inch page scanned at 300 pixels per inch uses approximately a 1 Mbyte of storage at just 1 bit per pixel. Color images can easily require 4 Mbytes just to show 16 colors.

Compression schemes are vital for storing color, black and white, and halftone images. Very significant reductions in storage can be gained by employing an efficient compression algorithm. At least one developer has achieved enough reduction to enable the storage of 1 hr of full-motion video with audio on a single CD ROM disc. Earlier versions got 30 seconds of full-motion video and sound, so a gain of 120 to 1 was obtained with good compression.

Any storage compression scheme, no matter how efficient in terms of storage, must also lend itself to real-time expansion, especially for full-motion video and sound applications. In fact, this requirement is usually the roughest part of any attempt to design a compression scheme for CD ROM.

Other types of visual data include the geometric or vector class of graphics, where lines, points, and arcs need to be specified. There are many significant applications where vector graphics are best, mostly in the CAD/CAM and cartographic area. Over the years numerous encoding schemes for vector graphics have been developed and used, creating incompatibility problems. Fortunately, standards are now becoming available.

The Computer Graphics Metafile standard, ANSI Standard X3.122-1986, contains three encoding techniques: ASCII, binary form, and clear text (human readable form). This standard is referred to as a picture-defining protocol, because it allows one to reconstruct a picture from an encoded description. ISO will adopt the same standard in 1987.

Ultimately, an application designer must choose an encoding scheme that will most effectively support and the application and meet the needs of the end user. All kinds of encoding schemes can be used to create CD ROMs. With certain types of applications, such as motion video, image compression is mandatory if one wants to store a reasonable amount of video on a single disc.

Access Methods

The two basic access methods, sequential and random, are available on CD ROM. If application needs can be satisfied with sequential access, significant access time gains can be realized over random access methods. With either approach head movement and latency times can be minimized with proper file layouts on the disc.

File Attributes

Two attributes concerning files are important for the CD ROM environment: file placement and file structure. An application designer can and should plan the location of data placed on a CD ROM disc. Choosing appropriate areas of the disc, and structures for the data, are two of the most important design tasks for optimizing CD ROM application access times.

For file attributes, the designer should adhere to the appropriate national and international standards. At the present time there are three such standards. The first published standard for file formats by an official standards writing body was from the European Computer Manufacturer's Association (ECMA 119) in the fall of 1986. A close parallel to that document was approved by the National Information Standards Organization (NISO) in the United States in the spring of 1987. Their standard is NISO Z39.60-1987. In the fall of 1987, the International Organization for Standardization (ISO) approved their version, ISO 9660. All three versions are to be fully compatible.

File Placement on Disc

Minimizing access time normally translates into finding data placement patterns that minimize head movement and/or latency times.

There are some general rules of thumb that are useful when considering placement of files on CD ROM:

1. Place data that is frequently accessed together with blocks physically near one another (cluster the data).
2. Use inner tracks for most frequently accessed data to reduce latency.
3. Place files that are used in conjunction with each other physically near each other on the disc.
4. Interleave files when application will use them concurrently (most appropriate for sequential access files).
5. Avoid situations where the head must move frequently across a large file to get to another file.

File Structures

There are four general file structures that are suited to CD ROM:

1. Sequential
2. Indexed Sequential Access Method
3. B-Tree
4. Hashed

This section will discuss each of these structures and review their advantages and disadvantages for CD ROM applications. Figure 9-3 to 9-6 show logical views of the four file structures to be discussed. The data and retrieval keys are the same for each example, allowing the reader to make reasonable comparisons among the four structures.

For information regarding these four structures beyond what is presented below, please consult the references at the end of the chapter. This list is not intended as an exhaustive bibliography on the subject, but merely as a guide to representative texts.

Sequential Files. Sequential files have been the workhorse of data processing since the notion of a computer file first occurred. They are by far the most efficient file type for CD ROM, in terms of access time, if the application can use the data in a strictly sequential order. Certain data types, such as video and audio, require that the data be stored in a sequential manner, given the nature of its use. If an application can be implemented using a sequential file structure, a designer of a CD ROM application should seriously consider this possibility.

Figure 9-3 shows a sample layout of a sequential file using fixed length records blocked one record to a block, sequenced on the name field. The records are simplified versions of typical personnel file entries. This format usually takes less space than the other three formats, but you pay for that in terms of access times, particularly when you need to find records on a random basis.

For example, to find "Francisco" and the related data, an application program would have to read the previous six records, comparing on name until finally matching with the seventh record. This translates to seven I/Os to find one record. However, if one wanted to process the entire file sequentially, this format is very efficient in space and access times.

Indexed Sequential Access Method Files. Indexed Sequential Access Method (ISAM) files can give you the advantages of both sequential and random access files. In purest form, ISAM files contain two types of blocks: index blocks and data blocks. Index blocks contain ranges of keys with pointers to other index blocks, or to data blocks containing actual records. The indexes are arranged logically in a tree shaped hierarchy, with a root index pointing to index nodes

NAME (KEY)	HIRE DATE	AGE
ADAM	800115	30
BILL	760130	34
CASSANDRA	821015	27
DEBRA	870701	40
ELOISE	750102	33
FRANCINE	790214	55
FRANCISCO	770815	42
FRANKLIN	860201	22
GEORGE	800229	35
HORACE	830401	60
JULIO	700101	65

Figure 9-3 Personnel file — sequential structure.

which point to lower level index nodes or terminal nodes, which are data blocks.

To search the file randomly, a specific key is searched in the indexes. Eventually, the last index searched contains a pointer to the relevant data block. Sequential access begins by searching for a record with a given key, but then each record accessed after that will be the one with the next highest key value.

Figure 9-4 shows a sample layout of an ISAM file with a single index block and four data blocks. The size and layout of the types of blocks can be dissimilar in ISAM and in this example that is the case. This allows for optimization of both record types with regard to their useability and efficiency.

In this example, a search for "Francisco" and related data would begin with a sequential search of the index block, I0. One would be looking for either an exact match or for a key greater than "Francisco." Once either condition is met, than the next block pointer associated with the qualifying key will take the search to the next level down. In this case "Franklin" is greater than "Francisco," so the search goes to the D2 data block. A quick sequential search of D2

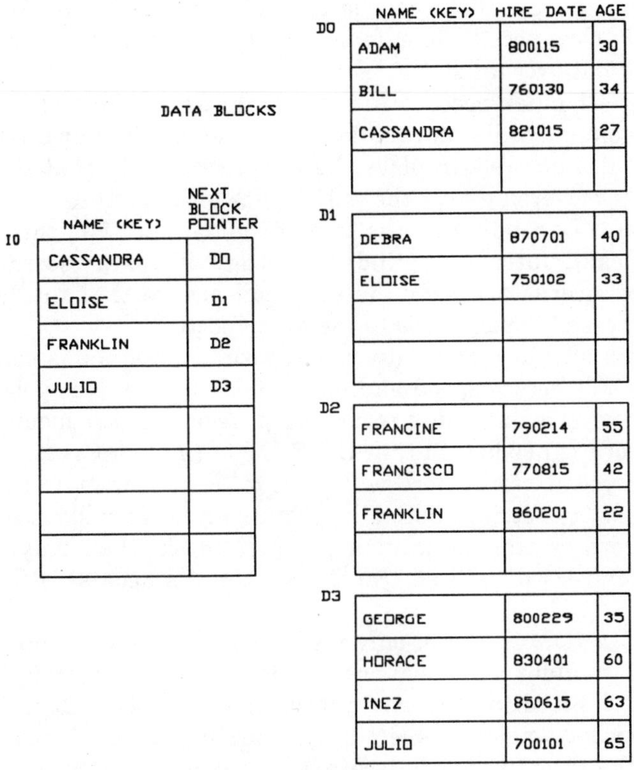

DATA BLOCKS

D0

NAME (KEY)	HIRE DATE	AGE
ADAM	800115	30
BILL	760130	34
CASSANDRA	821015	27

I0

NAME (KEY)	NEXT BLOCK POINTER
CASSANDRA	D0
ELOISE	D1
FRANKLIN	D2
JULIO	D3

D1

DEBRA	870701	40
ELOISE	750102	33

D2

FRANCINE	790214	55
FRANCISCO	770815	42
FRANKLIN	860201	22

D3

GEORGE	800229	35
HORACE	830401	60
INEZ	850615	63
JULIO	700101	65

Figure 9-4 Personnel file — ISAM structure.

results in finding "Francisco" and the related data in the second position of the block.

This search took two I/Os, assuming that I0 is not kept in memory. This compares quite favorably with the seven I/Os used in the sequential file. If we wanted to process the entire ISAM file sequentially, five I/Os would suffice. One I/O would get I0, then four more I/Os would be needed to retrieve D0, D1, D2, and D3. The sequential file, blocked one record to a block, would take twelve I/Os. This is the worst case, and could be improved with a reasonable blocking factor, such as six or even twelve records to a block.

The primary advantages of ISAM are that there are two methods of access built into the structure. Disadvantages lie in the same fact. Overhead for supporting random access in the form of searching and maintaining the indexes can slow the system down. Placement of the indexes on the CD ROM can be critical. Finally, CD ROM, with its inherently slow access time, forces the designer to consider carefully index and data record size.

Placing all index records in a separate area will assure minimal head movement while moving down the tree looking for a record key. But it is also possible to place the index records so that the head is constantly traversing over the entire data block area to read the next data record. Depending on the size of the data section, this time can be significant. Intermixing index records with data records so that the index records are near the data can ensure that the last index record accessed is very close to the data record.

In terms of index and data record size, a designer is constrained by CD ROM's access speed and physical block size. It is good to have as many keys in an index record as possible, which means a large index record is needed. But, in CD ROM, if the index record is larger than a physical block there will need to be two or more accesses to the disc just to retrieve one index. That can be very slow. And if the index record is smaller than a physical block, then maybe one or more index records will be transferred than is necessary for searching.

Since CD ROM is a read-only medium and does not support updating of files, index maintenance overhead is not an issue. Indexes should be built with care and precision since this task is only performed once. A major problem with searching ISAM indexes on CD ROM is the time needed to locate an index and read it into memory to be searched. If some or all indexes can be read at start-up time, search time can be reduced at the expense of additional start-up delays. A 100K index file will obviously take longer than a 20K file. All of these trade-offs must be considered.

B-Tree Files   B-Tree files are characterized by the fact that the keys to the data records all reside in a multiway search tree structure. A pointer to each data record is associated with the appropriate key. This is different from most implementations of ISAM files in that not all key values are necessarily found explicitly in the indexes for ISAM files. ISAM generally has pairs of key values to indicate a *range* of keys, with a data block containing *multiple* data records with keys that fall within a given range. B-Tree files, on the other hand, can have one or more logical records per data record, but multiple keys per index block. This latter attribute results in the "multiway" designation for B-Trees, since it means there are multiple paths leading down the tree from an index node.

Figure 9-5 shows the logical layout of a particular type of B-Tree, the B+ Tree, a very popular form because of certain built-in efficiencies. For one, the index blocks do not contain the actual keys; instead they contain a value that can be compared against a search key to determine the path to be followed down the tree. This is a space-saving efficiency. A time-saving efficiency realized by B+ Trees is that the leaves of the tree contain the data records and are stored with the index records. Normally B-Trees are implemented as two files — one containing the indexes, the other containing the data (Comer, 1979).

"Francisco" can be found by searching the I0 index block for a value greater than "Francisco." Once found, the pointer to the left of that index value is used to continue the search. If no index value is greater than the search key, than the desired data is not in the file. In this case, index value "F" is too small, but "Z" is greater. Using the pointer, "I2," leads us to search the I2 index block. Here, "g" is found to be larger, so the pointer "D2" tells us to go to the D2 data block. Searching D2 sequentially yields the record we want. This

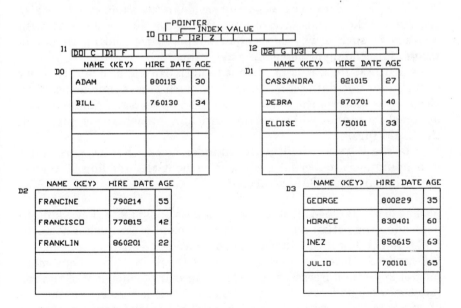

Figure 9-5 Personnel file — B-Tree structure.

search took three I/Os, comparing favorably with ISAM. Obviously, the number of index block levels and number of data records per data block affect the efficiency of the search.

With reasonable care in the design, the B+ Tree can afford an application efficient sequential access as well as random access. Placing pointer in each data block to the next one in order allows one to process the file very quickly, with only the overhead of going down the index tree one time to find the first data block. Thus B+ Trees offer the same advantage as ISAM, giving the user two access methods. Normal B-Trees do not have this advantage.

Files based on the B-Tree structure are very common in current applications based on magnetic media requiring random access capability. Random retrieval is reasonably quick, and the time and space overhead necessary for maintaining the B-Tree structure through a series of updates is fairly low. In fact, it is the low overhead factor for updates that makes them very popular. However, since CD ROM does not support updates, that aspect of B-Trees is not significant, leaving the random retrieval capability as the major asset for B-Trees on CD ROM.

Sequential access, while possible with B-Trees, is not necessarily as efficient with them as with ISAM. Finding the next key is not simple, since it does not necessarily reside in the same index node as the current key. One way around this is to thread the tree with pointers in such a way as to allow simple sequential movement in terms of ascending or descending key value.

As in ISAM files, it is important to optimize the size and capacity of the index and data blocks to save as much access time as possible. Keeping as much of the index tree in memory as is possible is a good approach, though it will affect the start-up time negatively, just as in the ISAM files.

In fact, a B-Tree is built with full index blocks that are spread out in a minimum number of levels and sequential threading of keys is quite similar to an ISAM structure.

Hashed Files   Hashed files, or direct access files, use a key value to determine the actual address of the associated record using a "hashing" function to convert the key to an address.

Usually the hashing function does not result in a one-to-one mapping of keys to addresses, but instead there are "collisions" of records into the same address. On magnetic media this is resolved by the use of "buckets," i.e., multiple records are held in the same bucket, if their key values all "hash" to the same address. This results in some time lost searching the bucket for the correct record. Buckets normally have a fixed size and may overflow when too many keys map into the same bucket.

Hashed files on magnetic media have to be designed with all of the above points in mind. Again, on CD ROM updating will not be performed. In special cases the CD ROM designer can take the time to devise a "perfect" or near perfect hash function. All keys are known from the beginning, so the designer can put extra effort into making a hash function that comes close to a one-on-one mapping.

Even without "perfect" hashing, one can assure that buckets do not overflow during the building process and that bucket size is optimal for minimizing access times.

Figure 9-6 shows a logical view of a hashed file. The left-hand side, labeled "Main Hash Area," contains space for 13 records, correspond-

MAIN HASH AREA

NAME (KEY)	HIRE DATE	AGE	OVERFLOW POINTER
ADAM	80015	30	
BILL	760130	34	
CASSANDRA	821015	27	
DEBRA	870701	40	
ELOISE	750102	33	
FRANCINE	790214	55	00
GEORGE	800229	35	
HORACE	830401	60	
INEZ	850615	63	
JULIO	700101	65	

OVERFLOW AREA

	NAME (KEY)	HIRE DATE	AGE	BUCKET POINTER
00	FRANCISCO	770815	42	01
01	FRANKLIN	860201	22	

Figure 9-6 Personnel file — hashed structure.

ing to the 13 logical hash addresses A through M of the alphabet.
The right-hand side indicates 13 more record hold areas. These will
accommodate any overflows from the Main Area caused by two or
more incoming keys "hashing" to the same logical address.

"Francisco" is found by running the key through the hash function
to obtain its logical address. In this example the hash function is
simply taking the first letter of the key, "F," and using it as the logical address. Retrieving the record at "F" reveals that "Francine"
resides there. However, "Francine"'s overflow pointer indicates that
there are records for that logical address, "F," in the Overflow Area.
Retrieving the record at 00 gives us "Francisco." If we had been searching for "Franklin" we would have continued from 00 to 01, where
we again would have been successful.

Two I/Os found us "Francisco," which is highly comparable to
ISAM and B+ Trees for random access. If the key had been any besides "Francisco" or "Franklin," than one I/O would have sufficed.
This reflects the desirability of finding the "perfect" or near-perfect
hash function. If one had such a function, then sequential access of a
hash file would be as efficient as sequeitial files, which is beyond the
capability of the ISAM and B+ Tree files.

Alternatives to Total In-house CD ROM Application Building

Depending upon the application, there are several alternatives that
can be used to bring a CD ROM product to market besides doing it
from the ground up with in-house staff and facilities.

If the goal is to provide a retrieval capability for a large database,
there are a number of commercially available generic retrieval packages. One could select an appropriate package, have a CD ROM
mastered with the data in the format required by the package, and
distribute the CD ROM with the software necessary for accessing the
data. This approach can be relatively painless, simple, cost effective,
and is generally a fast implementation method.

The criteria for selecting retrieval software are the same as the
criteria used to evaluate and design one's own application. The
software should access the data within acceptable time limits,
provide user-friendly access capability, error-recovery, be usable in
an acceptable number of hardware and operating system environments, and, if necessary, provide support for use in all any required
foreign language.

Besides designing the data layouts and writing the software needed, a large part of any CD ROM application development project is the preparation of the data itself for placement onto the CD ROM. This can be done in-house and usually involves creation of special programs to convert the data to its new format and the use of an in-house data conversion center to prepare the data in a production environment. This latter element is particularly necessary if the application involves a serial publication of the data, such as a quarterly or monthly basis.

Another approach is to use a commercial data preparation service. Commercial services will convert a given set of data into the format required for CD ROM mastering. Using such a service can eliminate many internal costs and problems, especially if an organization has no in-house database expertise.

Using commercially available retrieval software, data preparation services, or both, can save a prospective CD ROM application provider time, money, and headaches. On the other hand, doing as much of the job in house as technically feasible, gives the developer greater control over the quality of the end-product. By designing and writing software, a developer can give the application a specific look and feel that will differentiate it from the crowd.

The various alternatives for producing a CD ROM based product are all viable, depending upon the developer's own requirements and constraints.

CD ROM Example Applications

OCLC (Online Computer Library Center) Inc., is involved in a number of on-going CD ROM-related activities. For purposes of providing an example, we will briefly describe the design of one of those projects — *Graph-Text*.

The *Graph-Text* project reflects OCLC's desire to devise a low-cost, high-quality, easy-to-use, alternative to journals. A major goal was to display the content as a reproduction of the original typesetting and graphics. The introduction of full text searching was also an objective.

Starting from scratch, the developers needed to do the following:

1. Acquire journal articles in a usable format or at least convertible form.

2. Develop retrieval software.
3. Develop display software (screen and print).
4. Process journal articles into formats required by *Graph-Text* software and CD ROM mastering process.
5. Master a CD ROM disc with all the data files.

Acquiring and formatting the data for an application can sometimes be one of the most difficult, and certainly the most expensive, parts of a project. In the case of *Graph-Text*, the publisher agreed to allow OCLC to use their data and supplied OCLC with tapes containing the typeset material.

If the data is not already in a machine-readable form, then steps must be taken to prepare the data. In *Graph-Text*, the graphics (charts, drawings, and halftone pictures) in the journal articles had to be captured as raster images, since typesetting tapes contain only textual data.

The retrieval system we designed uses a key word–based algorithm. The user enters key words as their query and the system displays the titles of all articles in the database relevant to the query. The user then selects which article he or she wishes to view. The system then displays the requested document. A search can be qualified later to reduce the set of retrieved documents.

On the display side of the system, *Graph-Text* seeks to display the content of the articles in fonts that resemble the original published version, both on a CRT screen and laser printer output. Since the output devices are different, this design criteria required that two different views of each journal article be stored on the CD ROM, the screen version and the print version. Also, fonts that are used for each article are stored in separate files. All together, this means that there are three files specifically related to each article on the CD ROM disc:

1. CRT output control file
2. Laser printer output control file
3. Article-specific font file

There are 300 separate files for fonts that could be used in any of the articles. Graphics are stored at 400 dpi, with scaling occurring as required for each output device.

The data from the typesetting tapes was formatted into a common typesetting format that the display software could handle easily.

Typesetting languages present many of the same problems that natural languages do, so programmatic translations are never totally accurate. Manual intervention is mandatory. Font and placement information was extracted at the same time as the text itself. If an article required fonts that were not in the 300 common fonts, then a file of fonts specific to that article was generated.

The three files per article were always stored adjacent to each other, since they usually are opened two at a time — sometimes all three. Since there was no way to know which articles would have the most use, no optimization of file placement in terms of hit rate was possible. The index files were large, approximately 100 Mbytes. Since these are accessed during all sessions, the best that could be done was to place them in the lower latency areas of the disc, i.e., the inner tracks.

The best form of optimization that *Graph-Text* could make use of was internal to the software. The low-level CD ROM access driver keeps all the directory and pointer information in buffers, eliminating the need to access the CD ROM more than once for such information. The retrieval and display software also have intelligent buffering algorithms whose main objective is to minimize the need to access the same information more than once directly from the disc during a single session with a particular article.

Summary: Getting Started from Scratch

Slow access time is the primary negative aspect of CD ROM that applications designers must deal with. Optimizing file structures, file placements, and file accessing algorithms are the best approaches to improving access time performance.

Some rules of thumb for design:

• Never access the disc twice, when once is enough.
• Never place a file where it slows down overall performance.
• Never structure a file so that multiple accesses are needed to get a single piece of data if it can be structured for one access.

These three rules epitomize the goals of CD ROM file design and layout. The closer a design comes to these ideals, the better the application's performance is likely to be.

Despite slow access time, CD ROM has significant strengths. Large capacities (500 Mbytes and up), and multiple data types (binary, text, audio, and video) are the primary positive aspects that designers are blessed with for CD ROM applications. Used judiciously, these attributes can make possible applications that once were only dreams.

About the Authors

Bradley Watson

Mr. Watson holds advanced degrees in library science, English literature, and computer science. He has worked as a programmer/analyst for the Air Force Logistics Command on foreign military sales systems, for Mead Data Central on LEXIS/NEXIS, and for NCR, Inc. on PC-based retail Point of Sale systems, before joining OCLC as a staff scientist for technology assessment in the Office of Technical Planning. Mr. Watson is currently pursuing a Ph.D. in English literature at The Ohio State University.

Terry Noreault

B.A., computer science, State University of New York at Oswego; Ph.D., information transfer, Syracuse University.

Before joining OCLC in 1985, Dr. Noreault was an assistant professor of information science at the University of Pittsburgh. Prior to that, he was an assistant professor in computer science at Colgate University. Dr. Noreault's research interests are in information retrieval. His published works are in the areas of ranking algorithms and efficient techniques to calculate statistical relationships between terms.

Dr. Noreault is manager of the Database Department of OCLC. He is responsible for the development of database software for the online system, currently supporting 3000 simultaneous users worldwide, and CD ROM–based systems. The CD ROM database system, Search CD450, is an information retrieval system being offered by OCLC with subscriptions to various databases such as ERIC.

Howard Turtle

B.A., English/mathematics, University of Wisconsin M.S., computer science, University of Wisconsin.

As director of the Office of Technical Planning, Mr. Turtle is responsible for technology assessment activities, coordinating work on national and international technical standards, and providing technical input to and review of OCLC development and strategic plans. His principal research interests include mass storage and information retrieval architectures, advanced processor technologies, and the implications of distributed architectures, particularly those based on OSI (Open Systems Interconnection) protocols.

Before moving to the Office of Technical Planning, Mr. Turtle was a Senior Research Scientist in the Office of Research, where he directed the Human-Computer Interaction program and was actively involved in the Electronic Document Delivery project and Distributed Processing program.

Prior to joining OCLC, Mr. Turtle was a Research Scientist at Battelle Columbus Laboratories, specializing in the design and implementation of information retrieval software and the analysis of telecommunications networks.

OCLC, Inc. (Online Computer Library Center)
6565 Frantz Road
Dublin, OH 43017
1-800-848-5878

References

Aho, A. V., J. E. Hopcraft, and J. D. Ullman (1985). *Data Structures and Algorithms*. Computer Science and Information Processing Series. Reading, Mass.: Addison-Wesley.

Bradley, J. (1982). *File and Data Base Techniques*. New York: Computer Science Series. Holt, Rinehart, and Winston.

Claybrook, B. G. (1983). *File Management Techniques*. New York: John Wiley & Sons.

Comer, D. (1979). "The Ubiquitous B-Tree." *Computing Surveys. 11* (2): 121–137.

Ullman, J. D. (1980). *Principles of Database Systems*. Computer Software Engineering Series. Potomac, Md: Computer Science Press.

10

Data Conversion: The First Step Toward Publishing On CD ROM

John W. Bottoms & Linda W. Helgerson

The big question is: Are you going to do it yourself or have somebody else do it? And, if you are going to do it yourself, do you just need a scanner or do you need a system that can reformat data or process images? What resolution do you need to scan with? Should the scanner attach to a PC or does it need its own computer. Should images be kept in bitmap form or should they be converted to vectors? The answers to these questions depend upon many factors such as the size of the system, the volume of material to be scanned and, most of all, your budget.

The processing of converting data from printed page to electronic form involves several identifiable, quantifiable steps. The manager who understands the process of identifying these steps and determin-

This chapter is reprinted by permission of Diversified Data Resources, Inc., publisher of The Scanning Sourcebook, in which this chapter appeared.

ing the outcome at each will be better able to communicate the need for resources and understand the benefits accrued from each correct decision. To facilitate the discussion we have broken our information into two sub-articles. The first is on the technical steps involved in assembling a scanning system. The second sub-article deals with the process of making or buying a scanning system.

Article I: Designing the Electronic Publishing Pipeline

One way to look at complex electronic publishing systems is to consider them as pipelines in which a significant portion of the work is performed at each stage of the pipeline. The pipeline is filled with work and stays full as long as new material is entered into the system. This approach allows the design of a cost-effective system that levels the workload peaks and cost justifies the specialized personnel to run the system.

The workstations at each point in the pipeline are optimized for a particular task. Among the tasks are: input, scanning, format conversion, verification, markup indexing and output. Some of these steps are optional, as we will see in the next section, but should be considered in their proper order.

Input Stage

The input stage of electronic publishing consists of those steps necessary to make sure that the data is received in the correct format, assure that all data is accounted for, schedules are created, and all material is available which specifies the input and output formats. The associated documentation for the Input stage should include the following:

1. Schedules
2. Material tracking forms
3. Error reports and tracking forms
4. Input/output specifications
5. Change notices and procedures

Input/output specifications should include descriptions of the format(s) that data is submitted in and complete descriptions of the changes for data as it is processed. For example, if spelling checking is required on textual data, the accuracy, percentage and reference work for spelling should be described. If the input source is from a British company, it may not make sense to use an American English dictionary or spelling program to check the spelling of words. Likewise, if the accuracy of the spelling checking is to be 100 percent and the source work is a medical document, there may be additional costs to hire a medical transcriber to check the document. Input specification should include scanning resolution if it is to be specified by the client.

Scanning

The scanning step performs the paper-to-electronic-image conversion for all types of media. The scanner used for the conversion may be a page scanner, a large blueprint scanner, or a camera which outputs images of material. Some scanners output a binary signal of black or white data for each picture element scanned. Others output a multi-level signal that can take on one of many different gray levels. Typical values for these "continuous tone" systems range from 16 to 256 gray levels for each picture element. As the data is scanned, data is accumulated in a file for each image. Usually this data file is quite large. In the simplest case at 300 dots per inch the data from a page is:

8 1/2" * 300 dpi * 11" * 300 dpi
/8 bits per byte
= 1.05 million bytes

For a large blueprint at the same resolution the figure is 16.8 million bytes. It is then easy to see that for a typical building with hundreds of blueprints, the amount of space to store the images becomes very large. However, the data is rarely stored in this form. It is usually compressed in some fashion to allow many more documents to be stored.

The resolution used in scanning determines the quality of the reproduced image compared to the original. The scanning resolution should be selected as the minimum required to produce acceptable results for the output material. For example, if the scanned material is to be processed for optical character recognition, then it is not required to scan the material beyond 300 dots per inch unless the source material is in a very fine type size. Typical type sizes of 10 to 20 points can be recognized by systems that scan at 200 dots per inch. Scanning for commercial art and typography storage may take place at 1000 to 6000 dots per inch.

The scanning stage may output images in color. The color information requires more storage space than does black and white images. Most scanners or cameras output from 5 to 8 bits of color information each, for red, green and blue colors. From these three colors all other colors can be derived, but only to the resolution that the system can represent them. For example, if a system uses 5 bits of information for each of the red, green, and blue (or RGB) data, then that is a total of 15 bits of color information. Then the system could represent each color using (or not using) each color bit. This results in a system that has 2^{15} colors or 32,768 different colors. At the upper extreme, a system that uses 8 bits for each color has a total of 24 bits for its RGB system which results in 16.8 million colors.

Thirty-two thousand colors seems like a lot, so how many are required? The answer depends upon the color requirements of the system. If the images to be scanned are real estate images of houses or commercial buildings, then color may not be a critical element as long as the buildings are presented as they look. In this case 32,000 colors should be more than enough. But if the application is for the storage of commercial graphic art that is used for the cosmetic industry, then accurate color presentation is critical and a sophisticated system with 16 million colors should be used.

Format Conversion

Format conversions take the form of data format conversions and information conversions. By data conversions we refer to the process of modifying the internal representation of information without changing the information or changing it only to a small degree. For example, the compression of an image may change some small portions of the image as an aid to compression but the overall image should be recognized as the same picture. Information conversions take place when the output information material for a conversion is not the same as the input information material. This happens when we translate a printed page of English into a printed page of French. Similar translations might be from FORTRAN into Ada or another computer programming language.

Data Conversions

The most common data conversions are string compression, image compression, color image compression, optical character recognition (OCR), and color compression. These conversions are usually performed to reduce the storage space for documents. For example simple image compressions result in typically 10:1 reductions while OCR can result in 1000:1 compressions.

Data Compression

String compression is further divided into run length coding and Huffman coding. Run length coding is the process of assigning a series of identical numbers a count. This is typically performed after scanning a drawing. If the drawing is a simple drawing, it consists of a few lines on a white paper. The white space would be read in by a scanner as a long sequence of zeros which represent the white space. If the white space consisted of 33 zeros, the number of zeros could be represented by a code such as "W33" instead of 33 zeros written out.

Huffman coding is more sophisticated because it adapts to the most common occurrences of strings. If the string of 33 zeros occurred as the most common length of white space, it could be encoded by a single character such as "#." This symbol is shorter than "W33" and coding in our example compressed 33 symbols to 1, resulting in a compression ration of 33:1.

In actual practice the resulting compression ratio is rarely a fixed value. It is dependent upon the compression technique and the statistical nature of the data being compressed. Images that have a lot of detail involving a lot of different colors will not compress to the same extent as images with lots of broad areas of the same color.

Image Compression

There are two common techniques for image compression. These are both based on standards for data representation. The first is referred to as CCITT Group III or Group IV coding. These coding techniques are run length coding techniques developed for the transmission and reception of facsimile images. Group III coding is pure run length coding of each FAX scan line.

Group IV coding takes into consideration that most of the time adjacent scan lines contain identical or nearly identical data. Increased compression usually results from the use of Group IV coding. Both of these compression techniques require significant computing time to perform the coding algorithm. Some companies have recently offered PC boards which perform these (and other more general) algorithms in specialized hardware. The second type of image compression technique is raster-to-vector conversion. This approach requires the conversion of all the picture elements in a line to the start and end points of the line. The results in greatly compressed images but it is difficult to develop the computer programs to do the conversion. First, it is difficult to determine the start and end points of a vector if the drawing is not clear. Often in scanning, lines appear to be wider than originally drawn.

And secondly, it is often confusing to try to determine the end of a line when several lines are running through the same point at nearly identical angles. This compression is often needed with engineering drawings because of their size and data storage requirements but those are also the drawings with the most exacting requirements for accuracy in the specification of vector end points.

Color Image Compression

Color image compression is extremely difficult because most images are derived from TV cameras using NTSC coding. The design approach for the NTSC results in small phase shifts of the color signal for each picture element. This was done to keep the color signal in the original TV channel which was designed for monochrome images. But the result is that each picture element resulting from the capture of an NTSC image is of a different color. The resulting image is faithful to the original image but, upon close inspection, the image can be seen to be a mosaic of many different colors that are nearly the correct color. The result is that the NTSC artifacts have introduced color noise into the picture. This noise is not noticed by the user but makes image compression more difficult.

To do compression on a color image then usually means smoothing out or averaging these colors to reduce the amount of information in the picture. Often images are filtered to reduce the effects of large areas that are the same color. Since the human eye is more interested in medium levels of detail than in small or large detail in a picture, it makes compression easier, resulting in larger compression ratios. Once the picture has been filtered, areas of the image that are similar can be grouped together and coded, usually using a Huffman code or a similar technique. In the case of pictures the Huffman coding must be two-dimensional instead of one-dimensional as used for scan lines or strings of symbols.

A feature of the human eye that determines the filtering level is the number of different colors that can be determined at a given instant. Earlier we had discussed systems that could display 16.8 million colors. That is certainly more than could fit on a display of 512 X 512 color picture elements. It is also much more than the human eye can distinguish. The issue becomes the proper number of colors to allow adequate compression without degrading the image.

Many systems allow the display of 256 colors at a given time from a palette of 16.8 million colors. This results in a very lifelike image without excessive loss of picture quality. The 256 colors to be displayed are indicated in a table referred to as a Color Look-Up Table (CLUT) and the colors must be selected to provide a faithful rendition of the original image. This is done by performing a careful selection of the colors to be selected. Usually they are weighed against the number of colors that are similar in the original image. If this is performed in software the process is slow, taking about 20 or 30 seconds before a 512 X 512 image can be displayed. Recent integrated circuits for graphics display have incorporated the CLUT algorithm in the integrated circuit resulting in fast response times for display. The hardware CLUT also allows rapid modification of the image if necessary.

Optical Character Recognition

Text that must be searched should be converted to computer codes for alphanumeric characters so that the computer can perform the necessary comparisons during the search. It also greatly reduces the storage space for the information. OCR is performed by a computer program that compares each image of a character to information known about all characters from a library. The character from the library that most resembles the the unknown character is considered a match and the computer code for that character is added to the output file.

Because of the number of comparisons that must be made in comparing characters from a wide range of size and type fonts, the OCR program must execute tens or hundreds of millions of instructions just to convert a single page of image data to characters. If the program is executing on a PC, the time may be excessive. It might be quicker or more cost effective to type the page into the system. Some systems implement the recognition program in special hardware that executes very quickly. The hardware may be contained in a special board that is added to the PC or the hardware may be resident in the scanner. Some sophisticated scanner systems contain as many as four or five computers to aid in the OCR task and while their prices may be higher than other desktop scanners they produce more accurate recognition and process data more quickly.

Most OCR programs operate on one of two principles, template matching or topology. In template matching, a comparison is made between each character image and the known image for a character. If there is a high degree of correlation between the two, then it is considered a match. This approach suffers from two problems. First the match has to be performed for many different types of fonts and sizes to be sure that the highest possible correlation is known. And, there are some cases in which the classifier is mistaken because of minor size or rotation differences.

Another technique for OCR involves the topology or optical features of a character. For example, the characters a, b, d, e, g, o, p, q all have a closed loop in them. Other characters, such as i, k, l, t, v, w, x, y, z, all are made of straight lines. By determining all the common features of characters it is possible to classify characters independent of size or even rotation. Both techniques sometimes have trouble distinguishing between "one" and the letter "l" or even the letter "i." Characters that touch are unreadable in some systems while the more expensive systems are designed to decipher them correctly.

Some of the more expensive scanners can determine characters attributes, such as "bold" or "italic." If this information is required at some later step in the publishing process, then this attribute information must be preserved. Usually, it is added to the output material at the markup stage (see below). If the scanner cannot return attribute information, it will have to be manually added by keying in the data.

Information Conversions

Some conversions are merely substitutions of data which result in a new database. Typical of this transformation are conversions from Celsius to Fahrenheit temperature. Other conversions involve more sophisticated processing which reflects an understanding of the basic rules of a particular grammar. An example might be translation from English to French. These two types of transformations are referred to as "data record" and "content" conversions.

Data Record Conversions

There are times in which the data being prepared is tabular data that must be modified before it can be used. One option to perform the conversion is to import the data, after it has been scanned, into a database system. The database system should be selected that can import the data easily and easy to use for modifying data formats. Then, using the database system, convert the data to the new form and write it out. It may also be just as easy to write a program as to perform the conversion, but this depends upon the level of complexity of the conversion. It may be necessary to break the data into common types to perform the conversion, and this process of breaking the data up can simplify the process considerably.

Content Conversions

If the data is to have modifications made to it beyond the simple conversion of a database format, then other methods become necessary. Simple find and replace functions can be performed by most word processors and some feature find and replace functions that work on regular pattern replacements. If the data is very large or if the modifications are done on a regular basis, it may be necessary to write a program that recognizes the data structure and makes changes based on the structure and content. This type of program is called a "parser" and useful for very powerful types of processing. One type of parser, a compiler, is used for converting programming languages to assembly or machine language. Others are being developed to convert between English and foreign languages.

Verification

The degree of verification of the output data significantly affects the project cost because of the high degree of human involvement. The electronic publishing pipeline should be designed to minimize human involvement at all stages including this one. The only elements that should be left to the human should be those that a computer is not able to check. For the 100% correct OCR of text, the normal procedure is to scan the material twice, have it corrected by a spelling program, perform checking of each copy by a human and then compare the two resulting copies. Experience with the electronic publishing system performance and the quality of the material can often be used to predict the quality of the output product.

If the input material is of high enough quality for a high- end OCR system, the output material may be close to 99.95% The accuracy of drawings can be checked but true verification involves a draftsman or engineer sitting with each drawing, verifying that dimensions are correct and that the total of the related dimensional figures make sense. Scanning may introduce overall image compression or expansion along one of the axis and careful attention must be paid to its effects. Verification of color images is difficult but reflecting densitometers could be used as a final check on the process.

Document Markup

After text material has been scanned and converted to computer codes, it may be necessary to add markup to the document to aid in the publishing process. Markup in the broadest senses falls into three categories:

• Processing markup
• Structure markup
• Content markup

Processing markup refers to the addition to the material of commands that control the printing of the material using a "smart" printing system. The printing commands may control gray scale, type size and fonts, or graphics commands. Most laser printers and many page printers contain some ability for processing printing commands. Adobe's specification, PostScript, and Xerox's Interpress are two examples of complete processing markup systems.

Structure markup refers to the additional information added to a manuscript to indicate the start and end of chapters, sections, paragraphs, and other structural elements. Structural markup contains more information about a document than does processing markup and it has evolved out of the typography and printing industries. There are now international and American standards for markup. The American standard has been adopted for the markup of documents that are placed on optical discs.

Some applications require more information than is provided by structural markup. It may be necessary to identify exactly the contents of a particular chapter. In this case content markup can be used to identify structural elements by name. For example, in a company profile, one element might indicate the company history, while another might indicate the financial section.

One type of markup that is popular today allows the user to trace references through a document without using the index. This type of lateral browsing, referred to most often as "Hypertext" is a type of structural markup like footnotes and footnote references. During the publishing process, these links between different portions of the document must be indicated. Upon presentation for the user there must be a means of following the links through the document.

Classification

Before documents can be stored in a library, there should be some thought given to the structure of the library and how users are going to find specific documents. It is not sufficient to assume that the computer is going to search all the documents in the library for the information. The search of all the documents in a library unit or "jukebox" may take hours while a selective search of a few or just one document may be done in seconds. The classification step should provide the ability to determine the type of document that is to be stored away and to assign a system identifier to it and a location for it within the logical and physical system.

In a classic paper in 1985, Blair and Maron pointed out that full text retrieval in the systems examined resulted in the retrieval of less than than 16 percent (on average) of the documents relevant to a particular search. In the study cited, these researchers studied the use of full text retrieval in a system with a large number of documents constituting over 350,000 pages of text. Today, despite the accurate reporting of this study, full text retrieval is being performed on CD ROM and optical discs in much the same manner as reported in the study.

What Blair and Maron were stating is that when a search is performed across a large number of documents that have been accumulated in a document database, there is an inverse relationship between the precision of the search query and the successful retrieval relationship of information. Simply put, if you are very precise in framing a query, then the document retrieval system may not return all relevant documents. If the query is too broad, the user is flooded with a large number of responses.

In order to cope with the poor response characteristics of these types of systems, the full text retrieval vendors have developed creative approaches to allow users to correctly locate desired information. Proximity searches have been used to determine if the words in a query are located near each other in the source document before notifying the user of a successful response.

Another approach creates statistics about word usage. Statistical retrieval systems weigh the number of occurrences of the words in a query to determine if the words in the response documents are being used in the way words are typically used. Both of these approaches have achieved some improvement in response but the basic problem remains.

At a recent trade show I watched a demonstration of a full text retrieval system. The vendor mentioned to observers how hard the system was working as it searched for the requested information. He proudly pointed to the screen which indicated that there were over 35,000 responses to the query and he then entered further qualifying information to reduce the number of query responses. This was repeated several times and each time the number of responses diminished until there were just a few which could easily be browsed. In this demonstration the initial query took about 20 seconds and the entire query process took over a minute. The vendor once again proudly indicated the power at the user's fingertips for searching a very large body of information.

The system demonstrated used the same approach as many other systems on the market. These systems have very poor response times when compared with most interactive systems and their accuracy figures are poor. In systems such as these, database responses are qualified blindly by the user without seeing the data, because it would be impossible to browse across the vast ocean of responses.

This is not unlike walking into a library and asking the librarian to show you all occurrences in the library in which word A was within a five word proximity of word B. She would probably look at you silently for just a second before politely asking if you knew how to use the card catalog. If she were to try to fulfill your request, the library would have to hire teams of librarians to roam across the book stacks searching for word combinations. Instead, libraries do not try to do searches across unstructured databases. The books are arranged in shelves and stacks which reflect the structure used by the library.

Returning to Blair and Maron's paper for a minute, let's find out how we got led down this garden path of searching for information in large unstructured databases in an unstructured fashion. The findings of this classic paper were precisely correct but the results should be restated. The results should have been stated thus: "If a search is performed at the word level across a large unstructured document database, the results will always be poor." What we have done by allowing users to put unrelated information together on an optical disc is to repeat the sins of the early 1970s when users felt that if they could move their book-keeping system to a computer, their accounting problems would be solved. Instead, the accounting problems remained and the use of the computer simply compounded the problems.

We cannot expect full text retrieval to solve the problem of the poorly organized filing cabinet. We should not let ourselves believe that users will embrace CD ROM systems when searches are being done blindly and response times are on the order of 15 seconds or even minutes. The same tight requirements of 1- to 2-second responses should apply to optical disc applications as well as hard disk applications. The user has little comprehension of how much information 550 Mbytes is and cannot appreciate the number of machine cycles required to search this volume of information.

In order to alleviate this problem, the electronic publisher needs tools for putting storage information on a document before it is placed into the database. This information should be appended to the document much like the numbers on the spine of a library book. Then retrieval systems could be developed which allow searches in the same way one uses a library. Documents could be grouped according to the same filing system used in the reference system, whether it is a library or corporate office. If the reference system is a corporate file cabinet, then the user should search just office memos for an interpersonal reference rather than having to pay a penalty for searching across technical manuals as well as memos.

Retrieval systems should have a facility to restrict searches to one or two sections of the library rather than having to search every book or document type in the library. Users should see the responses of queries immediately before qualifying the search further. Structured browses can then be performed in less than a second, giving users responses that are typical of today's interactive systems.

Indexing

Because typical electronic publishing systems deal with large amounts of material, it is important to consider the storage and retrieval aspects of controlling the information. Often it is sufficient to place the final document in a particular place, with a corresponding entry in a system catalog as to its location. However, if the information is to be later searched using full text searches, then it may be necessary to perform the database indexing or "inversion" before it is stored away. Indexing all the words and references to images in a document may take as much as 1 hour/Mbyte of source material. For systems handling data that is intended for storage on a library unit or "jukebox," the use of a dedicated machine for indexing may be required.

Final Output Formatting

After the documents have been placed into their final form one last step remains to complete the process. The output media determines the type of final processing. If the output is to paper, then the markup needs to be converted to typography codes so that a composition program can be executed to create the page layout necessary for printing. If the output is to an optical disc then formatting is necessary for the particular type of disc. If the output disc is a CD ROM then a High Sierra Group (now DIS 9660) directory is created to hold the documents. Other file formats may be necessary for 8-, 12- or 14-inch write-once disks. All due effort should be made to store the documents in electronic form along with their electronic publishing markup, whatever it may be.

Article II — Procuring Systems and Services

Determining the "Make" versus "Buy" Decision

The first step in the process of transferring data from the printed page to electronic form involves determining who is going to perform the work. Another term for this decision process is the "Make-Buy" decision. This phase is another way of stating that the electronic publisher has three choices. First, the publisher can select to buy and integrate the components ("Make" the system) that are needed for the conversion effort. Second, the publisher can purchase ("Buy") the entire system as a complete package. Or, the publisher could contract with a service bureau to perform the conversion effort. The first two decisions result in an in-house conversion operation. The obvious factors involved in making this kind of decision involve the traditional business concerns necessary to justify the decision. These typically include:

- Skills of the technical staff
- Cost of the conversion approach
- Length of time to project completion
- Size of the project
- Capital available for equipment purchases

Making the Decision Based on Extraneous Influencing Factors

In addition, there are often underlying, nonverbalized influencing factors that should be considered. The influencing factors are important and should be recognized early in order to understand what the selection team is experiencing. These factors may be subtle, such as the opinions of someone in the car-pool, or they may be very coercive, such as political pressure to award a contract to an industry insider.

These lobbying efforts usually appear early in the project, just after the project becomes public knowledge. In addition, early in the decision making process there probably is a good idea of the approach that will be followed to handle the volume and type of data. For example, if there are only a few documents to be processed, then contracting with a service bureau is probably the most cost-effective solution. If the president's nephew is in the business of selling scanning equipment, perhaps the decision is already made. Or, if the scanning equipment is unique to an in-house CAD system, then the decision may be predetermined.

Areas to be avoided are emotional appeals to buy or lease equipment based on nonobjective influences such as:

1. The sales rep was in my engineering class at school and he's a nice guy.
2. They are located right down the street so service has got to be great (or at least convenient).
3. If you buy this firm's system they will throw in the database management system and the report generator at no charge.
4. The sales rep that sells you tapes also sells scanners so you can buy all you need from one person.
5. The discount for the unit is 50 percent and that's a lot.
6. The vendor really cares about us, they take us to the ballgames.

Whatever situation the company is in — and every company has these pressures — it will have some influence in determining the "Make/Buy/Contract" decision. It is best if managers identify those factors and address them before attempting to select a course of action.

Make: Assembling a System

The "Make" decision involves assembling the equipment for scanning, along with all the software elements necessary to make the system operate smoothly. This approach requires a technical staff that can solve the time-consuming problems of interfacing hardware and software together. This approach is warranted in one of two situations. The first is a situation in which there are a very large number of documents to be scanned, probably in the hundreds of thousands of pages. The other is the situation in which the number of types of documents is small, such as business size documents (8 1/2 X 11 inch).

The "Make" decision poses the most difficult problems for a firm in terms of time and skills, and the publisher should be sure that the situation indicates this direction is justified, in a business sense, before embarking on this approach. If this course is selected but a strong in-house technical staff is not available, then consultants or contract engineers will be needed to aid in the integration effort.

The steps involved in the "Make" decision include:

• Developing a system specification
• Identifying hardware
• Procuring hardware
• Developing software
• Integration and testing

Buy: Purchasing a Complete System

The "Buy" approach is useful for those that find themselves lacking in-house technical staff but that anticipate a large number of documents to be processed on a regular basis. The fact that a system vendor has already solved the technical problems of systems integration means the user can get on with the task of conversion without having to worry about the most severe development and interfacing problems. This approach is not warranted when document conversion involves frequent custom services, such as those that are required to process many different types of documents or those in which the electronic output formats are diverse. In other words, a "Buy" decision is warranted if the data to be converted is extensive and uniform.

The steps in procuring a system include:

• Developing a system specification
• Identifying systems
• Procuring the system
• System installation
• Acceptance testing

Contract: Hiring a Service Bureau

The "Contract" decision is useful for those companies that have a one-time project or a series of one-time projects to convert a number of documents, or when the conversion involves a type of formatting that will not be repeated. Situations include those in which the electronic data output is to a seldom-used optical disc format or when special image processing is required. The "Contract" decision consists, for the most part, of determining the user requirements, selecting a data conversion firm with the appropriate capabilities, and conveying the users requirements to the service bureau.

The steps involved in contracting with the service bureau include:

• Developing a system specification
• Identifying engineering firms
• Selecting the service bureau
• Transferring source material
• Evaluating the response

System Procurement Issues

There are some administrative issues that arise in all three approaches for procuring a scanning system or service. To avoid repetition in the discussions of the various procurement procedures, these issues are discussed collectively.

The Bottom-Up Estimate

In order to determine if there are sufficient funds to complete a project, an initial spending estimate must be made. Make a quick determination of the system design based on the approach that has been identified. If the resulting figure is not close to the amount of money budgeted for the project then the system design should be reconsidered. Alternatives should then be explored to lower system costs. This can be achieved through trading off capital expenditures against increased labor costs which result in lower costs. Off-shore keypunching could be considered to lower labor costs and equipment leasing can reduce capital equipment expenditures.

Estimating the Labor Effort

A first cut should also be taken to estimate the expertise needed to complete the project, i.e., operate the data conversion process. If additional expertise is required, it may be necessary to find a consultant to support the project on a temporary basis or to train in-house personnel, for example. Skills to be identified in the labor effort estimate should include engineering skills necessary for providing hardware compatibility for equipment, software compatibility, and technical management personnel who understand the data management aspects of the system.

Identifying Technical Expertise Concerns

Like the preliminary spending estimate, there should also be a preliminary estimate of the technical expertise required for assembling a system. If the goal is to put together a simple scanning system that reads page images into a PC, then the work can be performed by most office workers with initial training and then telephone support from the dealer or manufacturer. Complex systems that require the integration of many software and hardware components will require a full-time person dedicated to the integration task. If the system integration requires more personnel time than is available, a different approach should be explored to provide technical expertise. Avenues for exploration include borrowing personnel from other departments or hiring temporary contracting engineering or computer science personnel.

Professional Job Descriptions

The tasks for each job title should be identified before those positions are filled. The following are brief descriptions of three of the job titles:

System Design Engineer. The system design engineer (SDE) shall be responsible for the system design and architecture. He (she) shall develop all system and component specifications and assure that these specifications meet the previously developed user specifications. The SDE shall evaluate vendor responses to the Request for Proposal and shall develop system acceptance test plans for the system and components acceptance. The SDE shall be responsible for all software and hardware interface control specifications, maintenance procedures, system software specifications, and system operational procedures. The SDE shall maintain a log of all system design and performance issues during procurement and implementation and shall assure that all technical aspects of issues are resolved.

Consultants. The consultant shall provide design assistance to the system design engineer as required. He (she) shall be responsible for the development of white papers that provide a design approach that solves a particular problem or resolves an outstanding design issue.

System Programmer. The system programmer shall be responsible for converting software design specifications into computer language codes as defined by system software procedures. He (she) shall also be responsible for the development of the loading and operating procedures and the software test plans and procedures necessary to verify the execution of the computer programs.

Identifying New Requirements

During the process of obtaining a new system, there may be new requirements that are recommended by vendors or that are discovered by the publisher for inclusion in the system specification. Each of these recommendations should be examined closely to determine its utility relative to the original charter of the system. The acid test for each new requirement is:

Will the system absolutely not work without obtaining this new requirement?

If the answer is that the system will not work without the additional requirement then it should be included; otherwise, it may be considered for inclusion as a "nice to have" item in the specification or added later when the system is operational.

Initial Cost Estimating

Make a quick estimate of the costs for each component. This estimate will be used to make sure the system will be within the projected budget. Be sure and include all the hardware and software components. Most system component costs can be determined from the source product hardware and software sections of this book. Make a list of each of the items to be purchased. Total these figures and see if they are within 20 percent of the desired budget. If not, it is time to either rethink the basic design approach, lower the requirements, or see if there is a more creative way to design the system which results in lower system costs.

Initial Requirements Specification

One factor that is common to all "Make-Buy" system approaches is the need that for the volume of data to be processed be estimated accurately. With this determination it is impossible to select the needed equipment or talk with service bureaus in an informed manner. To determine the volume of material to be processed within a routine period, start by listing all the types of documents to be scanned, their size, some information about the number of characters or images on each page, and the total number of each particular page size. For each document type list the anticipated number of characters, vectors, and images. For example, if you are going to scan microfiche and business documents, make the following list:

24 X microfiche
8 1/2 X 11 inch (blow-back size)
1200 chars/page
1200 pages/day

If you are going to work with D-sized drawings then the list should reflect the volume:

D-sized drawing
300 vectors/page
500 chars/page
50 drawings/day

The list should be in a spreadsheet format, should include all page types and should include columns for adding the data volume for each page type. There should also be different columns for adding the number of characters on a page and the number of drawings lines (or vectors) on a page. A page count for each type of page should be included so the total number of each type of information element can be calculated. After all the basic information is listed in your spreadsheet, go to the columns which indicate the total volumes, perform the calculations for each page type volume, and add the totals for each type of information format.

For example, if you have listed both B- and D-sized drawings with a corresponding number of documents/day, and they have a number of vectors/document, then multiply the figures to get the number of vectors/day for each document type, and then add up all the vectors for all the document types. Do the same for images and characters. (Include illustration of spreadsheet.)

Once all the figures have been listed and totaled you should have a good idea of the volume of work the system must be capable of handling. It is a good idea to include a figure for margin of safety in your calculation. For most systems this figure should be about 20 percent, but for some large systems it might be as much as 50 percent.

Final Requirements Specifications

After the system performance figures have been assembled, whether the data conversion effort is a "Make" or "Buy" decision, a plan — knows as system requirements — is required. These requirements are extracted from the spreadsheet list of system and component features. For the system requirements, write down each of the features that is attractive for your operation. Next indicate an order of importance for each of the features indicating those that are (1) absolutely required, (2) should be included, or (3) would be nice to have. Reorder the list and review the priorities. In your discussions with vendors or service bureaus, insist only on those items that are absolutely required. Discuss the other features, but only when they are offered at no cost or at next to no cost.

This list should include system or equipment features necessary to provide compatibility with existing equipment or user operation. Among these features are items such as:

- Environmental requirements
- User interface requirements
- Processing throughput requirements
- Physical and logical interface requirements

Procurement requirements are best stated as required items; for example, "The system shall operate on an average voltage of 115 Volts dc." The use of "shall" makes it easy to determine whether a product meets the requirement or not. Each requirement should consist of a positively stated requirement containing the word "shall" or "must."

Avoid ambiguity in stating requirements. If there are system or component features that are desirable or which can be exercised at the vendor's discretion, then the desirability of those feature should be stated as desired options. This is done by using "may" in the procurement specification. An example might be: "The component chassis may be light or dark blue, but it shall not be green." Keep a list of all requirements; it will be used later to score the responses of each of the vendors.

Examples of correctly stated requirements include:

• The modem shall transmit at 1200 bits/second.
• The unit shall be capable of running on supplied power of 110 Volts ac plus or minus 5 percent.

Incorrect specifications include those which may be interpreted in various ways. Examples include:

• The modem shall transmit at 1200 bits/second or faster. (Is 1205 bits/second desirable or was the intent to allow 2400 bits/second?)
• The unit shall be capable of running on supplied power of 110 or 220 Volts ac plus or minus 5 percent. (Was the intent to operate with only one of the two voltages or was it to have the unit work with both, at different times?)

Final Cost Estimates

Final cost estimates should be closely in line with the initial cost estimate prepared at the beginning of the project. If there are significant differences, the funding level to cover the differences should be discussed. The final cost estimate is used as a final check on the procurement process to assure that the vendors providing bids on equipment understand the requirements in the same manner as the client. This also gives the client the opportunity to do a line-by-line comparison of the equipment and services to be supplied by each vendor.

System Technical Issues

During the system design process there will be technical issues to be considered that affect system performance and that have a significant impact on system cost. Each of these should be carefully considered and, if necessary, additional assistance should be sought. Some of these issues include:

* Average versus peak loading
* Component costs erosion curves
* Converting back files
* Levels of verification
* Hardware/software trade-offs
* Indexing
* Minimizing labor
* Modifications
* Pipeline backup and overflow
* Segmentation
* Information Standards

Average Versus Peak Loading

The data that will be passing through the system will not be at a constant level. At times it will be heavy; while at other times there may be just a trickle. The capacity that the system is designed to handle also determines the system's ability to handle this fluctuating data load, and in then, it also affects system cost. If the system is designed to handle the heaviest estimated load, then costs will be at a maximum. A system designed to handle a light load will cause most of the work to wait, but will minimize costs.

One generally accepted approach is to design for an average system load and then work backwards to identify ways to smooth out the workload that the system is expected to handle. This averaging process can be accomplished through rigorous scheduling of work, offering lower costs to users for longer turnaround times, or staffing additional shifts during the evenings or on weekends. Each of these trade-off has its own costs, and these costs should be examined and compared with the costs of a system designed for higher or maximum throughput.

Component Costs

In order for an in-house conversion facility or service bureau to stay competitive and offer the best services at the least cost, it is often desirable to obtain the latest, most efficient technology. And, while these new technical developments in hardware and software may offer direct cost savings, their costs may be at a premium when they are first introduced or until competitive systems are introduced. Additional products enter the market and cause prices to slide. An "erosion curve" is predictable. Sometimes, the vendor can offer projections on prices 6 months or a year from the date of consideration. Substantial savings can be realized by delaying purchases until the item is absolutely needed, waiting for the introduction of competitive products or when the premium paid for an early purchase is less than the savings realized from an early procurement.

Converting Back Files

It is often desirable to convert the old files or "back files" to be compatible with the newer data that is added to the system. This decision adds substantial time and dollar investments for this type of conversion. In actual practice, it is usually only necessary to convert 10 percent to 30 percent of the older files. An attempt should be made to identify the critical portion of the back files to see if savings can be realized through partial conversion.

Levels of Verification

Verification is one of the most expensive portions of the publishing pipeline because it is usually labor intensive; it is however, a necessity. Some types of checking can be automated. If the underlying rules of grammar can be specified (or there are programs already available within an industry that accomplish this), then a parser can be used for verification. A parser could be used as a proofing system to check a book's structure against a publisher's style guide.

Hardware/Software Trade-offs

In selecting system components, there are trade-offs that can be made between hardware and software that provide for flexibility between the rate of capital expenditures versus the system performance. For example, the OCR function can be performed in software at a slower rate, but with a lower capital cost. A low-cost OCR system can be purchased, at the expense of additional cost in keypunching, if that trade-off is attractive. Data can be moved between machines on floppy disks or magnetic tapes as opposed to capital expenditures for the purchase of a local area network (LAN). Each of the system components should be examined for possible savings if the budget is tight.

Data Indexing

There is no one indexing approach that will work for all possible applications. Some are more efficient in terms of speed while others are more conservative of storage space. The system designer should look carefully at the overhead in terms of system storage space and machine cycles in determining the indexing approach. The system architecture will also determine the type of indexing: (1) a structured or unstructured data storage facility, (2) short files stored in quickly accessible locations, or (3) larger files which take longer to retrieve.

Minimizing Labor

Some scanning devices are designed to accept autofeed adapters. These scanner additions reduce the manual labor necessary to keep them active. Likewise, there are often network interfaces for some input devices which will reduce the human time necessary to move data from one system to another.

Modifications

In the performance of in-house publishing services there are often requests that are made for specialized publishing services. In electronic publishing they are most often centered around the acceptance of data formats or interface of hardware which is different from that of the publishing system. Modification requests should be reviewed

with the same scrutiny that was applied to original system requirements.

Pipeline Backup and Overflow

The electronic pipeline shares some characteristics with its analog,
the real pipeline. When the pipeline is empty, it must be primed to
get data flowing, and when the pipeline gets plugged, there must be
an effort to clear the blockage. Contingency plans must always be
available to identify the process for starting and/or continuing the
flow through the pipeline. If the pipeline gets clogged due to an excess amount of data, then additional data processing equipment and
human resources must be made available to cope with the blockage
and allow data to start flowing again.

Segmentation

The large volumes of data available in some corporations results in
more data than can fit on a single optical disc. The decision then is
to use additional discs. Once this decision is made, a further decision
must be made as to how the data is to be segmented across the
several discs. For example, corporate records could be segmented by
year, by divisional group, by subject matter — alphabetically, or by
some other figure of merit, such as gross revenues or geographic
location. The segmentation decision affects many different types of
users and the option selected should consider the needs of all users.

Information Standards

System designers should attempt to design to industry standards.
The use of standards results in compatibility within the company or
agency, lower costs, reliability, and less "finger pointing" when
problems arise. Standards in the following areas should be examined
for use:

• Device physical and logical interface
• Electronic document markup
• Image compression algorithm

- Image file format
- Optical disc directory and file structure

Make: The Top-Down Design Stage

This section is for those who feel qualified to assemble a system, provide the computer programming necessary for operation, and bring the system to operation with a minimum amount of outside technical support.

Developing a System Specification

The system specification should be a compendium of the needs of the users within the company for the scanning system. It should be carefully pruned to include just those items that are minimum requirements for operation. The system will soon evolve with appropriate bells and whistles over time as the requirements grow. It is most important to get the system working first; embellishments can occur at some later date. By implementing a minimum system first, there is much valuable experience gained which is useful at a later time.

Identifying Hardware

Now you are ready to determine the kinds of equipment necessary to complete your system. Using the Scanning Sourcebook or magazines that have articles or reviews of systems, identify at least three vendors for each piece of equipment and, if possible, get as many as six or seven. List their addresses, phone numbers and the type of equipment they manufacture. This Scanning Sourcebook is designed to assist you with this step. If a vendor does not manufacture the desired equipment make a note to determine if they are an authorized agent of the manufacturer and whether the manufacturer or the agent will provide warranty service through the agent.

Once the list has been assembled, contact the vendors and ask them for literature about the scanning products that you have identified. At this point they will try to ask you questions to determine exactly what you are doing so they can help you further. Do not give any specific information about your project at this step. Simply state that you are at the initial planning stage, and are just gathering product information. If they insist on learning about your project, or want to come to visit, tell them that you are assembling a list of vendors for a competitive bid and that further contact is not allowed.

Do not sign any contractual or nondisclosure agreements at this time. Before long you should start receiving information from each of the scanner vendors. If you do not receive information from each of the vendors within 3 weeks, call them back and remind them that they must send the information requested in order to be included in the consideration process.

As the product literature arrives, read it all thoroughly and determine for each type of scanner (i.e.,for a particular document type) the product features that you think are important. If the volume of data conversion material is particularly high, then throughput and ease of service may be important. If the volume is small, then ease of use and user training may be more important.

After you have read the literature, list the features or aspects of all the products that you think are important. This list is going to become the standard for evaluating all the vendors' products. It is best to keep the requirements as broad as possible. For example, if the speed of a printer is to be at least 100 characters per second, then do not state that the requirement "shall be 100 characters per second." This excludes those printers that are capable of printing at 120 characters per second. In general, if the list is too restrictive, then there will only be one or two vendors in each product category and you will not have the broad choice of vendors that you need. This list is now referred to as the user requirements specification.

Selecting Equipment

Using the requirements list, indicate for each product whether the product meets your requirements or not. Remember that requirements are just that, they are required. If the requirement contains a numeric value, indicate the vendor's offering as a numeric value also. For example, if, for a specification called "sheet feed," one vendors literature says "yes" while the other indicates "100 page stack," put down the quantity "100 pages" and then plan on filling in the data for the other vendor during further investigation. You may find that some vendors only list a few of the specifications that are important to you and a phone call may be needed to fill out the list.

When you have finished the product summary list, it can be used to "read across" all the vendor's specifications to determine which ones best meet your needs. If you want to get very analytical, you can assign weights to each of the categories and add up the scores to rank each of the vendors. Usually, that is not important unless the products are very similar to each other.

Some product's performance figures are difficult to specify. This occurs, for example, when trying to specify the optical character recognition capabilities of a text scanner. Many scanners can correctly identify characters that are printed by a laser printer but some have trouble with even the first copy off a duplicating machine. For these kinds of circumstances, you may want to ask the vendor for a demonstration and for the demonstration, take real samples of your own material to be scanned.

If your scanning requirements are very extensive, pay particular attention to the throughput specifications for each product. Often the figures are stated under very specific conditions which may not reflect your work environment. Ask the vendor if this figure for throughput refers to peak or average throughput. If the purchase is a critical purchase — for a large piece of equipment, for example — or if you are buying several of the same pieces of equipment then you may want to request a demonstration of the throughput. Again, bring your own material and use the same material for all demonstrations.

Procuring Hardware

The final act in the decision process is to review the whole process with decision makers and assure that the company will be comfortable with the final decision. The culture of any company figures in here. Does the company typically buy complex systems at one time, or are systems acquired in pieces with the company growing into the larger, more complex versions over time? Is this a one time purchase or will the system continue to grow across several years? Each of these questions must be considered for any one company to be comfortable with the recommendation.

When the final selection has been made, it is submitted to upper management for final review, to the legal authorities, and to the finance department for proofing and finally to the purchasing department for procurement.

Developing Scanning System Software

A full discussion of software development is beyond the scope of this article but a few pointers may be in order. Software development should be closely tied to the environment that the program is to be used in. When possible, programs should be broken into simple tasks that can be tested on an operational test system before being integrated into the production system. Programming efforts requiring more than a man year may require the assistance of experienced software development specialists.

If the staff is not available in house for this effort it may be possible to locate a software product that is similar to that required and then contract to have the software modified. Before embarking on the task of developing a program that requires additional staff, consider the decision carefully. Once software development is started in house it is difficult to live without the immediate availability of a programming staff.

Integration and Testing

Integration and testing plans should be built into the design and development of the system. This process consists of assembling the various hardware and software components to make sure that they interface correctly. "Testing" refers to final system testing to assure that the system output meets the output specification.

Buy: Purchasing a Complete System

Developing a System Specification

If expertise is not available in house to assemble a system then buying a system is a good choice. The first step in procuring a system is to develop a system specification. This step should be performed the same as Initial Requirements Specifications and Final Requirements Specifications above. Because it is more difficult to get a match between systems than between components, list just the minimum performance requirements for the system operation. This helps ensure that the system specification is not overly restrictive resulting in a set of requirements that cannot be met. Do not attempt to specify how the system will perform to meet the requirement. For example, when writing the system specification, it is better to indicate the system throughput without attention to manpower required to operate the system. The manpower requirements for system operation should be considered in a separate step after it has been determined that all systems under consideration meet the minimum performance requirements.

Identifying Systems

Systems can be identified by reading the "Systems" section of this Sourcebook, by attending trade shows, and by combing trade journals for the scanning and electronic publishing markets. Again, avoid getting deep into discussions with vendors until you have a specification and then treat all the vendors exactly the same. If you give one vendor a tour of your facilities, be sure to offer the same amenities to other vendors. Do not let vendors monopolize your time or they will prevent you from listening to presentations from others.

Procuring the System

Procuring a system should not be significantly different from procuring services or system components, with the exception of the requirement for interfacing with other systems and/or departments. If the system is tied in to other departments' systems within the company, then those departments should be part of the specification review process. Once their inputs have been made a part of the system specification, there should be little involvement with those departments during the procurement process. Their opinions (and therefore their sign-offs) should be captured within the system specification. Changes in the specification that may be negotiated during the procurement process should be discussed with those departments if it varies significantly from the original. As long as system requirements are met, how they are achieved is (or should not be) an issue for other departments.

System Installation

System installation includes the delivery, connection, and initial testing, debugging, and operation of the system. Usually, the vendor is required to execute a series of tests that indicate the system is operational before the installation is considered completed. Make a schedule for the installation that indicates the resources to be supplied to the vendor for the unloading and installation process. The installation checklist should include power, lighting, and space requirements, designated unloading area, technical point of contact during the installation, and other company facilities as required for the hosting of visiting guests.

Acceptance Testing

Once the system is installed the customer gets to watch the vendor perform the approved suite of acceptance tests. The test suite should be reviewed and approved beforehand so that everyone understands the limits of the test and understands that the tests are representative of the final system specification. Prior to the acceptance testing, there should be an understanding, between parties, as to the definition of "failure" and "success" in passing the acceptance testing phase as well as the time period allowed to remedy system failures. Vendors are usually given three opportunities to perform the acceptance tests. If the vendor's system cannot pass in the given number of opportunities, the vendor usually has a fixed period of time to repair the system before it must be removed by the vendor at vendor expense, or it is designated that it is removed immediately following the third failure. This should be stipulated in the purchase order or purchase contract.

Contract: Let Someone Else Scan It

Identifying Service Bureaus

The companies that provide scanning services advertise in trade periodicals and attend the trade shows for the electronic publishing and optical disk markets. Often, companies that sell components or systems will be willing to provide scanning services as well. Most companies that provide optical disk data preparation services also offer scanning services.

Selecting a Service Bureau

Provide samples of the material to be scanned, the time requirements for the documents to be scanned along with specifications for the data output format(s) to each of the companies being considered for scanning services. Each of the samples packets supplied to the service bureaus should be identical to allow a basis for comparison. Define in the request for proposal that all the services will be required. If this is not explicitly stated, some companies may provide the services that are the most attractive for them, leaving the more difficult problems undone.

Evaluating the Proposals

Once responses have been received, narrow the candidates to two or three and perform a pilot test. Deliver the same material to all candidates and then evaluate the response time and quality of results. Finally, select the service bureau that provides the best service.

Submitting Material to Service Bureaus

To clearly state the delivery format for material to be scanned, an output specification is needed. The output specification should be developed before submitting material to a service bureau it describes the media, format, times, and other pertinent information about the delivery formats. A sample of output specifications appear below.

Text Output Specifications

All text not associated with graphics or artwork shall be delivered using ASCII codes. Text shall be shall be delivered using either 7 or 8 bits of each ASCII character. Parity shall not be used and the parity bit shall be set to a constant value. The accuracy for conversion of text material shall be less than one character error per 1000 characters of ASCII output text. Each chapter of textual material shall be placed in a separate file on a 5 1/4-inch IBM PC compatible double density (720-kbyte) floppy diskette. Chapters shall be placed in sequence on floppy disks using multiple diskettes as necessary.

Images Format Specifications

Images shall be scanned at a resolution of 300 dots per inch. Each illustration on a page shall be compressed using CCITT Group II compression algorithm and placed in a file on an IBM PC compatible, double density (720-kbyte) floppy disk. Image files shall be placed in sequence, by file name, on floppy diskettes, using multiple diskettes as necessary. A master image list shall be provided by the service bureau that indicates the floppy diskette number and file name that corresponds to each illustration number from the source document. The list shall be ordered by source illustration number.

Scenarios for Procurement

Single Desktop Scanner

Desktop scanner systems are available that are easily interfaced with PCs. All come with complete instructions that an office worker can understand. Some require the addition of a PC board to the PC while others interface with the serial port. Before purchasing a unit, ask to see a demonstration, and take the time to learn to operate the system during an in-depth demonstration. If possible, operate the unit, performing all the initial program loading and actually scanning several pages of paper. By doing this with several systems, it is possible to identify the desirable and undesirable features of a system.

Don't be shy about taking sample material for such a demonstration, taking samples of work that is typical of that to be scanned in your facility. Don't expect OCR systems to faithfully read the twelfth photocopy of a page that was shredded in the mail. Even the most expensive system will have trouble with that one. Take samples that are typed on typewriters and laser printers for testing. You may want to make a copy of one that is slightly tilted (no more than 5°) to see the effect on the OCR programs.

Once a purchase is made, be sure and fill out the warranty registration card and get the name and phone number of the customer service department in case there are problems installing or operating the unit.

Images and Text Systems ("A" size)

Systems that are designed to store 8 1/2 X 11 inch pages are typically used in commercial offices. These systems typically perform OCR, which provides the user a savings benefit because of the reduction in cost compared to the cost of storing images of pages. To provide the most cost-effective storage solution it should be determined if the system used for scanning can also be used for the retrieval and display of the scanned material. If possible, separate these various units into groups optimized for particular functions.

If the display unit is only to be used occasionally for viewing images, then CGA/EGA displays may be sufficient. If the display function is to be viewed for long time periods, then full page sized monitors that display 150 dots per inch, or more, should be considered. For applications that have limited distribution (in terms of the number of copies) of a large volume of material the use of write once optical disks should be considered. Generally, if there are more than 100 copies of the image and text material, then CD ROM should be used, for it is more cost effective than write-once discs for large quantities.

Because of the large storage space required for drawings, these systems often include write once disks and large amounts of hard disk space. Review the storage capacities available of the different systems in terms of the number of images and pages that can be stored on the media.

Drawings Systems ("B" through "F")

Most of the systems for larger drawing sizes require significant amounts of disk space. This means that they are generally complete systems that include scanner, computer, and hard disks. These systems should be procured as any scanning system by preparing a system specification of requirements which is then submitted to the vendors under consideration. Visits to vendors' facilities to observe the system in operation is almost a requirement for these types of systems.

Aperature Cards Systems

Aperature card scanners are available from only a couple of companies. Since the cards are generally used for the storage of drawings, system components for handling drawings should be considered as part of the system design. In addition, the aperature card image when scanned requires considerable space for storage of each image. Each image should be scanned at 300 dots per inch or greater. The image on the aperature card may be any size, typically up to "F" size which requires 12.6 Mbytes of storage when scanned at 300 dots per inch and stored in an uncompressed form.

Aperature card scanners are precision instruments that must be able to scan large blow-back image areas compared to their resolution. These features result in high prices for the units. Computers that are used in systems which contain aperature card scanners should be selected to be able to move large volumes of data quickly. The addition of compression boards to the computer is is necessary if many drawings are to be handled. The compression of images allows them to be stored more quickly on disk, and allows the storage of more images.

Future Components

By the second quarter of 1988 there will be new types of scanner components on the market. These components are multifunction scanner interface boards for IBM compatible computers. These boards will contain many of the features needed to support imaging systems, and with the board, the features can be easily incorporated into specialized scanning and imaging handling systems. Among the features anticipated on these boards are CCITT Group III and IV compression and decompression, high-speed scanner and printer interfaces, modems, and optical character recognition.

By adding one of these boards to their system users will be able to input page images from scanners, compress them or convert them to ASCII and then transmit them to a distant location. These new boards will take up only one slot in a PC compared to four or five boards in older designs.

About the Authors

John W. Bottoms is president of Taunton Engineering, Inc., a software engineering firm in the Boston Metropolitan Area that specializes in the design of integrated applications for building and retrieving databases using the Standard Generalized Markup Language (SGML). This core activity has provided a framework for related projects in the design and implementation of local area networks and modems, or network protocols and management systems, of error recovery procedures, optical disc systems, and electronic publishing systems.

Recent efforts at Taunton Engineering have included the development of an indexed retrieval system for large databases stored on magnetic, optical write-once, or CD ROM systems, and a program that performs automatic SGML markup. As a member of the Electronic Manuscript Committee for the Association of American Publishers, Bottoms contributed to the commercial definition of the electronic style guide for SGML used in electronic publishing. Bottoms also participated on the Computer Acquisition Logistics System (CALS) working group in the development of the Document Type Definition for MIL-M-28001.

John Bottoms is a highly regarded contributor to professional and trade journals. Sample articles include "Structured Document Storage Plus Full-Text Retrieval Equals Successful Queries," *CD Data Report*, September 1987, "Full Text Retrieval Systems Explained," *CD Data Report*, January 1988, "An SGML Tutorial," forthcoming in EPB, and "Selecting Media for Electronic Publishing," forthcoming in *CD ROM Review*.

Bottoms has presented papers at the Optical Information Systems Conference, CD ROM Expo, LaserActive, CEPS: Corporate Electronic Publishing Systems.

John Bottoms is also the coauthor with Linda Helgerson of the forthcoming compendium, *The Optical Disk Sourcebook*.

Linda W. Helgerson is president of Diversified Data Resources, Inc. (DDRI), a consulting firm in Northern Virginia that specializes in optical storage technologies and directly related fields, and editor and publisher of *CD Data Report*, the leading CD ROM industry newsletter since 1984.

Helgerson consults with large and small organizations worldwide, including electronics manufacturers, optical disc mastering and replication firms, software development companies, industry associations, traditional and electronic publishers, online database service firms, federal agencies, the Department of Defense as well as DoD contractors. The types of consulting projects include analysis of user requirements, market trend analysis, hardware and software evaluation for integration within specific systems, technology evaluation, competitive product analyses, as well as overall industry watchdog. For many clients, Helgerson provides a continuous series of industry reports on areas of specific interest.

Helgerson is co-Editor of *The CD ROM Sourcebook* and co-author of *The Scanning Sourcebook* and *The Optical Disk Sourcebook*, all three published by DDRI. She is the author of two books published by the Association for Information and Image Management: *The Introduction to Scanning* and *The Introduction to Optical Technology*. She is the author of a three-part series of analytical articles appearing in *Library Hi Tech Journal* — "CD ROM Public Access Catalogs" — describing the features, the database creation and maintenance, and the user interface for each existing CD ROM PAC system. She is also the publisher and coeditor of a new series of popular books for users and producers of CD ROM products, published by Langley Publications, Inc.

In addition to being a prolific contributor to trade and professional journals, a regular speaker at industry conferences and forums, and a well-recognized name in the industry, Linda Helgerson has consulted extensively for the past 8 years with both users and suppliers in the planning, marketing, and production of optical storage and dissemination technologies.

Taunton Engineering
505 Middlesex Turnpike Suite 11
Billerica, MA 01821
617–663–3667

DDRI
6609 Rosecroft Place
Falls Church, VA 22043
703–237–0682

References

Apperson, Gene, and Rick Doherty (1987). "Displaying Images," in *CD ROM Volume Two: Optical Publishing* (Suzanne Ropiequet, JohnEinberger, and Bill Zoellick, eds.). Redmond, Wash.: Microsoft Press.

Bridge, Raymond, and James Morin (1987). "Preparing Text," in *CD ROM Volume Two: Optical Publishing*, Suzanne Ropiequet, John Einberger, and Bill Zoellick, eds.). Redmond, Wash.: Microsoft Press.

Helgersen, Linda W. (1987). "Scanners Present a Maze of Options," Mini-Micro Systems, January, pp. 71–81.

Helgersen, Linda W., and John W. Bottoms (in press). *The Scanning Sourcebook*. Falls Church, Va.: Diversified Data Resources, Inc.

Helgersen, Linda W., and William Pferd III (1986). *Market Report on Scanning Products and Systems*, Falls Church, Va.: Diversified Data Resources, Inc.

McFaul, James P. (1986). "Image Capture and Processing for CD ROM," in *CD ROM: The New Papyrus* (Steve Lambert and Suzanne Ropiequet,eds.). Redmond, Wash.: Microsoft Press.

"Optical Character Recognition, January 1970– February 1988" (citations from NTIS database). Springfield, Va.: National Technical Information Service, March 1988, 75 pages.

Smith, Truett Lee (1986). "Compressing and Digitizing Images," in *CD ROM: The New Papyrus* (Steve Lambert and Suzanne Ropiequet, eds.). Redmond, Wash.: Microsoft Press.

11

Full Text Indexed
Retrieval Systems

John W. Bottoms

Overview of Indexed Retrieval Systems

In the broadest sense, an index is a distillation of information that is
used as an aid in recovering information about real objects. The first
indices used were simple knotted strings or notches whittled into a
stick. These basic reminders allowed owners of livestock to accurately record the count and types of their stock.

Lists from 300 B.C. have been found which showed the names
of people in local cults that were sorted alphabetically by the first
letter of their name. Works have been found from the middle ages
(c. 630 A.D. and c. 725) which contained lists sorted by the first two
letters. The first known work which contained a full description of
the alphabetic sorting process was written in 1286 by Giovanni di
Genoa (Knuth, 1973).

This article first appeared in the December 1987 issue of CD Data Report,
published by Langley Publications, Inc., of McLean, Virginia.

These early sorting techniques have now evolved to more sophisticated techniques that can refer to items by name, part number, description, or even pictures of the item. This article will examine a couple of techniques for creating indices for full text retrieval.

Preliminary Topics

Full text systems generally consist of two portions. The first the user invokes is the inverter, which creates the index; then a retrieval engine is used to search for data. In order to provide a common vocabulary for the user, we will first look at some of the common terms associated with full text indexing.

The Index

To find information in a document we could use a program that starts at the beginning of the document and searches through the document, looking for the words of interest. This approach is easy to implement and fast for small documents, but for very large documents or databases of hundreds of documents, it is cumbersome. What is needed is the equivalent of a card catalog that can quickly indicate the location of desired information. This information is contained in the index and not all indices contain the same information. One might indicate the equivalent of a Dewey Decimal System number, while another might indicate a bookshelf number.

Creating The Index

In its most common usage, the term "indexing" refers to the process of creating a list of offsets for words or tokens of a document. As an example, throughout this article we will use the Gettysburg Address as an illustration. If you have trouble remembering it, we have included it in the Appendix at the end of this chapter. An example of word indices for the word "devotion" shows that the word occurs two times at offsets of 1179 and 1249 characters from the beginning of the document. Offsets are indicated as bytes with each byte holding one character. (Two bytes are allowed for the end of each text line for the "carriage return" and "line feed" control characters.)

In examining the text a few things come to mind immediately. First, some of the words have hyphens. Are we to consider these as one word made up of two words joined by a hyphen, or are they two words separated by a hyphen. In searching we would not be able to anticipate that these two particular words are joined and would not be able to find them if we were searching on the basis of these separate words. So we index them as separate words. Every complete full text system must contain some internal representation of what constitutes an English word.

Another item that is noticed is that many of the small words are not of prime importance in the document. If we were searching for information on the Civil War we might be interested in "battlefield" and "war," but we are probably not as interested in words such as "it," "the," and "thus." By leaving these relatively unimportant words out of the index, we can save index space and little will be detracted from the systems search capability. These omitted words are referred to as "noise" words or "stop" words. Some inverters keep track of all word counts and automatically omit words that occur more than a previously set number or percentage of all words. This approach to identifying noise words is of some use but also tends to discard important words that occur often. Most systems allow the user to specify the noise words to be used for during the inversion process. A typical noise word list of the 100 most common English words is shown in Table 11-1.

A basic concern in the creation of the index is how to keep it as small as possible. The elimination of noise words is a good first step. In our example we started with a total of 274 words. The elimination of noise words reduced the word total to 123. Some of these words were duplicated, and by eliminating the duplicates the list was reduced to 98 words. In terms of word counts this list contains only

Table 11-1 100 Most Common English Words

*a	*be	*from	if	me	*now	own	*the	*to	*what
about	been	*great	*in	*might	*of	said	*their	two	when
after	*but	had	into	more	old	*shall	them	up	*which
*all	*by	has	*is	most	*on	she	then	upon	*who
an	*can	*have	*it	much	one	*should	there	*us	*will
*and	could	he	its	must	only	*so	*these	very	with
*any	*do	her	like	my	*or	some	*they	was	would
*are	even	him	made	*new	other	such	*this	*we	yet
*as	first	his	man	no	*our	than	*those	well	you
at	*for	I	may	*not	out	*that	time	were	your

*The words that also appear in the Gettysburg Address are noted with an asterisk.

36 percent of the number of words but retains all the significant words in the document. In actual practice there is information added to the index so the index size will vary.

As a computer index is created, each word is entered into a list along with the number of occurrences of that word. This way file space can be allocated for each word that is dependent upon how many times that word occurs. The amount of space determines how many times the word can occur before the system is not able to record further occurrences of that word. For example, if 2 bytes are allocated for the number of occurrences of a word, then a document may have 65,536 occurrences of that word before no further occurrences will be recorded.

In selecting the occurrence space the system designer makes a choice between an index size that is small and efficient versus one that is comprehensive but bulky. The actual choice is a compromise of many factors. While 2 bytes may not seem like much, it is necessary to allocate those 2 bytes for each word used in a document. Some system designs can eliminate the need for the occurrence count space by indexing a document using just the computer's memory. But systems that provide indexing beyond the memory size of the computer used for indexing must be able to track the number of occurrences of words to allocate memory space. Some systems index by individual characters, but this approach requires additional indexing time.

In addition to providing a count of each word, the indexing system must be able to track all the different words used in a document. If the system uses a number to represent a particular word and the number is kept in 2 bytes, then the maximum number of words that can be used in the document is 65,536. Some systems combine the number of words with other information, such as paragraph numbers, and end up with differing document sizes. In these systems it is difficult to tell how large a document can be because of the maximum sentence, paragraph, and chapter counts.

Factors Affecting Indexing Speed

Some methods for creating indices are faster than others. If the index being created fits into the computer memory, then indexing is faster than using a hard disk. Indexing efficiency also affects time to index. If the index has to be rearranged during the indexing, then the process is slowed. A good inverter design attempts to place data in the final location as the data is first encountered.

The Retrieval Engine

Once the index has been created, the user can invoke the retrieval engine to locate information. Retrieval engines allow the user to access the document in several ways. Most are designed to allow access similar to that of a book. The user can look up words in the index or the more curious may want to browse from page to page. Some systems allow the user to specify a word from the text and use that word as an index term. This "lateral" or "sideways" browsing allows the user to find related information quickly.

Search systems provide boolean operators to be used with search terms. Using a boolean function, the user may search on "war" and "battlefield" but not "Europe" within a document. Some systems may contain a synonym list or thesaurus to aide in searching. Once information is found, the user may want a copy of it. Most systems allow searches to be made using a wildcard. The wildcard indicates that any replacement characters can be used in place of the wildcard indicator. This allows the user to search for all occurrences of the word "dedicate" by specifying "dedi*." In our example this search would result in the location of the words "dedicate," and "dedicated." Some systems only allow wildcard indicators to be used as suffixes.

Retrieval systems provide the means to print the information or move it to a file where it can be used with a word processor. Usually the user will specify the start and end of a section of text to be moved to the printer or a text file. The user may also be able to print the screen currently being displayed. Some systems that work with proprietary information may limit the use of this feature to limit the amount of information that can be excerpted.

Factors Affecting Retrieval Speed

Retrieval speed is affected by the construction of the index and the complexity of the search request. If the search request specifies a word that is a noise word, the retrieval system will probably perform a linear search for the word in combination with other words in the search. This results in a lengthy search for large databases. Likewise, searches using wildcards take increased time. Powerful wildcard systems tend to be slow because the user has the ability to request information in many ways, most of which are not in the index.

Multimedia Retrieval Systems

Often it is desirable to locate information other than text, such as still images, sound, or video images. Special techniques must be developed for indexing and retrieving multimedia information.

Text Only Systems

Full text retrieval systems provide capability for most office and commercial applications, because over 90 percent of all information that is communicated in the office today is communicated using text alone. However, that does not mean that the design of a full text retrieval system is an easy task. The usage of English is modified by each industry in the English speaking world. Each of these modifications has the capability to compound the task of full text retrieval.

Retrieval of text is accomplished by a system that understands the differences between words. Lexical rules are built into the inverter that tell it how to separate words. For example, it is easy to see that characters separated by spaces belong to different words, but it is more difficult trying to determine when characters separated by punctuation marks belong to different words. Is "drive-in" one word or two. The lexical rules adopted for use by the inverter should reflect the lexical rules that the user is familiar with. If the retrieval system is used by a group or industry that commonly uses punctuation in words, then the indexing system should follow that usage. In applications for the U.S. Armed Forces, the common names of equipment, such as "AN/FGC-56," should be stored by the inverter so that the name "AN/FGC-56" can be located by the retrieval system.

Full Text with Images

In looking at text with images the first impulse might be to store information just as it would appear in a book. This would allow the rapid display of information by simple retrieval and display of the page containing the requested information. However, this complicates the task of the inverter, for now it must be capable of reading a book and locating the placement of the words (and images) that are on each page of the book. If the book is written with two columns per page and captions on the images, then the inverter must be able to read each page and associate the correct information with each image. If paragraphs and chapters are to be searched as a unit, then the inverter must be able to determine the start and end of these structural units.

Systems that provide image retrieval along with text retrieval face a basic output difficulty. The display monitor of the retrieval system is used for the output of two types of information in these systems. The system designer is then faced with the question of how to share the screen between these two types of data. Ideally, the display should reflect the presentation of multimedia documents, books, and magazines that contain pictures.

However, this is compounded by two issues. First, to format the text and images for display, as you would see in a book, requires that the retrieval system perform the composition that is done when a book is published. And this is a complex task. The second issue is that by requiring that the display be similar to a book, we have limited the display capabilities that may be possible with an electronic delivery system. It may be desirable to have pages that are 15 feet wide and 20 feet tall, or images that are overlaid on each other and that can be peeled by the reader to reveal images below.

Neither of these issues renders text and image systems inoperable. There are concessions that can be made to easily implement these systems. To simplify the output approach, it is necessary to separate the identification of the material from the output formatting of the material. The separation of these units is accompanied by a system of identifying where the images and text are stored in the computer along with information about how the material is to be displayed for the user. This will be discussed in a later section on "Markup."

Text, Images, and Sound

The complication of adding sound, in addition to text and images, to a retrieval system does not compound the indexing process so much as it does the display and output process. The basic problem here is how to keep the user from being flooded with sounds and how the connections between sound and images are conveyed to the user. These are formatting problems that are part of the human interface and display portions of the retrieval system. These issues will be addressed as part of the discussion on style sheets.

Development of an Indexed Retrieval System

Memory Resident Model

The simplest approach to building an index is to keep all the words in the index in memory. The issue here is in what form to keep the words. Two forms are shown in the following diagrams. The first approach is to keep the words in a tree structure where the tops of the tree are the first letters of the words in the text. In this example just the words starting with the letter "D" are shown, but in actual practice all would be catalogued.

(top)

a	b	c	d	e

(word)	dead	dedicate	dedicated	detract	devotion	did
(count)	(3)	(2)	(4)	(1)	(2)	(1)
(locations)	709	400	137	790	1179	897
"	1151	620	305	1249		
"	1297		946			
"			1078			

The advantage of the tree structure is that we quickly get to the words of interest, those starting with "D" in just two moves. The first to the pointer "D" and the next is to the first word starting with a "D." The disadvantage of the tree structure is that it is more difficult to construct than other types of data structure.

Index Tables

The words in an index can also be kept as a simple linked list, also referred to as a threaded list. In this case only the start and end of the list are known. To find a particular word, the program must know the start and end of the list. It can then perform a binary search of all the words in the list. In the list of all unique words in our example, there are 98 unique words. A binary search could find any word in this list in less than seven attempts with most words being located within three or four attempts.

In Table 11-2 we have not shown the count or locations of each word as we did in the previous data structure. This data usually is appended to the word and complicates the procedure for locating the next item in the list. Because the words have different numbers of occurrences, 1 to 4 in our example, the search mechanism must be able to skip around the count and occurrence pointers to find the next word in the list.

The advantage of the linked list structure is that it is easy to construct and easier to search than a tree structure, but the search process takes longer since the data increases.

The techniques we have discussed thus far have been built in the resident memory of the computer. However, if the number of different words is large, then all the words will not fit into the memory space. Then some of the words will have to be stored on disk temporarily while the document is being indexed. The process of accessing the disk to see if words have been indexed greatly slows the indexing process but it allows the creation of indices for very large documents. The programs for the creation of this type of index are difficult, but generally one of three techniques are used.

Virtual Memory Models

A true virtual memory system can be developed that simulates a larger computer that keeps track of pages that data has been stored on. These systems keep the most active or recently used pages in the

Table 11-2 Sequential List of Words through "E" in the Alphabet

above	altogether	brought	consecrate	dedicate	died
add	battlefield	cause	consecrated	dedicated	earth
address	before	civil	continent	detract	endure
advanced	birth	come	created	devotion	engaged
ago	brave	conceived	dead	did	equal

active memory of the computer and only accesses the disk as required.

Other systems may create many small indices in the memory of the computer and then merge them when all the indexing has been completed, discarding the duplicate words as the merge is performed. Some systems merge the indices as they are created, creating a final index that grows larger as the document is read and indexed.

Usually, the process of creating an index is performed in two passes. The first pass recognizes all the unique words, and counts the number of times that each word occurs. It then allocates space for the final index and then reads the source document once again, noting the location of each word. When the final pass has been completed, the index is done and searching can be performed.

Preparation of Documents

The preparation of documents for indexing and storage involve steps to supply information about the document structure and classify a document according to its function or subject.

Markup Codes

Usually the search procedure is enhanced by the addition of information about the document structure. It is useful for the retrieval application to know where chapters, paragraphs, and other document structural elements start and end. This information can be added by the inclusion of "markup" codes. These codes designate the start and end of particular structural elements.

Some markup codes are unique to a particular vendor and are proprietary. Often they are nonprinting control characters. One particular markup approach is based on the international standard for markup specifications. The approach, Standard Generalized Markup Language (SGML), specifies the use of markup that is printable. Examples of markup are shown in Table 11-3.

The commercial standard for markup which has been adopted for use on optical discs has over 260 predefined markup codes for such diverse items as publisher information, font types, lists, tables, and mathematical expressions.

The need for a common approach to markup grew out of the interchange between publishing companies and printing and typography companies. Initially, typography and printing markup codes were

Table 11-3 **Examples of SGML**

SGML Markup	Meaning
<chp>	Chapter start
</chp>	Chapter end
<para1>	Paragraph start, level 1
<fig, id=pix2>	Figure, file identifier = "pix2"

unique to each company. They evolved over many years and became difficult to document because of the numerous changes. Today, it is possible to recover some of this information from the typography codes and convert it to more meaningful markup through an automated process. Similarly, word processor codes can often be converted to generalized markup.

Once markup codes have been added to a document, this information can be used as an aid in the retrieval process. The markup codes can indicate the start and ends of sections that are to be searched. This allows the structured searching of documents that have been carefully organized. The result is much faster searches and meaningful browsing for the information desired.

Classification and Segmentation

Before the indexing and storage of documents, it may be necessary to perform a classification process on the document. This allows similar documents to be stored together and even indexed together to allow faster retrieval. This process is similar to the function of filing of documents in an office filing cabinet. Retrieval occurs more rapidly when there are folders which contain the papers related to a particular subject, compared to an unorganized file cabinet full of unrelated papers.

In this step each paper is examined and sorted according to a predetermined criteria. In an encyclopedia the sorting criteria is alphabetic. Company histories may be kept by year or by geographic location. Other figures of merit may be used but some attempt should be made to organize the documents similar to the organization used in the company or agency. If there are many documents that are to be stored in an optical disc jukebox, the classification may be designed to reflect the locations of the discs in the jukebox.

Display of Documents

The display of information that has been stored can be handled by the retrieval system based upon embedded rules or it can be specified by the use of a style sheet.

Style Sheets

Data that has been stored on CD ROM may contain markup information or other information about the structure of the document. This data may not be appropriate for the display of the document on the user's monitor. The reformatting of the display is then specified by a guide or "style sheet" which describes how the output image should look.

The style sheet may also be referred to as a "generic layout specification." It may be embodied in the program that performs the retrieval function or it may be a list of substitutions or processing instructions that are related to the generic markup of a document. Special concerns may be required for the display multimedia information.

A sample style sheet is shown in Table 11-4. In this example the output display is controlled by substituting printer commands for the tags found in the document. A markup tag is replaced by a command for a laser printer and an explanation of each command is shown at the right. The command codes are for an unspecified laser printer.

Multimedia information is more difficult to deal with in terms of a style sheet, but physical descriptions of image placement can be described. The problem with image display during retrieval is one of formatting the page using sophisticated composition rules. Sound

Table 11-4 Sample Style Sheet

Tag	Command String	Meaning
<title>	<esc>(5W<esc>(s12V	Roman 12 pt font
<para>	<esc>(s74	Pica typeface
<section>	<esc>&k2J	Skip to page top

Note: <esc> is the ASCII value 1B in hex (027 decimal).

and image output may be indicated and the user can then elect to invoke their "display" or not.

Advanced Topics

Now that we have discussed some of the general topics about indexing and searching, it is useful to add some topics that can lead the reader to more interesting problems.

Precision Versus Recall

A basic problem involved in searching is the question of how to find the exact information needed, without knowing beforehand what it is, and avoid finding information that is not desired. Most systems search blindly and literally without any understanding of the intent of the user. Then if the user states the query too broadly, the information that is located by the search will flood the user. If the search query is framed too narrowly, there will be insufficient results and the user will not locate the information desired. This is referred to as the "precision-recall" problem. That is, as the precision of a query increases, the recall of the number of documents located will decrease.

However, this observation is true only for certain types of document databases. In a classic paper in 1985, Blair and Maron pointed out that full text retrieval in the system examined resulted in the retrieval of less than than 16 percent (on average) of the documents relevant to a particular search. In the study cited, they studied the use of full text retrieval in a system with a large number of documents constituting over 350,000 pages of text. In actual practice there are no mechanisms to solve the precision-recall problem but some techniques can minimize its impact. The only real solution is to provide a classification means to order documents in the way a file cabinet or library is organized.

Proximity, Context, Clustering, and Other Statistical Searches

All these terms refer to techniques designed to reduce the effect of the precision-recall problem in searching large, unstructured databases. Most of these techniques involve measuring the number of keywords that are used in a document and comparing that to the keywords used in other documents. If the set of keywords overlaps to a great extent, there is some assurance that the subjects are closely related and the document is retrieved for the user.

These statistical approaches to searching should not be considered the best approach to providing the user with the desired information. By far it is much better to structure the data beforehand just as publishers do when preparing printed material. Statistical searches suffer from the basic problem of retrieving incorrect information if classification of the material has not taken place first. Consider the person looking for information about automobile engines in a large set of material. Consider a statistical search for the words "sparkplug" and "fanbelt," because information about the repair of engines is desired. The search may also retrieve parts purchase invoices in which those items were purchased which is not at all what is desired. However, if the original material were placed into electronic folders, the folders could be searched much more reliably yielding the user the desired information.

Often search techniques attempt to verify that the search result is valid and does not contain a negating term in the same sentence. For example, if the search is for "house" and "garage" and there is a sentence in a particular document that reads, "This barn, once used to house pigs and cows, is not suitable for a dwelling or garage," then the selection of this sentence as qualifying the search criterion would be erroneous. This is referred to as a "false-drop" and if detected would not be part of the search results. False-drops are located by examining the sentence for negating terms, such as "not," "nor," or "never."

Search Tracing and Electronic Notepads

Some searches are lengthy and involve lateral browses through many documents making it difficult for the user to remember or recreate the steps in locating the information. Other related information may have been encountered during the search but, if it cannot be located by backtracking, it is lost to the user.

Some systems provide tools to keep track of searches as they take place. This usually takes the form of an audit trail that indicates the documents that have been visited and some may allow the user to attach "electronic notes" to the documents much like a user might insert bookmarks in a book.

Dynamically Updating Documents

Because CD ROM is a read-only medium there is no way to update the data contained on it. However, there are situations in which it is desirable to provide updated information. This can be done by remanufacturing the CD ROM, but this involves additional time and expense. Another alternative is to build a text retrieval system that can be updated. The impact this has is on the index structure. If the index structure is on the CD ROM, it cannot be modified to allow the addition of new material.

The answer is to provide an auxiliary index on floppy disk or tape that can be searched before the CD ROM is searched. Some refer to this as an electronic looseleaf because pages can be added or subtracted. The typical implementation assigns revision numbers to sections, paragraphs, or chapters and allows them to be overridden by corresponding sections, paragraphs, or chapters on the floppy disk. Using this technique, elements can be added, replaced, or omitted altogether.

Cleanup of Index Structures

When a large amount of material is indexed, the index structure may have to be optimized at the end. This is usually needed with tree structures that have branches broken and new branches added onto existing ones. The problem usually occurs that the index tree contains too many pointer nodes that just point to other branches instead of data. The tree may become unbalanced and searching in some parts may be executed quickly at the expense of other searches. The final act of rebalancing the tree can repair this problem.

Searching Across Multiple Files

When many documents are held in an unstructured database, it is necessary to search across many files. This is also useful when there is more data than should be placed into a single index file. The index files then need to contain information with each word about what document the word occurs in for each instance. This allows the retrieval systems to provide the user with a count of the number of different documents that fulfill the search query.

Hierarchical Document Structure

Searches across structured documents that are arranged according to a predefined hierarchical structure provide the opportunity for sophisticated searches. The tree can then be searched down a branch such as "chapter" to "paragraph" to "section," restricting the domain of the search at each level until just a small amount of text is searched. Alternately, all the leaves of the tree can be searched, such as all "sections." With this type of system, the user could search for all instances of "artwork" and see all the images in a document.

Document Security

In some applications there is a need to separate data by levels of security. These levels may be the government levels of unclassified, confidential, secret, and top secret or they may be levels developed for other purposes. Companies working on a common project may want to isolate trade secrets or financial information from other participants.

To protect this information, it is necessary to tag each element, such as "chapter" or "paragraph," with the security information. Then the retrieval system application must be sure that a user is authorized to access the data before retrieval is accomplished. The determination of authorization and access control can be enforced through the use of passwords or other software means, or secure systems hardware keys can be provided.

Conclusions

The results of the discussion in this article are a better understanding about the issues surrounding the indexing of documents that are to be stored on CD ROM.

Retrieval tools must match the application. It is important that all the retrieval tools are closely matched to the user community they serve. If the display is for the storage and retrieval of high-quality commercial art, then a high resolution display system is needed to provide the image quality that the users need. The same system is not needed for salespersons involved in the sale of commercial property. For the retrieval of text, systems developed for general English usage may not be appropriate for other languages or for the medical community. Some users demand near immediate response for searches within a single document while others are more interested in searching across many unrelated documents.

Documents should be structured as much as possible before indexing. A major responsibility of a publisher is to distribute a document that immediately communicates the ideas of the author. This means that the document should be structured around a central premise or theme. If this structure is clear to the reader, then very complex ideas can be communicated quickly and with efficiency. It also allows the retrieval and display of the information in that document to be done efficiently.

Costs are a major consideration. The development of an indexing and retrieval system is a major programming effort. In order to minimize the development time and resource requirements, it is necessary to understand how information is used, how inverters are designed, how searches are performed on indices, and how information is best displayed for the user. A well directed effort in these skills that serves a broad audience by those well versed will minimize the development costs of a retrieval system.

What's Ahead in Indexed Retrieval?

Now that standardization is available in document formats with the availability of SGML, vendors have started developing compatible text processing tools that meet the standard. Several companies have introduced word processors that automatically insert standard markup tags while authors prepare material. The insertion of the tags is unseen by the author and frees the writer from the fuss of inserting tags correctly. Block move instructions in the word processor environment assure that blocks are moved in their entirety.

For program developers the future should bring ease of integration of dictionaries and thesauri. A standard structure for a dictionary allows application developers to create indices and retrieval modules for their applications. Then, when a user wants a definition or synonym for a word, the application will be able to provide further information. At the present time the application developer would have to build the dictionary in addition to the application.

One area that has been neglected is the standardization of indexing structures. Text retrieval software developers use proprietary index structures largely for two reasons. First, there is no standard on which to base the index. Second, if the index structure is not accessible, then the data in the source document has an added measure of protection. The result of this approach is that every time there is an application that uses a large database of the same source material, the source material is duplicated along with a new index structure. There is little incentive for standards in this area but the problem is attracting increasing attention.

By far, the greatest effect of indexed retrieval will be in the development of corporate publishing systems. The increase in the amount and speed of information processing, along with the decrease in clerical tasks, means that each person in a corporation will be responsible for larger amounts of information. As the mountains of data grow, the company that will be the most successful will be the one that is most capable of accessing, analyzing, and using its historical data.

About the Author

John W. Bottoms is president of Taunton Engineering, Inc., a software engineering firm in the Boston Metropolitan Area that specializes in the design of integrated applications for building and retrieving databases using the Standard Generalized Markup Language (SGML). This core activity has provided a framework for related projects in the design and implementation of local area networks and modems, or network protocols and management systems, of error recovery procedures, optical disc systems, and electronic publishing systems.

Recent efforts at Taunton Engineering have included the development of an indexed retrieval system for large databases stored on magnetic, optical write-once, or CD ROM systems, and a program that performs automatic SGML markup. As a member of the Electronic Manuscript Committee for the Association of American Publishers, Bottoms contributed to the commercial definition of the electronic style guide for SGML used in electronic publishing. Bottoms also participated on the Computer Acquisition Logistics System (CALS) working group in the development of the Document Type Definition for MIL-M-28001.

John Bottoms is a highly regarded contributor to professional and trade journals. Sample articles include "Structured Document Storage Plus Full-Text Retrieval Equals Successful Queries," *CD Data Report*, September 1987, "Full Text Retrieval Systems Explained," *CD Data Report*, January 1988, "An SGML Tutorial," forthcoming in EPB, and "Selecting Media for Electronic Publishing," forthcoming in *CD ROM Review*.

Bottoms has presented papers at the Optical Information Systems Conference, CD ROM Expo, LaserActive, CEPS: Corporate Electronic Publishing Systems.

John Bottoms is also the coauthor with Linda Helgerson of the forthcoming compendium, *The Optical Disk Sourcebook*.

Taunton Engineering
505 Middlesex Turnpike, Suite 11
Billerica, MA 01821
617–663–3667

References

James, Geoffrey, Document Databases, New York, Van Nostrand Reinhold, 1988.

Knuth, Donald E., *Sorting & Searching, The Art of Computer Programming, Volume 3*, Reading, MA, Addison-Wesley, 1973.

Transactions on Office Information Systems, Association of Computing Machinery, New York, New York.

Special Interest Group on Information Retrieval, Association of Computing Machinery, New York, New York.

Appendix

1 Gettysburg Address
21 Four score and seven years ago our fathers brought forth on
84 this continent a new nation conceived in liberty and dedicated
148 to the proposition that all men are created equal.
200 Now we are engaged in a great civil war testing whether that
264 nation or any nation so conceived and so dedicated can long
325 endure. We are met on a great battlefield of that war. We have
392 come to dedicate a portion of that field as a final resting place
459 for those who here gave their lives that that nation might live.
525 It is altogether fitting and proper that we should do this. But
591 in a larger sense we can not dedicate-we can not consecrate-we can
659 not hallow this ground. The brave men living and dead who
719 struggled here have consecrated it far above our poor power to add
787 or detract. The world will little note nor long remember what we
854 say here but it can never forget what they did here. It is for us
922 the living rather to be dedicated here to the unfinished work which
1991 they who fought here have thus far so nobly advanced. It is rather
1060 for us to be here dedicated to the great task remaining before
1124 us-that from these honored dead that we take increased devotion to
1192 that cause for which they gave the last full measure of
1249 devotion-that we here highly resolve that these dead shall not have
1318 died in vain-that this nation under God shall have a new birth of
1385 freedom-and that government of the people by the people for the
1450 people shall not perish from the earth.

Chapter

12

Artificial Intelligence Systems

Michael Pincus, Kathy Pincus, and James B. Golden III

*"The apparent complexity of (man's)
behavior over time is largely a reflection of
the complexity of the environment in which
he finds himself."*
— *HERBERT A. SIMON*
FATHER OF ARTIFICIAL INTELLIGENCE

A primary target of artificial intelligence technology is toward automated information analysis and correlation. In the area of information retrieval, especially in such a specialized field as information analysis, the goal of the human analyst is a correlation between different, seemingly irrelevant or abstract data. The analyst hopes to discover some kind of cascade effect, relating various dissimilar factors. There are very few tools to aid the analyst in making intuitive links or inferences between the data points. Such a tool can be built using two examples of the current technology: CD ROM mass storage and artificially intelligent software.

CD ROM

In study or research of information whether directed toward science or management, an optimal situation would be to employ a large static database containing all examples of a domain — a database containing information, research, articles, journals, studies, and questionnaires. The database could be static (unchanging) except for updates from other studies and new research approximately once per year.

Trappl (1986) estimates that approximately 20 percent of the "knowledge base" of a manager is altered each year. A knowledge-based information system should presumably undergo a yearly 20 percent overhaul. To contain such a database, a highly efficient mass storage/accessing device is necessary.

Optical disks allow a higher density of data storage than any other computer memory system currently available or imminently anticipated. One CD ROM stores 550 Mbytes of data with an uncorrectable error rate below 10-12. A system running at 1 million bits/second with an error rate of 10-12 gives an average of only one bit error every 11 1/2 days, assuming the system runs at 1 million bits/second all around the clock, 7 days a week. The entire static database could be stored on three to four optical disks, adding an additional disk every 4 to 5 years. "Jukebox" style disk drives are available that can automatically access up to 50 disks, resulting in a total data capacity of 160 Gbytes.

Most of the information necessary to compile these types of databases is currently available from the Library of Congress, and from information retrieval companies. All professional journals and published articles are stored with the Library of Congress and are available for inexpensive downloading on magnetic tape. Magnetic tape is easily transferable to CD ROM. Such a database would give the human analyst and the accessing software a wide range of information to study.

The second database would be a relational or nonstatic database where questions to the software, current problems and studies, and prospective articles could be contained. Current hard drive technology is adequate for this, either in the micro or mainframe environment. Any data that was marked for permanent storage could be easily added to the CD ROM.

Methods

When an analyst performs the task of data reduction and filtering, he or she reads and understands the data and how to correlate it. The understanding process can be represented in terms of the syntactic analysis of the message into a tree structure, which identifies the relations of subject and object. Software can achieve this analysis if it is equipped with the linguistic and other special knowledge an analyst is familiar with, including concepts of word meaning and equivalence that a human employs to understand a message as well as the procedures for using these types of knowledge in the analysis process.

A few programs currently exist that idealize retrieval and correlation algorithms. These programs operate through various word meaning processors and computational linguistic methods to distill surface or deep inference accurately and dynamically, appearing intelligent to the user. Some of these systems are also driven by natural language almost exclusively and so are very easy to use. These are the most advanced software programs available in the field of natural language and information retrieval. Most of these systems are currently employed in proprietary government applications and niche markets. But this trend of privitization is changing.

Expert systems technology has received considerable attention as the "buzzword" of artificial intelligence marketed internationally. Since expert systems do occupy a role in conventional AI systems, we will discuss their relevance to CD ROM.

Ostberg (1986) addresses six main themes in his discussion of current expert systems. They are:

1. Development of nontrivial expert systems and the experts "rule" extraction process is very costly and time consuming.
2. Off-the-shelf Expert System Shells are no good for the design of nontrivial expert systems.
3. Building expert systems is an art, and few artists are available.
4. An expert system is never finished and requires continuous revision.
5. An expert system is not portable and only works within a narrow domain.
6. Choosing an appropriate application domain is very important for the in-house selling of future expert system work.

But with the development of intelligent text analysis software, CD ROM–based enthusiasm for AI expert systems need not be curbed. Text evaluated with software capable of correlation can extract analysis "rules" used by the author of the text. It can be used for eliciting operational expertise in differing occupational specialties. These rules can immediately be incorporated into rule-based expert systems or used operationally for various problem analysis and decision-making tasks. Expert systems distilled from information articles or journals can mimic the author's analysis skills. For example, rules extracted from mishap reports, research data, scientific reviews, forecasting studies, and other types of information can be built and referenced at will. The skill of the analyst is never lost, even when the human analyst is not present. Company employees could have the knowledge of all previous presidents, employees, analysts, psychologists, pathologists, scientists, researchers, or writers.

With text knowledge domains, the rule base is very easy to add to. True, the intelligent database or expert system designed from a text database is never finished, but that is to the advantage of the user. Information can constantly be added or changed, making the system resilient over time. Because the text files can be manipulated, the system is not limited to one domain. Natural language processing makes the expert system "artist" (knowledge engineers) unnecessary and acts as the user interface. If a formalized rule-based expert system is necessary, than a knowledge engineer is needed. But, using an intelligent CD ROM–based information analysis system will take a great deal of effort out of the information correlation process as well as the rule extraction process, making the job of building conventional expert systems considerably easier.

Information forms a sprawl of knowledge across the fuzzy boundaries between disciplines, subjects, and fields. An artificially intelligent environment for research creates a cohesion of universal ideas resident in diverse context and architecture. Using such a system, an information researcher is able to see whether a linkage of various text and sources support a concept or dismiss it. This system can help support foresight and prediction.

While rule-based expert systems are powerful software tools that help many organizations and government groups to solve difficult and complex problems, others are using alternative methods that provide a spreadsheet capability for "symbolic thought patterns."

They are being highly developed for use in very sophisticated AI applications which could include CD ROM.

Not all problems lend themselves to a rule-based approach. In the past, a lot of emphasis has been placed on rules and some problems are very rule oriented. But, humans do not "think" in the same way that a computer manipulates rules. Therefore, the rule-based expert systems tend to be limiting in many domains.

The ability to accomplish information transformation (analysis) and data correlation of naturally occurring networks allows an intelligent human analyst to examine the complex relationships between pieces of symbolic information and make decisions based on that evaluation. This type of information transformation is more akin to the way humans really "think."

For example, a high-altitude supersonic jet plane has wings and the wings may fold out or be swept back allowing better control at higher altitudes and faster speeds. What's important is not that the jet plane has wings (most planes have wings) but that the wings on certain supersonic jets retract as the altitude, speed, and goal of flight varies.

It is possible to parse word units into information via an inference engine consisting of many root words with their conventional meanings. By using this inference engine and through other inventive methods, intelligent response can be generated. These letter substructures constitute the architecture and conceptual foundation of the English language. These word substructures are defined in part, in terms of themselves. You could call them primal word or letter patterns. A very large number of these English words would have to be present in this inference engine (word network or web) for it to work properly.

Words have transformational qualities, i.e., synonyms, acronyms, and equivalent expressions, which are part of their formula. It is not a large leap of logic to see the metaphor that human cognitive faculties can be modeled in software when any self-referencing meaning transformation is accomplished. This can be seen crudely in recursive functions where a particular pattern is continually repositioned and recognized inside of other patterns iteratively.

Information transformations are specialized knowledge structures often naturally encoded inside of a general body of information where the relationships among the nodes in a network are more important than all the nodes themselves. These transformational nodes are interconnected (coded) through meaning and relevance in various ways.

For software to effectively analyze and correlate information, it has to be able to parallel both sides of the coin. It has to be able to decode the code.

It is possible to parse a user's query into the information being queried. This is essentially self-referential information transformational networking. The resulting correlations are located through an analysis of their word meanings. The result is intelligent retrieval.

The basic idea here is founded on one concept. The iteration of a real-valued mathematical function, i.e., the actions of a sequence of values x, $f(x)$, $f(f(x))$, $f(f(f(x)))$, where f is a function. The idea is that f can be representative of a word or string of symbols like a sentence, paragraph, or file, as easily as it could represent any list of things. By doing this we are inventing a function f with the property that for any real value of x, $f(x)$ is also real, and when $f(f(x))$ equals possibly -x, then information is likely to exhibit interesting cyclic or semicyclic logic. This is the structure of meaning relevance. The values simply continue to influence each other, representing various patterns containing replications of earlier patterns as information transformation in organized interconnected networks.

In order to understand this process better, we suggest you study how one goes about translating something someone has said in a "foreign" language into one's own native tongue. It is almost the same process. Much of this process consists of the referencing and rereferencing of various interrelated linguistic subsets.

Thought and Nature

When information is studied things of interest (attractors) in the information are often perceived as relative. Ideas are built up from patterns of words and theoretically any word could be viewed as an attractor. When studying information, one can never be sure of what ideas will emerge either in the material being studied or in the mind as information is assimilated. Learning is often a random chaotic affair. Attractors continually represent patterns of themselves inside of themselves and as one studies information a trace recording of these abstractions can appear. It is at this point that we observe connection and interchange within the information. These become the ghostlike "strange attractors" which almost mysteriously emerge in our minds from the chaos of abstracted connection. The "strange attractors" then are cognitive bits which can be restructured and constitute the foundation upon which new ideas emerge.

The "strange attractors" then are cognitive bits which can be organized with logic and feeling to aid the human in understanding. They represent a type of learning.

A patterning of seeming randomness inside a body of data produces structure. This constitutes a natural internal architecture which can be further controlled by human learning feedback to decrease problem complexity and improve human analysis skills. This is a process which occurs through the cooperation of a human user, a computer, and artificial intelligence software.

In life, randomness models the complications we have in our world. Economics, politics, philosophies, technologies, people, war and where to eat tonight are all levels of density of random fields. The only distinguishing feature of this randomness is its density. Within a body of information, abstraction and relevance are correlated to levels of density with a random field. As connection is correlated, patterns change and density slowly decreases. Gaps appear and grow. As time goes on, stable objects appear. Points of further correlation are isolated as density drops, and "strange attractors" are more pronounced in the "mind" and begin to form patterns of their own. They move from subcognitive feeling dawnings (human pattern recognition) to fully developed logical states as they begin to aggregate (a patterning of a pattern) in the mind of the human.

The Future

It is really no longer workable for computer scientists to model computational systems in ways which are different from the universe in which we find ourselves. We now know that by studying the phenomenon of small nuclear particles, we are actually influencing them in ways which prevent absolute analysis. We have also been forced to notice that we cannot measure a signal inside of a cluster of closely interfaced microchips without disturbing it. Our existing hardware models are changing, and as they do, our software concepts will change as well. Man is part of the universe. It would be naive and scientifically irresponsible to continue to create thinking systems which do not cybernetically interface in a natural way with the human.

The whole idea here is to take information in any form and liken it to an ocean. Using retrieval of these networks to further model information plastically, for example, building laminar flows (like cars moving in a multilane highway) or molecules of fluids moving inside of larger fluid jetstreams at 10,000 feet. What was once a dimensional field of patterns, of symbols, letters, numbers, and words now becomes a multidimensional world of order and chaos interacting to generate new data structures.

Within this transformational network we can establish interconnection and interchange by observing the patterning of patterns of meaning with some mutual frequency contingent on requisite considerations made by the human. The product for the human user is increased information correlation or accelerated learning rate and improved problem analysis and decision making skills. CD ROM offers an ideal environment in which to build these types of systems.

Conclusion

In some applications, it may be difficult to encode human knowledge directly into a rule-based expert system. A solution may be to give up altogether the goal of attempting to encode human expert knowledge directly into conventional expert systems and instead derive an appropriate model of the domain from a database of past cases (Ostberg, 1986). In any event, a CD ROM–based intelligent information correlation tool may appropriately model this type of approach.

Artificially intelligent systems, seen in this light, do not try to replace human intelligence, only to support it smartly.

A human analyst tends to be a cybernetically self-organizing structure. By using such a system the analyst can become an expert as a natural by-product.

Man is generally considered to be intelligent. The universe has equipped us with a richly structured neural cellular system possibly connected sub quantally to a larger macro system. This interfaced system, while serving a variety of functions, specifically enables us to learn and store information. A certain critical degree of structural complexity is required of this network before it can become significantly self-metamorphizing. System interfacing is of major importance.

These concepts embodied in useable technology constitute a fresh approach to data analysis and correlation. Its relevance to the field of artificial intelligence goes without saying. This allows hope that a design science for accelerating man's knowledge and ability to evolve his world is possible. Environments incorporating CD ROM mass data storage support these goals.

About the Authors

Michael and Kathy Pincus are the principals of Expansion Programs International, Inc./Thunderstone, an AI (Artificial Intelligence) software company in NE Ohio specializing in text retrieval and analysis systems with competitive intelligence applications. They currently devote the majority of their time and efforts toward the embodiment of advanced computing concepts in a product called Metamorph™. The implementation of concept into software has been made possible through their association with P. Barton Richards, who has made considerable breakthroughs in the area of pattern matching using the C programming language.

Lt. James B. Golden, III, is currently a graduate student at the University of Tennessee majoring in Artifical Intelligence. His interests are in natural language processing and expert systems for command and control. His experience spans a number of related fields including uses of advanced computing methods in aeronautics and aerospace.

Thunderstone/EPI, Inc.
P.O. Box 839
Chesterland, OH 44026
216–449–6104

References

Ashby, W. R. (1970). Information flows within co-ordinated systems. In: *Progress of Cybernetics* pp. 57–64. J. Rose (ed.). New York: Gordon and Breach.

Bach, E. (1964). *An Introduction to Transformational Grammars*. New York: Holt, Rinehart, and Winston.

Banerji, R. B. (1971). Some linguistic and statistical problems in Pattern Recognition. In: *Pattern Recognition*. (Vol. 3, pp. 409–19). New York: Pergamon Press.

Barr, Avron, and Edward Feigenbaum (1981). *The Handbook of Artificial Intelligence*. Stanford, Calif.: Heuristech Press.

Barron, R. L. (1968). Self organising and learning Control system. In: *Cybernetic Problems in Bionics*. H. L. Oestricher and D. R. Moore (eds.). New York: Gordon and Breach.

Bates, M. (1984). "Accessing a Database with a Transportable Natural Language Interface." Proc. IEEE First Conf. Artificial Intelligence Applications, Computer Society of the IEEE, 10662 Los Vaqueros Circle, Los Alamitos, Calif., pp. 9–12.

Bell, G. I. (1973). Predator-prey equations simulating an immune response. *Math. Biosci.*, 16(3–4):291–315.

Carnap, R., and Y. Bar-Hillel (1953). An Outline of a Theory of Semantic Information. MIT Research Laboratory, Electronics Rech. Rep. 247.

Gabbay, D. M. (1969). A Model Theory for Tense Logic. Report nos. 1 and 2. Applied Logic Branch. The Hebrew University of Jerusalem.

Golden, Lt. James B. (1986), An Artificially Intelligent System for Human Factors Research. HQ AFISC/SERY, Norton AFB, (1986).

Hammer, M., and D. McLeod (1981). "Database Description with SDM: Semantic Databse Model," *ACM Trans. Databse System*, 6(3): 341–386.

Hayes, P. J. (1984). "Entity-Oriented Parsing," Proc. 10th Int'l Conf. Computational Linguistics, Assoc. for Computational Linguistics, Bell Communications Research, 445 South St, MRE 2A379, Morristown, N.J. 07960, pp. 212–217.

Hendler, J. et al. (1981). "Issues in the Development of Natural Language Front Ends," Proc. AFIPS NCC, AFIPS Press, Reston, Va., pp. 643–648.

Hesse, M. (1963). *Models and Analogies in Science.* Sheed and Ward.

Hobbs, L. C., D. J. Theis, J. Trimble, H. Titus, and I. Highberg (eds.) (1970). *Parallel Processor Systems, Technologies and Applications.* Spartan Books.

Kerner, E. H. (1959). Further considerations of statistical mechanics of biological associations. *Bull. Math. Biophys.*, 21:217.

Lilly, J. C., and D. Shirley (1968). Perception of Repeated Speech. I.E.E. NPL Conference on Pattern Recognition. NPL.

Louguet-Higgins, C., and D. Michie (1971). A holographic model for memory. *Nature.*

Manna, Z. (1970). Correctness of non-deterministic programmes. *Artificial Intell.*, 1:1.

Markov, AA. (1961). Theory of Algorithms. Works of the Math. Inst. I.M.V.A. Steklov. Vol. 42. Trans. Israel Program for Scientific Translations. Oldbourn Press.

Mesarovic, M. D. (1962). Self-organisational systems. In: *Self-Organising Systems.* M. Yovitz, G. Jacobi, and E. Goldstein (eds.). Spartan Press.

Minsky, M. (1967). *Computation: Finite and Infinite Machines.* Englewood Cliffs, N.J.: Prentice-Hall.

Ostberg, Olov (1986). Expert Systems in a Social Environment — Human Factors Concerns. Proceedings of the Human Factors Society — 30th Annual Meeting.

Pask, G. (1954). Self-organising systems involved in human learning and performance, pp. 247–335. In: Proceedings 3rd Bionics Symposium, Dayton, Ohio (1963). USAF ASD-TDR-63-946, ASTIA.

Pask, G., and B. N. Lewis (1964). Research on the Design of Adaptive Teaching Systems with a Capability for Selecting and Altering Criteria for Adaptation. Annual Summary Report, No. 4, USAF Contract No. A F 61(052)-402. System Research Ltd.

Pekelis, V. (1974). *Cybernetics A to Z.* Moscow: Mir Publishers Moscow (1974).

Schrefl, M., A. M. Tjoa, and R. R. Wagner (1984). "Comparison-Criteria for Semantic Data Models," Proc. IEEE Int'l. Conf. Data Engineering, Computer Society of the IEEE, 10662 Los Vaqueros Circle, Los Alamitos, Calif., pp. 120–125.

Shroedinger, E. (1944). *What is Life?* Cambridge University Press.

Sondheimer, N. K., R. M. Weischedel, and R. J. Bobrow (1984). "Semantic Using KLONE," Proc 10th Int'l Conf. Computational Linguistics, Assoc. for Computational Linguistics, Bell Communications Research, 445 South Street, MRE2A379, Morristown, NJ 07960, pp. 101–107.

Trappl, R. (1986). Impacts of artificial intelligence: An overview. In *Impacts of Artificial Intelligence.* R. Trappl (ed.),. Amsterdam: North Holland, p. 3–51.

Turing, A. M. (1969). Intelligent machinery. In: *Machine Intelligence*, vol. 5. B. Meltzer and D. Michie (eds.). Edinburgh University Press.

Von Foerster, H. (1971). Molecular ethology. In: *Molecular Mechanisms of Memory and Learning.* C. Ungar (ed). New York: Pergamon Press.

Zadeh, L. A. (1971). Toward a theory of fuzzy systems. In: *Aspects of Network and System Theory.* R. E. Kalman and N. DeClaris (eds.). New York: Holt, Rinehart and Winston.

Creating a CD ROM: The Process

13

Data Preparation and Premastering

Allen L. Adkins

Guidelines for In-House or "Do It Yourself" Data Preparation

Since data preparation will probably be the most time-intensive part of any CD ROM publishing project, it is worthwhile allocating initial budget dollars and time for some serious upfront planning. Good decisions during implementation planning in the early stages of a project will always be helpful and may sometimes save many thousands of dollars over the course of a CD ROM project. The following guidelines are provided as a stimulus list to assist in the upfront planning stages of a CD ROM project or to act as sign posts along the way to finishing a project. These guidelines are just that, only guidelines. Once you have a good understanding of the basic issues, you'll be able to take that knowledge and apply it appropriately to your own particular application.

Each CD ROM program will inevitably have differences. The requirements for data preparation for one project will often have very

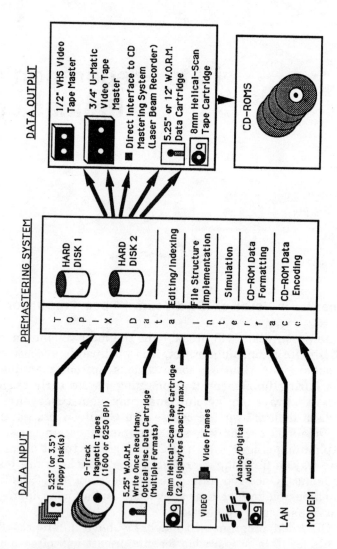

Figure 13-1   CD ROM publishing: How it happens.

different implementation objectives than others. On the other hand, CD ROM programs that *are* similar can take advantage of the similarity; for example, databases that are updated have to undergo less data preparation than the very first one. Subsequent updates often only require minor editing, updating of indexes, etc. Since it is likely that no two CD ROM projects are exactly alike, effort is made here to be somewhat general, and cover a range of issues potentially relevant to most CD ROM publishing projects.

Some of the basic questions to consider in data preparation planning are as follows:

1. *The concept.* Is the idea or concept for the CD ROM project valid? Does it "fit" with what CD ROM has to offer versus some other type of publishing media such as write-once read-mostly optical disc (WORM), laser cards, or microfiche, or just plain old print media, for example?

2. *Copyright issues.* Who owns the data? Do you know if you have the legal right to publish, distribute, and resell any and all of the data? If not, can you acquire or negotiate for the rights?

3. *Data capture.* Is the data machine readable? Has the data been used in some kind of on-line or other type of electronic database environment? If so, is the user interface design and database search and retrieval software available or does it need to be created? Will you create it in house or buy off-the-shelf products that already do the job you require? If the data is not machine readable, will the data be converted inhouse or by a service bureau of some kind? Is the data just text or does it combine numerical data, graphics, diagrams, drawings, video, audio, or some other type or form of information?

4. *Project management.* Is there a standard method of capturing the information in place that works well on your data preparation system? Is there a central or networked managed data editing, formatting, and indexing system? Are you taking full advantage of your existing computer processing equipment?

5. *Experience.* Is this the first CD ROM project you have done? Are you sure you are aware of the issues? Have you consulted with those who *do* know and can share at least their own ex-

perience? Will the whole project be performed in house or will a service bureau be utilized? If it is to be done in house, do you have all the necessary resources to complete the task(s) required? If you are considering a service bureau, does the firm have sufficient experience doing similar enough projects, and do they have sufficient manpower to give your project proper attention during the whole project, not just during the first phase?

6. *Quality assurance.* Is the data a small amount or a large amount of data, for example, is the database 10 or 20 Mbytes or is it 500 Mbytes? Will the data fit on three or four floppy disks or will it fit on one CD ROM (665 Mbytes of user data per disc)? Whether the data is a little or a lot, has the data been thoroughly edited, properly formatted, and completely checked for accuracy? Do you have enough hard disk storage interfaced to your data preparation system to allow for ease of editing, index building, etc.? Do you have a thoroughly valid method of verifying that all your data in the database is correct, bit for bit?

7. *Data formats and adherence to industry standards.* Will the data be published to conform to an existing industry standard file structure, such as High Sierra (ISO/DIS 9660, etc.) or will it be a proprietary file structure, possibly with extensive data encryption for added protection? Have you thoroughly thought through the trade-offs between adhering to industry standards and going with a proprietary file structure that potentially provides more data security?

CD ROM Characteristics

What is CD ROM? How can it be used? In the attempt to understand whether or not CD ROM is the right media choice for a given project, it helps to understand what the basic characteristics of CD ROM are. If one fully understands what CD ROM is, what the relative strengths and weaknesses are, then the choice of whether or not to use CD ROM or how to use it can be made much easier. Let's quickly review some of the more salient points.

- Compact Disc Read-Only Memory (CD ROM is a *permanently* pre-recorded polycarbonate plastic disc metalized with a reflective surface read by a laser beam).

- The CD ROM is approximately 4.72 inches in diameter and spins counterclockwise during reading.

- The data on a CD ROM is organized into consecutive data blocks, each consisting of 2352 bytes of data (12 synchronization bytes, 3 CD Time Code Address bytes expressed in minutes, seconds, and blocks), one mode byte, and 2048 bytes of user data, and 288 extra error detection and correction bytes in CD ROM mode 1. See Figure 13-2.

- A CD ROM spins at a constant linear rate of 75 data blocks per second which yields a 150 kbyte/second data transfer rate. The rotation speed of the disc varies as the head moves from inner to outer tracks, so that a constant number of blocks are read every second during reading. Initially the disc spins at a rate of approximately 500 rpm in the inner diameter area, and then gradually slows down to around 200 rpm at the outer edge of the disc.

- The CD ROM's data storage capacity can vary depending on which data mode you specify. There are three valid data modes available. These are 0, 1, and 2. In mode 0 you have no data stored. In mode 1 you have 2048 bytes user data with an additional 288 bytes used for the added layer of CD ROM data error detection and correction (EDC). In mode 2 the added layer of error detection and correction is not used. This allows the 288 bytes ordinarily used for EDC to be used for additional user data, for a total of 2336 bytes of user data per block.

- The average access time to the beginning of a data block can be as long as 1.5 seconds or longer, depending on the brand of CD ROM drive used, overhead of the operating system, and the efficiency of the device driver used. This needs to be taken into account when designing an application, particularly when multiple reads may be required in the actual use of the program. The possible delays during multiple seeking is the reason why index tables are built into databases — they can shorten the search time, thereby offering the user a better response time.

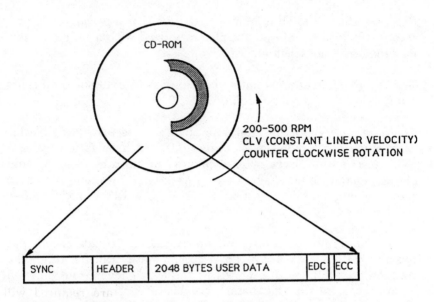

Figure 13-2   CD ROM Mode 1 block structure.

- A CD ROM disc is essentially the same as a CD Audio disc except for the method of encoding the data, the precise structure of the data on the disc, and the manner in which the data is decoded by the player. Some CD ROM drives can now recognize and play both audio and data CDs.

- CD ROM can store audio as well as digital computer data. In this *mixed* mode, you must allow for a 2-second pre- and post-gap between tracks of computer data and audio. The CD Audio specification allows for a maximum of 99 tracks on a disc. Each track can also have 99 index points. CD ROM discs made according to the ISO9660/High Sierra format specification must have the data track appear first, always starting at CD time code 00:02:00. Any CD Audio tracks are placed after the first CD ROM track, followed by a 2-second CD ROM block of structured zeroes and then by a 2-second gap of nonblock structured zeroes, for a total of 4 seconds of zero gap between different types of CD tracks (data or audio).

CD ROM Data Preparation

CD ROM data preparation is a general term which covers all the various kinds of data manipulations that may occur to data, in one form or another, on its way from its original format to its final data structure on the CD ROM. CD ROM data preparation is too general and all-encompassing a subject to fully describe here. There are so many ways to prepare data for CD ROM that is is impossible to fully cover in the limited number of pages in this book. CD ROM data preparation is the activity performed *after* you have defined your application and acquired the data, and *before* a master tape (or other type of intermediate data storage used for submission to a CD factory) is generated and sent to the CD ROM manufacturer for disc replication. It is the time when all the information you plan to put on the CD ROM is converted to a machine readable format, if it is not already machine readable, and formatted into a "program image" for premastering and placement on the disc.

The kind of data preparation functions that are required will depend on the kind of data that will go on the CD ROM. The original source data format could be virtually anything. The database could be an amalgamation of many kinds of data, or it could be just a collection of large data files that already exist on a mainframe computer and have, ideally, the addition of an index to help find and shorten the seek time to the data. Refer to Figure 13-3 for an overview of the process flow from data preparation to finished CD ROM application.

Preparing Text for Publishing on CD ROM

Of course, since CD ROM is a digital media, any and all information stored on it must first be converted to a computer readable format of some type or another, if it is not already in a format that can be read by or input to the computer. Text, regardless of the particular nationality or dialect, must be "machine readable" or, in other words, able to be read or input to the computer performing data preparation functions such as editing or indexing.

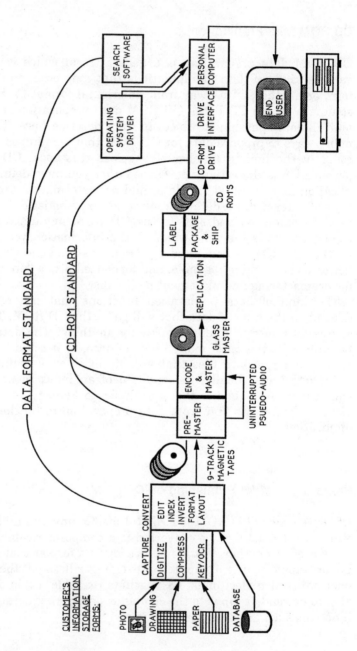

Figure 13-3   The CD ROM product development process.

Representing Text on a Computer

There are many methods of getting the text into the computer, but there are primarily two common ways to represent text on a computer. One is as character coded text, where a character is represented by a specific pattern of pixels (picture elements) on the screen, where each character, punctuation, or diacritical mark and other symbols are comprised of a pattern of pixels, with each pixel represented by 1 byte, or 7 or 8 bits, of binary data. The second is as a bit mapped image of the text, where the entire page or portion of a page of text is scanned in, or digitized, and stored as a single "whole page" image.

Text Stored as Characters

Computers generally store text as characters which can be individually or collectively displayed on a CRT (cathode ray tube) monitor. These characters are usually stored using one of two standard formats: ASCII or the American Standard Code for Information Interchange; and EBCDIC, which stands for Extended Binary Coded Decimal Information Code. These character codes use either 7 or 8 bits of data to represent the character and are stored usually on a computer readable media, such as floppy, hard disk, magnetic 9-track or DAT (digital audio tape), optical disc (CD ROM, WORM, or other type), or from an integrated circuit form of memory and read into computer memory or directly displayed on the CRT.

ASCII is probably the most common form of character coding used by most computer displays, though EBCDIC is used widely in writing tapes for data interchange between larger mini- and mainframe type computers. ASCII is used almost exclusively on smaller computer systems and personal computers. For this reason, you will most often find that conversion from EBCDIC to ASCII is required prior to placement on CD ROM, as most CD ROM programs are or will be read by personal computer workstations. Of course, you should keep in mind that CD ROM can store data in virtually any form, and as long as you have a way to display or utilize the data output in the desired manner, it can be viewed as a universal data publishing and distribution media.

Text Stored as a Bit Mapped Image

In order to store text in a bit mapped, or digitized, form you must scan the image or text with a scanning device. The scanner will generally read an entire page or part of a page at a time and store the scanned "image" in computer memory, then as one big file of data, instead of individual ASCII characters. In order to display the text, you must display the entire scanned portion of the page where the text is located, instead of as a group of one or more 7- or 8-bit ASCII character bytes. This approach inherently limits the kinds of text manipulation that can be performed with the text, but allows, in some cases, faster conversion of document pages to machine readable format where display of the entire page is adequate for the application.

OCR (optical character recognition) scanners are available with differing degrees of scanning resolution usually ranging from 150 dpi to several hundred dots per inch. However, for most applications the scanning resolution will usually be between 150 and 600 dpi. Scanners with higher resolution are very expensive to buy and also expensive to rent.

A consideration when choosing the scanning resolution is whether or not an output option will be made available to the user and, if so, on what kind of output device will the user print out the text and/or image(s).

When storing text as bit mapped images, expect to use up a larger amount of hard disk, optical disc, or mag tape storage. For example, a standard size page of text, when scanned at an average resolution of 300 dpi, will require approximately 1 Mbyte of data storage. If compression is used, for example, Group 3 or 4 facsimile transmission coding, the requirement can be reduced to only 100 kbytes, still 30 to 50 times more than that required by ASCII representation.

Comparison Between Storing Text as Characters or as Bit Mapped Images

Choosing between storing text as characters or as bit mapped image pages is a potentially important issue with far reaching implications in terms of user requirements, user expectations, flexibility, budgetary costs, conversion time, etc. Each kind of format has its relative strengths and weaknesses. Table 13-1 lists some of the main advantages and disadvantages of text as characters and as bit maps.

Table 13-1 Some Strengths and Weaknesses of Character Coded Text and Bit Mapped Text

Text as ASCII or EBCDIC	Text as Bit Mapped Images
Long established international standards	Potentially faster and easier to scan
Wide-ranging compatibility	Limited capability
Requires manual key entry or OCR scanning for data conversion	Any page can be scanned easily with the right equipment, could be expensive
Requires only 1 to 3 kbytes of data to store a page of text	Requires about 1 Mbyte per page
The largest majority of existing databases worldwide are stored in either ASCII or EBCDIC format either on-line or on mag tape	Standards for bit mapped images and text input, storage, and printing are just now being created and are not yet in wide use
Text stored as ASCII or EBCDIC can be fully indexed using key words or as full text and can be retrieved by a character or word or phrase or paragraph at a time.	Text cannot be indexed. Only the page itself can be referenced unless extra database fields are created, requiring significantly more data prep time

A CD ROM disc can store between 175,000 and 300,000 pages of text as ASCII or EBCDIC characters and can store between 600 and 6000 pages as bit mapped images. Retrieval of text in bit mapped form is all but impossible and is not recommended. Retrieval of the entire page or parts thereof is possible, but even here access time will probably be longer than for an ASCII page of text.

The kind of situation where it makes the most sense to scan documents as bit maps instead of ASCII is when the document will always be displayed as a full page unto itself or connected with other adjacent pages, for example, old manuals, catalogs, forms, and other types of documents that would be complicated to convert any other way than by scanning. In other cases, and certainly for databases being created in the present time, ASCII is much preferred.

Attention to file formats and resolution compatibility is important, and much more so when dealing with bit mapped images because of the fact that there are fewer standards in place for graphics pages than for ASCII text. Usually, only laser printers with fairly good printing resolution are acceptable for printing bit mapped images. Since laser printers usually cost much more than dot matrix printers, you should consider the cost factors required for the end-user workstation requirements.

The subject areas of character coded text and bit mapped graphics are well covered in the literature.

Data Capture

Keyboard Data Entry. The most straightforward, and, surprisingly, sometimes the least expensive and most reliable way, is just to type data in, using standard keyboard entry. Careful consideration should be given as to just how fast it is to use OCR scanners versus the more traditional keyboard entry approach. Many service bureau firms will convert text oriented databases by key entry and can offer very high levels of accuracy and well-managed, timely conversion within budget planning guidelines. Oftentimes these service bureaus will perform the actual keyboard entry offshore, for example, in the Philippines, to reduce labor costs. You can expect costs to range from 50 cents per page to more than $2.00 per page. The total number of pages, the degree of complexity, and the degree of accuracy required will largely determine the actual price. Usually, you must key in the data twice and compare to achieve near perfect accuracy.

Optical Character Recognition. OCR technology has been evolving for the past few years and has been steadily advancing to a more reliable and cost effective level. However, great caution should be exhibited when deciding the exact text conversion methodology one should use for a given database conversion project. Generally, when the project is very large, when it must be done in a timely manner, and when budget and data accuracy are extremely important, keyboard data entry is the hands down winner. But OCRs *are* getting better. The key point to remember here is that you should always try out sample pages of the document(s) on the given OCR device you are thinking about using to confirm that the per page time and accuracy of scanning and final cleanup and editing are as fast and as inexpensive as key entry. The only way to know which way to go for sure is to try it out and see which is faster in your particular application.

Data File Formats and Conversion. The issue of what file format to create when you perform data conversion or when you are preparing a database that is already machine readable is a most important one. The primary deciding factor should be the end user and what kind of file structure is required by the delivery system. Typically, in the MS- DOS world this means using either the May 28, 1986 draft mode High Sierra specification or the ISO/DIS 9660 specification, as they are compatible with the Microsoft CD ROM Extensions, release one and two, respectively. In the Macintosh or other type of PC environment, the choice is to either buy or write a device driver that can read High Sierra or ISO/9660 CD ROMs or a device driver than can read the native file structure of the intended host computer of the information delivery system.

Preparing Machine Readable Text for CD ROM Publishing

The main issue here is to render the text file(s) into a format that can be handled by the search and retrieval software you are using in a manner that will suit the user the best when it comes time to access the information. In many cases the text information will be indexed using the index build function of a related search and retrieval engine. In this case, the particular software requirements should be documented to allow you to know the exact format the data must be in prior to performing the actual data input to the index build program. The data formatting required to get the data ready to be indexed is often called data cleanup or text preparation. There are many options in this area of text retrieval, and the developer is well advised to check out all available existing software packages prior to writing custom software, as there could well be one that meets your needs very closely and can be acquired for a reasonable cost. Other CD ROM industry resources exist to assist in this selection process and are easily found by reading industry trade publications such as *CD Data Report, CD ROM Review, Optical Memory News,* etc. Remember, nothing is better than an actual demonstration of a particular indexing, search and retrieval software package running with your own data to determine if your needs are properly met by a particular company's software. If you can't find what you need on the open market, perhaps you can customize an existing program or write your own, but be prepared for some long hours of development, testing, and/or customizing in order to achieve a quality user interface and data search and retrieval performance.

The Data Structure of the Database

The key element in any electronic database publishing project, whether or not it is to be published on CD ROM, is the ease of information search and retrieval, based on the request(s) of the user and the usefulness of the presentation of information to the user. The indexing will allow the information search and retrieval, and the search and retrieval software should handle the presentation of the information to the user. The data must be put into a format that can be read by the indexing software being used. This process, often called data cleanup, if properly performed, can save large amounts of time in the data preparation of a database.

Full Text

There are a great variety of ways to store text on CD ROM. In many cases, however, the text will be stored in an industry standard format such as ASCII or JIS Kanji (or SHIFT JIS), except for very small files for use as messages, help files, etc., the text in most databases should be indexed to allow for rapid retrieval of the data. There are really two primary ways to store data in a structured format, the first being the storage of the text as a full text document oriented database, and the second a record/field/keyword oriented database. We may also anticipate some applications using a combination of both the full text and record/field or multimedia data structure.

The primary focus should always be for the publisher and/or the database builder to determine how the information will be used by the various users, and choose the data structure, indexing, and user interface that will most likely facilitate the searches that the end user will want.

If the text oriented database is already in a machine readable format, then use the data structure that is desired in the new database and devise a plan for running the text through a formatting program that preprocesses the data to prepare the text for indexing. The basic idea is to use the computer to do what it can do faster and more efficiently than a human editor can do by hand. This formatting process requires a good bit of upfront planning, decision making, and understanding about the precise functionality of the index building or file inversion software and how you want to index and later query the database.

With a good structural design of the database in hand it is then possible to write a special software program to preformat (or preprocess the data into an optimum format) the text data so that the index software program can more readily create the appropriate indexes. This preprocessing period is also the time when effort may be applied to performing text compression or delimiting the database by using stop words or other methods to achieve a reduction of the size of the resulting index.

In full text databases, each word may be indexed or certain nonessential words may be left out. In addition, certain key words may be used during indexing to allow for rapid search and retrieval of specific words, phrases, or subjects within a full text or record oriented database. Also, in the case of full text databases on CD ROM, great attention should be given to the number of seeks required to complete a given search. Various indexing methods, such as balanced B-Trees, hashing, "tidy" hashing and/or combinations or hybrid variations of the above may be required to achieve acceptable search and retrieval performance.

Page Description/Page Display

The information age is bringing with it a gradual evolution of how information workers have access to information. For centuries we have been using the printed page as the primary information presentation metaphor. Now, as electronic information access grows in use we find the page metaphor a strong determinant in affecting how we are presented with information on an information workstation computer display screen (CRT). In fact, we now have special computer software known as page description or page display software that enables information to be displayed in a pagelike manner. However, unlike the printed page, with the electronic or digital page we have an added dynamic information search, retrieval, and presentation capability that is synergistically enhanced by the computer and the page description, the indexing software, and the search and retrieval software.

In order for the user to see the information on a CRT screen in the specified manner, the preparation of the information, the indexing, and the search and retrieval software must have been previously accounted for it as much as possible. The display format should ideally be flexible, allowing the user to at least minimally decide where on a page display certain information is displayed.

Maybe the user wants to browse or look at short phrases or lists before going into more depth in the case of full text databases. Maybe the user wants to choose how the numeric or record oriented databases are displayed on the screen. In addition, as is often the case, one search leads to another and then yet another and so on. Thus we see a need to create links between words, concepts, phrases, or subjects so that the user can quickly and easily go from one reference or records to others which have certain relationships — maybe even more easily discovering new relationships — thereby providing a knowledge leverage factor to an otherwise ordinary information search.

One of the developments in the page description area during the last few years is the effort being made in the publishing and electronic publishing industries toward a more standard or uniform procedure for defining electronic documents or manuscripts. One such standard is known as Standard Generalized Markup Language (SGML). Since it is necessary to insert special codes into documents to allow for specific kinds of display after searching, there has been an effort to unify or standardize what codes to use, when and how to use them, and efforts to integrate these standards into database publishing software and systems. Various preparatory efforts were initiated by interested industry groups in the mid 1960s. By the late 1970s ANSI and ISO approved SGML as an international standard — ISO8879.

SGML as a standard data structure description language seeks to accomplish the following:

• To provide a uniform standard for electronic documents that are usable on a wide range of systems, including text and word processors in general widespread use, CAD systems, desktop publishing systems, and other related systems.

- To ensure ease of use by computer systems and information editors (human operators).
- To ensure device and character set independence (i.e., ASCII, JIS KANJI, EBCDIC).
- To provide a way for other forms of media such as bit mapped images, audio, related data files to be referenceable and callable from within an SGML processed document.
- To provide a well-defined standard to allow for SGML oriented or compatible hardware and software information processing system to be developed and progressively evolve.

Since the early 1980s SGML has been implemented in many government and electronic information oriented companies as part of complete document processing and display/printing systems. For example, SGML systems are in use at the U.S. Air Force, U.S. Navy Publications and Printing Service, the Association of American Publishers (which includes a very large number of major publishing firms) and increasingly electronics information publishing companies of all kinds.

The use of SGML based information publishing software tools and systems is likely to increase dramatically, especially the creation of intelligent software that can more or less automatically mark up an electronic document or greatly reduce the amount of time required by an operator when using an SGML system. Additionally, more index building and search and retrieval software will take advantage of SGML and there may eventually be quasi standards for indexing and search and retrieval, partly due to the level of standardization offered by SGML.

It is strongly recommended that any serious database publisher become familiar with SGML through the American Association of Publishers, ANSI and ISO, and companies offering SGML based or compatible information processing products.

Multimedia Search and Retrieval

One of the most significant characteristics of optical discs (of which CD ROM is but one type or format) is that it is possible to store almost any form of digital media on a single disc. Virtually any form of data can be stored on a CD ROM. Depending on how the data is encoded on the disc, the media can be analog, digital, or a combination of both. For example, the laser video disc has the video data encoded in a type of analog format. It is also possible to encode the video in a digital format. We can expect an increasing trend toward all-digital video, as the video images are potentially much more flexible and easier to manipulate in a digital format. There is a clear trend toward all-digital media workstations used for all sorts of multimedia program productions.

One of the reasons why optical discs allow for the integration or mixing of various media is the large storage capacity and the random access to any part of the disc. This allows highly interactive programs to be created. As soon as we talk about mixing different types of media together on a disc, we also must consider the methodology of searching and retrieving the different forms of media and presenting the information to the user or viewer. For this, one needs special capabilities which allow the simultaneous access realtime (or interleaving) and display or presentation of text, graphics (vector or bit mapped), animation, video and audio. This also implies that the delivery system must also have the facility to support the display (CRT, color, high-resolution) and presentation of audio (digital-to-analog converter, speakers, headphone).

The simultaneous display of text, graphics, animation, and audio on CD ROM also makes it necessary to allow for interleaving of files which contain the different media for display. The data transfer rate and seek time limitations of CD ROM require careful judicious use of interleaving in many cases to achieve a dynamic, acceptable delivery of multimedia. In later sections of this chapter I will refer to the notion of hypertext, hypersound and the eventual goal of fully interactive, seamless digital hypermedia. There are many different kinds of software and hardware components that are required to first develop, simulate, and then allow end user interactive access of the multimedia database or program. We see the beginnings of the building blocks for digital multi- media authoring systems appearing from such companies as Optical Media International, Meridian Data and TMS and others who have been developing CD ROM data preparation systems and other software companies who are developing multi-media authoring tools such as OMI, Electronic Arts and MacroMind (VideoWorks II™).

Before we will see really significant applications of digital multimedia CD ROMs, we must first have fully capable multimedia authoring workstations that can be used by noncomputer literate artists, writers, and interactive program designers from various backgrounds and disciplines. It is an essential aspect of multimedia program design that full and complete simulation of the program be possible at every stage of development. Thus, we must tightly couple the design, development, testing, simulation, and final use of the program into the authoring system. The end user run time search and retrieval will in effect be a subset of the system software of the development system, and in some cases, end user functional requirements may require dynamic updating in which case the full development capabilities are part of the end user delivery/data acquisition system.

Necessary components of the multimedia development system are as follows: computer, Virtual CD Hard Disk Storage, Image Scanners/Film Scanners, Digital Video Frame Grabber, Image Editing Software, Hi-Res Display Monitor, OCR/Scanner, Bit Pad, A/D Converter, Pulse Code Modulation (PCM) Processor, Adaptive Differential Pulse Code Modulation (ADPCM) (a technology for achieving high quality compression of PCM audio data) Encoder/Decoder, powerful Multimedia File Editing and Interleaving Software, Retrieval Software with Multimedia File support for iterative development, simulation, and final end use.

Graphics Scanning and Other Forms of Image Capture

Graphic Images

Graphic images can be created or captured (converted to a digital format) in a variety of different ways. Images can be scanned in from photographs, 35-mm slides, drawings on paper, frame-grabbed from a live video camera; video tape or videodisc captured and edited with a video/raster image paint program. Further, images can be entirely created using a paint program (such as Apple's MacPaint and other fine, more advanced drawing and paint programs), end-point computed, or they can be created using algorithms that form an image by computing polygons using a graphics rendering capability, such as PIXAR's RenderMan™, for example. Graphics can be traced, either by hand or using image analysis software that autotraces an image, bit mapped, scanned, or otherwise, and creates a vector graphics image file.

Almost any type of image can be stored or converted and then stored on CD ROM. The issues are really what kind of image is appropriate or desired for a given application, how will the image be created or captured and then ultimately displayed to the end user. Let's look at the kinds of images, their generation or conversion, image storage and their relative aspects in view of their applicability in CD ROM applications with emphasis on how to deal with each in the data preparation of an image or multimedia database or program and the eventual retrieval and presentation of the image(s).

Digitizing an Image

Digital images are either created or converted or "captured" using an electronic device, such as a graphics scanner, film or slide film scanner, video camera and frame grabber, bit pad with paint program or algorithmic or end-point (fractal, image formula based) computed.

Graphics scanners are improving in quality, becoming easier to use while decreasing steadily in cost. The issues in graphics scanning are scanned image resolution and the graphics image file format that the image file is stored as when recorded on a permanent or interim storage media. Generally, images should be originally scanned at as high a resolution as possible, then scaled to meet a given application requirement. Scaling, in this context, is the process of decreasing or increasing the resolution of an image, for example taking a 1024 x 1024, 24 bits per pixel image and "scaling" it down to 640 x 480, 8 bits per pixel. This approach allows more flexibility and upward compatibility with higher resolution image formats and display monitors. It is always easier to produce a quality image when you are starting with an ultra high resolution and going to a lower resolution. Any subsequent processing may take away some of the resolution, thus making an original of high resolution very desirable. Images scanned with a scanner can be black and white, gray-scale, or color. The scanner chosen should allow for rough and fine adjustment of parameters relevant to the kind of image being scanned. There are many types of scanning and image input devices to choose from.

The choice should really be based on what type of image you want to have displayed to the user and what type of display monitor or device will be required by the user to display a given type of image. High resolution monitors can be expensive. Low cost video monitors, though less expensive, may not offer sufficient resolution for many applications.

Types of Image Capture/Creation Devices

- Flatbed scanners. Varying scanning resolution, typically 75 dots per inch (dpi) to more than 1000 dpi. The price increases as the resolution capability increases.
- Rotating drum scanners
- Laser image scanners
- Digitizing tablets (bit pads)
- Video digitizers/frame store devices
- Video cameras
- Film scanners
- Flying spot scanner
- Paint programs (software)
- Drawing programs (software)
- Computer animation systems
- Conversion of digital images to other digital image formats
- Converting bit-mapped images to vector images (raster-to-vector image conversion)
- Storing a lot of images in a small space — digital image compression

Graphic images can be digitally represented, stored, and displayed in a variety of different file formats, such as Tagged Image File Format (TIFF), Pict I, Pict II, Postscript, etc.

CD ROM Data Preparation Issues for Video

The addition of video to CD ROM databases can be handled in a number of different ways. Primary issues are whether or not you need full motion video or just still frames and how the images will be displayed by the user.

Video

Video has become a very ubiquitous form of image representation and a successful consumer and professional technology. There are many established world standards for video, and there is a large amount of support technology to assist developers with the production, editing, and presentation of video to a wide variety of viewers.

Video standards do not currently have the luxury of being the same worldwide, as does the Compact Disc. Consequently, there is the issue of which video standard format you will use if you want to add video to a CD ROM database, or even if you just want to place a number of video images on a CD ROM. The United States, Japan, and a number of other countries use the NTSC (National Television Standards Committee) video standard. Europe, Australia, India, and parts of Africa and Asia use the PAL (Phase-Alternate-By-Line) video standard. Other parts of the world, for example, France, the USSR, and most Eastern Bloc countries, use the SECAM (Sequential Color with Memory) video standard. Since there are several different formats, you must choose how you want to store the image on the CD ROM and in what image format will it be displayed on the screen to the user.

It is possible to convert from one video format to another, but the right equipment has to be available and it costs extra, whether you buy or rent your own equipment or just rent time in a video production facility that can handle such conversions. Since CD ROM is inherently digital, the video image must first be converted to a digital format in order to be added as a data file to a CD ROM database.

The new CD Video, offered by Philips and Sony as another standard CD format, allows the video to be stored on a Compact Disc in basically the same manner that it is stored on an analog Laser-Vision-type video disc. Currently, due to the diameter of a Compact Disc, you can only store 5 min of full motion video on a single disc. If you want to store full motion video in a digital format on a Compact Disc, you must first convert the image to a digital format, then perform what is called image compression to reduce that amount of digital data required to represent the image while being stored on the Compact Disc. Conversely, when the video is played back, the compressed image must then be decompressed to be viewed on the screen. This decompression must be performed fast enough to allow 30 video frames per second to be continuously sent to the video display.

Since the fixed, maximum data transfer rate of CD ROM is 150 kbyte/second, in CD ROM mode 1 and 171 kbytes in CD ROM mode 2, you must use a very sophisticated video compression and decompression scheme in order to accomplish full motion video. The recently introduced Digital Video Interactive (DVI) technology developed at the David Sarnoff Research Center of RCA/GE offers this capability (see Chapter 7). The DVI method allows a full 72 minutes of NTSC video, digitally encoded, to be stored and played back as normal video. A very impressive feat, to be sure. This accomplishment, however, requires a relatively expensive special video compression system to first compress the video and a relatively expensive external printed circuit board to decompress the video prior to display on the screen. Effort is under way by RCA/GE to cost reduce this technology, but it will be several years, at best, before it is practical as a consumer technology. Certain professional applications, however, can be well served by this impressive technology once a less expensive system is made available to developers for the encoding of the video and a less expensive printed circuit board is more widely available for the end user delivery system. One of the advantages of this format is that it can utilize a standard CD ROM drive in conjunction with the decompression PC board. If the decompression hardware can be made less expensive, then the use of DVI will expand. However, the availability of delivery hardware is but one part of the required development system. The program authoring tools that allow more streamlined production of the content, and authoring of the program for a particular media, will ultimately play the largest part in the success of that particular media format.

Another approach, Compact Video Disc (CVD™), developed by SOCS Research, Inc. of Los Gatos, California offers a completely different technique by innovating a new way of video encoding allowing approximately 20 min of video to be stored on a Compact Disc. A special type of player, which allows the disc to rotate at 1800 rpm and that has the special CVD video demodulation circuitry, is required to play a CVD disc.

The SOCS Research CVD disc format also allows CD quality digital audio and digital data to be stored on the disc along with the video, adding to the potential applicability to a wide range of uses.

Up to 18,000 still frame TV quality video images can be stored and randomly accessed on a single disc. This compares very favorably with a CD ROM, which, without significant image compression, using something such as DVI, offers considerably less storage capacity.

Several hardware player manufacturers have agreed to offer CVD players, so we should ultimately see this technology introduced in the marketplace.

Another approach to accomplishing full motion video is to consider a hybrid system that uses both an analog laser videodisc player together with CD ROM. It will be some time before full motion digital video can be offered cheaper than using two players, one video disc and one CD ROM. Both can easily be interfaced with a computer and the CD ROM can offer many nice enhancements to the video disc. For example, one CD ROM could store more than 10 separate soundtracks in 10 different languages and could synchronize with the video disc during playback. It is certainly something that merits serious consideration for many applications.

Video can be stored in CD ROM more easily if you don't require full motion. The next section will deal with more straightforward approaches to storing video on CD ROM.

Still Frame Video

Still frame video images can be captured in a variety of different ways. The most common is to use what is called a "frame grabber." A frame grabber is a device, often taking the form of a printed circuit board installed in an image capture computer workstation, that is capable of "grabbing," in less than 1/30th of a second, a single analog video image or frame and performing an instant analog-to-digital conversion (A/D conversion) and then storing it in computer memory, called a frame buffer. Once in the computer memory of the frame buffer, the now-digital image can then be stored as a normal computer data file and written to hard disk or to some other form of intermediate storage such as magnetic tape or write-once optical disc. The image can also be edited or manipulated in numerous ways to enhance or change the image to suit one's particular purpose, using a variety of image editing software programs on the market. In addition, the video image can then be easily converted to a number of other industry standard image file formats

Video Slides

One way of using video in CD ROM databases and in multi-media programs is to display video one video frame at a time, or, in other words, a video slide.

The process of doing this is to "capture" the video image of choice using a video frame grabber, usually one that allows "grabbing" a video frame in less than 1/30th of a second. The frame rate of video is 30 frames per second and therefore usually requires that a frame be placed in a memory buffer in less than 1/30th of a second to allow for complete capture of a frame before the next frame is played because the content of the next frame may not have the same content as the one you want. Image capture or video frame grabbers with real-time video frame grabbing ability are available in the market for use with a wide variety of computers.

Once the video frame is placed in the memory buffer of the development system computer, a data file can then be made and stored on the hard disk. The next step would be to index the image or tag it to fit in with the particular CD ROM database or program being developed.

Issues to consider when developing CD ROM programs that include video slides are the amount of time required to read in the video frame during program execution. Remember that the CD ROM data transfer rate is 150 Kbytes per second. A video frame will require more than 1 Mbyte of data and will therefore require several seconds, at best, to read and display on the user's screen. This will require some user interface decisions and program design approaches that would perhaps load in the video frame into a buffer while the user is looking at something else on the screen. In any case, it is probably a good idea to not cause the screen to go blank during the time it takes to read in a video frame and display it. Of course the other issue is that the end-user delivery system may require much more RAM memory and require a display screen or other electronics that allow for the display of a video image.

If a normal video image takes too much memory or takes too long to display, another approach would be to compress the video frame(s) using a video compression scheme. This then would need either a software or hardware decompression scheme to allow display of the video image to the user. The software decompression would be less expensive, but may not be able to decompress the video image very quickly or fast enough to meet the program design requirements. A well designed hardware decompression scheme would allow very fast decompression but would definitely cost more to implement. These are the main tradeoffs to consider.

Other potential strategies would include decreasing the size of the image to be displayed on the screen by putting the video image in a small window on the screen, perhaps along with some text or other graphics. This would allow the image to be stored using less memory and displayed quicker in an application.

Any data file, whether it is video data or whatever, can be converted to the High Sierra/ISO 9660 file format in the normal way.

Partial Full Motion Video

Another approach to take with video on CD ROM is to either do some compression and decompression such that several frames (say from 5 to 20 frames) are displayed in succession at a somewhat less than normal video frame rate, perhaps accomplishing the desired result and still allowing the ability to have motion video or graphics. The issues here are essentially the same as with video slides. You would still have only the standard CD ROM data transfer rate to consider and the amount of time required to read the images and display them to the user.

It is quite possible, however, to start with video and then scale down and convert the video image to, for example, 640 by 480 resolution and display the images on a Macintosh II or IBM PC or compatible computer. The IBM VGA graphics allows 640 by 480 resolution display as does the Apple Macintosh. This fact is encouraging as this immediately means that the end-user equipment requirements to display the partial motion video or graphics is overall much less expensive for both the developer and the end user.

Full Motion/Video Compression

The issue of full motion digital video on CD ROM (or CD-I) or some other CD format is an exciting one and one that will continue to evolve for many years. RCA's DVI is an early front runner in this area. MIT has a research project, partially funded by Apple Computer, that is also making excellent progress in this area (see Chapters 6–8).

The main issues here are the availability of cost-effective systems to compress the video images, author interactive programs, simulate the program fully prior to disc production and then having a low-cost solution to decompress the video transparently integrated into the end-user delivery system, as mentioned earlier.

The basic process is to first capture the video images required for the program using as good a quality video camera as possible, editing the video into segments that will be used in the program and then inputting them into the video compression module or system. The resulting output would be some kind of compressed video data file (for example either MS-DOS, Macintosh HFS, or UNIX, etc.) that could then be either interleaved with other data such as audio or text and then used by the authoring system and simulated on a system that has a virtual CD playback capability.

The simulation system would also need to have a decompression circuit capable of decoding the compressed video and displaying it in the required fashion in real time (30 video frames per second).

Audio and CD ROM

Since CD ROM is a derivation of the Compact Digital Audio disc, adding audio to CD ROM is a natural and relatively straightforward task, assuming you have access to the right kind of development system.

There are, in fact, several different types of audio which can be combined on a CD. The standard type of audio found on all audio CDs is called Pulse Code Modulated (PCM) digital audio which is digitally sampled at a sampling frequency of 44.1 kHz, 16-bit resolution, two's complement.

Almost every audio CD is produced by either analog or digital recording, mixed down to a two-track master, and then processed into the standard CD Audio format using a PCM digital audio processor and recorded on to a 3/4-inch U-Matic videotape cassette. This digitally recorded audio is placed on the videotape as video, being modulated by the PCM processor. The same PCM processor is then used at the CD manufacturing facility during mastering to demodulate the video data back into the standard 16-bit, 44.1-KHz bit stream. This serial bit stream is then input to a CD encoder simultaneously with the CD subcode data, synchronized by SMPTE time code, in realtime. This type of mastering procedure is standardized worldwide as dictated by the "Red Book" CD Audio specification administered by Philips and Sony.

The most common type of professional PCM processor is the Sony PCM 1610 or 1630. In fact, there are only two manufacturers of professional PCM processors, Sony and JVC. JVC offers a very similar system known as the DAS-900 system, of which the VP-900 is the PCM processor. Any type of standard CD Audio must be processed by a professional 16 bit stereo PCM processor prior to CD mastering.

Generally, any type of audio, analog or digital can be converted into the standard CD Audio format. The key to mixing CD Audio with CD ROM data is the ability to combine the audio with the data onto a standard input media, such as the defacto standard 3/4-inch U-Matic video tape cassette, or DAT tape.

The program designer must decide where to place audio on the disc and then actually construct a tape master, using an in-house system or by delivering the data and audio separately to a facility equipped with the necessary system to accomplish this task.

All CD players, including those CD ROM players which support audio, can play any standard CD Audio track, whether the disc is a normal audio CD or a CD ROM combined with one or more CD Audio tracks.[1] As mentioned previously, CDs can have a maximum of 99 tracks. Each track can be either a CD Audio track or a CD ROM data track. A subcode bit set during PQ subcode editing, prior to mastering, will allow the CD player to recognize a CD Audio track or a CD ROM data track. It is important that the PQ subcode bit be properly set, as CD ROM drives cannot read a CD ROM data track that has been inadvertently flagged as an audio track. Each audio track can have a maximum of 99 index points, also added during PQ subcode editing.[2]

If you make an audio disc that has 99 tracks and 99 indexes per track, you will have a maximum of 9801 individually addressable audio segments (or double that many in mono) if you use the subcode index points to seek the audio segments. You can also randomly seek audio segments using explicit CD time code (minutes, seconds, blocks) addressing. Most current CD ROM device drivers allow this

---

1   CD Audio players *cannot* play a CD ROM disc with CD ROM data tracks. However, some CD ROM drives can play CD Audio discs and CD ROM discs which include CD Audio tracks.

2   Not all subcode editors in use support the full specification 99 tracks and 99 indexes per track; therefore, it is important that you check with the facility that will perform the PQ subcode editing to determine their capability if you plan to make a disc that uses a large number of tracks and indexes.

type of audio random access, i.e., the Microsoft CD ROM extensions, for example.

Generally, CD ROM data tracks and CD Audio tracks can be mixed in any order on a CD, except that all High Sierra or ISO/DIS 9660 formatted CDs must always have the first track as the High Sierra/ISO data track partition, located at CD timecode address 00:02:00. Any audio tracks or additional non-High Sierra/ISO data tracks must be added after the first High Sierra/ISO track.

Converting Analog Audio to the CD Audio Format

When preparing analog audio for inclusion to a CD ROM, remember that the analog audio should be as free as possible of any hiss or noise, as the digital audio system used by CDs will accentuate any background noise that may be present on the analog input media after analog-to-digital conversion. Just remember, garbage in, garbage out has never been more true than with digital audio. Any type of analog audio can be converted into a 16-bit, 44.1-kHz PCM digital audio format, for example, by using the Sony PCM 1630 Digital Audio Processor. This PCM processor has built-in 16-bit, 44.1-kHz A/D and D/A converters that will perform realtime conversion. Remember that many analog audio sources will require equalization or normalization prior to being rendered into the digital audio domain to avoid unwanted audio artifacts. Consult a knowledgeable facility with experience in this area, particularly if you are new to this kind of endeavor. It's not really complicated, but there is an art to it.

Digital Audio

Digital audio covers a wide range of different types and formats, of which the CD Audio format is only one of many. Generally speaking, the quality of digital audio is determined by the sample rate and digital bit resolution; for example, a sample rate of 100 kHz and a 24-bit resolution would theoretically be superior to a 16-bit, 44.1-kHz digital audio recording. However, in real life practice, there are many additional factors that determine the overall quality of a particular digital audio sound. Special digital filters, oversampling, and other special digital circuits and digital recording techniques can make a profound difference, aside from the sample rate and digital resolution of a particular sound. This chapter is not sufficient to cover the vast area of digital audio technology; there are many fine books widely available on the subject. (See Chapter 16.)

Prior to the introduction of the Compact Disc Digital Audio format, there was a large amount of study and contribution and heated debate over the optimum sample rate and digital resolution to be used in the CD format. Many of the best minds in the field of digital audio contributed their suggestions and opinions and, for better or worse, a middle of the road compromise was decided. Actually, the format is proving quite satisfactory for all but the most die-hard analog fanatics, with the advent of specially designed digital filter circuits and oversampling chips that are widely used in many consumer CD Audio players. It is in the area of the original digital recording technique that the most work and evolution is needed.

If you have a digital audio recording that exists in a different sample rate or different format from that of CD Audio, you will need to have it converted to the correct format prior to final premastering of your program. There are many facilities that offer this service. You should contact the CD pressing facility you plan to use and ask their advice if you're in doubt as to how to proceed.

Adaptive Delta (or Differential) Pulse Code Modulation (ADPCM)

Another type of digital audio that is starting to be widely talked about and will soon see wide use is a type of compressed PCM audio known as ADPCM, or adaptive delta (or differential) pulse code modulation. This ADPCM format also has many different forms and sample rates and digital resolutions that are possible, and any can conceivably be used in conjunction with CD ROM. The only requirement is that the particular type of ADPCM must have a decoder that is capable of decoding and playing back the particular ADPCM format used.

The CD-I specification (known as the "Green Book" to CD Licensees) explicitly defines three levels of ADPCM. The CD-I type of ADPCM is one type that will undoubtedly see wide use, not only in the CD-I player system but in background music applications and mixed-mode, interleaved audio applications, where the CD ROM drive is either equipped with a built-in-in CD-I decoder chip or with an external CD-I format ADPCM decoder chip to allow the ADPCM audio to be played, while any CD ROM data is sent to its intended destination, such as a host computer.

Interactive Multimedia CD ROM

One of the exciting prospects of CD ROM is the fact that the compact disc is so well suited to multimedia applications. It is capable of storing vast amounts of digital information. Text, graphics, animated graphics, video (depending on the capabilities of the particular format used), and audio can all be combined on a single disc.

However, one of the areas that has been lacking in the CD ROM standards is the ability to play audio as well as the other data formats at the same time. In order to accomplish synchronized audio with data and/or graphics you must either seek and read the data segment(s), place them in a memory buffer, then seek to the audio segment and then have the computer display the required data on the screen while the audio segment(s) play through the CD player. This is how most multimedia programs have been accomplished with CD ROM thus far. This method, though certainly minimally adequate, is not the optimum method. A far better approach is to "interleave" the audio segment(s) with the related data or graphics, video, or other digital data that you may wish to display, accompanied with some sort of audio. This interleaving, if properly done, can allow near perfect synchronization with the other data.

The problem, however, is that standard CD Audio cannot be interleaved such that a segment can be played in realtime, or in other words, to have the data and audio play continuously at the maximum data rate a CD is capable of playing (either 150 or 171 kbyte/s). This is due to the fact that CD Audio requires the full bandwidth of the CD data channel to play the audio, leaving no space available for other data, or vice versa. In addition to the fact that CD ROM data tracks and CD Audio tracks must be physically located separately on the CD (as strictly specified in the CD standard), thus making it impossible to interleave data and audio while adhering to the normal CD Audio specification. This brings up the significance of what ADPCM has to offer interactive multimedia CD ROM applications.

In order to achieve realtime or nonrealtime data and audio interleaving, you must compress the audio (reduce the amount of data required to represent a given audio segment) and then interleave this compressed audio with data (text, graphics, video, etc.) according to the desired interleave factor, for example 8 kbytes of data, followed by 6 kbytes of compressed audio, allowing the data to be played, immediately followed by the compressed audio. Of course, the compressed audio must be able to be decompressed, in realtime, and sent to a digital-to analog converter to be played back through either a speaker or headphones. ADPCM is a widely used technology in many areas, particularly in the telecommunications industry. One possible format is to use the CD-I ADPCM specification, or at least something similar.

Currently, no CD ROM drives support the decoding of ADPCM audio, only standard CD Audio, which, as previously mentioned, does not allow for the interleaving of data and audio. In order for the truly meaningful interactive multimedia CD ROM programs to be implemented, some form of compressed audio will need to be offered. This brings up several possibilities.

The Need for a Compressed Audio Standard for Multimedia CD ROM

Of course, anyone can create their own format of compressed audio and the required decoder to play it back with a custom application. This approach would work well if the application was only for a strictly controlled, vertical application where the end-user delivery system CD ROM player/decoder was sold along with the program. But for widespread use of interleaved data and audio to become a reality, there must be at least one (or possibly more than one) standard specification widely available and easily utilized by program developers. The specification must define how the audio will be encoded, using APDCM, for example, and how it will be decoded during playback. This will require cost effective ADPCM encoding, simulation, and decoding systems for program development and testing, as well as inexpensive ADPCM decoders, easily interfaced to existing or future CD ROM players.

The function of the ADPCM decoder is to allow any ADPCM format data on any CD to be sent through the decoder's D/A converter and then on to a speaker of headphones, and any normal data to be sent through the interface to the host device, such as a PC, during playback. This format specification must be widely adhered to or the true potential of multimedia CD ROMs will not be fully realized. This means that CD ROM player manufacturers must consider how they will support the multimedia feature of interleaved data and audio in their players. There are three possibilities: Manufacturers can build decoding chips into the players they can offer external decoders that are interfaced to the player, either in a host PC or as a completely external decoder device; or third party companies could offer the required decoder.

We should eventually see the CD ROM player manufacturer's supporting data and audio interleaving with built-in ADPCM decoders based on either the CD-I format ADPCM and/or some similar format. We will also see third party companies offering ADPCM decoding solutions as well as ADPCM Development Systems that will perform the required encoding, simulation, and decoding of programs that contain ADPCM audio interleaved with various types of data.

There are, however, several technical issues relevant to the issue of the interleaving of ADPCM audio with data in the CD ROM format that are yet to be fully resolved and that must be resolved before a widespread use can be achieved. First and foremost is the issue of the ADPCM block length and structure.

In the CD-I ADPCM format, the data block length is 2336 bytes. As you may recall, it is CD ROM mode 2 that allows 2336-byte data blocks. In CD ROM mode 2 you do not have the added layer of error detection and correction. Further, the most widely used CD ROM data standard, the High Sierra and ISO/DIS 9660 CD ROM File Structure, explicitly specifies 2048-byte data blocks. All High Sierra/ISO CD ROM device drivers support 2048-byte data blocks. Of course, device drivers can be rewritten to support a modified version of the standard, but the fact remains that the current widely used standard specifies 2048 byte data blocks.

Another approach, that taken by Optical Media International with its CD ROM CA format, is to support both the CD-I ADPCM format, as well as a somewhat similar format that is 100 percent compatible with High Sierra/ISO and that has 2048-byte data blocks for the ADPCM audio as well as data, thus requiring no changes in any existing software device drivers in order to implement interleaved data and audio files. The additional advantage is that the ADPCM audio is in the CD ROM mode 1 format, and thereby protected by the additional CD ROM layer of error detection and correction. Since the ADPCM is a compressed form of audio it is imperative that the data be 100 percent correct after decoding or audio distortion will likely occur.

The main point here is that there must be widespread industry support and acceptance of a compressed audio standard. In all likelihood, ADPCM audio will emerge as the most practical form of compressed audio, if for no other reason than the ADPCM decoding chips will be mass produced in the CD-I players and thus a practical, cost effective choice.

It is, however, important to remember that the ADPCM format should ideally fully conform to other CD ROM standards already in widespread use, thus allowing for maximum use by the industry with the least amount of additional development.

Many exciting applications can be created with interleaved audio: Talking books; totally new kinds of interactive training and educational programs; and innovative audio-enhanced programs of virtually every description. Indeed, it is the audio component of the CD that first created enormous success for the new optical media. It will be the audio component mixed with the data component that will help the CD ROM rise to new heights of utility and widespread use for many years to come.

Multimedia CD ROM Editing and Authoring

The issue of multimedia CD ROM editing and program authoring perhaps sounds complex, but actually, upon careful examination, you will find that it is straightforward when viewed as separate elements that are individually created and then combined to make the eventual multimedia program. The steps are analogous to making a movie, though if the program is interactive it requires a program designer that can think "interactively," much like a movie director thinks, but with the added component of non-linear interactive imagination. Many talented computer programmers are very good non-linear, interactive thinkers. Perhaps movie directors who want to get into interactive program design would do well to take some courses in computer programming or vice versa, or just become familar with Apple Computer's HyperCard™ or other hypertext oriented program such as Guide from Owl International.

The video components of a multimedia program are created using the techniques appropriate for the given application, ideally using some kind of storyboard application. The audio is recorded in a way that meets the requirements of the program such as budget and the appropriateness of the audio to match the video or graphics that it will be heard with. The development system should allow dynamic placement of the various multimedia elements within the program and the real-time playback of all elements as they currently exist at any given time during program design or implementation. In fact, such a system would also be very useful to movie makers or Broadway play producers who want a way to test out or simulate their ideas and offer a way for others to interact in the creative process using a dynamic real-life simulation on computer metaphor.

The authoring software should also ideally allow the program designer/artist to make the storyboard, create interactive relationships and actually build be runtime software code to play back the program at a high level using regular English and/or icons. This is the direction that all multimedia authoring systems are heading. The creative artist must have at his or her disposal all of the tools required to implement the program, complete with simulation capabilities without having to do any actual lower level programming, unless the creative artist is a programmer and wants to do programming at a lower level.

Interleaving ADPCM Audio with Text, Graphics, Animation, and Compressed Digital Video

The process of interleaving compressed audio, such as either the Philips/Sony CD ROM XA format ADPCM or OMI's CD ROM ICA format (compatible with the CD ROM XA format) with text, graphics, animation and compressed digital video will depend upon the level of program implementation you plan to do in house. The cost of a development system that allows ADPCM encoding/deconding, text formatting and editing, graphics design, editing, scanning and/or digital paint program drawing, graphics animation and compressed digital video encoding/decoding along with the desirable simulation capabilities will be fairly expensive in the near term. Many companies can start with the basics and add components as their needs grow or become more clearly defined.

The basic idea is to implement the graphic elements you want and store them as files on the development system hard disk(s). Encode the ADPCM audio into the format you want and place the ADPCM sound data files on the development systems hard disk(s). Ditto for any compressed digital video or animated graphics. After the elements to be interleaved are stored as files on the computer, an interleaving program can then interleave them according to the desired interleave factor. You may want five frames of graphics or animation followed by three frames of ADPCM audio and so on. The interleaving program should ideally automatically create the desired interleave factor out of the various program media components, whether they be text, graphics, animated graphics, ADPCM audio (or some other form of compressed audio) or compressed digital video. Of course, immediately after the interleaving it would be highly desirable to simulate the program and "play back" the segments or real-time files (if any) to make sure that the interleave factor and other timing related elements are properly displayed and/or synchronized.

Interactive Digital Hypermedia

Interactive multimedia is ultimately moving toward fully interactive, digital hypermedia that will allow very flexible interactive relationships to be designed into programs using the concepts of hypertext with all forms of media, including sound, digital video, text or graphic images. This is the vision that will drive the creative developments during the next ten or twenty years and that will influence software programming, graphics and any form of digital video and audio technology and that will be used to create the ultimate type of media programming that will reside on CD or CD-like media of the future.

We are just now beginning to see the emergence of the vision from the efforts of such groups as the RCA/DVI developers, MIT's Advanced Media group, the Apple Computer HyperCard group, OMI's Digital Hypermedia Group and many, many other groups and individuals that have caught the vision of creating lifelike (or nonlifelike, as the case may be) realities in the digital domain. We will see the continual convergence of the different forms of entertainment media, such as video, movies and music along with the microcomputer into the new digial hypermedia metaphor. The processes of image, sound and data capture will become more and more straightforward to the point where a creative artist can have an idea or concept and be able to express it quicker with less distraction and frustration from the actual mechanics of the underlying technology. For it is our underlying desire to create and to express our creative visions, whatever they may be, that is acutally motivating the vision and keeping it alive.

The CD system, the computer, the digital samplers and music synthesizers, video and other forms of technology are the things we have collectively developed and supported as consumers and users that are the outer tools we use to express our creative energies.

It is the concept of interactivity, the concept of being able to personally influence our experience, that is the exciting quantum jump. We are adding another dimension to our media experience. Sometimes passive viewing or listening is fine, but sometimes we need or want to get more involved in the experience, put our own energy into it. This is the direction of what we call digital hypermedia and it will be the content of the media of the future for our learning, for our work and for our entertainment, and, most importantly, for our creative expression as individuals.

CD ROM Program Simulation

One of the most important steps in the development of a CD ROM program is the iterative and final test of the program and data structures to determine whether or not all the efforts of the development team have produced an error-free disc. Certainly, since the CD ROM is a permanently recorded disc you will not have a chance to change errors, should any exist, after the discs are pressed — thus the importance of program simulation prior to disc replication.

There are several commercially available CD ROM simulation systems on the market. OMI offers the TOPiX CD ROM Publishing System, with a complete CD ROM simulation capability as does Meridian Data (CD-Publisher™), TMS (Disc Architect™), and Electroson (CD Simulator™). Other options may also be available on the market, though some offer varying degrees of full CD ROM simulation capability.

A good CD ROM simulation system will allow the search and retrieval software to run on the host computer and access the CD ROM database while still residing on a hard disk (oftentimes the same hard disk used during development). Additionally, a good CD ROM simulation system will allow various CD ROM player characteristics to be simulated, such as data seek times and overall data transfer speeds.

It is, of course, possible for simple in-house CD ROM simulation to be performed by just running the program on the host development system making sure that all of the data is correct and that all the required content has been added to the database. If the program will run on the hard disk using the same application software that will eventually be used with the final CD ROM, then chances are that all is okay. But, there is still the issue of overall performance, and it is here that commercially available CD ROM simulation systems can be of considerable value. You can get a much better idea of how the databases will perform in the actual end-user environment and have the ability to try changing the position of data files to optimize data locations on the disc for optimum seek times and thus overall performance. It should be noted here, however, if you do certain optimization of the data base, you will only be optimizing the database accesses that you tested for, and some databases will be used differently by each user, therefore greatly complicating the optimization task. Generally, the best advice is to not get too carried away with files locations, but rather, have adequate indexes, good search algorithms, and choose the highest performance CD ROM drives that you can afford.

It is in the area of multimedia CD ROM simulation that the current effort is being directed by the major vendors of commercial CD ROM simulation systems. The ability to completely simulate a multimedia CD ROM program, with interleaved audio and graphics, is a nontrivial task, and systems with this capability are becoming available on the market. Systems that offer this function must have the ability to play CD Audio, as well as encode and decode the ADPCM audio, in realtime, and exactly simulate the environment of the end user. This added function of mixed-mode multimedia simulation is one of the most important functions of the optimal CD ROM Multimedia Development Workstation. Unlike the development of databases with text or numeric data, an interactive, multimedia program is much more likely to require extensive iterative development, requiring almost constant simulation of the program up until the final completion. Partial simulation is dangerous, as mismatches of audio and data synchronization are easily overlooked. It is the availability of such CD ROM development systems, with multimedia development and simulation capabilities, coupled with interactive program authoring tools that will empower the industry to realize CD ROM's full potential.

CD ROM Simulation Using Microsoft's CD ROM Extensions (MSCDEX)

When testing a CD ROM program that is intended to be used with the Microsoft CD ROM Extensions operating in the MS-DOS or PC-

DOS operating system environment, a good CD ROM simulation system will allow the virtual CD ROM on the simulation system hard disk to be simulated through the CD ROM Extensions just as though the application program was being executed using a real CD ROM player. In fact, if you are using either the High Sierra May 1986 Draft or ISO/DIS 9660 CD ROM file format in the MS-DOS or PC-DOS environment, you will most certainly be using the MS CD ROM Extensions (MSCDEX). In order to fully test the program prior to outputting a program image tape to the CD ROM manufacturer for final premastering and mastering, you must run the actual application program utilizing the hard disk as if it were already on an actual CD ROM. This, of course, requires special software, customized to work with the operating system of the host computer. OMI's Universal SCSI CD ROM simulation system allows full and complete testing of the CD ROM program from the virtual CD hard disks of the simulation system through a standard SCSI interface. This optional approach allows any host computer to be connected to a CD ROM simulation system through the SCSI interface. The simulation system will then fully emulate the CD as if it were an actual CD or CD ROM player.

The Advent of CD PROM — The Write-Once CD

Another option for CD ROM simulation and low-quantity database production is the introduction of recordable CD PROM (CD-Programmable Read-Only Memory, or Write-Once CD). The ability to record a CD using a special player that is, in effect, a mini-mastering system will soon be a reality, though certainly a bit pricey to start with. The availability of this type of system, however, even if you can't afford to purchase your own in the near future, will mean greatly reduced prices for test CD ROMs, or for a limited quantity run of production CDs. The key breakthrough is the media. The important recent advance in CD media that can be recorded in a special CD recorder, and then taken out and played in most standard CD ROM or CD Audio players, will bring a whole new dimension to the industry. Look for this new type of capability to appear as an added service at all CD factories and many new kinds of CD Data Service Bureaus, and to eventually be affordable enough to have one for your very own.

Implementing the High Sierra or ISO/DIS 9660 Standard CD ROM Volume and File Structure

At the current time in the industry, there are basically three options open to developers wishing to place their CD ROM program or database in the High Sierra/ISO file format. You can research the High Sierra/ISO Specification and write a utility to perform this task in house (though certainly feasible it could take several months), use an outside service bureau (or have the CD ROM manufacturer perform this function in conjunction with premastering), or you can purchase a turn-key CD ROM data preparation/publishing system that offers the High Sierra/ISO File Origination feature.

Of the three options mentioned above, the one best suited to your company or particular project will depend on how heavily involved in CD ROM you plan to be. Typically, if you think you will produce more than three or four relatively complex CD ROM programs per year, then purchasing a commercial grade CD ROM publishing system could be money well spent. On the other hand, if your company has a wealth of software programming talent with an interest in CD ROM, you might consider in-house development of your own system from scratch. If you will only produce one or two programs per year, or relatively simple databases, then having your data converted to High Sierra/ISO file format during premastering at the disc pressing facility is the best way to go. Most, if not all, CD ROM disc manufacturers offer High Sierra/ISO file structure conversion as a standard service.

One of the reasons for having a professional, commercially available CD ROM publishing system is the tight integration of all of the necessary utilities and functions required of simple and very complex database production, High Sierra File Origination, Simulation, and Program Image Tape Output for CD pressing factory submission, not to mention industrial grade hard disks made for continuous editing, index building and other types of data preparation. Good CD ROM publishing systems take years to fully perfect and are generally quite reasonable at the current state of the industry.

CD ROM Premastering, Encoding, Mastering, and Replication

The process of taking the final database or CD ROM program from the data preparation system through to the physical CD ROM is a multi-step function that is useful to understand. The various steps are completely specified as part of the CD standards published in the "red, yellow, green, and blue books" which collectively make up the CD family.

What is CD ROM Premastering?

CD ROM premastering actually is the process of rendering a CD ROM program into the specified final CD ROM data structure so that it can be input into the CD encoder. This means the process that takes each 2048 bytes (CD ROM mode one) or 2336 bytes (CD ROM mode 2) and adds the 12 synchronization bytes, the binary coded decimal CD ROM address header, the CD ROM mode byte prior to each user data block and the calculation and addition of the 4 error detection bytes, the placement of the 8-byte gap, the calculation of the P and Q parity layered error correction and detection bytes and the final scrambling of the data block according to the CD ROM "Yellow Book" mode 1 specification. (See Figure 13-4.)

For CD ROM mode 2 data tracks, each data block may have 2336 bytes of user data and, in this case there are no EDC/ECC bytes. The full CD ROM mode 2 data blocks have the 12 sync bytes, the address header, and the mode byte (2 BCD) but not the 288 bytes of EDC/ECC. The bit scrambling function is also performed as with mode 1 data blocks.

The basic requirement is to output an exact image of the CD ROM program content onto a media that the CD ROM factory can use to input to the "Red Book" CD Audio CD Encoder which is interfaced to the Laser Beam Recorder (LBR) that "writes" the final modulated

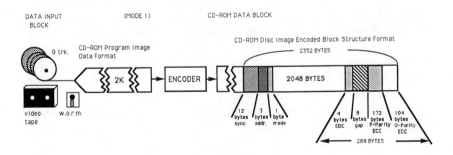

Figure 13-4 CD ROM data premastering and encoding process.

pits onto the actual CD master disc. This CD encoding function first adds the CD ROM program PQ subcode data to the main user data by a specific interleaving of the subcode data with the main program channel data, the additional CD Audio layer of Cross Interleaved Reed-Solomon code (CIRC), and finally performs the 8-to-14 bit data modulation and sends a continuous single serial bit stream to the laserbeam recorder of the CD mastering system, which causes the data to be modulated onto either the photoresist prepared glass master disc, or in the case of a recordable CD PROM, onto the recordable CD PROM disc. This process is done in realtime (176.4 kbyte/second), meaning that the program image data must be properly transferred to the CD Encoder, in very exact time code synchronization, with the PQ processor continuously, without even so much as 1 bit lost or out of sync during the entire process. This step is the actual mastering/recording process and cannot be interrupted, by even 1 bit, during the entire time of mastering.

Program Image Media Versus CD ROM Disc Image Premaster Media Production

The main requirement to be fulfilled in order for a CD ROM manufacturer to be able to take your data and make a CD ROM is to provide either what is called a program image media, such as 9-track magnetic tape, a WORM disc cartridge, R-DAT tape, or some other media that can be input into the actual premastering system that generates the CD ROM disc image. The resulting CD ROM disc image is then input to the CD Encoder which in turn delivers the final single serial bit stream to the CD Laser Beam Recorder.

The Program Image format means simply a contiguous recording of the CD ROM program divided into 2048 byte divisible data blocks onto the Program Image Submission Media (9-track tape, WORM disc, DAT tape, etc.). The Premaster/Encoding System will then add around each 2048 byte block the required CD ROM sync, address header, mode byte and the 288 bytes of EDC and ECC codes to form the final 2352 byte CD ROM data block structure.

Most commercially available CD ROM Data Preparation/Publishing Systems will automatically output, for example, one or more 9-track magnetic tapes that are formatted as a CD ROM Program Image. The primary requirement here is that the 9-track tapes have an acceptable tape block size, which is either a multiple of 2048 bytes, in the case of a CD ROM mode 1 program, or 2336 bytes, in the case of a CD ROM mode 2 program. This Program Image Output tape (or some other type of output media) is then deliverable to a CD ROM factory.

The other option is for the data publisher to produce a fully encoded CD ROM disc image on either a 3/4-inch video tape or a WORM disc and then submit the encoded CD ROM disc image master tape to the CD ROM factory. The advantage in doing this is that the factory will not have to perform the CD ROM block structure encoding and can proceed directly to the mastering step, usually after a final verification that the CD ROM tape (or disc) master is error-free and completely readable by the tape (or disc) player interfaced to the PCM processor and the CD Encoder.

Often, if a fully encoded tape master is submitted to a CD ROM factory, they will offer up to as much as a 50 percent discount in the mastering charge because they don't have to perform the encoding step at the factory. In fact, almost every single CD factory in the world is primarily set up to handle 3/4-inch video CD program tape masters as the standard input to the CD Encoder and Mastering System. All CD Audio discs made worldwide are mastered from 3/4-inch U-Matic tape cassettes (and in some cases 1/2-inch Professional VHS cassettes, as is possible using the JVC DAS-900 System).

Another method used in some CD ROM factories is to load the Program Image Data onto the CD ROM Premaster/Encoding Computer System that is directly interfaced to the CD Encoder and CD Mastering System. In some such systems, such as the TOPiX CD ROM Premaster/Encoding System, the Program Image Data is input, converted to the final CD ROM Disc Image format, data verified, and then transferred in realtime (176.4 kbyte/second) directly to the CD Encoder, bypassing the intermediate storage onto 3/4-inch video tape. This method can save time at the factory, assuming that the factory is set up with this type of CD ROM mastering production procedure and has the requisite premaster/encoding system. Originally, all Program Image tapes were input into VAX computers that were interfaced to the CD Encoder and Mastering System. This type of system was, and still is in use at, for example, Sony and Philips's CD factories, worldwide. OMI, in late 1986, introduced a system to essentially perform what the more expensive VAX Minicomputer did with a standard IBM PC/AT using specially developed custom hardware printed circuit boards to perform the CD ROM data format encoding and the transfer of the data to either the 3/4-

inch U-Matic video tape master or directly to a CD Encoder and mastering system, all for less than one-third the existing cost.

The Final Encoding and Mastering Process

Whether or not the CD ROM program image data is transferred to the CD Encoder via hard disks from a directly interfaced CD ROM Premaster/Encoding System or from a 3/4-inch U-Matic Video Cassette, the following processes to make the CD master, stampers, and replicated discs are the same. The data is input into the CD Encoder, the CD program subcode data is also simultaneously input into the CD Encoder, synchronized by SMPTE time code, the CD glass master disc is modulated with the recording laser, and the photoresist exposed surface is then developed, metalized, and transferred to the CD stamper electroplating process. This process produces one or more metal stampers that are then placed in the injection mold cavity of the CD injection mold machines and the discs are replicated, typically at a rate of 8 to 15 discs per minute, depending on the type of injection molding machine used and how fast a cycle time the particular injection molding machine is capable of. Please refer to Chapters 14 and 15 on CD ROM mastering for in-depth descriptions of the actual mastering and replication process.

Future Trends in CD ROM Premastering

The CD ROM industry, today, almost exclusively uses 9-track magnetic tape as submission media to CD factories for pressing. Though an increasing number of publishers are submitting CD ROM programs on the 3/4-inch U-Matic Video tape CD ROM Disc Image format to the CD factory. We will soon see a trend toward using write- once optical discs, including recordable CD PROMs, as well as DAT tape.

Along with the growth of multimedia CD ROM programs in the market, we will see a further integration of the CD ROM premaster/encoding functions with the CD ROM data preparation systems, particularly in the cases where CD ROM programs will be written to recordable CDs. A fully functional CD ROM Premaster/Encoding System properly interfaced to the CD PROM drive is required to be able to properly record a CD ROM program onto the recordable CD.

Additionally, the data preparation and premaster/encoding functions will also become more tightly coupled with multimedia authoring and program simulation systems, as the need to have all of these capabilities in one system will greatly increase, particularly in the case of CD-I or interactive multimedia CD ROM. The use of DAT tape is definitely a good candidate because of the ability to store a gigabyte of data on one tape, more than enough to store the largest fully encoded CD ROM program, and it is due to the fact that DAT tape is so convenient and inexpensive. The main issue to be resolved here before this can become a truly viable option is the issue of proven data integrity and overall data transfer speed to the CD Encoder. When these issues are solved we will certainly see DAT playing a role in CD premastering and mastering.

The CD ROM Data Preparation Workstation

The CD ROM data preparation workstation is usually the computer environment wherein you will prepare the CD ROM database. In some cases, the database will be created on a mainframe or super minicomputer and then transported to a smaller system for final preparation, CD ROM simulation, and testing and program image premastering. The CD ROM development workstation should be configured to allow for all functions that you might want to use during the implementation, testing, and premastering stages. Following is a discussion of the various components and issues to be considered in either building or purchasing a CD ROM data preparation workstation.

CD ROM Data Preparation System Component Requirements

A CD ROM data preparation system may be established in an incremental fashion or installed as a fully functional, fully featured system. Understanding immediate needs, how they will evolve over time, and how these needs fit with current industry standards will ensure a smooth transition into the burgeoning field of optical disc publishing.

There are several key components to a CD ROM data preparation system. Further, there are several degrees of functionality and performance that can be expected, depending on the specific configuration. CD ROM publishers may enter the data preparation cycle at any level, and build up or down as they learn more about their needs.

The Computer

The most important part of the CD ROM data preparation system is the computer, because it largely determines your software and hardware options. The operating system, utilities, I/O devices, and processing speed are all defined or at least heavily affected by the type of computer you choose. Some are readily available, simpler to operate, and less costly to purchase and maintain — but often at the cost of speed and performance.

The best way to evaluate what you need is to determine how often you will produce CD ROMs, and how much data processing power will be necessary. After you have a clear idea, make sure that the peripheral interface bus can handle the loads you intend to impose on it, as this will have a major impact on the overall processing throughput of the system. Also, check that the required device drivers for the peripherals are available and that they are properly and tightly integrated into the operating system. And last, but not least, evaluate the software and operating systems that are available for the computer you have in mind — they may not be adequate.

Small personal computers already perform many CD ROM data preparation functions. As the Apple Macintosh continues to expand in memory and processing power, especially the Macintosh II, it will also being supporting larger peripherals. The IBM PS/2 and its more powerful relatives in the PC family will play a dominant role from data preparation to a widely used delivery system. The DEC VAX family of mini and super minicomputers will remain industry workhorses. Mainframes, IBM or the others, will be used, but mainly for dedicated applications, and for more rapid calculations of indexes for very large data files, and in some instances, as a central processor in distributed and networked configurations.

The goal is to assemble data in files of various sizes from small to very large. A minimum system configuration will call for a computer capable of supporting medium-size to large hard disks and a 1600-bpi, 9-track magnetic tape drives which which will store the final encoded data on 9-track tape to send to the CD ROM manufacturer. IBM ATs and compatibles can do the job, though be sure to check the processing throughput for your particular kind of data preparation. Smaller computers can be used as terminals or for storing pieces of your final program.

Generally, put as much memory into your system as possible and familiarize yourself with every available software processing utility. Also confirm that you have enough expansion slots or the ability to add an expansion chassis. There is always a need for more space than you think.

A true multimedia system will be able to adequately support the graphics and audio data acquisition, editing, and file formatting that is needed to produce the CD ROM premastered tape.

A CD ROM Premaster/Encoding System can produce a final CD ROM data-packet encoded professional videotape (computer with sync, header, 2-kbyte blocks, and error detection and correction). The advantage of the videotape version is that you can send it to any CD Audio disc manufacturer and have it replicated as a regular audio CD.

The computer must be able to calculate the CD ROM data packet (sync, header and error correction algorithm) and support the Sony 1630 PCM processor interface complete with software.

Hard Disks[3]

Hard disks are absolutely essential and can vastly increase the overall system performance during almost every phase of CD ROM data preparation. Hard disks are becoming increasingly smaller, faster, of larger capacity, and remarkably cheaper. No doubt, the eminent rise of optical disc data storage is putting pressure on the magnetic disk manufacturers to squeeze out every drop of performance physically possible and to sharpen their focus on the niches where magnetic media are now and will continue to be required. In the meantime, optical disc technology keeps getting more and more refined and systematically starts stepping into various areas previously held by magnetic technology.

---

3 Hard disk unit — it is recommended that you have at least twice the size of the largest file or total number of files you will work with in hard disk storage. Optimum is 1.4 Gbytes though not required.

For now, the erasability and speed of large, high-performance hard disks are almost indispensable to CD ROM data preparation. Here, the interface bus decision is important. Check out what is available with a SCSI interface. Many large drives on the Storage Module Device (SMD) bus are tried and proven and are a good value these days. However, SCSI is an up and coming, flexible interface that will be worth considering for integration into many development systems.

Generally, in the area of CD ROM data preparation, the more hard disk space the better. A couple of gigabytes is really not unreasonable, and in some cases is required for fast, efficient processing of large files. If possible, use two storage areas, each the size of the total amount of data you intend to store on the CD ROM (including all directory files, index files, hash tables, etc.).

To say that 10 or 20 Mbytes of hard disk is adequate is probably stretching it, unless you are assembling a collection of fairly small files. In any event, you should also allow enough disk space to accommodate the total cumulative file I/O, including indexes.

"Floppy ROM" types of CD ROM programs can be composed of sequential files, assembled in pieces, and then properly cataloged, indexed and copied to magnetic tape. This process can then be repeated, over and over, until you have loaded all the data.

For those with a smaller system, this kind of preparation is fine for transferring sequential files, or to incrementally load data to tape for later final processing at a fully equipped CD ROM data processing facility. In fact, the more preprocessing you do, the better. Your efforts will often reduce the premastering charges, compensating for the additional time required up front.

It should be emphasized here that you *can* make a CD ROM on a small system. With enough care and creativity, some really useful and popular programs can be implemented. Large, powerful systems do not hold the exclusive license on creativity.

Magnetic Tape Storage[4]

Magnetic tape storage is the standard data interchange format between large and small computers. Consequently, most static databases currently in existence are now archived on some form of 9-

---

4   Magnetic tape storage unit — 1/2-inch, 9-track 1600-bpi type is minimum specification, 6250 Group Coded Recording (GCR) type recommended.

track magnetic tape — the same as the premaster tape specification. There are several data recording densities that are used, typically 800, 1600, 3200, 6250 bpi and newer high-performance drives that are well over 10,000 bpi. For the immediate future, the most widely used and supported will be the 1600- and 6250-bpi formats. If another format must be dealt with, there are numerous data processing service bureaus that can convert the format into either 1600- or 6250-bpi tapes for ease of processing. For small systems the 1/4- and 1/2-inch data cartridge formats can be used to input data incrementally, as long as your development system also contains one of these tape drives. They are usually much less expensive than the 1/2-inch 9-track magnetic tape drives and have standard interfaces to most common interface buses.

Each type of configuration can use the same type of tape drive as long as an appropriate interface is available. In some instances with high-volume environments, it is preferable to have a two tape drives because it allows quick and easy tape-to-tape copies and tape backups. If SCSI is fully supported, you can transfer directly from one tape drive to the other, or directly from hard disk to one tape drive while the other is writing data out to another hard disk. Look for these intelligent interfaces to become major industry standards and vastly increase the longevity and utility of these often expensive data storage peripherals.

In the near future we can anticipate that write-once, WORM, and erasable optical discs will store the final CD ROM disc image and be interfaced to the various CD ROM disc manufacturers' premastering and mastering computer systems. We can also expect DAT (Digital Audio Tape) to be used for intermediate and final input and output media for CD ROM data preparation, premastering and mastering. This will eventually reduce premaster storage space and, ultimately, cost — not to mention the inherent flexibility and data integrity it offers.

Operating Systems

The operating system is the command center and heart of your computer system. A good operating system can make all the difference in providing you an easy way to perform certain kinds of data manipulation. As you might expect, the newer ones have nice buzzword-filled features, but in some cases have yet to be thoroughly and reliably debugged. Additionally, many of them simply are not robust enough to offer the really powerful standard utilities of the older, more mature, and proven operating systems. The industry standard on micros, MS-DOS, has been evolving and will continue to do so. As this happens it will become increasingly more adept at handling large amounts of data, with more power and flexibility.

Although MS-DOS has its place in the world of operating systems, it may not be the system of choice for larger systems. Here you will want to consider a standard version of UNIX, such as System V, or 4.2 BSD.

It is always a good idea to test each component, hardware and software, before relying on the system's integrity. This can be especially true with newly acquired peripherals from third-party vendors. One should never be too busy to double-check each component and its operation in the manner in which it is to be used during processing. If you wait until the last minute, you may not have time to adjust, replace, or fix any problems. Every effort should be made to acquire all useful utilities that are available for your operating environment and stay up to date on new versions.

Multimedia System. More than an operating system is needed to manage the various kinds of media that will be used on mixed mode or multimedia CD ROMs. You'll need a bona fide authoring system. This enhanced operating system should support emerging graphics protocols, various audio standards, and the file I/O required for these media. Evolving user interfaces such as the Macintosh's have demonstrated that a little can go a long way in allowing more non-technical artistic creators access to the potential of the new optical disc technology.

Systems Software Utilities[5]

Perhaps the key to fast, efficient CD ROM data preparation, given the proper hardware and operating system environment, is the

---

5 System software utilities — good text editor and directory manager, file format converters, file inversion program or utility for creating index file(s), flexible disk-to-tape data I/O utilities, volume manager and volume table generation utility and file location table generation utility, ANSI tape I/O utility (x3.27, level 3).

functionality of the various system software utilities that actually manipulate the data, helping to place it in the proper format for premastering. Naturally, good text editors and graphics editors are important. File conversion programs and protocol converters are also very useful, and in some instances absolutely essential to perform certain kinds of data acquisition. Data file inversion utilities (indexing programs) are in high demand and will become increasingly more sophisticated as they are integrated with various search and retrieval programs, providing quicker access to the CD ROM data.

Ideally, these utilities should automatically generate the appropriate table or directory. In the case of mixed mode CD ROMs, they should be able to specify or determine whether a data block is to be mode 0, mode 1, or mode 2, flag each block, and create an input so that during the final premastering stage the correct mode bytes are set.

ANSI tape label utilities are required to generate all premaster tapes for submission to those CD ROM replicators that request ANSI × 3/27 level 3 labeled tapes. It should be noted that each individual disc manufacturer should be contacted directly at the time of premastering tape submission for the applicable data tape submission specification.

File Structure Creation Programs.[6] This may be one or more programs that read the assembled CD ROM data and create the appropriate file structure required and expected by the end user, and delivery system.

An active CD ROM data preparation service should expect to be able to create several more-or-less standard file structures or, in some cases, produce discs that have more than one file structure. It is conceivable that certain publishers may wish to achieve a very proprietary, more secure data format and request a nonstandard file structure.

Of course, proper device driver software needs to be available for different hardware peripherals to access the particular file structure on the disc. Most currently used CD ROM file structures are compatible and offer these device drivers. It is important to note, however, that because of subtle differences in the drive

---

6 File structure creation program — program to create the desired file structure such as the ISO/9660 "High Sierra" File Structure or other subsequent industry standard or proprietary file structure.

manufacturers' interfaces for the standard computer systems, a specific device driver may be required for a specific combination of CD ROM drive, interface, and program. This situation should become less of an issue over time, but should in any case not be overlooked.

Issues of interest with regard to CD ROM file structure are such items as:

- Physical data block to logical data block I/O system
- Logical block size (variable or fixed)
- Disc identification and disc contents identification
- Logical handling of multiple disc sets (as in the case of multidisc players or juke box type drives)
- Management of file attributes
- Creation and disc mapping of hash tables and/or index files (if used)
- Standardized location and specification of disc file directory and/or volume directory (if required)
- Support of mixed mode or multimedia CD ROMs, i.e., audio and graphics in various protocols
- Provision for company-specific, preassigned mode bytes (as in the MIDI interface spec used by most electronic musical instrument manufacturers)
- Perhaps allowance for multiple operating system compatibility and/or multiple file structures or a so-called "Universal ROM File Structure"

Multimedia CD ROM Development Workstation. Recommended system configuration:

- Computer (PC/AT or compatible, DEC Micro Vax II, PDP-11, Sun MicroSystems or other comparable computers capable of supporting large hard disks and GCR 9-track magnetic tape storage on PC Bus, SCSI, SMD, Multi-Bus or VME Bus), and a special purpose interface between the computer and the PCM processor in NTSC video format.
- Hard disk unit (It is recommended that you have the size of a full CD ROM or approximately 700 Mbytes in hard disk storage, 1.4 Gbytes is optimum.)
- Magnetic tape data storage unit (1/2-inch, 9-track 1600-bpi type is minimum specification. 6350 GCR type recommended.)

- Graphics Bit Pad
- Video Digitizer/Frame Grabber (optional, for multimedia CD ROMs)
- Graphics Scanner, Flat Bedtype (300 dpi or higher)
- Color Film Slide Scanner
- PCM Audio Processor (or Analog-to-Digital Converter) and Companion VTR (or audio tape recorder for CD Audio on non-CD Audio). Also for creating a final, fully encoded CD ROM premaster tape in professional videocassette format than can then be delivered to any CD Audio manufacturing facility for mastering in the same manner as an audio CD. Extra care must be taken, however, to ensure data integrity.
- Operating system utilities — enhanced MS-DOS, OS/2, MAX-VMS, UNIX, or comparable
- System software utilities — good text editor and directory manager, file format converters, flexible disk-to-tape data I/O utilities, File Inversion program or utility for building index files, volume manager and volume table generation utility and file location table generation utility, ANSI tape I/O utility (×3.27, level 3 or higher). For the videotape CD ROM premaster encoding system you must be a Philips/Sony CD technology licensee and have the encoding program to generate the CD ROM sync, header, and error detection and correction data packet on each 2-kbyte block of data before writing the final video tape.
- File structure creation program — program to create the desired file structures such as the draft High Sierra or ISO/DIS 9660 CD ROM Volume and File Structure Information Interchange File Format, DEC's Uni-File, UNIX, or the subsequent industry standard file structure.

Conclusion

Whatever the outcome, the importance of industrywide standardization cannot be overemphasized. The pace, and perhaps, the ultimate potential of CD ROM as a publishing medium will hinge on its ability to synergistically enhance or coexist with other technologies, and become properly supported by all of the related manufacturers and publishers.

About the Author

Allen L. Adkins is founder and president of Optical Media International (OMI). He has been very active in optical disc technology for many years, having pioneered several new concepts in interactive media, such as interactive training by interfacing computers to videodiscs and having previously founded two companies that dealt with interactive videodiscs. Over the past 3 years he has spent his time developing new applications for CD ROM and establishing an experience base in the various aspects of CD ROM data preparation and premastering by designing and developing the widely known TOPiX and mac TOPiX CD ROM data preparation and premastering systems. Mr. Adkins has been responsible for many new concepts and applications of optical disc technology. His company, Optical Media International, developed the first CD ROM interface and CD ROM application program for the Apple Macintosh computer and many for the PC environment. OMI has also produced, published, and is marketing the first digital sound databases on CD ROM for the professional audio industry. The programs, collectively known as "The Universe of Sounds," contains multiple thousands of digitally sampled musical instrument sounds and sound effects which are used in conjunction with digital sampling keyboards. The programs are sold with the OMI Professional Universal CD System which contains a number of industry standard interfaces, such as SCSI, RS-422, AES-EBU Digital Audio interface (both balanced and unbalanced), analog audio, and optional ADPCM audio.

Optical Media International performs a variety of contract CD ROM and CD Audio data preparation services, consulting, and program development services. Reflective Arts International (OMI's CD publishing label) is active in the production of unique, high-quality CD ROM, Multimedia CD ROM and CD Audio programs. CD ROM interfaces, device drivers, data preparation, multimedia authoring and premastering workstations developed by OMI such as the TOPIX hypermedia workstation are available on an OEM and/or license basis.

Optical Media International
485 Alberto Way
Los Gatos, CA 95032
408–395–4332

14

CD ROM Mastering

Robert Harley

Mastering Overview

Mastering is the first step in CD ROM manufacturing. During mastering, data is transferred to a master disc from which replicated discs are made. This stage of the process is crucial since the finished discs will be nearly exact duplicates of the master disc.

Figure 14-1 shows a simplified mastering system. A glass disc coated with photoresist is placed on the turntable of the mastering machine and rotated. Data to be stored on the disc is encoded into the CD format and this encoded signal drives an optical modulator. A laser beam directed at the spinning glass first passes through the modulator which either allows the beam to continue toward the disc or deflects the beam away from the disc according to the data appearing at the modulator input. In addition to rotating, the turntable is slowly moved relative to the beam (or vice versa), forming a spiral track of exposed and unexposed areas on the glass master disc.

When the transfer of data is complete, the glass master is chemically developed. Areas of the disc that have been exposed to the laser beam are etched away, creating "pits" in the photoresist. Unexposed

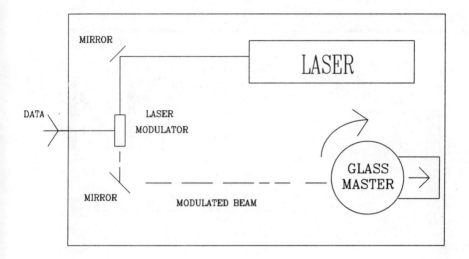

Figure 14-1   Mastering overview.

areas are not affected by developing and are called "land." Binary data is thus encoded in pit and land formations. This alternating pattern of land and pit is shown in the scanning electron microscope photograph in Figure 14-2.

After developing, a thin layer of silver or nickel is vacuum deposited on the master, making it electrically conductive. The master is checked on a special player that analyzes data integrity and signal quality. The metalized master is then electroplated to make stampers from which replicated discs are injection molded.

Data Retrieval and Encoding

Before discussing CD ROM mastering in depth, it is helpful to understand two concepts: (1) how data is retrieved from pit and land formations on the disc and (2) how data is encoded on the disc.

Data Retrieval

In the CD ROM drive, the playback laser beam is focused on the disc and reflected back to a photo-detector. The wavelength of the playback beam is four times the effective depth of the pit. When the

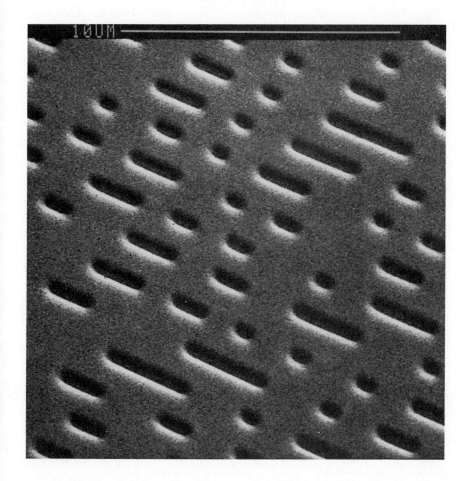

Figure 14-2 5000X magnification. Scale at top line is 10μM. (Photo by Alvin Jennings, Jr.)

beam strikes a pit part of the beam traverses the depth of the pit while part is reflected from the land. The portion of the beam reflected from the bottom of the pit is 180° out of phase with the beam reflected from the land, causing destructive interference (phase cancellation), hence reduced output from the photo-detector. The resulting variable intensity beam reflected from the disc thus carries the information encoded on the disc. Figure 14-3 shows this relationship between binary data and pit formations. In this scheme, the pits do not represent binary data directly. Instead, pit edges (either leading or trailing) represent binary 1s while all other surfaces (land or pit bottom) represent binary 0s. This type of encoding is called Non-Return to Zero Inverted (NRZI).

EFM Encoding

Since pit and land do not directly represent data, an encoding system is required. The encoding system used in CD ROM (and all other CD formats) is called Eight-to-Fourteen Modulation (EFM). In EFM encoding, symbols of 8 bits are assigned unique 14-bit words (by a look-up table), creating a pattern of 1s and 0s in which binary 1s are separated by a minimum of two 0s and a maximum of ten 0s. An excerpt from an EFM conversion table is shown in Figure 14-4. In addition, blocks of 14 bits are linked by 3 "merging" bits, resulting in a

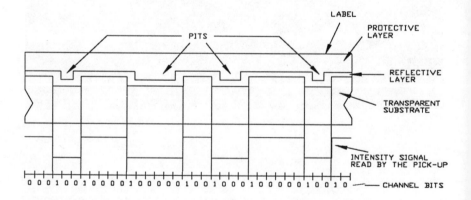

Figure 14-3   Relationship between pits and binary data.

Data	EFM
00001000	01001001000000
00001001	10000001000000
00001010	10010001000000
00001011	10000100100000
00001100	01000001000000
00001101	00000001000000
00001110	00010001000000

Figure 14-4   An excerpt from an EFM conversion table.

ratio before and after encoding of 8:17. The final data ouptput of the EFM encoder is referred to as "channel bits."

The bit stream is thus given a specific pattern of 1s and 0s that result in nine discrete pit or land lengths on the disc. Although the number of bits has been more than doubled by EFM, data density is increased by 25 percent over unmodulated coding. In addition to facilitating data retrieval, EFM has other inherent advantages: The bandwidth of the playback signal is limited (196 to 720 kHz), allowing slower disc speed, and the EFM clock signal helps control the motor of the playback drive.

As a result of EFM encoding, the playback signal from the CD ROM is comprised of nine discrete frequencies labeled I3 (720 kHz) through I11 (196 kHz). The highest frequency, I3, represents the shortest pit or land length (100) while I11 represents the longest pit or land length (10000000000). Figure 14-5 shows pit and land dimensions. These pits are among the smallest manufactured structures. A human hair is about the same width as 50 tracks.

The resultant EFM playback signal, shown in Figure 14-6, is known as the high-frequency (HF) signal. This signal is alternately referred to as the "eye pattern." It is then the job of circuitry in the CD ROM drive to decode this signal, returning the data stream to an unmodulated condition.

Data Retrieval During Mastering

Since CD ROM mastering is performed on equipment designed for digital audio, data to be mastered must be formatted to conform to the CD Audio standard. The EFM encoder expects to receive two serial TTL signals, each with a data rate of 705 kilobits per second

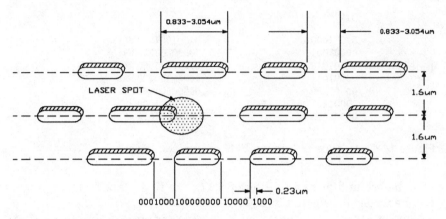

Figure 14-5 Pit and track dimensions.

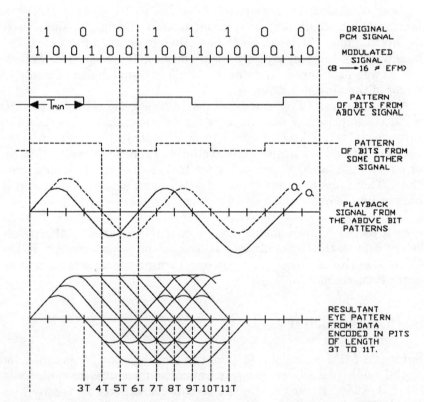

Figure 14-6 EFM encoding produces eye pattern (HF) signal output.

(kbs). This number is derived by multiplying the digital audio sampling rate of 44.1 kHz by 16, the length of each quantization word. In digital audio, two signals are required for left and right stereo audio channels, which are multiplexed by the EFM encoder.

Typically, data is retrieved during mastering by one of three methods: directly from a Digital Equipment Corp. VAX computer, from a personal (or workstation) computer, or from 3/4-inch U-Matic video tape.

Each of these methods requires that the data first be structured into addressable data blocks of 2352 sequential bytes each. Each data block contains the following data fields:

Sync field	12 bytes
Header field	4 bytes
User data field	2048 bytes
Auxiliary data field	288 bytes

Mastering from VAX and Personal Computers

In mastering from a VAX, user data, usually on 9-track magnetic tapes, is downloaded to a hard drive. Hardware and/or software formats the data into the addressable data blocks previously described. The extra layer of error correction data (auxiliary data field) is added at this time.

The formatted data from the hard drive is then converted into two serial bit streams, each with a data rate of 705 kbs. This signal is now identical to the digital processor output previously described and is ready to drive the EFM encoder.

Mastering from a personal computer or workstation computer is similar to VAX mastering except that data formatting is performed by the PC. User data is formatted by the PC into addressable data blocks and stored on hard disk. During mastering, data is retrieved from the hard disk and transferred to the glass master.

Premastering systems have been developed that accept a variety of formats including 9-track magnetic tape, WORM (Write Once Read Many) data cartridges, floppy disks, and hard disks. The systems then format the user data to a large hard disk. Once on hard disk, data can be read out at the required frequency directly during mastering, or stored on 3/4-inch U-Matic tape.

The 3/4-inch U-Matic Format

The primary format for CD ROM mastering is the 3/4-inch U-Matic video cassette. The proliferation of this format is largely due to the fact that 3/4-inch video tape is the worldwide standard for digital audio CD master tapes. The U-Matic format is widely used in broadcast and industrial video applications.

The requirements of a storage medium for the large amount of data transferred to the glass master are met by the U-Matic format: wide bandwidth, high storage density, and the provision for synchronization with other equipment using SMPTE time code. The storage density is sufficiently high to allow error detection and correction data to be added. In fact, error detection and redundant data account for about half the tape's data capacity.

The U-Matic format has other inherent advantages: a large base of existing hardware and error correction schemes developed for digital audio can be utilized.

However, before data can be recorded on a video tape recorder (VTR), it must be converted to a format acceptable to the VTR. The VTR expects to receive a "composite video" signal at its input. A composite video signal, shown in Figure 14-7, is comprised of horizontal sync pulses, vertical sync pulses, and video information. The video information for one horizontal line falls between two horizontal sync pulses. In the National Television Standards Committee (NTSC) system used in North America, 525 horizontal lines form one video frame (picture), with a rate of 30 frames per second. Luminance

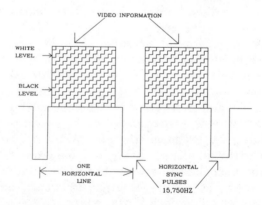

Figure 14-7   Composite video.

(brightness) information is represented by the amplitude of the video signal.

In order to record data as a video signal, it is necessary to retain the timing information of the video signal (horizontal and vertical sync pulses), while substituting data for the video information. A video signal converted this way is called "composite digital." The term composite digital applies to both digital audio and computer data in the video format. Data formatting is performed by a digital processor designed for digital audio applications. This processor converts serial data into composite digital and vice versa.

In the composite digital format, binary 1 is represented by a high luminance level (white). Binary 0 is represented by a low luminance level (black). Each horizontal line stores 193 bits. Since the composite digital signal possesses all the attributes of a video signal, it can be displayed on a television monitor. The appearance of data on the monitor takes on a rapidly changing "salt and pepper" effect as the individual bits toggle.

The storage capacity of a standard length U-Matic tape can be calculated by multiplying 193 (bits per line) by 490 (active lines) by 30 (frames per second) by 3600 (seconds per tape). Thus, a 60-minute tape has a capacity of about 1.27 Gbytes. Since error detection and redundant data consume about half this figure, data yield is approximately 635 Mbytes — sufficient for CD ROM applications. It should be noted that data on the tape has been previously structured into standard data blocks of 2352 sequential bytes, of which 2048 bytes are actual user data.

The error detection and correction scheme used in encoding data on 3/4-inch tape is called "Cyclic Redundancy Check Code" (CRC). CRC encoding involves adding redundant data and interleaving. Interleaving is scattering data to different parts of the medium to be reconstructed (deinterleaved) upon playback. Interleaving converts a long burst error (the most common form of error) to many shorter errors which are more easily corrected. With CRC, burst errors as long as 11.7 horizontal lines (2240 bits) are completly corrected. CRC encoding and decoding are both performed by the digital audio processor. Once data is retrieved from the tape and demodulated, CRC has performed its function and is no longer part of the bit stream.

Another development that increases the robustness of data stored on 3/4-inch tape is called "Read-After-Read." A VTR equipped with Read-After-Read has a second pair of video heads ("B" heads) that read the same data as the primary heads ("A" heads). Errant or missing data from the "A" heads is replaced by correct data from the "B" heads, greatly reducing the possibility of an uncorrectable error. The digital processor used in conjunction with a Read-After-Read VTR must be equipped to accept both "A" and "B" signals. Selection and substitution of data occur within the digital processor.

A new development, available in mid-1988, promises to further solidify the position of the U-Matic cassette as the worldwide standard for CD ROM mastering. This development, called "Extended Interleave" (EI), is a set of three PC boards that replace boards in a conventional digital audio processor. These boards, used exclusively for CD ROM and data applications, greatly increase the error correction capability of the digital processor.

The Cross Word Coding (interleaving) scheme can correct errors lasting one-third of the interleave length. In a standard digital audio processor, the interleave length is 35 horizontal lines, allowing correction of burst errors up to 11.7 horizontal lines (2240 bits). In a processor retrofitted with EI boards, data is interleaved over one TV frame (490 horizontal lines), thus permitting correction of burst errors up to 162 horizontal lines (31,360 bits). As a result, bit error rate has been improved to $10^{-12} \sim 10^{-13}$.

Analysis of data integrity is possible with a peripheral device called a Digital Tape Analyzer. Location and severity of errors are displayed by the analyzer. In addition, the analyzer makes the distinction between completely corrected errors and concealed errors. Error concealment techniques (such as linear interpolation), while sometimes acceptable for digital audio, are not acceptable for CD ROM.

The 3/4-inch U-Matic format provides two independent audio tracks. In a video application, these tracks would be used to record stereo audio. In a CD ROM application, however, these two tracks serve other purposes.

Audio track 1 of the U-Matic tape is used to store the "Q" subcode. The "Q" subcode is timing, control, and display information for the CD ROM drive that is read from the master tape just prior to mastering, reformatted, and multiplexed into the bit stream, and then recorded on the glass master.

Audio track 2 is used to store Society of Motion Picture and Television Engineers (SMPTE) time code. SMPTE time code is an absolute address assigned to each frame of video or composite digital. SMPTE time is counted in hours, minutes, seconds, and frames (HH:MM:SS:FF). Events on the CD ROM master tape (data start and stop) are referenced to SMPTE time code. During mastering, time code is read from the tape and used to trigger events in the mastering sequence that are time critical in relation to events on the tape.

Programming the "Q" Subcode

When some CD ROM drives seek a certain area of the disc, they locate specific areas based on timing information retrieved from the "Q" subcode as the laser head scans radially across the disc. When the laser head stops and begins reading data blocks, the player receives more accurate location information from the block address contained in the header field of the 2352 byte CD ROM block. The timing information retrieved from the "Q" subcode during disc playback must closely match the block address or a "seek error" may result.

To synchronize the block address with the "Q" subcode, the starting point of data on the 3/4" UMatic tape (SMPTE time) must be correctly identified. Before user data begins, two seconds of "pre-gap" is recorded on the master tape. The start time of the disc (according to the "Q" subcode) must be in pre-gap, just before the start of user data.

Pre-gap consists of data structured into the 2352 byte blocks with sync, header, user data and EDC. However, the user data field (2048 bytes) is filled with zeros. Pre-gap provides an area on the disc formatted as CD ROM data but without any user data. This area allows the laser head to overshoot the user data area and still see the block structured format. In addition, the same data structure, called post-gap, is recorded after user data for the same reason pre-gap is used.

Typically pre-gap is exactly two seconds, accurate to the CD ROM block. To identify the transition from pre-gap to user data, the transition from digital silence (all zeros, not block structured) to pregap is first found using a digital audio editor. The editor identifies the first SMPTE frame of pre-gap. The first frame of user data is calculated by adding two seconds. Then, to ensure that user data begins after the disc "Q" subcode start time, one SMPTE frame (1/30th of a second) is subtracted. This SMPTE time is stored in memory of the subcode encoder which generates "Q" subcode data based on SMPTE time read from the tape during laser mastering.

The accuracy of this method can be verified by reading data from the tape into a premastering system and displaying the data blocks (in hex) on a computer monitor. The transition from pre-gap to user data is readily apparent.

Identifying the end of the disc (according to the "Q" subcode) is not as critical. The last SMPTE frame of post-gap is specified as the end of the disc. This method prevents possible truncation of user data while preventing the CD ROM drive from reading non-block structured data.

Master Tape Specifications

The following master tape specifications are typical of most CD ROM manufacturing facilities.

1. Record 2 minutes of digital silence at the head of the tape before data, and 30 seconds of digital silence after data.
2. Record nondrop frame SMPTE time code on analog audio track 2. Time code must be continous, unique, and upcounting beginning at 00:00:00:00 and should run through lead-in, active data, and lead-out.
3. Record subcode on analog audio track 1. In lieu of this, a log should be provided indicating start and end of data points including pregap and postgap.

CD ROM Mastering

Preparation of the Glass Master

The mastering process begins by polishing a piece of glass 240 mm in diameter and 6 mm thick. The polished glass is spincoated with an adhesion promoter, spincoated with photoresist, and cured in an oven. Preparation of the glass master must be performed in a extremely clean environment to avoid contamination of the photoresist. A "clean room" with fewer than 100 particles per cubic foot of air (class 100) is required. The typical office or home contains about 100,000 particles per cubic foot and a hospital operating room about 10,000. Workers wear clean suits that completely cover their bodies and enter the clean room through an air shower that blows off any particles on the clean suit. This contamination-free environment is maintained throughout the entire CD ROM manufacturing process.

The photoresist is formulated to react to a narrow band of light which is the same wavelength as the blue recording laser. To prevent exposure of the photoresist by the blue component found in normal room lighting, the glass master is prepared under filtered lights.

Maintaining very tight tolerances of photoresist thickness is critical to the quality of the master. Typically, resist thickness is held to a tolerance of ±30 Å. Resist thickness is measured by a laser elipseometer system. This narrow tolerance is required since the depth of the pits created in the mastering process is a function of the thickness of the photoresist. Correct pit depth is vital to data retrieval.

The Mastering Machine

Transfer of data to the glass master is performed by a CD mastering machine. A mastering machine costs about $1 million and is used to master CD Audio as well as CD ROM. A mastering system consists of a cutting lathe and control racks. The lathe is typically 6 feet long by 4 feet wide by 4 feet high and, as in glass preparation, is located inside a clean room. The laser, optical modulator, turntable, and optics are mounted on the lathe.

CD ROM mastering (and all other CD formats) is performed in the CLV (Constant Linear Velocity) mode. In CLV recording, turntable speed decreases as recording radius increases. This is contrasted with CAV (Constant Angular Velocity) recording in which turntable speed is kept constant, with the resultant increase in writing speed as the recording radius increases. A phonograph record is an example of a CAV medium.

The mastering machine turntable rotates at approximately 500 rpm at the innermost recording radius (23 mm) and at approximately 200 rpm at the outermost recording radius (59 mm), thus maintaining a constant linear recording velocity of 1.4 meters/second.[1] In addition to rotating tangentially, there must be relative motion between the recording beam and the glass master to create the spiral

---

1 The Philips specification for linear velocity is 1.2 meters/second minimum and 1.4 meters/second maximum. Variations within one disc must not exceed .01 meters/second.

track. To accomplish this, the turntable can be mounted on an air-bearing sled and driven proportionately to the rotational velocity. Alternately, the optics can be translated during recording. In both cases data is recorded from inner to outer radius.

The heart of the mastering machine is the recording laser and modulator. The laser, emitting at a wavelength of either 442 or 458 nanometers (blue), is mounted on the top of the mastering lathe. This laser is typically argon or helium-cadmium. The beam is directed by mirrors into an optical modulator. Data to be recorded on the master disc appears at the modulator input after EFM encoding. The modulator is generally one of two types: electro-optical (E-O) that operates on the Pockels effect, or acousto-optical (A-O). In the A-O scheme, the EFM signal causes the modulator to diffract the beam toward the glass, exposing the photoresist (creating a pit), or the modulator transmits the beam away from the glass, leaving an unexposed area (land). An E-O modulator selectively rotates the polarization of the beam according to the electrical signal driving its input. A polarizer then allows only one polarization to exit the modulator. Whichever method is employed, electrical data is converted to a modulating laser beam which is converted to physical contours in the photoresist on the glass master.

It should be noted that in this process pits are not directly formed in the photoresist during mastering. Instead, the exposed master is chemically developed later, etching away photoresist only where exposed by the recording laser. This step is discussed in detail later in this chapter.

Other mastering machine subsystems include a focus servo system to maintain focus on the spinning glass despite any surface irregularities, a laser power servo to ensure correct exposure, and a phase lock system that locks the turntable's rotational speed to a reference frequency.

The control racks contain the majority of mastering electronics. These include:

- EFM (Eight-to-Fourteen Modulation) encoder
- EFM decoder
- Subcode encoder
- Computer terminal for mastering machine control
- Premastering system for user data retrieval
- 3/4-inch U-Matic VTR
- Digital tape analyzer

- Digital processor
- Mastering machine electronics
- Oscilloscope for monitoring machine functions.

Signal Flow

Note: The following description describes mastering from 3/4-inch U-Matic tape.

The signal flow between mastering machine components is shown in Figure 14-8. Prior to the mastering run, subcode data stored on audio track 1 of the VTR is loaded into the subcode encoder's memory. This information is the start and stop of data referenced to the SMPTE time code. SMPTE time code from audio track 2 is also input to the subcode encoder. When the subcode encoder "sees" a SMPTE time that corresponds to an event in memory, it outputs the correct "Q" subcode that will become part of the bit stream written on the master disc. Upon playback, the "Q" subcode is stripped from the data stream, providing the drive with timing, control, and display information. The data rate from the "Q" subcode is 7.35 kHz.

Composite digital from the VTR is converted into serial data by the digital processor and error correction is performed. Analysis of data validity occurs simultaneously with tape playback. An uncorrected error results in immediate rejection of the master.

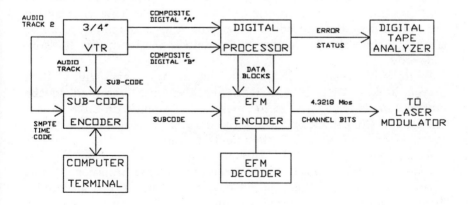

Figure 14-8 Signal flow between mastering components.

Serial data from the digital processor is input to the EFM encoder as is subcode data from the subcode encoder. The EFM encoder multiplexes the two data streams and performs EFM encoding. In addition, the EFM encoder performs Cross-Interleaved Reed-Solomon Code (CIRC) error correction encoding. With the addition of subcode, CIRC encoding and Eight-to-Fourteen Modulation, the 1.41-Mbs data rate is increased to 4.3218 Mbs at the EFM encoder output. This signal is now ready to drive the optical modulator.

The Mastering Sequence

The mastering sequence begins by placing a prepared glass master on the turntable. The recording optic is focused on the glass and the turntable is rotated at the correct linear velocity. These functions are computer controlled and monitored by the operator.

Subcode data stored on audio track 1 of the master tape is read into the subcode encoder before mastering.

Before transferring data to the master, an identification band is recorded at the inner diameter of the disc. This band contains human readable alpha-numeric characters, used to identify the master, stampers, and replicated discs as they are processed.

With the turntable spinning, the shutter is opened, allowing the modulating laser beam to expose the master disc. The signal driving the modulator is not yet user data but rather the "Table of Contents." This area of the disc is called "lead-in." The table of contents contains time and track information for the drive. This information is generated by the subcode encoder from the data read from audio track 1 of the VTR. Table of contents data is written in the "Q" subcode only.

While still recording lead-in on the master glass, the VTR is played back. During this period, "digital silence" recorded on the master tape is transfered to the master disc along with table of contents data. Digital silence means the data is all zeroes and is recognizable by a black screen on the television monitor.

At the correct disc radius, actual data transfer begins. The "Q" subcode changes from table of contents to timing information. This is verified by decoding the subcode data and monitoring the decoder display. Data is transferred at the rate of approximately 10.5 Mbytes/minute of which 9.2 Mbytes is actual user data. Thus a 550-Mbyte CD ROM has about an hour of active data.

When data transfer is completed, the beam continues to expose the glass, writing digital silence along with "Q" subcode that indicates end of data. This portion of the disc is called "lead-out" and continues to the maximum outer radius of the disc. The entire mastering procedure takes about 2 hours to complete.

Chemical Processing

After the exposed master is removed from the mastering machine turntable, it is transferred to a seperate area for the next steps in CD ROM manufacture: chemical developing and metalization.

Developing the master is considered part of mastering since the pit shape is influenced by both mastering parameters and developing parameters. There is a high degree of interdependence between the two processes.

The photoresist coating on the master is comprised of three components: an alkaline soluable novalac resin, a photosensitive dissolution inhibitor, and a carrier solvent. Exposure of photoresist to laser radiation photochemically nullifies the dissolution inhibitor, rendering the novalac resin polymer soluable in an alkaline developing solution. Photoresist not exposed to laser radiation remains insoluable. When the exposed master is subjected to the developing solution, pits are formed only where the photo- resist has been exposed to the recording laser.

Developing is performed while the master is spinning to ensure reaction uniformity. The developing cycle consists of subjecting the master to five stages:

• Prerinse of deionized water
• Overlap period of prerinse with developer solution
• Developer dispense
• Overlap period of developer and deionized water
• Postrinse of deionized water.

During development, the pits slowly evolve to their final shape. It is thus vital to stop development when optimum pit geometry is reached.

The developed master is then dried, inspected, and prepared for vapor metalization. In metalization, a thin film of silver or nickel is vapor deposited on the master. Metalization performs two functions:

(1) The master is made electrically conductive for the next stage of processing, and (2) the metalized master can be played on a specially designed player to monitor signal quality and data integrity.

Signal Optimization

The HF signal produced by optically retrieving the EFM signal encoded on the disc provides valuable information about the shape of the pits. Pit shape and depth are optimized in the mastering/developing process to yield the highest quality HF signal.

Among the parameters that affect pit shape and hence signal quality are photoresist thickness, laser power, duty cycle of the EFM signal, develop time, and developing solution strength. All these parameters are interrelated: Changing one affects the others. Optimum signal quality is a delicate balance between a multitude of factors.

Signal quality actually begins with preparation of the glass master. Defects in the glass substrate cause dropouts in the HF signal, resulting in an increased Block Error Rate (BLER). Surface flatness must also be held to a close enough tolerance that the mastering machine's focus servo can compensate for any irregularities.

The two main factors associated with signal optimization are photoresist thickness and exposure level. Since the CD ROM master is developed to the surface substrate (glass), the depth of the pit is a function of resist thickness (assuming adequate exposure). The effective exposure is a combination of laser power, laser beam spot size, develop time, and developer concentration.

Optimizing pit depth is a trade-off between maximum HF level and maximum radial tracking level. The radial tracking signal is the difference signal from two halves of the playback photodetector (Philips system). The radial tracking signal is used to servo the position of the lens during playback. A strong tracking signal is necessary to ensure the ability of the player to track the spinning disc.

Maximum HF level is obtained by a pit depth of $\lambda/4$. However, maximum radial tracking signal is obtained by a pit depth of $\lambda/8$. ($\lambda = 790$ nanometers). It is thus necessary to select a pit depth that yields both HF and tracking signals at adequate levels.

Another factor that influences signal quality is asymmetry. Asymmetry describes the duty cycle of the EFM playback signal which is determined by pit length. Asymmetry is specified by Philips to be

±20 percent. Laser power, beam spot size, and develop time all contribute to asymmetry level and must be optimized to obtain the desired level.

Alternate Processes

In addition to the process just described, several other mastering processes are currently available. These are known as the "dry process" and Direct Metal Mastering (DMM), respectively.

With the dry process, the glass master is coated with a photoreactive substance. Exposure of the coating by a laser results in localized vaporization of the coating, creating a pit. Since pits are created directly during mastering, a playback laser can "read-after-write," allowing real-time monitoring of master integrity. A disadvantage of this scheme is contamination of the master by partially vaporized particles.

Direct Metal Mastering (registered trademark of the Teldec Corporation) bears little resemblance to the laser-based processes previously described. In DMM, the recording blank is a disc coated with a thin layer of copper. A diamond coated stylus moves up and down, embossing pits in the copper surface. Like the dry process, DMM also allows direct "read-after-write" evaluation of master quality. DMM eliminates the steps of developing and metalization of the master. Since the master is already electrically conductive, electroforming mothers and stampers can begin immediately. One drawback of DMM is the difficulty of controlling pit geometry, which is more easily accomplished by laser-based mastering systems.

About the Author

Robert Harley works with the Compact Disc research and development group at Disctronics in Anaheim, California. He heads the CD premastering department and has contributed to building Disctronics' custom CD mastering machines. Mr. Harley also teaches the Recording Engineering program at Golden West College in Huntington Beach, California.

Disctronics is the largest independent manufacturer of Compact Discs in the world with plants in Anaheim, California, Huntsville, Alabama, Melbourne, Australia and Southwater, U.K. Committed to providing both high-quality discs and excellent customer service, Disctronics offers a worldwide "One-Stop-Shop" of CD ROM services where clients' raw data is processed, the product designed and developed and then CD ROM discs replicated at one of the Disctronics facilities. Disctronics' services include:

* Project Management
* Data collection and conversion
* Customized user interface development
* Search and retrieval software
* Pre-mastering, mastering and replication
* Service and support

Disctronics USA

Disctronics Manufacturing Inc.
1120 Cosby Way, Anaheim, CA 92806
Phone (714) 630-6700 Fax (714) 630-1025

Disctronics Manufacturing Inc.
4905 Moores Mill Road, Huntsville, AL 35810
Phone (205) 859-9932 Fax (205) 859-9932

Disctronics Inc.
405 Lexington Avenue, 47th Floor, New York, NY 10174
Phone (212) 599-5300 Fax (212) 599-3227/3229

Disctronics Australia

Disctronics Limited
Disctronics Optical Storage Systems Limited
4th Floor, 20 Queen Street, Melbourne, Victoria, 3000
Phone 61 (3) 629-2775 Fax 61 (3) 614-3711

Disctronics Manufacturing Pty. Limited
9 De Havilland Road, Braeside, Victoria, 3195
Phone 61 (3) 587-2633 Fax 61 (3) 587-2901

Disctronics Europe

Disctronics Europe Limited
24 Queen Anne's Gate, London, SW1H9AD
Phone 44 (01) 222-6878 Fax 44 (01)222-4407

Disctronics Manufacturing U.K. Limited
Southwater Business Park, Worthington Road,
Southwater, West Sussex RH137YT
Phone 44 (403) 732-302 Fax 44 (403) 732-313

Acknowledgments

The author wishes to acknowledge the contributions of the following individuals to this chapter:

Evalee Harley
Alan Hamersley
Ray Keating

References

Pohlmann, Ken C. (1985) *Principles of Digital Audio,*. Howard Sams & Co., Inc.

Philips Corporation. *CD ROM System Description* ("Yellow Book").

Isailovic, Jordan (1985). *Videodisc and Optical Memory Systems.* Englewood Cliffs, N.J.:Prentice-Hall, Inc.

Sony Corporation (1986). *Sony Digital Audio Seminar Manual.*

Sekiguchi, K. Y. Maruyama, and M. Tsubaki."An Extension of the CD Mastering System Format for CD ROM Mastering," presented at the 83rd Convention of the Audio Engineering Society, October, 1987.

Chapter

15

CD ROM Manufacturing

Robert Harley, Dwight Bancroft, Al Weeks, and Theodore Lindberg

All Photographs by Roy Mottram

Manufacturing Overview

The mastering and metalization processes described in Chapter 14 produce a metal-coated glass disc (the "glass master") with data encoded in pit and land formations on the surface. The next CD ROM manufacturing phases convert this master disc to replicated plastic discs for distribution and sale.

After mastering and metalization, the glass master is used to form stampers through a process called electroforming. Electroforming creates a stamper which becomes part of a mold for an injection molding press. The surface contours of the stamper are impressed on a clear plastic disc. Data in pit and land formations is thus transferred to a large quantity of discs.

The clear injection-molded discs are then coated with a thin aluminum film ("metalized") to reflect the playback laser beam from the surface. At this stage, discs are not yet ready for use: the surface is vulnerable to dust, scratches, and environmental conditions. To protect the disc from these hazards, an acrylic or lacquer coating is applied to the disc surface, rendering it nearly impervious to handling.

The final step before packaging is screen printing in which an identifying label is silk screened on the disc. All processes described are performed in a "class 100" clean room (fewer than 100 half micrometer-sized particles per cubic foot of air). The discs are then inspected and packaged in "jewel" boxes for shipment. A flowchart of this manufacturing process is shown in Figure 15-1.

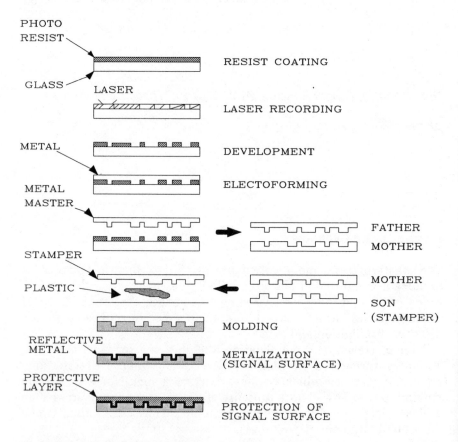

Figure 15-1   CD manufacturing process.

Electroforming

Electroforming is the electro-deposition of a metal on a substrate or "mold." The electroforming process creates a solid nickel stamper from the metalized glass master described in Chapter 14. This stamper is used to replicate quantities of plastic discs by injection molding techniques.

Electroforming, based on the principles of galvanics developed in the mid nineteenth century, is similar to the more familiar process of electroplating. However, unlike electroplating, electroforming requires that the deposited coating be separable from the substrate.

The electroforming process begins by immersing the metal master in a low chloride nickel sulfamate solution saturated with nickel atoms. Also immersed in this solution is a lattice of nearly pure nickel pellets. When a voltage is applied across the mold and the lattice, some of the atoms in solution become attached to the mold. Surface atoms in the solid lattice become hydrated, dissolving into the solution. Atoms removed from solution and deposited on the master are thus replaced by atoms from the solid lattice. In this way, a thin coating of nickel is slowly deposited on the master.

Any contamination of the master or the solution could cause improper deposition, resulting in areas on the disc devoid of pits. To reduce this possibility, all electroforming processes are conducted in a class 100 clean room. Although this contamination-free environment is necessary for manufacturing all CD formats, CD ROM requires the most stringent cleanliness.

Since the nickel is deposited slowly on the master, it is necessary to terminate the process once the correct thickness of nickel has been achieved. A typical deposition thickness of 0.3 mm is achieved in about 1 hour.

The resulting "sandwich" of glass, photoresist, silver, and deposited nickel is removed from solution and separated. Once the nickel coating is removed from the glass master, it is called the "metal master." The metal master is an inverted image of the glass master: pits on the glass master are bumps on the metal master. This separation procedure must be performed carefully since any abrasion of the master surface would destroy pit formations and thus binary data. Figure 15-2 shows a glass master and a metal master.

Once a metal master has been electroformed, it can be used as a stamper to replicate discs. However, should additional stampers be required or if the stamper becomes damaged, it would be necessary

Figure 15-2 A glass master and metal master.

to master the disc again. Consequently, metal masters are rarely used as stampers. Instead, the metal master undergoes further processing so that multiple stampers can be made from one glass master.

The metal master is again immersed in the electroforming tank. This time however, the metal master becomes the mold. Nickel is deposited on the metal master in the same way nickel was deposited on the glass master. The result of this process is a metal master coated with nickel. This nickel coating is separated from the metal master and is called the "metal mother." The metal mother is a positive image (identical to the glass master). To facilitate separation of the master from the mother, the master is passivated prior to this second stage of electroforming. Passivation of the metal master consists of dipping it into a chromate solution. This thin chromate film prevents fusion of the master and the deposited nickel.

After separation, the metal mother is passivated and immersed in the nickel solution. Nickel is again electro-deposited, but this time on the metal mother to form a stamper. Like the glass master/metal master pair and the metal master/mother pair, the stamper is separated from the mother. The stamper should retain the identical (but inverted) characteristics of the glass master such as pit depth and shape since these characteristics were optimized in the mastering and developing processes.

This three-step process is sometimes referred to as the master-mother-stamper process. This procedure allows the creation of up to 5 mothers per master and up to ten stampers per mother. It is thus possible to create as many as 50 stampers from a single master.

Before the stamper can be used to replicate discs, it must be undergo processing known as "dry operations." In dry operations, the stamper is trimmed to the correct diameter, the center hole is punched and the back is sanded smooth. Sanding the back of the stamper is necessary to ensure that the stamper fits flat in the injection molding press. A finished stamper is shown in Figures 15-3a, b.

The finished stamper is now ready for the next phase of CD ROM manufacture: injection molding.

Figure 15-3a Pre dry operation stamper.

Figure 15-3b   Finished stamper.

Injection Molding

The injection molding process transfers the surface configuration of the stamper to a plastic disc. Binary data encoded in pit and land formations is thus replicated on many discs.

Although other molding methods such as compression molding are available, injection molding remains the most common technique. The material used in molding CD ROM is transparent polycarbonate, chosen for its low optical distortion, mechanical strength, high heat and moisture resistance and great dimensional accuracy. It must also be exceptionally pure and contamination free. Contamination of the material would result in imperfect replication of the stamper surface. Figure 15-4 shows one disc's worth of polycarbonate (18 grams) in the form that it is received at a CD manufacturing facility.

Before being molded into discs, the polycarbonate is dried to reduce moisture content and vacuum loaded from the storage area

Figure 15-4   One disc's worth (18 grams) of polycarbonate.

into the molding machine. Once inside the molding machine, the material is transported toward the mold. Heating elements begin to melt the polycarbonate as it travels. Hot polycarbonate is then injected into the mold cavity containing the stamper. Fast material injection time combined with high material temperature ensure complete replication of pit geometry. The material is cooled rapidly and the disc removed from the mold as the machine readies for the next shot. This cycle typically takes about 12 seconds. A robotic arm removes and stacks discs either in vertical spindles or horizontal magazines. Figure 15-5 shows a molded transparent disc.

There are a variety of problems associated with injection molding optical discs. Among them are disc surface contamination and birefringence. Surface contamination is generally caused by airborne particles or contaminated material handling equipment. To reduce this contamination, stringent clean room conditions are maintained throughout injection molding rooms. In addition, polycarbonate handling and transportation is performed in hermetically sealed areas.

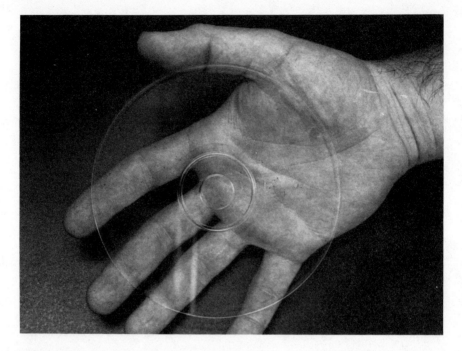

Figure 15-5   A clear injection molded disc.

Birefringence is a double refraction of the playback laser beam. When the beam enters the polycarbonate, part of the beam travels at a different velocity and polarization due to the changes in the refractive index of the polycarbonate. A certain amount of birefringence is inherent in injection molded polycarbonate discs and is acceptable. Excessive birefringence however, causes a degradation of the playback signal. Birefringence is caused by stress in the polycarbonate during molding. It is thus necessary to optimize molding parameters such as material temperature and injection velocity. Birefringence is measured by the relative phase shift of the refracted beams and is specified by Philips to be less than 100 nm (double pass).

Although the transparent discs contain data in the pit and land formations impressed in the surface, data retrieval is not yet possible. The discs must be coated with a thin metal layer to reflect the playback beam. This procedure is called "metalization."

Metalization

Metalizing Compact Discs is typically performed by one of two methods: vapor deposition or sputtering. Both methods achieve the same results with advantages and disadvantages to each.

Vapor Deposition

The vapor deposition method involves vaporizing a metal (aluminum) under vacuum and exposing the clear discs to the vaporized metal. The result is a thin, even coating of aluminum deposited on the disc. The process is analogous to dropping an ice cube in a hot frying pan and holding a glass plate above the pan.

Vapor deposition is a "batch" process wherein a number of discs are metalized in discrete groups. The clear molded discs are loaded pit side out onto trays mounted on a rotating planetary carriage. The carriage has large copper rods running through the axial center with "boats" attached to the rods. These boats are small trays which hold high-purity (99.999%) aluminum pellets. The carriage is placed inside a chamber and evacuated to a pressure of 2 X 10^{-5} Torr. A voltage is then applied across the copper rods. Current flow through the rods causes the boats to become extremely hot, vaporizing the aluminum pellets. Concurrently, the trays on the carriage rotate around the evaporative source, evenly exposing the disc surface to the aluminum vapor.

Deposition thickness is a function of chamber pressure and exposure time to the vaporized aluminum. To ensure that the discs are opaque and have high reflectivity, 1000 to 1500 Å of aluminum is deposited.

Sputtering

The second method of metalizing Compact Discs is called sputtering. Unlike vapor deposition, sputtering is an "in-line" process: discs are metalized one at a time in assembly line fashion.

The clear discs are loaded by robotic arm into individual trays on a track, pit side up. These trays are moved on a conveyor through the sputtering system. Masking rings are sometimes placed on the disc to prevent coating of the inside and outside diameters of the disc.

The disc then enters a chamber that evacuates air to a vacuum comparable to that used in vapor deposition.

Still under vacuum, the disc is moved into the "target" chamber. The target is a disc of high purity aluminum about 15 mm thick held parallel to and above the clear disc. A voltage is applied across the track that holds the disc and the target. When the disc enters the target chamber, a small amount of argon gas is discharged into the chamber. Simultaneously, the voltage across the target and the disc is rapidly increased. This voltage increase causes the argon gas to become positively ionized. This ionized gas is called "plasma."

Since opposite charges attract, the positively charged plasma is attracted to the negatively charged target, colliding with it at high speed. When plasma strikes the target, atoms of aluminum become dislodged from the target. These negatively charged aluminum atoms are deposited on the disc. To contain the aluminum atoms between the disc and the target, a powerful electromagnet rotates above the target.

One of the problems associated with Compact Disc metalization is pinholes. Pinholes are voids in the deposited aluminum layer that cause momentary signal loss and thus data errors. Pinholes are most often caused by particles on the clear discs during metalization. Aluminum is deposited on particles as well as the disc. When the particles become dislodged later, small unmetalized areas are left on the disc. Pinholes cause rejection of the disc.

To reduce pinholes and increase the yield through the metalization process, strict clean room procedures are maintained. Clear disc handling and metalization are both performed in class 100 clean rooms.

Disc Finishing

Protective Coating

At this point in the manufacturing process, the metalized discs are vulnerable to a variety of hazards such as moisture, oxidation of the aluminum coating and surface scratches. To protect the information (metalized) side of the disc, a layer of acrylic or laquer is applied. This procedure is called protective coating.

A robotic arm in the protective coating machine loads discs onto trays on a movable track. Discs move down the track to a spin chamber where liquid acrylic is dispensed on the slowly spinning disc. When the correct amount of acrylic has been dispensed, disc rotational speed is increasd to spin off excess liquid. The conveyor track then moves the disc under an ultraviolet curing lamp that hardens the acrylic coating. This curing method is called photopolymerization. Discs are removed from the track and stacked by robotic arm.

Screen Printing

Screen printing is the final stage of Compact Disc production. This label identifies the contents of the disc. A screen printing machine bears many similarities to a protective coating machine: both use robotic arms for disc loading and unloading, both utilize a moving conveyor system, and both have an ultraviolet curing station along the track.

Artwork supplied by the customer is photographed and the film is used to make a silk screen. The screen is saturated with ink and held in a fixture above the moving track. As the disc moves under the screen fixture, it is held stationary momentarily. The screen is then lowered toward the disc surface and a rubber squeegee wipes across the screen, leaving an ink impression on the disc.

After ink application, the disc moves down the track and underneath an ultraviolet curing lamp. The ink used is an ultraviolet-cured pigmented polymer. As in protective coating, photopolymerization hardens the ink. The printed and cured discs are then removed and stacked on vertical spindles or horizontal magazines by robotic arm.

Quality Assurance

Good quality assurance procedures are vital in the digital audio Compact Disc manufacturing process. CD ROM manufacturing, however, requires even more stringent quality assurance procedures due to the nature of the data replicated on the disc.

With digital audio, missing or errant data can be concealed with acceptable results by interpolation techniques. This is due to the high degree of correlation between samples of an audio waveform. Error concealment however, is not allowable on CD ROM: every bit must be retrieved from the disc with absolute accuracy (after error correction). The disc must play through with no uncorrectable errors.

If this is achieved, the data retrieved from the disc is identical to the source data. This requirement places extraordinary demands on both manufacturing processes and quality assurance procedures.

Each phase of CD ROM manufacturing is accompanied by a quality assurance inspection procedure. If the source data is on 3/4-inch U-Matic, a digital tape analyzer checks for missing or errant data and provides a printout of location and severity of errors. If errors are completely corrected (not concealed), the tape is passed to the mastering stage. The tape is analyzed again during mastering; any uncorrected errors result in rejection of the master disc.

Some premastering systems that allow direct mastering from a personal or workstation computer have a "simulation" feature. This feature allows retrieval of data from the premastering system to simulate data retrieval from the disc. Data integrity and operating software can thus be verified before mastering to glass disc.

The metalized glass master is played on a special player that analyzes a multitude of disc parameters including error rates, playback signal quality, and subcode programming. The master disc also undergoes an extensive visual inspection.

During the electroforming process, the metal master, mother, and stampers are visually inspected for imperfections. Voids or contamination are cause for immediate rejection of the metal parts.

To ensure stamper integrity, the first few discs from the molding machine are metalized and inspected. This inspection occurs simultaneously with injection molding of the production run. Consequently, if the stamper is found to be defective, discs molded during the inspection time must be scrapped.

Prior to protective coating, the discs are examined visually for pinholes or imperfections in the aluminum layer. Discs are again visually inspected after screen printing for print quality.

Among the electronic measurements made on replicated discs are:

• High frequency signal
• Asymetry
• Radial tracking level
• Block error rate (BLER)
• Subcode programming
• Error Detection Code and Error Correction Code analysis.

In addition, the following physical parameters are measured:

- Thickness
- Weight
- Diameter
- Track pitch uniformity
- Eccentricity
- Skew
- Lead-in and program starting radius.

Some premastering systems also allow direct byte-for-byte comparison of data read from a replicated disc with the source data. A finished disc is played back in a standard CD ROM drive interfaced to the premastering computer. The system then compares this data with the block-formatted hard disc data. This process is performed in real time — about 10.5 Mbytes per minute. If the data is not identical, the errant block is displayed (in hex) on the computer monitor. This feature is invaluable in assuring absolute integrity of data retrieved from a replicated disc.

As a final check, each disc is visually examined as it is inserted into the final packaging. A finished CD ROM is shown inserted in a jewel box in Figure 15-6.

Figure 15-6   A finished CD ROM inserted in a jewel box.

A Final Note

A Compact Disc manufacturing facility is extremely capital intensive, both for initial start-up and for day-to-day operations. In addition, a large pool of highly skilled labor is needed due to the technological nature of the finished product and the complex manufacturing processes involved.

Yet despite these facts, CD ROMs are readily available at relatively low cost. This paradoxical (and fortunate) situation is made possible by the unparalleled consumer acceptance of the Compact Disc as a medium for music reproduction. Worldwide, CD Audio sales are expected to approach 700 million units per year by 1990. Both manufacturing and research and development costs are thus amortized over a huge number of units. As a direct result, the Compact Disc becomes extremely cost effective, allowing the realization of a plethora of specialized CD formats that could not exist otherwise.

About the Authors

Robert Harley works with the Compact Disc research and development group at Disctronics, Inc. in Anaheim, California. He heads the CD premastering department and has contributed to building Disctronics' custom CD mastering machines. Mr. Harley also teaches the Recording Engineering program at Golden West College in Huntington Beach, California.

Dwight Bancroft is a graduate of the University of Michigan. He has worked in the electroplating and electroforming field since 1969. During this time he has been involved in both production and research and development of the optical disc including the videodisc and more recently, the Compact Disc. Mr. Bancroft joined Disctronics in 1985 and is currently manager of the Chemical Processing and Electroforming Departments at Disctronics' Anaheim facility.

Albert T. Weeks is a graduate of S.U.N.Y. at Morrisville, New York. He has worked in an R & D capacity for several large corporations and became involved in the development of the videodisc during his 5 years at Philips Labs in Briarcliff Manor, New York.

Mr. Weeks moved to southern California where he worked as a technical writer and test engineer. Joining Disctronics in 1982, he is currently manager of Disc Production.

Theodore Lindberg graduated from Golden West College with a degree in Recording Engineering. He currently studies mathematics at California State University, Long Beach.

He has been involved in many aspects of audio engineering, including sound reinforcement design/installation and digital audio. He currently works in the Quality Assurance Department of Disctronics' Anaheim facility.

Disctronics is the largest independent manufacturer of Compact Discs in the world with plants in Anaheim, California, Huntsville, Alabama, Melbourne, Australia and Southwater, U.K. Committed to providing both high-quality discs and excellent customer service, Disctronics offers a worldwide "One-Stop-Shop" of CD ROM services where clients' raw data is processed, the product designed and developed and then CD ROM discs replicated at one of the Disctronics facilities. Disctronics' services include:

* Project Management
* Data collection and conversion
* Customized user interface development
* Search and retrieval software
* Pre-mastering, mastering and replication
* Service and support

Disctronics USA

Disctronics Manufacturing Inc.
1120 Cosby Way, Anaheim, CA 92806
Phone (714) 630-6700 Fax (714) 630-1025

Disctronics Manufacturing Inc.
4905 Moores Mill Road, Huntsville, AL 35810
Phone (205) 859-9932 Fax (205) 859-9932

Disctronics Inc.
405 Lexington Avenue, 47th Floor, New York, NY 10174
Phone (212) 599-5300 Fax (212) 599-3227/3229

Disctronics Australia

Disctronics Limited
Disctronics Optical Storage Systems Limited
4th Floor, 20 Queen Street, Melbourne, Victoria, 3000
Phone 61 (3) 629-2775 Fax 61 (3) 614-3711

Disctronics Manufacturing Pty. Limited
9 De Havilland Road, Braeside, Victoria, 3195
Phone 61 (3) 587-2633 Fax 61 (3) 587-2901

Disctronics Europe

Disctronics Europe Limited
24 Queen Anne's Gate, London, SW1H9AD
Phone 44 (01) 222-6878 Fax 44 (01)222-4407

Disctronics Manufacturing U.K. Limited
Southwater Business Park, Worthington Road,
Southwater, West Sussex RH137YT
Phone 44 (403) 732-302 Fax 44 (403) 732-313

Chapter

16

Selected Bibliography: Search CD-450 in Action

Beverly A. Butler and Bradley C. Watson

This bibliography is a result of searching three databases produced on CD ROM by OCLC: COMPUTER, Current Index to Journals in Education (CIJE) 1982 to March 88, and Resources in Education (RIE) 1982 to March 1988. The first database is a subset of OCLC's Online Union Catalog (OLUC), while the other two are from ERIC. Each database resides on a separate CD ROM disc. Search CD-450, OCLC's CD ROM bibliographic database retrieval package, was used to find those records in the three databases that contained any mention of CD ROM. The records that were found were formatted and saved to a diskette. Once on a diskette, the records could be pulled into a word-processing package and edited. Not one 3" by 5" index card gave its life for this bibliography.

At the end of the bibliography is a list of some of the databases currently available on CD ROM.

Bibliography

Allen, R. J. The CD-ROM Services of SilverPlatter Information, Inc. *Library Hi Tech*, 1985, pp. 49-60.

The SilverPlatter system is a complete, stand-alone system, consisting of an IBM (or compatible) personal computer, CD ROM drive, software, and one or more databases. Large databases (e.g., ERIC, PsychLIT) will soon be available on the system for "local" installation in schools, libraries, and psychiatrists' offices.

Bardes, D. Attention Novices: Friendly Intro to Shiny Disks. *Library Software Review*, July-August 1986, pp. 241-245.

Provides an overview of how optical storage technologies — videodisc, Write-Once disc, CD ROM, and CD-I discs — are built into and controlled via DEC, Apple, Atari, Amiga, and IBM PC compatible microcomputers. Several available products are noted and a list of producers is included.

Bardes, D. Implications of CD-Interactive: Direction, Specifications, and Standards. *Optical Information Systems*, July-August 1986, pp. 324-328.

Looks at proposed standard for CD-I and its implications for product and market development, CD-ROM, and optical publishing. Possible roles of OS-9 (Microware's operating system), Polaroid's Colorcatcher, and products shown at the Microsoft CD ROM conference in the development of the CD-I market are discussed.

Barker, P. Video Discs in Education. *Education and Computing*, 1986, pp. 193-206.

This discussion of the use of images in learning processes focuses on recent developments in optical storage disc technology, particularly CD ROM and optical video discs. Interactive video systems and user interfaces are described, and applications in education and industry in the United Kingdom are reviewed.

Barlow, D. et. al. CD-ROM in a High School Library Media Center. *School Library Journal*, November 1987, pp. 66-68; 70-72.

Describes the experiences of high school students using microcomputers to access an electronic version of an encyclopedia in the school's media center. The topics discussed include hardware and software requirements of the CD ROM format, information seeking strategies and problems observed, student satisfaction with the system, and recommendations for similar projects.

Barrett, R. *Development and application of the Philips CD-ROM: Report to the British Library of a visit to Philips International BV, Eindhoven, Holland relating to grant number SI/V/87.* (Part of series: British Library Research and Development Reports.)

Becker, K. A. CD-ROM: A Primer. *College and Research Libraries News*, July-August 1987, pp. 388-390; 392-393.

Presents a "family tree" of optical technologies with a list of definitions, and briefly discusses some of the issues relating to optical technologies and their use in libraries.

Beiser, K. Microcomputing. *Wilson Library Bulletin*, April 1986, pp. 42-43.

Describes a product and a service, each of which revolve around the ultra-high-density storage capacity of CD ROM discs. The product is BiblioFile, Library Corporation's catalog production system. The service is reproduction of public domain software on CD ROM for sale to those interested. Criteria for selecting microcomputers are briefly reviewed.

Bovey, J. D. & Brown, P. J. Interactive Document Display and Its Use in Information Retrieval. *Journal of Documentation*, June 1987, pp. 125-137.

Describes software for displaying documents on computer graphics screens which provide the opportunity for interactive user interfaces. Based on a software system called Guide, this new approach relies on advances in hardware, such as the CD ROM, and can be used in the front end of a document retrieval system.

Brandhorst, T. Distributing the ERIC Database on Compact Disc: A Case History of Private Sector Involvement in the Distribution of Public Sector Data. *Government Publications Review*, 1987, pp. 541-557.

Describes the partnership between the public and private sectors in developing and marketing the ERIC database in CD ROM format. Particular emphasis is given to the marketing research and protocols of partnership that were developed.

Brandhorst, T. *Distributing the ERIC Database on SilverPlatter Compact Disc — A Brief Case History.* Paper presented at the ONLINE '86 Conference (Chicago, IL, November 5, 1986). November 1986. (ERIC Document Reproduction Service No. ED 277 394)

This description of the development of the Education Resources Information Center (ERIC) compact disc by two companies, Silver-Platter and ORI, Inc., provides background information on ERIC and the ERIC database, discusses reasons for choosing to put the ERIC database on compact discs, and describes the formulation of an ERIC CD ROM team as part of the development process.
A review of steps along the way in the development of a CD ROM version of the ERIC database includes discussions of agreements and contracts; division of labor; marketing information/surveys; product design; conversion/inversion specifications; retrieval system capabilities; alpha test sites; news releases, flyers, letters, status reports, and order forms; publicity (articles, conference exhibits, advertising); and documentation and user manuals.
The following information is appended: (1) ORI/SilverPlatter Division of Responsibility; (2) ERIC Database Conversion/Inversion Specifications; (3) Search Features — Comparison of ERIC on SilverPlatter with DIALOG 2; (4) Projected Retrieval System Improvements; (5) SilverPlatter order form and subscription agreement; (6) SilverPlatter pricing information; (7) Resources in Education (RIE) Sample Record; (8) listing of ERIC Clearinghouses; and (9) ERIC Fact Sheet.

Brandhorst, T. *ERIC on Compact Disc (CD-ROM). A Case Study.* Paper presented at the CD-ROM Based Information Dissemination Conference (Reston, VA, April 13-15, 1986). April 1986. (ERIC Document Reproduction Service No. ED 272 170)

ORI, Inc., and SilverPlatter, Inc., have joined together in a joint venture to offer the ERIC database to the public on compact laser disc (CD ROM). Data from both "Resources in Education" (RIE) and "Current Index to Journals in Education" (CIJE) will be offered on a single disc from January 1983 to the present (with the disc being updated every quarter). Data prior to 1983 will be offered on archival discs (two for RIE; one for CIJE).

This case study reviews the various reasons why ERIC is interested in CD ROM as a method of data dissemination and the reasons ORI chose to link with SilverPlatter in offering such a service. Some of the early experiences in developing the product are related: acquiring market information, configuring the product, developing the retrieval system, alpha testing, allocating corporate responsibilities, pricing, etc. It is noted that ERIC satisfies all five factors that have been cited as determining whether a product is likely to be successful if delivered on CD ROM technology: (1) large volume of data; (2) stable data not requiring frequent updates; (3) geographically dispersed user community; (4) most users have access to microcomputers; and (5) additional processing enhances the value of the data delivered.

Brito, C. J. Pan-American Health Organization CD-ROM Pilot Project. *Information Development*, October 1987, pp. 208-213.

Examines the difficulties faced by the implementors of information dissemination systems in developing nations, and explores the possible use of optical data disc technologies to overcome them. A pilot project of the Pan American Health Organization for the production of a CD ROM containing bibliographic references on public health is described.

Buddine, L. *The Brady Guide to CD-ROM.* New York: Prentice Hall Press, 1987.

CD ROM: the Current and Future State of the Art. Redmond, Washington: Microsoft Press, 1986.

Cerva, J. R. et. al. Selected Conference Proceedings from the 1985 Videodisc, Optical Disk, and CD-ROM Conference and Exposition (Philadelphia, PA, December 10-12, 1985). *Optical Information Systems*, March-April 1986, pp. 114-131.

Eight papers cover: optical storage technology, cross-cultural videodisc design, optical disc technology use at the Library of Congress Research Service and National Library of Medicine, Internal Revenue Service image storage and retrieval system, solving business problems with CD ROM, a laser disc operating system, and an optical disc for bibliographic databases.

Chen, C. Micro-Based Optical Videodisc Applications. *Microcomputers for Information Management: An International Journal for Library and Information Services*, December 1985, pp. 217-240.

This overview of optical videodisc technology focuses on microcomputer-based applications for information processing. Topics discussed include fundamentals of videodisc technology, interactive videodisc technology, and associated hardware systems; government-supported and commercial videodisc and CD ROM information projects; and speculations on future developments. Information-related videodisc and CD ROM products are listed.

Clark, J. E. & Finch, W. L. *Optical Disk Initiatives at the National Technical Information Service*. May 1986. (NTIS No. PB86-199973)

The National Technical Information Service (NTIS) is the central source for the public sale of reports, intellectual properties, and computer software and data files generated by the U.S. Government and many foreign sources in the fields of science and technology. The NTIS Bibliographic Database, which contains abstracts of these information products, has until how been available only in paper journals, magnetic tape, or online through the major information processors. Subsets of the database are now available on compact discs. CD ROM is an important new medium for database access by personal computers.

Cohen, E. & Young, M. Cost Comparison of Abstracts and Indexes on Paper, CD-ROM, and Online. *Optical Information Systems*, November-December 1986, pp. 485-490.

Describes a model enumerating cost factors for comparing paper, online, and CD ROM versions of indexes and abstracts. The model is applied to start-up as well as annual costs, and to the cost of storing and providing access to ERIC, Applied Science and

Fisheries Abstracts, and Excerpta Medica, based on anticipated academic library usage.

Compact Optical Disc Technology - CD ROM. April 1979-1986. Citations from the INSPEC: Information Services for the Physics and Engineering Communities Database. December 1986. (NTIS No. PB87-852885)

This bibliography contains citations concerning technology, applications and new developments in the rapidly growing field of Compact Disc and CD ROM disc players. Optical disc storage has proven to be capable of high density data storage, and is virtually indestructible to all but physical damage. Subjects addressed are CD players in data storage, audio and video reproduction, performance and production modifications, market developments, search and retrieval software for stand-alone database searching, full text document retrieval and printing, CD ROM publishing, and the latest developments in recording on optical discs and disc manufacture. (This updated bibliography contains 350 citations, 181 of which are new entries to the previous edition.)

Conference Proceedings. Videodisc, Optical Disk and CD-ROM Conference & Exposition, 1985, Philadelphia, Pa. Westport Connecticut: Meckler Publications, 1985.

Cribbs, M. A. The Invisible Drip...How Data Seeps Away in Various Ways. *Online*, March 1987, pp. 15-16; 18-26.

Discusses the preservation of electronically produced data focusing on the passive destruction of data due to lack of proper care in information storage. Three case studies are presented: two involve specific media, magnetic tape and CD ROM, and one the transfer of data from one system to another.

Demmon-Berger, D. & Hill, T. S. Schools and Technology: New and the Future. *Updating School Board Policies*, December 1985, pp. 1-3. (ERIC Document Reproduction Service No. ED 264 658)

School systems, by and large, are hesitating in integrating new technology into the educational process. The new technology includes computers, telecommunications, electronic blackboards, interactive video for simulations, editing devices, and the new optical storage disc, the CD ROM. Many believe the new technology can help to address such concerns as diverse population needs, equity in education, uniformity in curriculum, the shortage of qualified teaching personnel, and the need for lifelong learning and retraining experiences.

School boards involved in the purchase of new technology are advised to begin with a planning committee, involving teachers, for long-range planning and to formulate a district needs assessment. Policy statements need to be made concerning equipment purchasing, ownership, use, and maintenance. Since most school systems will not have the resources for immediate, full-scale computerization, priorities must be set. Planners can move from a generalized statement to more specific curriculum, hardware, software, and staff development needs.

Demo, W. *The Idea of "Information Literacy" in the Age of High-Tech.* 1986. (ERIC Document Reproduction Service No. ED 282 537)

The Information Age is being driven by an acceleration of technological breakthroughs including microcomputers, cable television, electronic publishing, fiber optics, satellite communications, videotext, online database searching, high-density CD ROM storage, and robotics. A new intellectual skill that will enable us to be masters of new communications and information technologies is needed.

This skill, which is called information literacy, has been written about from a number of different perspectives by information industry spokespersons, librarians, educators, and communications researchers. Some characteristics of information technology might actually be impediments to the attainment of information literacy for many: (1) generation of an over-supply of information; (2) cost of information machines; (3) cost of information access; (4) invisibility of the information revolution to the average person; and (5) the "de-massification" of mass media.

Libraries in secondary and higher education often provide the needed focus for information literacy programs. The public library can provide similar programs for the general population; however, under use and under financing may hinder such efforts. It is necessary to make the components of the online information environment more visible and accessible to potential users — those who are pre-information literate. Not to do so in an active, concerted manner will mean that information needs for significant parts of the population will remain unidentified, unexpressed, and unmet. Twenty-five references are listed.

Desmarais, N. Buying and Selling Laserbases. *Electronic and Optical Publishing Review*, December 1986, pp. 184-188.

Discusses factors that should be considered by buyers and producers of databases on CD ROM. The advantages and disadvantages of CD ROM are also discussed and compared with those of magnetic and print media, and market projections are provided.

Epler, D. M. & Cassel, R. E. ACCESS PENNSYLVANIA: A CD-ROM Database Project. *Library Hi Tech*, Fall 1987, pp. 81-92.

Describes ACCESS PENNSYLVANIA, a statewide program structured around school libraries which has two objectives: (1) production of a union catalog to facilitate resource identification and retrieval, and (2) development of automated support capabilities within the libraries served by the project. The CD ROM microcomputer technology used, Le Pac, is described by Virginia Gatcheff.

Essential Guide to CD-ROM. Westport, Connecticut: Meckler Publications, 1986.

The original limited edition of this volume included a sample CD ROM adhered in an envelope to the inside back cover of the book. While this current edition does not contain the disc, references to it remain in the text.

Essential guide to the library IBM PC. Westport, Connecticut: Meckler Publications, 1985.

Feasibility study of CD-Rom/Worm Optical Storage Technology. Cincinnati: Cincinnati Technical College, 1986.

Includes master plan, flowcharts, comparison and outline, etc. This study was undertaken to entitle upgrading the Student Record Department's present system with CD ROM/WORM drives to archive and retrieve student transcript records that are presently stored on microfilm and paper documents.

Feldman, T. *CD-ROM*. London: Blueprint, 1987. (Part of Publisher's Guide Series)

The First International Conference on CD ROM: Seattle, WA, March 4-7, 1986 (notes from the conference). Seattle: Compufair, Inc., 1986.

Forecast: Ten Trends for CD-ROM and OD-ROM. *TechTrends*, April 1986, pp. 17.

Rothchild Consultants, a market research and publishing firm, predicts how the market for optical disc read-only memory (OD ROM) products will evolve.

Glossary of CD-ROM-Related Technical Terms and Acronyms. *Optical Information Systems*, May-June 1986, pp. 230-234.

Defines approximately 95 of the most important and widely used industry terms, phrases, acronyms, and concepts for individuals new to CD ROM technology.

Graves, G. T. et. al. Planning for CD-ROM in the Reference Department. *College and Research Libraries News*, July-August 1987, pp. 393; 395-96; 399-400.

Outlines the evaluation criteria used by the reference department at the Williams Library at the University of Mississippi in selecting databases and hardware used in CD ROM work stations. The factors discussed include database coverage, costs, and security.

Hagan, D. L. The Tacoma Debut of Books in Print Plus. *Library Journal*, September 1, 1987, pp. 149-151.

Describes the Tacoma Public Library's experience with "BIP Plus," the CD ROM version of Books in Print. Memory requirements, search capabilities, automatic ordering, and the library staff's response are discussed. Keyword searching is explained as the system's most used feature, and price the area of most serious concern.

Halperin, M. & Pagell, R. A. COMPACT DISCLOSURE: Realizing CD-ROM's Potential. *Online*, November 1986, pp. 69-73.

The advantages and disadvantages of the compact disc version of the DISCLOSURE database are compared to the print version and other online formats. Timeliness of information, searching methods, users' perceptions taken from a student survey, price, availability, response time, and browsabiity are considered. Sample menus and screen displays are included.

Harrison, N. & Murphy, B. Multisensory Public Access Catalogs on CD-ROM. *Library Hi Tech*, Fall 1987, pp. 77-80.

BiblioFile Intelligent Catalog is a CD ROM-based public access catalog system which incorporates graphics and sound to provide a multisensory interface, and artificial intelligence techniques to increase search precision. The system can be updated frequently and inexpensively by linking hard disk drives to CD ROM optical drives.

Harvey, F. A. Emerging Digital Optical Disc Technologies: An Opportunity and a Challenge for Educational Researchers. *AECT-RTD Newsletter*, Fall 1987, pp. 2-10.

Description of new applications of digital optical disc storage technologies focuses on CD ROM, CD-I, and DV-I. Features of each technology are described in the context of instructional design and educational technology, and the role of educational research in their development is discussed.

Helgerson, L. W. Acquiring a CD-ROM Public Access Catalog System. Part 1: The Bottom Line May Not Be the Top Priority. *Library Hi Tech*, Fall 1987, pp. 49-75.

Compares pricing of seven CD ROM-based public access catalog systems for libraries of diverse sizes and groupings. Other features of the systems are outlined in the broad areas of database preparation, indexing, database updates, hardware, information retrieval, library controlled elements, interlibrary loan, reports, user support, future developments, and current installations.

Helgerson, L. W. CD-ROM Search and Retrieval Software: The Requirements and Realities. *Library Hi Tech*, Summer 1986, pp. 69-77.

Discusses search and retrieval software for use with CD ROM. Background trends, how data are made usable, supply and demand, data preparation services, and capabilities of search software are described. Vendors of significant information retrieval products are identified, and the characteristics of 12 packages are compared.

Herther, N. K. CD-ROM and Information Dissemination: An Update. *Online*, March 1987, pp. 56-64.

This current overview of optical disc technology describes the evolving marketplace for optical products, the use of libraries as test sites for prototype CD ROM products, CD ROM developments, new optical technologies, and advances in magnetics. A list of some compact disc manufacturers and a glossary of terms are included.

Herther, N. K. CD ROM Technology: A New Era for Information Storage and Retrieval? *Online*, November 1985, pp. 17-28.

Introduction to use of compact disc technology for storing digital data highlights history, background, and developments; technical features; standardization issues; current CD ROM applications; and the market for CD products. A production diagram, a sampling of CD manufacturers and disc replicators, and performance comparison of three storage media are included.

Hlava, M. M. K. et. al. CD-ROM vs. Online. *Bulletin of the American Society for Information Science*, October-November 1987, pp. 14-27.

This series of ten articles exploring users' reactions to optical data disc technologies focuses on comparisons with online retrieval systems. The opinions of users and vendors on cost effectiveness, searchability, equipment requirements and performance, effectiveness, and efficiency are presented and discussed.

Huffman, R. F. *In Praise of Mr. S. Platter and His Marvelous, Magnificent CD ROM Laser Disc Index for ERIC and PSYCHLIT.* July 1987. (ERIC Document Reproduction Service No. ED 284 579)

These instructions are designed to help patrons of the University of Missouri-Columbia library perform searches on PSYCHLIT, a CD ROM version of the Psych Abstracts database, and a CD ROM version of the ERIC database, both produced by SilverPlatter Information Services. Basic information is provided about the disc contents, use of the work station function keys, viewing and evaluating records, and printing search results.

In addition, a four-part set of instructions, "How to Do a Search on the ERIC/PSYCHLIT CD ROM Indexes," provides the following information: (1) instructions for performing a practice search using prescribed terms, displaying the retrieved records, and printing the search results; (2) instructions to enable a user to perform a search on a topic of his or her choice and to display and print the results; (3) helpful hints for completing a successful search; and (4) questions and answers about searching. A checklist of 22 items that a patron-trainee should be made aware of in order to use the ERIC and PSYCHLIT CD ROM indexes and four suggestions for the librarian-trainer is also included.

Jacobson, K. J. *Assessment of CD ROM (Compact Disk Read Only Memory).* June 1986. (NTIS No. AD-A169 259/9)

CD ROM is one of a group of optical disc technologies that offers great information storage potential. CD ROM Technology uses a laser to burn, or record, pits in the light sensitive surface of an optical or plastic coated disc. The typical 4.75-inch CD ROM disc offers enough storage capability to hold the contents of 1,200 standard 5.25-inch floppy disks. This report describes the current state-of-the-art and typical steps in preparing the CD ROM database, including data preparation (data indexing and reformatting), disc premastering, disc mastering, and mass replication.

The strengths of CD ROM technology include high data storage density, relatively low costs for widely distributed databases, relatively high random access speeds, and disc durability and integration in the normal office environment. Limitations include the current high costs of premastering and mastering discs, and the lack of standardization among CD ROM producers. CD ROM is not an acceptable storage alternative for databases that are highly volatile, however an erasable optical disc is currently under development.

Kennedy, H. E. *Information Delivery Options over Three Decades.* Miles Conrad Lecture presented at the Annual Conference of the National Federation of Abstracting and Information Services (28th, Philadelphia, PA, March 2-5, 1986). *NFAIS Newsletter,* April 1986, pp. 31-47. (ERIC Document Reproduction Service No. ED 274 365)

The rate of new technology-driven innovations for information delivery has accelerated over the past three decades. New information delivery formats in the 1950s and 1960s included microforms and, in response to demands from librarians, indexing and abstracting services began to make their publications available on this medium. Electronic processing and delivery of machine-readable records became a reality in the late 1960s; magnetic tapes were developed, and online distribution followed. Online usage on a broad scale occurred much more quickly than predicted, first as bibliographic entries, then as abstracts, and finally full-text formats became available online.

Recent information delivery mechanisms and issues include floppy discs, downloading, vertical integration, value added, electronic publishing, optical discs, and CD ROM. These technological applications have had a vast impact not only on the way information is processed and delivered to its point of use, but also on how it is used. During the decade ahead, the need for carefully weighed decisions will be greater than ever. Material pertinent to this topic is listed in an accompanying 34-item bibliography.

Kuhlman, J. R. & Lee, E. S. Data — Power to the People. *American Libraries,* November 1986, pp. 757-758; 760; 778.

The development of CD ROM following early computers and powerful personal computers will affect information retrieval by its accessibility and large storage capacity. Users will demand specific information and data sets from libraries, which could provide large research capacities. Librarians will act as database managers, thus enhancing their roles.

Lambert, S. & Ropiequet, S., Eds. *CD ROM. The New Papyrus: The Current and Future State of the Art.* Redmond, Washington: Microsoft Press, 1986.

This compendium of 44 articles written by leading authorities provides an in-depth and instructive overview of CD ROM for both the professional and the newcomer to the field. Three articles serve as an introduction to the book: (1) "As We May Think," Vannevar Bush; (2) "Finally It Works — Now It Must 'Play in Peoria,'" David C. Miller; and (3) "CD ROM and Videodisc: Lessons to Be Learned," Rockley L. Miller. The next section provides an overview of CD ROM technology via articles on the hardware, system software, and retrieval software.

The third section focuses on production techniques, including data preparation, data indexing, image capture and processing, and compressing and digitizing images. Section 4 considers the elements of design as it relates to the human factor, authoring and development, and project management. CD ROM publishing is discussed in Section 5, and the applications described in Section 6 include market considerations, CD ROM in libraries, medical and legal applications, geographic applications, and archive and research applications.

Additional resources listed in Section 7 include persons who contributed to the book either by writing an article or by answering questions and giving advice, and companies and individuals contacted during the compilation of the book. An index is provided.

Lampton, C. *CD ROMs.* New York: F. Watts, 1987.

Explains how CD ROM and optical information storage work and discusses their applications and possible future developments.

Lind, D. J. *Optical Laser Technology, Specifically CD-ROM (Compact Disc - Read Only Memory) and Its Application to the Storage and Retrieval of Information.* Master's thesis, 132 pp. June 1987. (NTIS No. AD-A184 111/3)

One of the significant problems of this information age is the production of vast amounts of information in a form that is neither convenient nor cost effective. A possible solution to this is the new optical laser technology, specifically CD ROM, and its use in the storage and retrieval of large amounts of information.

In many areas of DOD, the greatest benefit of CD ROM would be the regained space and weight associated with the storage of manuals and other paper documents. One CD ROM weighs less than an ounce and is capable of storing over 270,000 pages of text. The saved shipping and handling costs alone would be astronomically reduced. Also, the end user would have a more effective and efficient product.

The CD ROM is designed to work as a peripheral device to a microcomputer, and can therefore be made available to any user of an IBM compatible microcomputer.

For the application/demonstration portion of this thesis, over 2 million database records from the Transaction Ledger on Disc (TLOD) at the Naval Supply Center (NSC) in Oakland were pressed to a single CD ROM. The menu driven retrieval software with indexing on three criteria was also provided.

Looking for Strength in Diversity: ALA in San Francisco. *Wilson Library Bulletin*, September 1987, pp. 19-36.

This report of the American Library Association's 1987 conference in San Francisco summarizes meetings on: local area networks, personal liability of library trustees, librarian shortages, AIDS education, CD-ROM technology, literacy, black librarians and the political process, and restriction of young adult literature. Exhibit highlights are also included.

Mark, L. The Expanding Information World: SLA in Anaheim. *Wilson Library Bulletin*, September 1987, pp. 37-40.

The Special Libraries Association 1987 conference had the theme "Global Information Access — Expanding Our World." Topics discussed included: information access in the Third World, the value of information professionals, copyright fees and fair use, CD-ROM technology, and military libraries.

McGinty, T. Three Trailblazing Technologies for Schools. *Electronic Learning*, September 1987, pp. 26-30.

Provides an overview of the capabilities and potential educational applications of CD ROM, artificial intelligence, and speech technology. Highlights include reference materials on CD ROM; current developments in CD-I (compact disc interactive); synthesized and digital speech for microcomputers, including specific products; and artificial intelligence products for educators.

McLaughlin, P. W. New Access Points to ERIC: CD-ROM Versions. *Education Libraries*, Fall 1987, pp. 73-76.

Describes and compares three versions of the ERIC database that are available on optical data discs: (1) DIALOG OnDisc ERIC; (2) OCLC Search CD450; and (3) SilverPlatter ERIC. The database contents, software and search commands, hardware requirements, notable features, and costs of each version are discussed.

McLaughlin, P. W. *New Access Points to ERIC — CD-ROM Versions*. *ERIC Digest*. May 1987. (ERIC Document Reproduction Service No. ED 283 533)

This digest reviews three CD ROM versions of the ERIC (Educational Resources Information Center) database currently being delivered or tested and provides information for comparison. However, no attempt is made to recommend any one product. The advantages and disadvantages of the acquisition of CD ROM databases are discussed, and the vendor address as well as a description of the database scope and information on software capabilities, hardware requirements, and any notable features are provided for the following products: (1) DIALOG OnDisc ERIC, produced by DIALOG Information Services, Inc.; (2) OCLC Search CD450 for Education, produced by the Online Computer Library Center; and (3) SilverPlatter ERIC, produced by SilverPlatter Information, Inc.

In addition, a table presents a comparison of the current disc contents, archival disc contents, hardware, CD drives, and prices of the three products.

Melin, N. J. *Library Applications of Optical Disk and CD-ROM Technology*. Westport, Connecticut: Meckler Publications, 1987. (Vol. 8 of the Series: Essential Guide to the Library IBM PC)

Micco, M. & Smith, I. Designing an Integrated System of Databases: A Workstation for Information Seekers. *Library Software Review*, September-October 1987, pp. 259-262.

Proposes a framework for the design of a full function workstation for information retrieval based on study of information seeking behavior. A large amount of local storage of the CD ROM jukebox variety and full networking capability to both local and external databases are identified as requirements of the prototype.

Miller, D. C. Laser Disks at the Library Door: The Microsoft First International Conference on CD-ROM. *Library Hi Tech*, Summer 1986, pp. 55-68.

Description of First International CD-ROM Conference held by Microsoft, Inc., in March, 1986. Covers types of participants, hardware and support services, and technical standards and intellectual property rights as market barriers. The importance of librarians planning for CD ROM is stressed, and a detailed directory of references and contacts is included.

Miller, D. C. *Moving Information: Graphic Images on CD ROM*. Benicia, California: DCM Associates, 1986.

A special report to Fred Meyer Charitable Trust, Library and Information Resources for the Northwest.

Miller, D. C. Running with CD-ROM. *American Libraries*, November 1986, pp. 754-756.

An information industry analyst suggests ways for librarians to deal with the acquisition and use of CD ROM technology in their libraries. Practical information is provided on needs assessment, purchasing, system standards, and user access and fees, as well as sources of optical disc systems and titles.

Miller, D. C. *Special report: Publishers, Libraries & CD-ROM: Implications of Digital Optical Printing.* San Francisco: DCM Associates, 1987.

Client: Library and Information Resources for the Northwest, Portland, Oregon, a Fred Meyer Charitable Trust program; date — March 1987.

Moes, R. J. The CD-ROM Puzzle: Where Do the Pieces Fit? *Optical Information Systems*, November-December 1986, pp. 509-511.

Representing the point of view of Philips Subsystems and Peripherals on CD ROM and CD-I issues, this position paper attempts to point out differences and similarities between the basic CD ROM standard and the CD-I standard proposed for interactive use of data.

Morrison, J. W. *Role of Colleges in the Coming Demise of the Personal Computer Industry.* Paper presented at a Conference of NERCOMP (New England Regional Computer Programs) (Hanover, NH, January 18, 1986). January 1986. (ERIC Document Reproduction Service No. ED 273 257)

The concept of the personal computer (PC) as a stand-alone, single-user computer has had its day. The 8-bit processors cannot support the newer applications, and, although there have been some advances in 16-bit microprocessors, the "second generation" software is immature and does not work well.

The immediate problem for colleges and universities is how to replace and/or upgrade their obsolete computing equipment. The trend is toward 32-bit PC's as well as connecting, sharing databases, and linking departments. The "age of the peripherals" is beginning, and add-ons will include 640K RAM, enhanced graphic boards, laser printers, local area networks, high-resolution graphics monitors, fixed disks, hard disk boards, and CD ROM players.

Future enhancements to existing PC DOS operating systems will incorporate multi-tasking, which will allow users to run a variety of applications simultaneously. The evolution from 16-bit to 32-bit technology will enable users to protect their investment in hardware and software, and software will take full advantage of increased memory, storage, and multi-tasking capabilities. The PC of the future will have to be a strategic education tool for learning. It must be able to program major languages; be capable of accessing library databases; be a remote, online tutorial unit; be able to download instructional databases to fixed disk storage or a CD ROM device; be a terminal for electronic mail, class assignments, and campus news; be an efficient word processor with a full keyboard; and have graphics-based software and sound/voice capabilities. Advanced versions of the laptop computer will be especially important for student use.

Murphy, B. CD-ROM and Libraries. *Library Hi Tech*, 1985, pp. 21-26.

The CD ROM data format is explained and illustrated, noting current and potential applications. The "5-inch" compact laserdisc is described and photographs of an IBM PC/Hitachi CD ROM system adopted by Library Corporation to support its MARC database, BiblioFile, are presented. Screen displays for BiblioFile are included.

O'Connor, M. A. Education and CD-ROM. *Optical Information Systems*, July-August 1986, pp. 329-331.

Discusses role of CD ROM as a catalyst bringing together libraries, publishers, technology companies, and education in the development of creative solutions to educational problems. CD ROM applications in the educational environment, specific efforts by libraries, and product development by publishers and technology companies are reviewed.

Olson, L. Experiencing CD-ROM ERIC. *Education Libraries*, Fall 1987, pp. 77-80.

Briefly describes DIALOG OnDisc and gives an example of an actual search of the ERIC database using this system. The screen displays and search commands are used to illustrate the differences between the easy menu search method provided for novice users and the command search method provided for experienced users.

Optical Media in Perspective. Eindhoven, The Netherlands: Philips International B.V., 1987.

Paisley, W. & Butler, M. The First Wave: CD-ROM Adoption in Offices and Libraries. *Microcomputers for Information Management: An International Journal for Library and Information Services,* June 1987, pp. 109-127.

Predictions for the future of optical disc technology are based on three phases of development: feasibility testing; use as a replacement technology for older technologies; and the introduction of new applications not possible in older technologies.

Papers presented at the International Federation of Library Associations (IFLA) General Conference (52nd, Tokyo, Japan, August 24-30, 1986). IFLA General Conference, 1986. (ERIC Document Reproduction Service No. ED 280 501)

Papers on social science libraries presented at the 1986 International Federation of Library Associations (IFLA) conference include: (1) "Efforts at Computerization in Nigerian Libraries — A State of Development Review" (A. Olugboyega Banjo, Nigeria); (2) "The Information Activities of the National Library of Economics in the Federal Republic of Germany — Transition from Traditional Library Services to Computer-Based Information Systems" (Ekkehart Seusing, West Germany); (3) "Library Automation Activities at Helsinki School of Economics Library and in Finland" (Kyllikki Ruokonen, Finland); (4) "The Impact of Optical Disc Publishing on the Information Community (CD-ROM: Memory)" (W. Bartenbach, United States); (5) "Databases Created by Japanese Economists" (Yoshiro Matsuda, Japan); and (6) "The Role of the Libraries for the Assistance of Research in the Field of Social Sciences" (A. Kasyanenko, USSR).

Peters, C. Databases on CD-ROM: Comparative Factors for Purchase. *Electronic Library,* June 1987, pp. 154-160.

Describes databases available on optical discs, compares the databases with their print and online analogs, and suggests that the librarian should call such products to the attention of users needing information available in CD ROM format. Five features desirable to most libraries are listed.

Plans and Activities for 1990 Decennial Census. Part 2: Hearings before the Subcommittee on Census and Population of the Committee on Post Office and Civil Service. (House of Representatives, Ninety-Ninth Congress, Second Session, May 1 & 15, 1986). Washington, D.C.: U.S. Government Printing Office, 1986. (ERIC Document Reproduction Service No. ED 280 872)

Hearings on the 1990 Decennial Census were held on May 1, 1986, and May 15, 1986. The May 1 session focused on data processing procedures. Speakers included John G. Keane, Daniel G. Horvitz, William Eddy, Judith S. Rowe, Benjamin F. King, and Stephen E. Fienberg. Topics included automation of address files and questionnaire check-in; dissemination of data on a variety of media including microfiche and CD ROM; cost effectiveness of proposed procedures; linking of household records; and use of microcomputers for data processing.

Two areas were mentioned in which the Subcommittee could best assist the Bureau of the Census: the procurement of computer equipment and the oversight of plans for adjustment of census counts. The second hearing, held on May 15, concerned the census questionnaire and automation. Topics included the design of a shorter census questionnaire form; data conversion methods such as Film Optical Sensing Device for Input to Computer (FOSDIC) and optical mark recognition (OMR); cost effectiveness; and the National Content Test. Speakers included Susan Miskura, Gene Dodaro, and Gail Franke.

Pruett, N. J. *State of the Art of Geoscience Libraries and Information Services.* International conference on geoscience information, Adelaide, Australia. June 1986. (NTIS No. DE86011188)

Geoscience libraries and geoscience information services are closely related. Both are trying to meet the needs of the geoscientists for information and data. Both are also being affected by many trends: increased availability of personal computers; decreased costs of machine readable storage; increased availability of maps in digital format (Pallatto, 1986); progress in graphic displays and in developing Geographic Information System, (GIS) (Kelly and Phillips, 1986); development in artificial intelligence; and the availability of new formats (e.g. CD ROM).

Some additional factors are at work changing the role of libraries: libraries are coming to recognize the impossibility of collecting everything and the validity of Bradford's Law. Unobtrusive studies of library reference services have pointed out that only 50% of the questions are answered correctly. It is clear that the number of databases is increasing, although good figures for specifically geoscience databases are not available. Lists of numeric database are beginning to appear; evaluative (as opposed to purely descriptive) reviews of available bibliographic databases are beginning to appear; more and more libraries are getting online catalogs and results of studies of users of online catalog are being used to improve catalog design; and research is raising consciousness about the value of information.

All these trends are having or will have an effect on geoscience information.

Reese, J. & Steffey, R. ERIC on CDROM: A Comparison of DIALOG OnDisc, OCLC's Search CD450 and SilverPlatter. *Online*, September 1987, pp. 42-54.

Discusses the use of optical disc technology in online searching and compares three versions of the ERIC database currently available on optical disc in terms of hardware requirements, ease of installation, scope and cost of the system, search procedures, displaying and printing results, and documentation and user support.

Rice, J. The Golden Age of Reference Service: Is It Really Over? *Wilson Library Bulletin*, December 1986, pp. 17-19.

Argues that reference services will not only survive changes brought about by new technologies but will be improved and enhanced as a result. Examples given include online public access catalogs, automated record-keeping operations, CD ROM as an information storage medium, the continuing need for intermediaries in online searching, and copyright law.

Rodgers, D. Data Preparation for CD-ROM. *Optical Information Systems*, May-June 1986, pp. 209-213.

Explains steps in process of transforming data from current form to one ready for publication on CD ROM, i.e., disc layout, file format, building the master tape, and input to mastering facility. The conversion of a product currently existing in book form into a computer-based searchable database is described.

Rosen, D. History in the Making: A Report from Microsoft's First International Conference on CD ROM. *Educational Technology*, July 1986, pp. 16-19.

Reviews important developments of Microsoft's first international conference on CD ROM, focusing on the announcement of a new medium called Compact Disc-Interactive (CD-I). Discussion covers CD-I's design, applications, kinds of programming made possible, compatibility with current CD ROM products, impact on consumer market, and impact on overall CD ROM market.

Saviers, S. S. Reflections on CD-ROM: Bridging the Gap between Technology and Purpose. *Special Libraries*, Fall 1987, pp. 288-294.

Provides a technological overview of CD ROM, an optically-based medium for data storage offering large storage capacity, computer-based delivery system, read-only medium, and economic mass production. CD ROM database attributes appropriate for information delivery are also reviewed, including large database size, wide distribution, and infrequent updating.

Teasley, T. L., Ed. *Finding Ways: Excellence under Pressure.* Proceedings from the 1986 Spring Meeting of the Nebraska Library Association, College and University Section (Lincoln, Nebraska, May 2, 1986). May 1986. (ERIC Document Reproduction Service No. ED 276 458)

Based on the conference theme, "Finding Ways: Excellence under Pressure," papers presented at the 1986 meeting of the association include: (1) "Coping with Budget Pressure: A Public Services Librarian's View" (Janet C. Lu); (2) "The Librarian, the Accession List, and the Database" (B. C. Wehrman); (3) "New Start: Bibliographic Instruction for Non-Traditional Students" (Thomas A.

Tollman, Laura K. Dickson, and Carol J. Zoerb); (4) "The Philis- tines Are Coming, Are Coming!" (G. A. Rudolph); (5) "CD-ROM: What's in Store for Libraries in the Coming Year?" (Melvin M. Bohn); (6) "Turnover of Professional Librarians" (Dee Ann K. Al- lison); (7) "The State of Preservation and Microfilming and Its Im- plications" (Louis E. Jeffries); (8) "Inadvertent Personalized Reference Service" (Paul Frantz and Thomas Cashore); and (9) "On-Line Searching in Times of Retrenchment: An Informal Sur- vey of Regional Academic Libraries" (Virginia Moreland).

A brief abstract is provided for an additional presentation, "Librarians and Collective Bargaining at UNO (University of Nebraska at Omaha)" (Carole Larson, Mel Bohn, and Bob Nash).

Tenopir, C. Publications on CD-ROM: Librarians Can Make a Dif- ference. *Library Journal*, September 1987, pp. 62-63.

Describes optical data disc products currently on the market and discusses publishers and users' needs. Ways in which librarians can influence product development and design are suggested.

Vandergrift, K. E. et. al. CD-ROM: An Emerging Technology. Part 2: Planning and Management Strategies. *School Library Journal*, August 1987, pp 22-25.

Outlines the stages in the decision-making process for libraries ac- quiring optical data disc systems, including the establishment of a project manager or task force, feasibility studies, creating a plan- ning document, hardware and software evaluation, devising processes and policies, and analyzing contracts.

Vandergrift, K. E. et. al. CD-ROM: Perspectives on an Emerging Technology. *School Library Journal*, June-July 1987, pp. 27-31.

Discusses library applications of several specific CD ROM products, including library catalogs, book reviews, databases, en- cyclopedias, and interactive video programs. Such factors as cost effectiveness, ease of use, and user satisfaction are discussed, and a bibliography of books about CD ROM is provided.

Vanderstar, J. Optical Storage. *International Library Review*, April 1987, pp. 153-159.

Classifies and briefly describes several types of optical storage media available today: read-only and write-once analog discs, read-only and write-once digital discs, and erasable discs. The appropriateness of CD ROM for use in libraries of developing nations is discussed in terms of users' information needs and costs.

Videodisc and Optical Digital Disk Technologies and Their Applications in Libraries. A Report to the Council on Library Resources. March 1985. (ERIC Document Reproduction Service No. ED 257 433)

This report examines the potential impact of optical media, videodiscs; compact audio discs; optical discs; tapes; and cards, in library related applications. A detailed consideration of the technology includes discussion of the underlying principles, the various forms in which the technology is marketed, production methods and costs, and the capabilities of each different medium.

An introductory chapter outlines the different forms of optical media and their potential applications in libraries. Each of the remaining 11 chapters then addresses the details of one of the following technologies: videodiscs; interactive videodiscs; recording digital data on videodisc; videodisc production; compact audio discs and CD ROM; videodiscs and CD ROM as digital publishing media; optical digital discs; optical digital products; and erasable optical media.

A number of video and compact audio disc projects currently being developed or investigated in library settings are examined in the appropriate chapters, including audio and video applications at Video Patsearch, the National Library of Canada, the National Library of Medicine, and the Library of Congress; digital data publishing projects at MiniMARC, Information Access Corporation, Carrollton Press, the Library Corporation and other companies; and library applications of optical digital disc technology at the Library of Congress, the National Library of Medicine, the National Air and Space Museum, the Public Archives of Canada, and Disclosure Information Group.

An appendix explains the process of converting text, graphics, and audio to digital form.

Watson, J. A. et. al. Special Education Technologies for Young Children: Present and Future Learning Scenarios with Related Research Literature. *Journal of the Division for Early Childhood*, 1986, pp. 197-208.

The article surveys computer usage with young handicapped children by developing three instructional scenarios (present actual, present possible, and future). Research is reviewed on computer use with very young children, cognitive theory and microcomputer learning, and social aspects of the microcomputer experience. Trends in microcomputer, interactive videodisc, and CD ROM technology are noted.

Watson, P. D. & Golden, G. A. Distributing an Online Catalog on CD-ROM...The University of Illinois Experience. *Online*, March 1987, pp. 65-74.

Description of the planning of a project designed to test the feasibility of distributing a statewide union catalog database on optical disc discusses the relationship of the project's goals to those of statewide library development; dealing with vendors in a volatile, high technology industry; and plans for testing and evaluation.

Whitney, M. A. & Strub, P. M. *Development and Use of Interactive Videodisc Instruction for Navy Medical Corpsmen.* Paper presented at the 1985 Videodisc, Optical Disk, and CD-ROM Conference (Philadelphia, PA, December 9-12, 1985). December 1985. (ERIC Document Reproduction Service No. ED 272 134)

The University of Maryland's Center for Instructional Development and Evaluation has developed interactive video material for the Navy Medical Department to teach Navy medical corpsmen appropriate response procedures for each of seven emergency medical conditions: angina pectoris, acute myocardial infarction, congestive heart failure, stroke, diabetic coma, insulin shock, and epileptic seizure.

An underlying philosophy of the design team and subject matter expert was that the student could best master the process tasks by practicing them; the properties of computer-based interactive videodisc (CBIV) make it uniquely suited to impleent this instructional principe. The videodisc simulation can include both patient attributes and environmental attributes that compare realistically with actual settings. A total of 15 emergency settings were developed to account for specific variations of the seven medical conditions. Since the material is to be used for evaluative as well as instructional purposes, a second set of parallel lessons was developed for each setting, making a final total of 30 lessons in the system.

Background information provided for the learner includes a glossary, reference lessons, and an introduction to the hardware and software. This paper briefly describes the system design and a representative lesson.

Whitaker, D. *CD-ROM and the Migration from Print*. London: CLSI, 1987. (Part of the series: CLSI Annual Lectures on Library Automation)

Wiget, L. A. *Computer Use in Primary School Education and the Trend of Educational Software: An Alaskan Perspective*. Paper presented at EDUTEC '86, the all Japan Annual Education Technology Research Congress (12th, Tokyo, Japan, October 25-27, 1986). October 1986. (ERIC Document Reproduction Service No. ED 280 445)

This examination of microcomputer use in primary schools begins by comparing the national data for elementary schools for 1984-1985 with the findings of a study of seven elementary schools in the Anchorage (Alaska) School District (ASD) which was conducted in the same year. Current research findings are cited in a discussion of assumptions about the instructional effectiveness of computers, and it is noted that the overall results of the ASD study failed to show that the computers have been either effective or ineffective in improving academic achievement.

A description of the process used by ASD to integrate computers into the primary school classroom highlights coordination, including the development of a scope and sequence guide together with long range goals and objectives to ensure uniformity within the curriculum; provisions for in-service teacher training; provisions for maintenance and repair of the microcomputers; the acquisition of hardware and software; and a systematic approach to instruction. A brief description of teacher use of computers includes the names of software used for various purposes, and a discussion of trends in educational software focuses on applications programs for students and the use of CD ROM for a district-wide union catalog of school library holdings.

It is concluded that, although computers in the classroom are still in the experimental stage, they can be successfully implemented at the elementary level if adequate leadership, funding, and in-service training are provided.

Wilson, B. & Hubbard, A. Redefining the Role of School Media Specialists...Bridging the Gap. *Online*, November 1987, pp. 50-54.

Discussion of the changing role of the School Library/media Specialist argues that skill requirements for this group should be redefined to include competency in online information retrieval techniques. Appropriate online databases available on CD ROM and sources for training are described. A role for academic librarians in providing training is also suggested.

Working Paper for Information Processing: Volume and File Structure of CD-ROM for Information Interchange. *Optical Information Systems*, January-February 1987, pp. 29-49.

These proposed standards prepared by the CD ROM Ad Hoc Advisory Committee (the "High Sierra Group") specify the volume and file structure of CD ROM for the interchange of information between users of information processing systems.

CD ROM Databases

Applied Science & Technology Index. Bronx, New York: H.W. Wilson Co.

Art Index. Bronx, New York: H.W. Wilson Co.

Books in Print Plus. New York: R.R. Bowker, 1986-

CD-ROM Prototype Disc. Reston, Virginia: TMS, Inc., 1987

Current Index to Journals in Education. Dublin, Ohio: OCLC, 1981-

Dissertation Abstracts Ondisc. Ann Arbor, Michigan: University Microfilms International, 1986-

Education Materials in Libraries: a Subset of the OCLC Online Union Catalog. Dublin, Ohio: OCLC, 1987-

Encyclopedia of Chemical Technology. New York: John Wiley & Sons

ERIC. Boston: SilverPlatter Information Services, 1986-

ERIC. Dublin, Ohio: OCLC, 1982-

Grolier, the Electronic Encyclopedia: a 20-volume Encyclopedia on CD-ROM. Danbury, Connecticut: Grolier Electronic Publishing and Activenture Corp., 1986

Hydrodata. Denver: US WEST Knowledge Engineering, Inc., 1987-

LaserCat. Olympia, Washington: Western Library Network, 1987-

LaserDOS. Stillwater, Oklahoma: TMS, Inc., 1986

LISA. Wellesley Hills, Massachusetts: SilverPlatter Information Services, 1987-

McGraw-Hill CD-ROM Science and Technical Reference Set. New York: McGraw-Hill, Reference Technology, Inc., Fulcrum Technologies, Inc., 1987

MEDLINE. Wellesley Hills, Massachusetts: SilverPlatter Information Services, 1987-

NTIS on CD ROM. Boston: SilverPlatter Information Services, Inc., 1987-

PAIS on CD-ROM. New York: Public Affairs Information Service, 1972-

PC-SIG Library on CD ROM Disks no. 1 thru 605. Sunnyvale, California: PC-SIG, 1986

Readers' Guide to Periodical Literature. Bronx, New York: H.W. Wilson. 1983-

Resources in Education. Dublin, Ohio: OCLC, 1976-

Selected Geomagnetic and Other Solar-terrestrial Physics Data of NOAA and NASA. Boulder, Colorado: National Environmental Satellite, Data and Information Service, 1987

About the Authors

Beverly Butler is Principal Interactive Designer for IVID Communications in San Diego. Ms. Butler, co-editor of *The Videodisc Book* with Rod Daynes, has been designing and developing interactive videodisc programs since 1983. Prior to becoming an Instructional Designer in 1979, Ms. Butler was a librarian. Her library experience includes research and reference work for the Motion Picture Division of the Library of Congress and the University of California at San Diego.

Bradley Watson holds advanced degrees in Library Science, English Literature and Computer Science. He has worked as a programmer/analyst for the Air Force Logistics Command on foreign military sales systems, for Mead Data Central on LEXIS/NEXIS, and NCR, Inc. on PC-based retail Point of Sale systems, before joining OCLC as a staff scientist for technology assessment in the Office of Technical Planning. Currently pursuing a Ph.D. in English Literature at The Ohio State University.

IVID Communications
4340-B Viewridge Ave.
San Diego, CA 92123
619–576–0611

OCLC
6565 Frantz Road
Dublin, OH 43017–0702
614–764–6000

17

Discography: Published CD ROM Titles

Steve Holder

The following information has been obtained from sources deemed reliable, in most cases directly from the publisher. However, IVID Communications makes no warranty concerning the accuracy or completeness of the information, and assumes no liability for errors or inadvertant misrepresentation of products. Prices and update frequency were as quoted in April 1987.

1982 CENSUS OF AGRICULTURE *Agriculture*
Database
$1200-5 yrs

Entire county file from the 1982 Census of Agriculture with complete data from every county in the U.S. with state and national summaries. Comparable data from 1978 census for most items.

Slater Hall Information Products, 1522 K Street NW, Su. 522, Washington, DC 20005 (George Hall, 202–682–1350)

AD ART   *Commercial Art*
                                                             Image Database
A CD ROM version of Ad Art's catalog of product clip art for retail
and advertising publishers. High-resolution images of familiar
products accessed by company name, general category, or universal
product code.

Ad Art, 723 South Wells St., Chicago, IL 60607 (Clark Riley, 312–
427–4047)

ADDRESS VERIFICATION SYSTEM PLUS   *Addresses*
                                                                Directory
The entire 47-volume National Directory of the US Postal Service.

Information Design Inc., 1300 Charleston Rd., Mountain View, CA
94039 (415–969–7990, 800–892–5159)

AGRICOLA   *Agriculture*
                                                            Bibliography
                                                              $1750/yr
                                                                  4/yr
CD ROM version of the AGRICOLA database with citations of publications relating to all aspects of agriculture as compiled by the National Agriculture Library.

SilverPlatter Information, Inc, 37 Walnut Street, Wellesley, MA
02181 (Christopher Pooley, 617–239–0306)

ANY BOOK   *Library*
                                                            Bibliography
                                                               $600/yr
                                                                 4/yr
A book identification and ordering database, for use with the
Bibliofile Catalog Production System.

Library Corp., P.O. Box 40035, Washington, DC 20016 (800–624–
0559)

APPLIED SCIENCES AND TECHNOLOGY INDEX
Science
Bibliography
$1495
4/yr

Indexes 338 key English language periodicals in applied science and technology.

The H. W. Wilson Company, 950 University Ave., Bronx, NY 10452 (Frank Miller, 212–588–8400)

ART INDEX
Art
Bibliography
$1495
4/yr

Indexes 200 foreign and domestic periodicals, yearbooks, and museum bulletins addressing important developments in the world of art. Indexes reproductions as well as articles and book reviews.

The H. W. Wilson Company, 950 University Ave., Bronx, NY 10452 (Frank Miller, 212–588–8400)

A–V ONLINE
Education
Catalog
$795/yr
1/yr

360,000 annotated bibliographic descriptions and addresses for sources of audiovisual educational programs.

National Education Center for Educational Media (NICEM) or Access Innovations, Inc., P.O. Box 40130, Albuquerque, NM 87196 (Berry Ives, 505–265–3591) SilverPlatter Information, Inc., 37 Walnut Street, Wellesley, MA 02181 (Christopher Pooley, 617–239–0306)

BIBLIOFILE CATALOG PRODUCTION SYSTEM
Library
Cataloging
$1750

Special software that uses the LC MARC and ANY BOOK CD ROMS to produce library catalog records. First issue of each CD ROM is included in purchase price; suscriptions to updates are available separately.

Library Corporation, P.O. Box 40035, Washington, DC 20016 (800–624–559)

BIBLIOMED   *Medical*
                                                                  Abstracts
                                                                  $1900/yr
                                                                  4/yr
Thesaurus-oriented retrieval for MEDLINE, the medical bibliography from the National Library of Medicine.
Digital Diagnostics, 601 University Ave., Su. 255, Sacramento, CA 95825 (Stephen Haden, 916–921–6629)

BIOGRAPHY INDEX   *General Reference*
                                                         Bibliography
                                                         $1095
                                                         4/yr
Indexes biographical material drawn from 2700 periodicals of all kinds, as well as current books and literature.
The H. W. Wilson Company, 950 University Ave., Bronx, NY 10452 (Frank Miller, 212–588–8400)

BLACK FICTION UP TO 1920   *Academic*
                                                                  Reference
(Not yet completed. The Black Literature Database is currently under development.)
Black Fiction Project, 472 Caldwell Hall, Cornell University, Ithaca, NY 14853 (Christopher Newfield, 607–255–4390)

BOOKS IN PRINT   *General Reference*
                                                         Bibliography
                                                         4/yr
Includes Books in Print, Subject Guide to BIP, BIP Supplement, Forthcoming Books, and Subject Guide to Forthcoming Books.
Bowker Electronic Publishing, 245 W. 17th St.,New York, NY 10114–0418 (Robert Allen, 800–323–3288)

BRADY GUIDE TO CD ROM   *Demonstration*
                                               Book on Disc
A demonstration disc based on the book by Laura Buddine and
Elizabeth Young published by Brady Books.
   Reteaco Inc., 716 Gordon Baker Road, Willowdale, ONT M2H 3B4
Canada (416–497–0579)

BUSINESSBASE   *Business*
                                                  Directory
                                                    $1000+
Lists 500,000 Canadian businesses, U.S. and Canadian standard in-
dustrial codes and business list headings.
   Tetragon, 5445 Pare St.,Mount Royal, Quebec H4P 1R1 Canada
(Charles DeMartigny, 514–737–3550)

BUSINESS PERIODICALS INDEX   *Business*
                                                Bibliography
                                                     $1495
                                                      4/yr
Indexes 304 international English-language periodicals, including
trade and business research journals.
   The H. W. Wilson Company, 950 University Ave., Bronx, NY
10452 (Frank Miller, 212–588–8400)

BUSINESS STATISTICS   *Business*
                                                  Database
                                                  $2200/yr
                                                     12/yr
Three databases originally published by the U.S. Department of
Commerce Bureau of Economic Analysis: National Income and
Product Accounts (GNP) 1929–1986; Business Statistics (Blue pages
from Survey of Current Business), annual 1961–1985, monthly
beginning 1981; Income and Employment by state, annual 1969–
1985.
   Slater Hall Information Products, 1522 K Street NW, Su. 522,
Washington, DC 20005 (George Hall, 202–682–1350)

CAB ABSTRACTS   *Agriculture*
                                                               Abstracts
180,000 records on agricultural related abstracts, from the Commonwealth Agricultural Bureau database.

CAB International, Farnham House, Farnham Royal, Slough SL2
3BN, UK (F. G. Jones, 02814–5807)

CCINFODISC   *Health*
                                                               Collection
                                                        $100/yr (Canadian)
                                                                      4/yr
One of the world's largest collections of occupational health and
safety information, with 17 databases, 6 videotex information packages, and 18 full text information packages.

Canadian Center for Occupational Health and Safety, 250 Main St.
East, Hamilton, Ontario L8N 1H6 (Gary Bannister, 416–572–2981)

CD/BANKING   *Financial*
                                                                 DataBase
                                                                 $9,500/yr
                                                                      4/yr
The first disc in this series, "Commercial Banks," describes deposits,
loans, profits, liquidity, and other data for 15,000 federally insured
U.S. banks.

Shesunoff and Company, P.O. Box 13203, Capitol Station, Austin,
TX 78711 (512–472–2244) Datext, Inc., 444 Washington St.,Woburn,
MA 01801 (Darlene Mann, 617–938–6667)

CD/BIOTECH   *Biotechnology*
                                                                  Journal
                                                                   $495/yr
                                                                      2/yr
Contains the NIH sponsored Genetic Sequences Databank (Genbank), the National Biomedical Research Foundation's Protein Identification Resource, the European Molecular Biology Laboratory's
Data Library, journal and magazine articles, and operational
software of scientific interest.

International Association for Scientific Computing, 1030 East Duane Avenue, Su. E, Sunnyvale, CA 94086

CD/CORPORATE

Financial
DataBase
$9600/yr
12/yr

Numeric and textual information on all public companies traded on the New York, American, OTC, and regional exchanges. Over 10,000 companies, 900 lines of business, 50 industries from 6 leading databases.

Datext, Inc., 444 Washington St.,Woburn, MA 01801 (Darlene Mann, 617–938–6667)

CD/CORPTECH

Business
Database
$7500/yr
4/yr

A directory of over 13,000 domestic high-technology companies, public and private. Includes business description, products, revenue, and officers.

Datext, Inc., 444 Washington St.,Woburn, MA 01801 (Darlene Mann, 617–938–6667)

CD-ROM SOURCEDISC

Demonstration
Book/Software

Contains all the data in the CDROM Sourcebook, plus industry related market studies, periodicals, reference sources, and services. Also includes samples of CDROM related software.

Diversified Data Resources Inc., 6609 Rosecroft Place, Falls Church, VA 22043 (Martin Ennis, 703–237–0682)

CD ROM TEST DISC 3   *Demonstration*

A collection of software and image files for demonstrating the
Hitachi line of CD ROM drives. Includes 30 min of classical music in
CD audio format.
　　Hitachi, 1200 Wall St. West, Lyndhurst, NJ 07071 (201–935–5300)

CD ROM: THE NEW PAPYRUS, 1ST EDITION   *Demonstration*
                                                             Book on disc
A fully indexed, full text version of the printed book, demonstrating
the Bluefish access software.
　　Computer Access Corp., 26 Brighton St., Su. 324, Belmont, MA
02178 (617–484–2412)

CENSUS TEST DISC #1   *Demographic*
                                                            Database
Prototype disc containing demographic data for zip codes, Location of
Manufacturing Plants, county level agricultural data, 1983 County
Business Patterns, and 1984 Population Estimates for Governmental
Units.
　　U.S. Bureau of Census, Data User Services Division, Washington,
DC 20233 (Forrest Williams, 202–763–4100)

CENSUS TEST DISC #2   *Demographic*
                                                            Database
Prototype disc containing latitude and longitude of the centroids of
census statistical areas, demographic and housing data for all places
over 10,000 population, and a longitudinal county-level data file.
　　U.S. Bureau of Census, Data User Services Division, Washington,
DC 20233 (Forrest Williams, 202–763–4100)

COMMUNICATIONS EXCELLENCE   *Demonstration*

Demonstration disc for Reteaco's FindIT retrieval software.
　　Reteaco Inc., 716 Gordon Baker Road, Willowdale, ONT M2H 3B4
Canada (416–497–0579)

COMPACT CAMBRIDGE ASFA

Scientific
Abstracts
$1250+/yr
2/yr

International coverage of research in aquatic biology, fisheries and living resources, oceanography, earth sciences, marine technology, nonliving resources, and related socioeconomic and legal issues.

Cambridge Scientific Abstracts, 5161 River Road, Bethesda, MD (Laurieann Greeves, 301–951–1424)

COMPACT CAMBRIDGE LIFE SCIENCES COLLECTION

Scientific
Abstracts
$1250+/yr
2/yr

Abstracts of articles on biological, medical, and ecological topics, with 18 subject-oriented subfiles.

Cambridge Scientific Abstracts, 5161 River Road, Bethesda, MD (Laurieann Greeves, 301–951–1424)

COMPACT CAMBRIDGE MEDLINE

Medical
Abstracts
$1,250+/yr
2/yr

Indexes to articles from over 3000 international journals covering virtually every subject in the field of biomedicine.

Cambridge Scientific Abstracts, 5161 River Road, Bethesda, MD (Laurieann Greeves, 301–951–1424)

COMPACT CAMBRIDGE POLLUTION/
ECOLOGY/TOXICOLOGY

Scientific
Abstracts

Abstracts of articles on research, engineering, legal and social issues in pollution, toxicology, and ecology.

Cambridge Scientific Abstracts, 5161 River Road, Bethesda, MD 20816 (Laurieann Greeves, 301–951–1424)

COMPACT DISCLOSURE   *Financial*
                                                        Database
                                                        $4500/yr
                                                        4/yr
Financial/text data on over 11,000 public American and non-U.S. companies.

Disclosure, 5161 River Road, Bethesda, MD 20816 (800–843–7747)

COMPUSTAT PC PLUS   *Financial*
                                                        Database
                                                        $18,000+/yr
Company financial database for security, acquisition comparative analyses.

Standard & Poor's Compustat Services, Inc., Englewood, CO (Frank Hermes, 303–771–6510)

COMPUTERIZED CLINICAL INFORMATION   *Medical Database*
SYSTEM (CCIS)   *4/yr*

Compilation of medical databases (POISINDEX, DRUGDEX, EMERGINDEX, IDENTIDEX), for toxicology, drug consults, trauma injury, and capsule identification.

Micromedex, Inc., 660 Bannock St., Su. 350, Denver, CO 80204–4506 (Lela Chambers, 303–623–8600, 800–525–9083)

THE CONFERENCE DISC   *CDROM*
                                                        Technology
                                                        Promotional
                                                        $20
Samples of multiple CD ROM products, databases, and retrieval software, plus speeches and documents from the Second Annual Conference on CDROM.

Philips and DuPont Optical, 1402 Foulk Road, Su. 200, Wilmington, DE 19803–0469 (Robert Fisher)

CONQUEST   *Marketing*
                                                          Database
                                                           $7500+
                                                            1/yr
Consumer information system containing U.S. demographic, economic, and other data for market research and strategic planning.

Donnelly Marketing Information Services, 70 Seaview Ave., Stamford, CT 06904 (Candice Longcore, 203-353-7207)

CORPORATE AND INDUSTRY RESEARCH   *Business*
REPORTS (CIRR)   *Abstracts*
                                                          $1750/yr
                                                           1/yr
A cummulative index with abstracts to over 70,000 corporate and industry reports written by securities and investment banking firms for 1979-1986.

JA Micropublishing, 271 Main St., Box 218, Eastchester, NY 10707 (Ralph C. Ferragamo, 914-793-2130) SilverPlatter Information, Inc., 37 Walnut Street, Wellesley, MA 02181 (Christopher Pooley, 617-239-0306)

CUMULATIVE BOOK INDEX   *General Reference*
                                                        Bibliography
                                                            $1295
                                                            4/yr
Data on English-language books published worldwide, including clothbound fiction and nonfiction, and paperbacks.

The H. W. Wilson Company, 950 University Ave., Bronx, NY 10452 (Frank Miller, 212-588-8400)

CURRENT BIOTECHNOLOGY ABSTRACTS   *Scientific*
                                                         Abstracts
                                                       (Temporarily
                                                      unavailable)
Royal Society of Chemistry's database of biotechnology abstracts.

Royal Society of Chemistry, The University, Nottingham NG7 2RD, U.K. (A. Bingham, 0602-507411)

DATATIMES *Newspaper*
Database
Soon-to-be-available newspaper and wire service databases.
DataTimes, Parkway Plaza, Su. 450, 14000 Quail Springs
Parkway, Oklahoma City, OK 73134 (Allen Paschal, 405–751–6400)

DELORME'S DIGITAL WORLD ATLAS *Cartographic*
System
Worldwide atlas at an average screen scale of 15 mi to the inch.
DeLorme Mapping Systems, P.O. Box 298, Freeport, ME 04032
(David DeLorme, Tom Tracy, 207–865–4171)

DIALOG ON-DISC ERIC *Education*
Abstracts
$750+/yr
4/yr
Contains Resources in Education (RIE) covering significant educa-
tional documents, and Current Index to Journals in Education
(CIJE), an index to more than 700 periodicals.
Dialog Information Services, Inc., 3460 Hillview Ave., Palo Alto,
CA 94304 (Veronica Corchado, 800–3–DIALOG, 415–858–3785)

DISC IN A DAY *Demonstration*

Demonstration disc prepared in one day at the Second Annual
CDROM Conference. Participating were Lo-Down (data supplier),
Optical Media International (premastering), and LaserVideo (master-
ing).
Optical Media International, 298A Quail Run Road, Aptos, CA
(Alan Adkins, 408–662–1772)

DISC NAVIGATION *Navigation*
System
2000 sea charts contained on a 4-CDROM set, used in a maritime
navigational system.
Disc Navigation Sales, Bryggegt. 1, Aker Brygge, P.O. Box 903,
Sentrum, N–0104, Oslo 1, Norway (47–2–41 36 90)

DISCON
Library
Cataloging
$800+/mo

6,000,000 REMARC and MARC records for retrospective conversion of library holdings.

Utlas International, 2150 Shattuck Ave., Berkeley, CA 94704 (Parke Lightbown, 800–523–0449, 415–841–9442)

DISSERTATION ABSTRACTS ON DISC
General Reference
Abstracts
$995/yr

University Microfilms International, Inc., 300 N. Zeeb Road, Ann Arbor, MI 48106 (800–732–0616)

DRUGDEX
Medical
Database
4/yr

Drug information and consults on over 4000 investigational and foreign, FDA approved and OTC preparations.

Micromedex, Inc., 660 Bannock St.,Su. 350, Denver, CO 80204–4506 (Lela Chambers, 303–623–8600, 800–525–9083)

EDUCATION INDEX
Education
Bibliography
$1295
4/yr

Indexes 353 key international English-language journals in all areas of education.

The H. W. Wilson Company, 950 University Ave., Bronx, NY 10452 (Frank Miller, 212–588–8400)

THE ELECTRONIC ENCYCLOPEDIA ON CD ROM   *General Reference*
Encyclopedia
$299
1/yr
The entire text of the Academic American Encyclopedia (20 volumes, 30,000 articles)
Grolier Electronic Publishing, 95 Madison Ave., New York, NY 10016 (John Cole, 212–696–9750)

THE ELECTRONIC MERCHANDISER   *Retail*
Marketing
A "smart catalog" system for industrial and retail marketing.
Del Mar Group, Suite M, 722 Genevieve, Solana Beach, CA 92075 (Mary Wiemann, 619–259–0444)

EMBASE   *Medical*
Abstracts
Summaries of the world's literature in biomedicine covering all aspects of clinical medicine and biomedical research.
SilverPlatter Information, Inc., 37 Walnut Street, Wellesley, MA 02181 (Christopher Pooley, 617–239–0306)

EMERGINDEX   *Medical*
Database
4/yr
Aid to diagnosis and treatment of medical/surgical diseases and traumatic injuries. Contains Clinical Reviews and Clinical Abstracts.
Micromedex, Inc., 660 Bannock St.,Su. 350, Denver, CO 80204–4506 (Lela Chambers, 303–623–8600, 800–525–9083)

ENFLEX INFO   *Legal*
Reference
A system for compiling, storing, and maintaining federal and state environmental regulations. Available CD ROM discs contain Federal Regulations, and state regulations for many industrial states.
ERM Computer Services Inc., 999 West Chester Pike, West Chester, PA 19382 (George Esry, 800–544–3118)

ERIC
Education
Abstracts
$390 to 650+/yr
1–4/yr
Bibliographic database sponsored by the U.S. Department of Education; Resources in Education (RIE) and Current Index to Journals in Education (CIJE).

ORI, Inc., Information Systems Division, 4833 Rugby Ave., Su. 301, Bethesda, MD (Ted Brandhorst, 301–656–9723)

EXXON MANUALS
Engineering
Manuals
CDROM version of an engineering manual that teaches basic practices for building oil refineries. For internal use at Exxon.

Amtec Information Services, 3700 Industry Ave., Lakewood, CA 90714 (Jerry Lindberg, 213–595–4756)

FAST PAST
Education
History
Soon to be available in CDROM form, 5000 articles on historical events, persons, and trends from 10,000 B.C. to the present. Based on the floppy disc version.

Interage Research, P.O. Box 267917, Chicago, IL (312–764–1892)

FIRST NATIONAL ITEM BANK AND TEST
Education
DEVELOPMENT SYSTEM
Database

A 100,000 item database of test questions for construction of test instruments in five basic skill areas.

Minnesota Department of Education

GENERAL SCIENCE INDEX
Science
Bibliography
$1295
4/yr

Indexes 111 major English-language periodicals on a wide variety of scientific topics.

The H. W. Wilson Company, 950 University Ave., Bronx, NY 10452 (Frank Miller, 212–588–8400)

GEODISC — METRO SERIES
Cartographic
Database
$1595/disc
1–2/yr

The 50 to 60 discs in this series contain maps at 1:24,000 scale for major metropolitan areas plus additional source material.

Geovision, Inc., 270 Scientific Drive, Norcross, GA 30092 (Greg Mohl, 404–448–8224)

GEODISC — STATE SERIES
Cartographic
Database
$1595/disc
1–2/yr

Each disc has complete state map at 1:100,000 scale plus utilities, roads, railroads, hydrography, place names, hypsography, and county boundaries.

Geovision, Inc., 270 Scientific Drive, Norcross, GA 30092 (Greg Mohl, 404–448–8224)

GEODISC — U.S. SERIES
Cartographic
Database
$1,595/disc
1–2/yr

Complete U.S. map at 1:2,000,000 scale including roads, railroads, hydrography, place names, hypsography, state, and county boundaries.

Geovision, Inc., 270 Scientific Drive, Norcross, GA 30092 (Greg Mohl, 404–448–8224)

GLOBE AND MAIL, 1985   *Newspaper*
                                                      Collection
                                                      $1800/yr
All issues of the Canadian Globe and Mail Newspaper for the year
1985.
   Globe and Mail, 444 Front Street West, Toronto ONT M5V 2S9
Canada (Barbara Hyland, 416–585–5259)

GRAN ENCICLOPEDIA DEL MUNDO   *General Reference*
                                           Encyclopedia
CD ROM version of the 20-volume Spanish encyclopedia.
   ComCal, Nicaragua 95, 08029 Barcelona, Spain (Manual Marin,
93/321–6850)

HOMEBASE   *Addresses*
                                                      Directory
                                                      $1000+
Names, addresses, postal codes, and phone numbers for 7 million
Canadian residences.
   Tetragon, 5445 Pare St.,Mount Royal, Quebec H4P 1R1 Canada
(Charles DeMartigny, 514–737–3550)

HONDA AUTO PARTS CATALOG   *Automotive Parts*
                                          Catalog
A system using CDROM to provide Honda mechanics with rapid access to the Honda parts catalog.
   Reynolds and Reynolds, P.O. Box 1005, Dayton, OH 45419 (513–
443–2000)

HUMANITIES INDEX   *Humanities*
                                                      Bibliography
                                                      $1295
                                                      4/yr
Indexes 294 English-language periodicals on a wide range of topics
in humanities.
   The H. W. Wilson Company, 950 University Ave., Bronx, NY
10452 (Frank Miller, 212–588–8400)

HYDRODATA   *Engineering*
Database
$75 to $395
1/yr
USGS Daily Values for the 17 western states including flow, water
quality, and climate data.
US WEST Knowledge Engineering, 4380 S. Syracuse St.,Denver,
CO (Patrick Call, 303–694–4200)

IDENTIDEX   *Medical Database*

A tablet and capsule identification system with manufacturer imprint codes, color, physical description, street terms, etc. Over 33,000
entries.
Micromedex, Inc., 660 Bannock St.,Su. 350, Denver, CO 80204–
4506 (Lela Chambers, 303–623–8600, 800–525–9083)

ILLUSTRATED YELLOW PAGES   *Demonstration*
Directory
Demonstration disc containing digitized images, maps, and directory
information covering South Florida.
Compact Discoveries, 1050 South Federal Highway, Delray Beach,
FL 33444 (Carol Place, 305–243–1453)

INDEX TO LEGAL PERIODICALS   *Legal*
Bibliography
$1,495
Indexes 476 leading legal periodicals in English, French, and
Spanish. Search by cases or statutes, 4/yr as well as by topic.
The H. W. Wilson Company, 950 University Ave., Bronx, NY
10452 (Frank Miller, 212–588–8400)

INFOMARK   *Marketing*
                                                      Database
                                                   $10,000+/yr
                                                          2/yr
U.S. demographic information by census tract, zip code, county, and
state. Business information on 7.5 million U.S. businesses, market
segmentation using geodemographic profiles, asset/liability information for FDIC/FSLIC institutions, and mapping.
  National Decision Systems, 539 Encinitas Blvd., Encinitas, CA
(Tom Holland, 619–942–7000)

INTELLIGENT CATALOG   *Library*
                                                 Public Catalog
                                                 3.5 cents/title
                                                   + $37.50/mo
                                                ($2495/system)
Public access catalog workstation for libraries. Each system includes
a CD ROM catalog developed specifically for the library that purchases the system. After initial conversion to CD ROM, updates are
produced monthly.
  Library Corporation, P.O. Box 40035, Washington, DC 20016 (800–
624–559)

INTERNATIONAL DICTIONARY OF MEDICINE   *Medical*
AND BIOLOGY   *Dictionary*
                                                          $195
Definitions of over 160,000 terms in medicine and biology.
  John Wiley & Sons, 605 Third Avenue, New York, NY 10158
(Patricia Rowe, 212–850–6189)

KIRK-OTHMER ENCYCLOPEDIA OF CHEMICAL   *Chemistry*
TECHNOLOGY   *Encyclopedia*
                                                          $895
CD ROM version of Wiley's 24-volume guide to chemistry and re-
lated industries.
  John Wiley & Sons, 605 Third Avenue, New York, NY 10158
(Patricia Rowe, 212–850–6189)

KOJIEN   *Japanese*
                                                       Dictionary
                                                            $125

CD ROM version of the standard reference work on the Japanese
language. Uses a specially marked keyboard to enter words in Kana,
Kanji, or Roman alphabet.

Iwanami Shotem, Ltd (Japan)

LASERCAT   *Library*
                                                       Cataloging
                                                   $900/yr 4/yr

1.9 million records of materials held by Western Library Network, 2
years of current records from Library of Congress, covering books,
films, serials, music, maps and other formats. WLN members represent 250 libraries in the western U.S. and Canada.

Western Library Network, Mail Stop AJ–11W, Olympia, WA 98504
(Dave Wasser, 206–459–6706)

LASERGUIDE   *Library*
                                                  Public Catalog

Public access catalog for libraries, including library floor plan. Each
CD ROM custom developed for individual libraries.

General Research Corporation, Library Systems, P.O. Box 6770,
Santa Barbara, CA 93160–6770 (Darcy Cook, 800–235–6788)

LASERNAV 20/20   *Navigation*
                                                          System

A marine navigation system containing 25 computerized charts from
the National Oceanic and Atmospheric Administration.

LaserPlot, Inc., 48 Sword St.,Auburn, MA 01501 (Michael
Belanger, 617–757–2831)

LASERQUEST *Library*
Cataloging
$6900 1st yr
$2600/yr
4 million MARC records on four discs representing the holdings of over 1000 libraries. Useful for retrospective conversions and on-going cataloging.
General Research Corporation, Library Systems, P.O. Box 6770, Santa Barbara, CA 93160–6770 (Darcy Cook, 800–235–6788)

LASERSEARCH *Book Store*
Bibliography
$600+
4–12/yr
Catalog of retail books for bookstore reference and ordering.
Ingram Book Company, 347 Reedwood Drive, Nashville, TN 37217 (Art Carson, 615–743–5000)

LC MARC ENGLISH LANGUAGE DISCS *Library*
Cataloging
$870/yr (4 discs)
$1470/yr (12 discs)
Library of Congress English-language cataloging data, including monographs, serials, GPO publications, maps, films and music. Designed for use with the Bibliofile Catalog Production System.
Library Corp., P.O. Box 40035, Washington, DC 20016 (800–624–0559)

LC MARC FOREIGN LANGUAGE DISCS *Library*
Cataloging
$500/yr
4/yr
Library of Congress foreign-language cataloging data. Designed for use with the Bibliofile Catalog Production System.
Library Corp., P.O. Box 40035, Washington, DC 20016 (800–624–0559)

LE PAC *Library*
Public Catalog
Public access catalog for libraries. Each CD ROM custom developed for individual libraries.

Brodart Automation, 500 Arch St.,Williamsport, PA 17705 (Carol Rickert, 215–543–4389, Joe Torres, 800–643–0523, in CA 800–821–1117)

LE PAC GOVERNMENT DOCUMENTS OPTION *Library*
Public Catalog
$2500/yr
24/yr
Catalog of government documents from the Government Printing Office.

Brodart Automation, 500 Arch St.,Williamsport, PA 17705 (Robin Cooper, 800–233–8467, Ext. 642)

LIBRARY LITERATURE *Library*
Bibliography
$1095
4/yr
Indexes 189 foreign and domestic publications in English and a dozen foreign languages, covering all aspects of library and information science.

The H. W. Wilson Company, 950 University Ave., Bronx, NY 10452 (Frank Miller, 212–588–8400)

LISA *Library*
Abstracts
$995/yr
1/yr
Abstracts of the world's literature in librarianship, information science, and related disciplines, as compiled by Library Association Publishing, Ltd.

SilverPlatter Information, Inc., 37 Walnut Street, Wellesley, MA 02181 (Christopher Pooley, 617–239–0306)

LOTUS ONE SOURCE   *Financial*
Database
$12,500+
52/yr

Eight industry standard historical and fundamental financial
databases with interface to Lotus 123.

Lotus Development Corp., 55 Cambridge Parkway, Cambridge, MA
(Jennifer Strayton, 617–225–1472)

MARK ENCYCLOPEDIA OF POLYMER   *Chemistry*
SCIENCE AND ENGINEERING   *Encyclopedia*
$3,200

CD ROM version of Wiley's 19-volume reference to polymer and plastics technology.

John Wiley & Sons, 605 Third Avenue, New York, NY 10158
(Patricia Rowe, 212–850–6189)

MASTER SEARCH TM   *Legal*
Database

Database of trademark information from U.S. Patent and Trademark
Office, including registrations, applications, and digitized images of
actual trademarks.

Tri-Star Publishing, 475 Virginia Drive, Fort Washington, PA
19034 (Spencer Nickel, 215–641–6400)

MCGRAW-HILL CD ROM SCIENCE AND   *Science*
TECHNICAL REFERENCE SET   *Encyclopedia*
$300

7300 articles from the McGraw-Hill Concise Encyclopedia of Science
& Technology, plus 98,500 terms and 115,500 definitions from the
McGraw-Hill Dictionary of Scientific and Technical Terms.

McGraw-Hill Book Company, 11 W. 19th Street, New York, NY
10011 (Eric Johnson, 212–337–5906)

MERRIAM WEBSTER DICTIONARY   *General Reference*
                                                 Dictionary

Contains all the special typography, phonetic representation, and illustrations of the print version, with pronunciation recorded for each word.

Highlighted Data, P.O. Box 17229, Washington, DC 20041 (David Drake, 703–241–1180)

MICROSOFT BOOKSHELF   *General Reference*
                                                 Collection
                                                 $295

Contains 10 reference works including American Heritage Dictionary, Bartlett's Quotations, Chicago Manual of Style, World Almanac, Roget's Thesaurus, Zip Code directory, and more.

Microsoft Corp., 16011 NE 36th Way, Redmond, WA 98073–9717 (202–882–8080)

NEWSBANK ELECTRONIC INDEX   *Newspaper*
                                                 Abstracts

Access to citations for over 700,000 newspaper articles on issues and events (health, business, law, social, biographical, arts). Full text of all articles is available on Newsbank Reference Library Microfiche.

Newsbank, Inc., 58 Pine St.,New Canaan, CT 06840

NEWS SCAN   *News Film*
                                                 Catalog

Computerized catalog of American, European, and Asian news films from 1894 to 1986, containing abstracts of over 200,000 pieces of news film.

Newsreel Access Systems, 340 East 93rd St., Su. 19E, New York, NY 10128 (Jonathan Pollard, 212–996–3035)

NOAA/NESDIS DEMONSTRATION DISC   *Scientific*
                                                 Database

Collection of data from National Oceanic and Atmospheric Administration.

National Geophysical Data Center, 325 Broadway, Boulder, CO 80303 (Carl Abstan, 303–487–6276)

OPTEXT ISSUE 101
Legal
Regulations
$395 / yr
1 / yr

Contains titles 28–50 of the Code of Federal Regulations.
VLS, Inc., 310 S. Reynolds Rd., Toledo, OH 43615 (Lisa Shuey, 419–536–5820)

OPTEXT ISSUE 102
Legal
Regulations
4 / yr

Contains the 1986 Federal Register. VLS, Inc., 310 S. Reynolds Rd., Toledo, OH 43615 (Lisa Shuey, 419–536–5820)

OPTEXT ISSUE 103
Legal
Regulations
1 / yr

Contains titles 1–27 of the Code of Federal Regulations.
VLS, Inc., 310 S. Reynolds Rd., Toledo, OH 43615 (Lisa Shuey, 419–536–5820)

OSH-ROM
Health
Abstracts
$900 / yr
2 / yr

Over 240,000 citations with abstracts or keywords from 500 journals, and 100,000 Monographs and Technical Reports, covering occupational safety and health-related topics dating back to 1960.
SilverPlatter Information, Inc., 37 Walnut Street, Wellesley, MA 02181 (Christopher Pooley, 617–239–0306)

OXFORD ENGLISH DICTIONARY   *General Reference*
Dictionary

The 12-volume printed version of the Oxford English Dictionary (Oxford University Press) recorded on two CD ROM discs. Primarily used for scholastic and linguistic research.

Tri-Star Publishing, 475 Virginia Drive, Fort Washington, PA 19034 (Spencer Nickel, 215–641–6400)

PAIS ON CDROM   *Public Affairs*
Bibliography
$1795/yr
4/yr

Data records for PAIS Bulletin from 1976 through 1986 and for PAIS Foreign Language Index from 1972 through 1986. Bibliographic reference database of material written in English, French, German, Italian, Spanish, and Portuguese on public and business policy issues.

Public Affairs Information Service, Inc., 11 West 40th St., New York, NY 10018 (Barbara Preschel, 212–736–6629)

PARTS-MASTER   *Product*
Catalog

Database of over 12 million parts and products that are stocked or procured by the U.S. government.

NSA, 5161 River Road, Bethesda, MD 20816 (800–638–8094, 301–951–1389)

PATENT INFORMATION DATABASE   *Legal*
Database

Database of patent information, soon to be available on CD ROM.

Tri-Star Publishing, 475 Virginia Drive, Fort Washington, PA 19034 (Spencer Nickel, 215–641–6400)

PATHFINDER
Navigation
System
$4,995 / system

A portable flight navigation system including Jeppesen Sandersen LZ electronic navigation charts. The system assists in preparing flight plans, and can locate all airports within a given radius.

Lasertrak Corporation, 6235–B Lookout Road, Boulder, CO 80301 (Robert Lewis, 303–530–2711)

PC-SIG CDROM DISC
Software
Collection
$199

15,000 public domain software programs.

PC-SIG, 1030 East Duane Avenue, Suite E, Sunnyvale, CA 94086

POISINDEX
Medical
Database
4 / yr

Detailed toxicology database to identify and provide ingredient information on commercial, industrial, pharmaceutical and botanical substances; and detailed treatment/management protocols for toxicology problems due to ingestion, absorption, or inhalation.

Micromedex, Inc., 660 Bannock St.,Su. 350, Denver, CO 80204–4506 (Lela Chambers, 303–623–8600, 800–525–9083)

PSYCLIT
Psychology
Abstracts
$3,500+ / yr
4 / yr

All journal articles published in Psychological Abstracts since 1974. Each record contains the bibliographic citation, full abstract, and indexing from APA's Thesaurus of Psychological Index Terms.

American Psychology Association, 1400 N. Uhle St., Arlington, VA 22207 (Nancy Knight, 800–336–4980, in VA 703–247–7829) Silver-Platter Information, Inc., 37 Walnut Street, Wellesley, MA 02181 (Christopher Pooley, 617–239–0306)

READER'S GUIDE TO PERIODICAL LITERATURE *General Reference*
Abstracts
$1,095
4/yr

Indexes 182 popular English-language, general interest periodicals from U.S. and Canada.

The H. W. Wilson Company, 950 University Ave., Bronx, NY 10452 (Frank Miller, 212–588–8400)

REGISTRY OF MASS SPECTRAL DATA *Scientific*
Database
$2895

Database for applications in mass spectrometry.

John Wiley & Sons, 605 Third Avenue, New York, NY 10158 (212–850–6331)

SHIP COUNTY AND METRO COMPENDIUM *Demographic*
Database
$1200–/yr
3 yrs

Over 1000 data items for all counties and metro areas including data on health, education, retail, and wholesale trade, banking, personal income, poverty, labor, and more.

Slater Hall Information Products, 1522 K Street NW, Su. 522, Washington, DC 20005 (George Hall, 202–682–1350)

SHIP POPULATION DISC *Demographic*
Database
$1200/yr
10 yrs

Population and housing characteristics from the 1980 census for all states, regions, metro areas, counties and congressional districts; population estimates for counties annually through 1986; estimates by age, race and sex for 1980, 1982, 1984; population projections through year 2000 for states and metro areas.

Slater Hall Information Products, 1522 K Street NW, Su. 522, Washington, DC 20005 (George Hall, 202–682–1350)

SOCIAL SCIENCES INDEX
Sociology
Abstracts
$1,295
4/yr

Indexes 300 English-language periodicals on topics related to social sciences.

The H. W. Wilson Company, 950 University Ave., Bronx, NY 10452 (Frank Miller, 212–588–8400)

SOCIOFILE
Sociology
Abstracts
$1950/yr
2/yr

Repository of the contents of the world's journals in sociology as compiled by Sociological Abstracts in Abstracts of Journal Articles and Abstracts of Dissertations.

SilverPlatter Information, Inc., 37 Walnut Street, Wellesley, MA 02181 (Christopher Pooley, 617–239–0306)

STATE EDUCATION ENCYCLOPEDIA
Education/Legal
Reference
$2000/yr
4/yr

All regulations, appeals, and statutes required to run a school district in Texas, fully indexed.

Quantum Access, Inc., 1700 W. Loop South, Su. 1460, Houston, TX 77027 (Draper Kauffman, 713–622–3211)

SWEET'S CATALOG FILES
Product Catalogs
Database

An indexed listing of manufacturers product catalogs including Sweet's Byline Service, Sweet's Update Service, and Sweet's Specification System.

McGraw-Hill Information Systems Company, Electronic Sweet's, 1221 Avenue of the Americas, New York, NY 10020 (Miriam Elder, 212–512–2242)

THE TEXAS ATTORNEY GENERAL DOCUMENTS　　　*Legal Reference*
　　　　　　　　　　　　　　　　　　　　　　　　$2000/yr
　　　　　　　　　　　　　　　　　　　　　　　　　4/yr
The official Opinions issued by the Texas Attorney General, organized by date and topical hierarchy, fully indexed.
　Quantum Access, Inc., 1700 W. Loop South, Su 1460, Houston, TX 77027 (Draper Kauffman, 713–622–3211)

TITLE 26 — US CODE OF FEDERAL　　　　　*Demonstration*
REGULATIONS　　　　　　　　　　　　　　　*Tax Law*
　　　　　　　　　　　　　　　　　　　　　　To loan
Demonstration disc containing the 1984 U.S. Tax Laws.
　TMS, Inc., 110 West Third, Stillwater, OK 74074 (Bruce Benge, 405–377–0880)

TLG PILOT CD ROM #A FOR EXPERIMENTAL　　*Academic*
PURPOSES　　　　　　　　　　　　　　*Classical Literatire*

Greek, Latin, Hebrew and Coptic literary works.
　Theseaurus Linguae Graecae, University of California at Irvine, Irvine, CA 92717 (Theodore Brunner)

TLG PILOT CD ROM #B FOR EXPERIMENTAL　　*Academic Classical*
PURPOSES　　　　　　　　　　　　　　　　　*Literature*

Complete works of Classical Greek writers to 700 A.D.
　Theseaurus Linguae Graecae, University of California at Irvine, Irvine, CA 92717 (Theodore Brunner)

ULRICH'S INTERNATIONAL PERIODICALS DIRECTORY　　*General*
　　　　　　　　　　　　　　　　　　　　　　　Reference
　　　　　　　　　　　　　　　　　　　　　　　Abstracts
　　　　　　　　　　　　　　　　　　　　　　　　4/yr
Bowker Electronic Publishing, 245 W. 17th St.,New York, NY 10114–0418 (Robert Allen, 800–323–3288)

THE UNIVERSE OF SOUNDS *Audio Data System*

Digital audio data for proprietary sound synthesizer system.
Optical Media International, 298A Quail Run Road, Aptos, CA
(Alan Adkins, 408–662–1772)

USGS PROTOTYPE DEMONSTRATION DISC *Geology Database $35*

Contains the FAR/FIRMR databases and USGS datafiles with six
different data retrieval packages.
US Geological Survey, 12201 Sunrise Valley Dr., Restar, VA 22092
(Bruce Benge, TMS, Inc., 405–377–0880)

VISUAL DICTIONARY *Prototype Dictionary $60*

Based on a book of the same title that contains proper terms for all
the parts of objects depicted in 3000 line drawings. The protype
CDROM contains 115 images and 1660 terms, with digitized audio in
French and English.
Facts-on-File, Inc., 460 Park Avenue South, New York, NY 10016
(Carol Collins, 212–683–2244) Software Mart, 7419 Lakewood Drive,
Austin, TX 78750 (Carolyn Kuhn, 512–346–7887)

WHO'S WHO IN ELECTRONICS *Marketing Database*

"Selectory of American Electronics Manufacturers," a database of
U.S. Electronics Manufacturers, searchable by location, product, industry, size, key executives, etc.
Harris Information Services, 2057–2 Aurora Road, Twinsburg, OH
(216–425–9000)

YOUR MARKETING CONSULTANT (Consumer)   *Marketing*
Database
$950/yr
1/yr
Demographic, economic, and retail store data for determining sales
potential of consumer products, and for managing sales performance.
Knowledge Access International, Inc., 2685 Marine Way, Su. 1305,
Mountain View, CA 94043 (Lewis Miller, 415–969–0606)

YOUR MARKETING CONSULTANT   *Marketing*
(Business-to-Business)   *Database*
$950/yr
1/yr
Business, employment and occupational data for determining sales
potential of business products, and for managing sales performance.
Knowledge Access International, Inc., 2685 Marine Way, Su. 1305,
Mountain View, CA 94043 (Lewis Miller, 415–969–0606)

Undocumented CD ROM Applications

The following CDROMs have been cited in the literature, but we
have not independently verified these applications.

1984 IEEE JOURNALS   *Prototype*

University Microfilms International, Inc., 300 N. Zeeb Road, Ann
Arbor, MI 48106 (800–732–0616)

ABSTRACT FILE   *Prototype*

Dun's Marketing Service, 49 Old Bloomfield Road, Mountain Lakes,
NJ 07046 (201–299–0181)

AUTOMATED FACILITIES   *Engineering*

National Institute of Building Sciences, 1015 15th ST NW, Suite 700, Washington, DC 20005 (202–347–5710)

COMPACT VIDEO DEMONSTRATION DISC   *Demonstration*

Information Dimensions, Inc., 655 Metroplace South, Dublin, OH 43017 (800–DATA–MGT)

COOKBOOK   *Demonstration*

Pin Point Publishing, P.O. Box 13323, Oakland CA 94661 (415–654–3050)

EAT OR BE EATEN   *Demonstration*

The Record Group, 3300 Warner Boulevard, Burbank, CA 91510 (Stan Cornyn, 818–953–3211)

ENGINEERING INFORMATION SYSTEM   *Demonstration*

National Institute of Building Sciences, 1015 15th ST NW, Suite 700, Washington, DC 20005 (202–347–5710)

EUROPEAN CASE LAW   *Legal*

Eurolex, 4 Bloomsbury Square, London WC1, England

THE FINE CHEMICALS DIRECTORY   *Chemistry*

Fraser Williams Ltd, London Road South, Poynton, Cheshire SK12 1N, England

HEALTH AND SAFETY IN CHEMISTRY *Health*

Chemical Abstracts Service, P.O. Box 3012, Columbus, OH 43210

IDI PILOT PROJECT DEMO DISC *Demonstration*

Information Dimensions, Inc., 655 Metroplace South, Dublin, OH 43017 (800–DATA–MGT)

IMAGES ON CD ROM *Demonstration*

Compact Discoveries, 1050 South Federal Highway, Delray Beach, FL 33444 (Carol Place, 305–243–1453)

INTERACTIVE AUDIOMATION *Demonstration*

Earth View, Inc., 6514 18th Ave NE, Seattle, WA 98115 (Bryan Brewer, 206–527–3168)

LIBRARY AND TECHNICAL SERVICE DISC

Library Sydney Dataproducts, Inc., 11075 Santa Monica Blvd., Su. 100, Los Angeles, CA 90025 (800–992–9778)

MICROREVIEWS *Demonstration*

Knowledge Access International, Inc., 2685 Marine Way, Su. 1305, Mountain View, CA 94043 (415–969–0606)

MILLION DOLLAR DIRECTORY *Prototype*

Dun's Marketing Service, 49 Old Bloomfield Road, Mountain Lakes, NJ 07046 (201–299–0181)

OPTI/SEARCH SAMPLER DISC   *Demonstration*

Amtec Information Services, 3700 Industry Ave., Lakewood, CA 90714–6050 (Jack Moran, 213–595–4756)

PAN AMERICAN HEALTH ORGANIZATION   *Medical Information*

Reportedly, PAHO will be publishing multilingual medical information discs for dissemination to a 150-site network of hospitals, medical schools, and health organizations throughout the western hemisphere.

Pan American Health Organization (World Health Organization) United Nations (Claude Brito, Chief of Information Coordination)

PERIODICAL CATALOGING DATABASE   *Library*

Faxon Company, 15 Southwest Park, Westwood, MA 02090 (617–329–3350)

PERSONNET   *Unknown*

Information Handling Services Inc., 2001 Jefferson Davis Highway, Su. 1201, Arlington, VA 22202 (703–521–5000)

PHINET TAX RESOURCE   *Tax*

Prentice Hall Information Network, 292 Madison Ave., New York, NY 10017 (212–373–8600)

REAL ESTATE DATA   *Real Estate*

First disc in the series reportedly will cover metropolitan Washington, D.C.

Real Estate Data, Inc., 2398 NW 119th Street, Miami, FL 33167 (Martin Zuckerman, 305–685–5731)

SAMPLERS I, II, AND III   *Demonstration*

Reference Technology, Inc., 5700 Flatiron Parkway, Boulder, CO 80301 (Mike Befeler, 202–682–1350)

THE SERIALS DIRECTORY   *Unknown*

EBSCO, P.O. Box 13787, Torrance, CA 90503 (213–530–7533)

SOFTWARE LIBRARY DATAPLATE   *Demonstration*

Reference Technology, Inc., 5700 Flatiron Parkway, Boulder, CO 80301 (Mike Befeler, 202–682–1350)

TAX FORMS ON DEMAND   *Tax*

Online, 20251 Century Blvd., Germantown, MD 20874 (301–428–3700)

TAX LIBRARY   *Tax*

Tax Analysts, 400 N. Washington St., Falls Church, VA 22046 (703–532–1850)

UK LIBRARY DATABASE DISC   *Library*

British Library—R&D Department, 2 Sheraton St., London W1V 4BH, England

VOYAGER IMAGES OF URANUS   *Scientific*

Jet Propulsion Laboratory, Bldg. 264, Rm. 115, 4800 Oak Grove Drive, Pasadena, CA 91109 (213–354–3343)

About the Author

Steve Holder is Vice President and co-founder of IVID Communications, an applications development and systems integration firm. IVID specializes in interactive videodisc and CDROM applications design and software development.

IVID Communications
4340 Viewridge Ave., Suite B
San Diego, CA 92123
619–576–0611

Index